D0714129

Social History of the United States

Titles in ABC-CLIO's
Social History of the United States

Social History of the United States
The 1940s

Mark Ciabattari

Series Editors
Daniel J. Walkowitz and Daniel E. Bender

A B C CLIO

Santa Barbara, California   Denver, Colorado   Oxford, England

WINGATE UNIVERSITY LIBRARY

Copyright © 2009 by ABC-CLIO, Inc.

All rights reserved. No part of this publication may be reproduced, stored in a retrieval system, or transmitted, in any form or by any means, electronic, mechanical, photocopying, recording, or otherwise, except for the inclusion of brief quotations in a review, without prior permission in writing from the publishers.

Library of Congress Cataloging-in-Publication Data

Ciabattari, Mark.
Social history of the United States : the 1940s / Mark Ciabattari.
    p.   cm.
Includes index.
ISBN 978-1-85109-911-5 (alk. paper) — ISBN 978-1-59884-127-5 (set)
EISBN 978-1-85109-912-2 (ebook)
1. United States—Social conditions—1933–1945.   2. United States—Social conditions—1945–   I. Title.
  HN57.C544   2009
  306.973'09044—dc22   2008032817

12 11 10 09   1 2 3 4 5

Production Editor: Vicki Moran
Production Manager: Don Schmidt
Media Editor: Julie Dunbar
Media Resources Manager: Caroline Price
File Management Coordinator: Paula Gerard

This book is also available on the World Wide Web as an eBook.
Visit www.abc-clio.com for details.

ABC-CLIO, Inc.
130 Cremona Drive, P.O. Box 1911
Santa Barbara, California 93116–1911

This book is printed on acid-free paper ∞
Manufactured in the United States of America

Contents

Contents

Series Introduction

Ordinary people make history. They do so in ways that are different from the ways presidents, generals, business moguls, or celebrities make history; nevertheless, the history of ordinary people is just as profound, just as enduring. Immigration in the early decades of the 20th century was more than numbers and government policy; it was a collective experience of millions of men, women, and children whose political beliefs, vernacular cultural expression, discontent, and dreams transformed the United States. Likewise, during the Great Depression of the 1930s, President Franklin Delano Roosevelt advanced a broad spectrum of new social policies, but as historians have argued, ordinary Americans "made" the New Deal at the workplace, at the ballot box, on the picket lines, and on the city streets. They engaged in new types of consumer behavior, shifted political allegiances, and joined new, more aggressive trade unions. World War II and the Cold War were more than diplomatic maneuvering and military strategy; social upheavals changed the employment patterns, family relations, and daily life of ordinary people. More recently, the rise of the Christian Right in the last few decades is the expression of changing demographics and emerging social movements, not merely the efforts of a few distinct leaders.

These examples, which are drawn directly from the volumes in this series, highlight some of the essential themes of social history. Social history shifts the historical focus away from the famous and the political or economic elite to issues of everyday life. It explores the experiences ordinary Americans—native-born and immigrant, poor and rich, employed and unemployed, men and women, white and black—at home, at work, and at play. In the process, it focuses new attention on the significance of social movements, the behavior and meanings of consumerism, and the changing expression of popular culture.

In many ways, social history is not new. American historians early in the 20th century appreciated the importance of labor, immigration, religion, and urbanization in the study of society. However, early studies shared with political history the emphasis on leaders and major institutions and described a history that was mostly white and male—in other words, a history of those who held power. Several cultural shifts combined to transform how social history was understood and written in the last half of the 20th century: the democratization of higher education after World War II with the GI Bill and the expansion of public and land grant universities; the entry of women, children of immigrants, and racial minorities into the universities and the ranks of historians; and the social movements of the 1960s. Historians created new subjects for social history, casting it as "from the bottom." They realized that much was missing from familiar narratives that stressed the significance of "great men"—presidents, industrialists, and other usually white, usually male notables. Instead, women, working people, and ethnic and racial minorities have become integral parts of the American story along with work, leisure, and social movements.

The result has not simply been additive: ordinary people made history. The story of historical change is located in their lives and their struggles with and against others in power. Historians began to transform the central narrative of American history. They realized that—in the words of a popular 1930s folk cantata, "Ballad for Americans"—the "'etceteras' and the 'and so forths' that do the work" have a role in shaping their own lives, in transforming politics, and in recreating economics. Older themes of study, from industrialization to imperial expansion, from party politics to urbanization, were revisited through the inclusion of new actors, agents, and voices. These took their place alongside such new topics as social movements, popular culture, consumption, and community. But social history remains socially engaged scholarship; contemporary social issues continue to shape social historians' research and thinking. Historians in the 1970s and 1980s who focused on the experiences of working people, for instance, were challenged by the reality of deindustrialization. Likewise, historians in the 1990s who focused on popular culture and consumer behavior were influenced by the explosion of consumerism and new forms of cultural expression. Today's historians explore the antecedents to contemporary globalization as well as the roots of conservatism.

The transformation of the questions and agendas of each new era has made it apparent to historians that the boundaries of historical inquiry are not discrete. Social history, therefore, engages with other kinds of history. Social history reinterprets older narratives of politics and political economy and overlaps both areas. Social historians argue that politics is not restricted to ballot boxes or legislatures; politics is broad popular engagement with ideas about material wealth, social justice, moral values, and civil and human rights. Social historians, naturally, remain interested in changing political affiliations. They have, for example, examined the changing political allegiances of African Americans during the 1930s and the civil rights movement of the 1960s. So too have they examined the relationship of socialist and communist parties to working-class and immigrant communities. At the same time, social historians measure change by looking at such issues as family structure, popular culture, and consumer behavior.

For the social historian, the economy extends far beyond statistical data about production, gross domestic product, or employment. Rather, the economy is a lived experience. Wealthy or poor, Americans have negotiated the changing reality of economic life. Social historians ask questions about how different groups of Americans experienced and resisted major economic transformations and how they have grappled with economic uncertainty. The Great Depression of the 1930s, for example, left both urban workers and rural farmers perilously close to starvation. During the 1970s and 1980s, factories in the Rust Belt of the Midwest and Northeast shuttered or moved, and many Americans began laboring in new parts of the country and working new kinds of jobs, especially in the service sector. Americans have also grappled with the unequal distribution of wealth; some people advanced new ideas and engaged with emerging ideologies that challenged economic injustice, but others jealously guarded their privilege.

As social history has broadened its purview, it has transformed our sense of how historical change occurs. Social history changes our conception of chronology; change does not correspond to presidential election cycles. Social history also changes how we understand sources of power; power is constituted in and challenged by diverse peoples with different resources. Social historians, then, look at the long history of the 20th century in the United States and examine how the terrain has shifted under our feet, sometimes slowly and sometimes dramatically and abruptly. Social historians measure change in complex ways, including but also transcending demographic and geographic expansion and political transformation. How, for example, did the institution of the family change in the face of successive waves of immigration that often left spouses and children separated by national borders and oceans? Or during years of war with rising rates of women's wage and salary employment? Or following moralist reaction that celebrated imagined traditional values, and social movements that focused on issues of sexuality, birth control, homosexuality, and liberation? Historical change can also be measured by engagement with popular culture as Americans shifted their attention from vaudeville and pulp novels to radio, silent films, talkies, television, and finally the Internet and video games. The volumes in this series, divided by decades, trace all these changes.

To make sense of this complex and broadened field of inquiry, social historians often talk about how the categories by which we understand the past have been "invented," "contested," and "constructed." The nation has generally been divided along lines of race, class, gender, sexuality, and ethnicity. However, historians have also realized that analysts—whether in public or professional discourse—define these "categories of analysis" in different ways at different moments. Waves of immigration have reconfigured understandings of race and ethnicity, and more recent social movements have challenged the meanings of gender. Similarly, to be working class at the dawn of the age of industry in the 1900s meant something very different from being working class in the post-industrial landscape of the 1990s. How women or African Americans—to cite only two groups—understand their own identity can mean something different than how white men categorize them. Social historians, therefore, trace how Americans have always been divided about the direction of their lives and their nation, how they have consistently challenged and rethought social and cultural values and sought to renegotiate relationships of power, whether in the family, the workplace, the university, or the military. Actors do this armed with differing forms of power to authorize their view.

To examine these contestations, social historians have explored the way Americans articulated and defended numerous identities—as immigrants, citizens, workers, Christians, or feminists, for example. A post–World War II male chemical worker may have thought of himself as a worker and trade unionist at the factory, a veteran and a Democrat in his civic community, a husband and father at home, and as a white, middle-class homeowner. A female civil rights worker in the South in the 1960s may have seen herself as an African American when in the midst of a protest march or when refused service in a restaurant, as working class during a day job as a domestic worker or nurse, and as a woman when struggling to claim a leadership role in an activist organization.

Social historians have revisited older sources and mined rich new veins of information on the daily lives of ordinary people. Social historians engage with a host of materials—from government documents to census reports, from literature to oral histories, and from autobiographies to immigrant and foreign-language newspapers—to illuminate the lives, ideas, and activities of those who have been hidden from history. Social historians have also brought a broad "toolbox" of new methodologies to shed light on these sources. These methodologies are well represented in this series and illustrate the innovations of history from the bottom up. These volumes offer many tables and charts, which demonstrate the ways historians have made creative use of statistical analysis. Furthermore, the volumes are rich in illustrations as examples of the new ways that social historians "read" such images as cartoons or photographs.

The volumes in this series reflect the new subject matter, debates, and methodologies that have composed the writing of the United States' 20th-century social history. The volumes have unique features that make them particularly valuable for students and teachers; they are hybrids that combine the narrative advantages of the monograph with the specific focus of the encyclopedia. Each volume has been authored or co-authored by established social historians. Where the work has been collaborative, the authors have shared the writing and worked to sustain a narrative voice and conceptual flow in the volume. Authors have written the social history for the decade of their expertise and most have also taught its history. Each volume begins with a volume introduction by the author or authors that lays out the major themes of the decade and the big picture—how the social changes of the era transformed the lives of Americans. The author then synthesizes the best and most path-breaking new works in social history. In the case of the last three volumes, which cover the post-1970 era, scholarship remains in its relative infancy. In particular, these three volumes are major original efforts to both define the field and draw upon the considerable body of original research that has already been completed.

The ten volumes in the series divide the century by its decades. This is an avowedly neutral principle of organization that does not privilege economic, political, or cultural transformations; this allows readers to develop their own sense of a moment and their own sense of change. While it remains to be seen how the most recent decades will be taught and studied, in cases such as the 1920s, the 1930s, and the 1960s, this decadal organization replicates how historians frequently study and teach history. The Progressive Era (ca. 1890–1920) and postwar America (ca. 1945–1960) have less often been divided by decades. This highlights the neutrality of this division. In truth, all divisions are imposed: we speak of long decades or short centuries, and so forth. When historians teach the 1960s, they often reach back into the 1950s and ahead into the 1970s. The authors and editors of these volumes recognize that social processes, movements, ideas, and leaders do not rise and fall with the turn of the calendar; therefore, they have worked to knit the volumes together as a unit.

Readers can examine these texts individually or collectively. The texts can be used to provide information on significant events or individuals. They can provide an overview of a pivotal decade. At the same time, these texts are designed to allow readers to follow changing themes over time and to develop their own sense of chronology. The authors regularly spoke with one another and with the series editors to establish the major themes and subthemes in the social history of the century and to sustain story lines across the volumes. Each volume divides the material into six or seven chapters that discuss major themes such as labor or work; urban, suburban, and rural life; private life; politics; economy; culture; and social movements. Each chapter begins with an overview essay and then explores four to six major topics. The discrete essays at the heart of each volume give readers focus on a social movement, a social idea, a case study, a social institution, and so forth. Unlike traditional encyclopedias, however, the narrative coherence of the single-authored text permits authors to break the decade bubble with discussions on the background or effects of a social event.

There are several other features that distinguish this series.

- Many chapters include capsules on major debates in the social history of the era. Even as social historians strive to build on the best scholarship available, social history remains incomplete and contested; readers can benefit from studying this tension.

- The arguments in these volumes are supported by many tables and graphics. Social history has mobilized demographic evidence and—like its sister field, cultural history—has increasingly turned to visual evidence, both for the social history of media and culture and as evidence of social conditions. These materials are not presented simply as illustrations but as social evidence to be studied.

- Timelines at the head of every chapter highlight for readers all the major events and moments in the social history that follows.

- A series of biographical sketches at the end of every chapter highlights the lives of major figures more often overlooked in histories of the era. Readers can find ample biographical material on more prominent figures in other sources; here the authors have targeted lesser known but no less interesting and important subjects.

- Bibliographies include references to electronic sources and guide readers to material for further study.

- Three indices—one for each volume, one for the entire series, and one for all the people and events in the series—are provided in each volume. Readers can easily follow any of the major themes across the volumes.

Finally, we end with thanks for the supportive assistance of Ron Boehm and Kristin Gibson at ABC-CLIO, and especially to Dr. Alex Mikaberidze and Dr. Kim Kennedy White, who helped edit the manuscripts for the press. But of course, these volumes are the product of the extraordinary group of historians to whom we are particularly indebted:

The 1900s: Brian Greenberg and Linda S. Watts
The 1910s: Gordon Reavley
The 1920s: Linda S. Watts, Alice L. George, and Scott Beekman
The 1930s: Cecelia Bucki
The 1940s: Mark Ciabattari
The 1950s: John C. Stoner and Alice L. George
The 1960s: Troy D. Paino
The 1970s: Laurie Mercier
The 1980s: Peter C. Holloran and Andrew Hunt
The 1990s: Nancy Cohen

Daniel J. Walkowitz, Series Editor
Daniel E. Bender, Series Associate Editor

Introduction

The decade of the 1940s in the United States was shaped by two global struggles. The first, World War II, which the United States entered in 1941 after the Japanese bombing of Pearl Harbor and two years after the German invasion of Poland, was the violent culmination of events and decisions set in motion after World War I. The second, the Cold War, began as World War II ended and the United States found itself facing an enemy perceived to be intent on destroying what Americans had fought for in World War II and, in fact, destroying what Americans began to see as their most defining characteristics and values. These twin struggles, one coming directly on the heels of the other, gave Americans living during this decade a unique set of realities with which to contend. Current descriptions of Americans who weathered these challenges of the 1940s (and the Great Depression of the 1930s) often recognize this uniqueness and celebrate the sacrifices and challenges faced by this "Greatest Generation."

This volume examines the social history of the United States from 1940 through 1949 and offers a place to examine what this generation of Americans faced and how they responded to the special challenges this decade offered. Using World War II and the beginning of the Cold War as large markers, this volume will address how everyday lives of Americans across the divides of race, class, ethnicity, gender, and region were affected in similar and different ways. Some of the key questions this volume seeks to shed light on include the following: As the world itself was transformed, how did ordinary Americans make sense of it? Was this a period of expanding or contracting opportunities for individuals? Did the transformations occurring during the decade affect women and African Americans differently than white males? How did war, both hot and cold, affect life for those not directly involved in the conflicts? How did the return of prosperity and the beginning of one of the longest periods of sustained prosperity influence day-to-day life and Americans' self-perceptions? How did unlocking the "atomic age" filter how American viewed the world around them? How did ideological struggles over capitalism and communism, democracy, and totalitarianism get played out in everyday life? Were these struggles distant to people's daily life or did they fundamentally inform and shape daily life?

Seven chapters provide the organizational structure for exploring the 1940s. The first two chapters, which focus on the United States in World War II and the beginning of the Cold War, contextualize the decade within these larger global struggles and explore the social implications of hot and cold war for soldiers and for those remaining on the home front. These first chapters examine broad social changes caused by international conflict while the following five chapters narrow the focus. Chapters 3 through 7 examine changes in business and labor, the expansion of educational opportunity, changes in family life, internal migrations and how they reshaped the landscape and politics of the United States, and how all these changes were reflected in and mediated by the popular culture produced during the era.

The 1940s witnessed two major shifts on the national level that would have tremendous impact on daily life for average Americans. The first transformation was the tremendous growth of the federal government that had begun under Franklin Roosevelt during the Depression years but received a tremendous boost from the imperatives of carrying out first a global war against Axis powers and then a cold war against perceived communist threats. For example, during World War II the government rationed items needed for the war effort and contracted for unprecedented military goods production. Government policies after the war continued allocating resources to military purposes and, as during the first half of the decade, changed daily life. The second major change at the national level was the country's transformation from isolationism to internationalism. Again, World War II became the catalyst for engaging in a global struggle despite a long-standing tradition to look inward, but this stance was continued and, in fact, reinforced, by the dawning cold war.

The United States' engagement in World War II brought on the rapid and dramatic expansion of the federal government. Although it is true that the federal government had seen periods of expansion before, such as in the Civil War, World War I, and the years of the Great Depression, the expansion that took place during World War II was on a larger scale and proved to be longer lasting. Along with the millions of people who served in the branches of the armed forces, the number of civilians employed by the federal government quadrupled to 3.8 million. The federal government's budget and debt also swelled to unprecedented numbers. By 1945, the federal budget was 11 times larger than it had been in 1939. The government created new offices and bureaucracies to mobilize the economic and labor resources of the nation. The Office of Price Administration, for example, organized rationing and fought inflationary trends. The government financed much of the war through the sale of war bonds. Science, most notably in the Manhattan Project established to develop atomic weapons, was brought into war service through the financing and organization of the federal government. The federal government promised higher wages to spur and maintain production, produced movies to build home-front morale, and produced hundreds of propaganda posters that effectively explained to Americans the purpose of the war and what they needed to do to bring about victory.

The expansion of the federal government during the war years did not recede as traditionally it does after times of war crisis. The need to maintain military preparedness as the enemy shifted from fascists to communists by the late 1940s kept the United States on a war footing and helped maintain and solidify the growth of the federal government. The ultimate effect of this change was that Americans from all walks of life had closer contact with a level of government that in years past was distant and filtered through state and local governmental bodies.

During the later 1940s, national efforts to fight the Cold War continued the tradition of government led by mobilization of the nation's resources. The infusion of federal funds into university-based scientific research solidified the connection between institutions of higher education and federally defined and mandated research agendas in support of the Cold War. The federal government, fearing that the United States was slipping in educating its youth in basic math and hard science skills began to explore ways to influence local elementary and secondary school curricula, an arena that was traditionally in firm local, or at most, state control.

The early Cold War years also saw the continuation of the United States' international involvement. Just as World War II broke the hold of isolationists, the Cold War maintained the arguments for international engagement rather than a retreat into isolationism. The United States led in the creation of the United Nations and became the physical home to this international body similar to the League of Nations, which was so soundly rejected by the United States after World War I. This fundamental shift toward international engagement signaled a permanent change in United States foreign policy and would bring with it tremendous domestic ramifications. The place of the United States in the world became a topic that affected all Americans, not just those at the top of the policy-making hierarchy. American treatment of minorities would now be compared on a global scale. The tensions in Eastern Europe would affect the millions of Americans who had immigrated from these lands. Events in areas of the world that earlier in the century would have seemed distant and exotic now became more prominent as America emerged from World War II.

These large changes—growth of federal involvement in day-to-day life and a firmly established global position and outlook—grew directly out of World

War II and the beginning of the Cold War, the events central to the 1940s. This volume will use these large changes as the foundation on which to explore the social history of the United States in the 1940s. Examining how Americans worked, how they were educated, what constituted familial arrangements, where Americans lived, and how they mediated their lives through popular culture will broaden our understanding of how Americans were shaped by, made sense of, and tried—with varying degrees of success—to control the rapidly changing world around them.

In general, work became more available in the 1940s, and standards of living went up. World War II obliterated the Depression with its demand for labor and goods. Blue-collar industrial workers, who by 1941 were largely organized as a result of the industrial union surge of the 1930s, enjoyed high wages and sustained employment during the war years. Before Pearl Harbor, labor unions were re-energized to push for a fairer share of the wartime windfall gained by American industries. Although wages increased by as much as 50 percent because of the war, this rate never outpaced profits or prices. Among other strikes, the most prominent occurred among Ford workers in Dearborn, Michigan. Ford became the last of the large auto manufacturers to recognize the United Automobile Workers, which made it one of the largest labor organizations in the world. Patriotism and the need for sustained production led many unions to sign no-strike pledges for the duration of the war, which curbed official labor militancy but not unauthorized or "wildcat" strikes by locals.

If blue-collar work experienced unprecedented increases in wages and benefits during the war years, it also experienced new challenges posed by the transformation of American industry to the world's largest supplier of war materials. The demand for labor brought millions of African Americans into the industrial labor force and thus into the ranks of organized labor. Tensions between African American and white rank-and-file workers often boiled over in factories and on the streets of industrial centers. Although African Americans joined unions in unprecedented numbers during the war, this did not always guarantee their acceptance into the brotherhood of labor.

Women were also employed in large numbers to fill the labor shortage. Women moved into jobs that were traditionally preserved for their male counterparts, and they experienced newfound economic freedom and, to a certain extent, social acceptance. The cultural image of Rosie the Riveter as the backbone of American industry during the war is powerful and captures the ability of wartime emergencies to transform rigid social boundaries. Women with wages were able to flex their consumer buying power and carve out an independent niche for themselves that was not possible earlier.

After the end of the war, fear that the days of economic depression would return as GIs flooded home and war contracts expired led to another rash of labor militancy in 1946. Congress, under control of Republicans for the first time since the early 1930s, began to chip away at the rights won by organized labor over the last decade and a half. Most damaging was the Taft-Hartley Act of 1947, which ended the closed shop, secondary boycotts, and the use of union dues for political activities. Reflecting the rising Cold War tensions, the Taft-Hartley Act also required union officials to swear under oath that they were not communists. Organized labor in turn began to purge itself of communists and left-leaning leaders who had proved so critical in earlier organization efforts.

White-collar work after World War II also increased in volume and began to lead to what, by the 1950s, would be called the beginning of postindustrial America. The transformation of the United States to a service-based rather than industrial economy began in the 1940s. The need for clerks, accountants, bankers, advertising and public relations professionals, and other office workers rose tremendously after the war, which led to the emergence of a thriving consumer culture and rising standard of living while also creating a corporate culture that would come under attack by the 1950s as stifling and monotonous.

Opportunities for economic mobility were also tied to changes in education. The 1940s witnessed the continued expansion of educational attainment for Americans, a process that began during the Progressive era of the early-20th century. The demand for more skilled and literate laborers combined with the decreased reliance on child labor in factories and on farms led to reforms in the early part of the century that mandated school attendance and transformed the curriculum of schools to include preparation for entry-level jobs. The Depression years drove even more students into schools, especially high schools, as job opportunities for youth deteriorated. During World War II, high school–age youth were encouraged to stay in school as a way of helping the war effort. Many high school boys took courses of study sponsored by federal funds that taught them the basics of skilled machine work, aeronautics, and other needed wartime occupational skills. Despite upheaval in the form of economic depression and global war, the trajectory of growing education attainment for Americans continued during the 1940s.

After World War II, the biggest change in American education occurred at institutions of higher education. The Servicemen's Readjustment Act, commonly referred to as the G.I. Bill of Rights, encouraged many returning soldiers to go to college by providing tuition and textbook money along with monthly stipends. Colleges and university enrollments swelled with returning servicemen, which changed the culture and physical landscape of these institutions. The college degree itself was transformed in the 1940s from a document earned primarily by members of the American upper class to a necessity for professional and white-collar employment.

The overall expansion of educational opportunity in the 1940s masked the persistence of limited educational opportunity for American minorities. In the South, African Americans were forced to attend inferior segregated schools. In the North, de facto segregation kept minorities in poor schools. Explicit discriminatory policies kept minorities out of many institutions of higher education. The hypocrisy of fighting a world war against fascism and regimes that used racial hierarchies in the development and promotion of their political agendas was not lost on individuals committed to the promotion and extension of civil rights in America. Education would become a prime battleground for organizations such as the NAACP in the 1940s. The fruition of this work would arrive in 1954 with the Supreme Court decision in *Brown v. Board of Education*, which declared segregated schools unconstitutional, but the efforts of the NAACP leading up to that landmark decision began in the 1940s.

Educational institutions as they developed in the 1940s also became the physical and spiritual home of a growing and distinct youth culture. Prior to World War II, most adolescents did not attend high school, and their social and economic life was integrated more closely with the adult world. As the length of school attendance increased and economic opportunities for youth diminished, the amount of time kids spent among their peers as opposed to in more mixed groups increased. This shift, which had been occurring since the turn of the century but by the 1940s reached a critical mass of youth, provided the catalyst for the creation of a culture that began to define the behaviors and mores of American youth. Teenagers became a distinct demographic group with their own ways of speaking, dressing, and thinking about the world. Adults reacted to this emerging culture by studying youth, appealing to experts to help understand their younger citizens, and, more crassly, marketing products explicitly to this group. By the 1950s, youth culture was firmly established and would dominate how Americans defined teenagers for the remainder of the century.

Teenagers and the emerging youth culture in the 1940s, however, can be viewed as just one aspect of a larger transformed family life. Changes were taking place in where families lived, the roles of mothers and fathers, and the importance of families to American political and cultural life. In terms of sheer numbers, family life began a dramatic change in the 1940s. More couples were getting married at younger ages. Childbearing, put off in the hard times of depression and war, was now pursued, which led to the beginning of the "baby boom," a demographic explosion that created a generation that would define the United States in the last half of the 20th century. The changing reality of family life in the United States was not a uniform phenomenon. In many ways, the changes were most clearly seen in middle-class white families. Working-class families and minority families actually changed less. That said, the changing nature of families for the middle class had profound effects in terms of redefining a culturally dominant, acceptable family definition.

More and more middle-class families found themselves moving to suburbs beginning in the second half of the 1940s. Returning veterans and a marriage boom followed by a baby boom combined to create a severe housing shortage in the United States after the war. The federal government through Veterans Administration mortgage programs and Federal Housing Administration loans made millions of dollars available to help Americans buy homes. The demand for housing created a boom in affordable, mass-produced suburban homes. Individual entrepreneurs such as William Levitt, who pioneered ways of making cheap affordable housing for the military during the war, recognized this need and began to apply mass-production techniques to home construction. In a process that reversed the moving assembly line, subdivisions would be created by moving teams of specialized contractors.

The suburban boom created the needed cheap housing but also created problems. Some commentators immediately recognized the sterility of these quickly built uniform communities and pondered the possible negative aspects that suburbanization would have on American life. Extended families living in close proximity became rarer for the middle class, and others noted that suburbs also isolated women and children from other aspects of community life. Minorities were often excluded from these communities, which increased racial segregation and created a pattern of white suburbs and minority urban areas. Suburbanization also led to increased reliance on automobiles rather than mass transportation. Many urban mass transit systems experienced difficulty after the war and eventually yielded to the dominant automobile. The American landscape was physically transformed by roads and businesses, such as fast food franchises that catered to the automobile-dependent consumer.

Families in the 1940s also began to rely increasingly on child-raising experts such as Dr. Benjamin Spock, whose 1946 book, *The Common Sense Book of Baby and Child Care*, became one of the best-selling books of all time. Expert advice stressed the need for parents to follow their instincts, be less authoritative and more indulgent, and recognize the psychological needs of children. Fathers, the experts stressed, needed to be more involved in raising children rather than solely the traditionally distant breadwinner. Parenting, experts like Spock stressed, could actually be fun and fulfilling rather than just a burden. This emphasis on redefining parenting and child raising based on the importance psychological well-being transformed the iconic family structure from one firmly rooted in hierarchy to one that was seen as more democratic. Children were encouraged to be part of family decision making. Their choices and needs were to be seriously factored into parental decision making.

The ideal family as it evolved in the late 1940s was clearly shaped by not only the return of prosperity and the changes wrought by depression and then war but also by the Cold War. Arguably, the emphasis on democratic child raising combined with the prevalence of abundant consumer goods could be seen as ways of providing superior alternatives to model families in authoritarian collectivist societies. As families real and imagined changed in the 1940s, the changes were shaped by not only changed physical conditions of living but also global political conflicts.

As families were redefined, they moved. The migration to the suburbs was just one of the many movements of people in the United States during the 1940s.

Americans have traditionally been a mobile people. From colonization, to westward expansion, to the continual search for better work opportunities, Americans have always moved around the country. In the 1940s, migrations would have a tremendous impact on the physical geography of the country, social relations, and political realities. Some migration was forced, as was most noticeable in the internment of West coast Japanese and Japanese Americans as a panicked and racist reaction to the threat of Japanese spies and infiltrators. The demands of war production provided the largest catalyst to internal migration during the first half of the decade. To escape southern poverty and racism and to take advantage of higher wages, southern African Americans moved north to established communities in northern industrial cities. White Appalachians also moved to northern industrial cities in great numbers during the war. Although many would stay, establishing a southern presence in northern cities, many dreamt, like immigrants, to return to their home region after establishing themselves economically. Mexican migrants also joined the flow of workers seeking the high wages offered during wartime.

Demands for war-time labor also drew millions westward to what later became known as the Sunbelt, especially to the booming aircraft and shipping industries and to work related to developing atomic weapons. Cities such as Los Angeles, Seattle, Albuquerque, and San Diego boomed during the war years and catered to the millions seeking high wages. Industries operated around the clock, as did entertainment and street life, which created bustling activity in previously sleepy western outposts. By the end of the 1940s, the Sunbelt emerged as a region with growing political power. Population increases and the location of critical industries and natural resources made the issues of the region into national issues. Representation growth followed population growth, and an increasing number of politicians from the West and South became national figures during the second half of the century.

The migration of workers and the mixing of cultures under strained conditions also brought tension. City residents complained of crowding, lack of housing, and the influx of strangers into their community. Often the tension erupted into outright violence. In Detroit, violence erupted in 1943 over white resistance to African American employment in defense industries and housing issues. Over the course of 36 hours, 34 people were killed, of which 25 were African American. More than 1,800 people, the vast majority of them African American, were arrested for looting and other crimes. Also in 1943, Los Angeles erupted in violence as Mexicans and Mexican American youth clashed with Anglo servicemen in what came to be known as the Zoot Suit Riots.

The migrations of the 1940s physically transformed the landscape of the United States. Road construction increased to serve once remote areas, and housing construction tried to keep up with the growing demand. The stress on urban infrastructures would cause problems and political debates, especially over water rights. The West would serve as the birthplace to an architecture built around an automobile culture. Suburban housing tracts serviced by strip malls with adequate parking, fast-food operations with drive-up service, motels, and all sorts of franchises would combine to create a manufactured landscape that began to be monotonously reproduced across the country.

All of these themes—World War II, the Cold War, working, education, family life, and migrations—were reflected in popular culture in the 1940s, which is the focus of the final chapter for this volume. We can get an idea of the attitudes, fears, and hopes of American citizens from the popular culture produced during the decade. As with all popular culture, interpretation can be tricky; popular culture is not a true mirror of any age but rather a refracting device that can highlight some aspects of American life but distort others. Movies, music, sports, and the emerging medium of television illustrate how Americans were interpreting the changes, large and small, that were transpiring as a result of World War II and the Cold War.

Movies in the first half of the decade were dominated by war themes. Moviemakers eagerly participated in helping the national war effort. Well-known directors and actors contributed by making films that spurred on the home-front effort and lent their celebrity status to raising war bond revenue and entertaining the troops. In the immediate postwar years, themes of World War II continued in film, but more complex themes such as difficulties in postwar readjustment also became popular. In the years of the early Cold War, movie Nazis became shorthand in many cases for communists as the lessons of World War II were being applied to the emerging global power struggle.

Big bands, swing music, ballads, blues, jazz, and country music reflected the rich diversity that characterized popular music in the 1940s. The marketing and reach of this variety of music reflected the growing commodification of culture and the wider exposure of previously regional forms of musical styles. Also important in the 1940s was the emergence of a distinct youth culture–based music personified by such performers as Frank Sinatra. Teenagers' tastes would begin to be influential in decisions made by recording and radio executives. This trend of popular music being music for the young would continue into the century.

Sports, especially after the war, would return to the trajectory that had begun earlier in the century. Baseball, especially, would continue as the national summer pastime but would also reflect new realities in the form of integrated teams. Jackie Robinson, the first African American in the big leagues, would become a symbol both of continuing racism and potential upcoming social changes. The marketing of sports, like the marketing of music and movies, continued the standardization of American culture from coast to coast.

The advent of television continued to speed up the process of cultural homogenization. Although still a minor form of media in the 1940s, the initial forms of television production and the types of shows that would later dominate American living rooms were being born in the 1940s. Television, after modeling much of its early programming on radio, would eventually create its own forms. The early decisions made about television broadcasting would have lasting impact on determining the eventual power of the medium in American society.

Throughout this book, the focus will remain on how these events, changes, and themes changed the way Americans led their lives. To do this successfully, it is necessary to recognize that large and small change affect individuals differently based on a numerous factors, the most important being their race, class, and gender. Individuals are constrained by these categories but, as social history shows, are continually redefining and stretching the boundaries of these categories to best reflect the democratic values Americans embrace. For true understanding of the 1940s, one must see the large picture of global conflict and—equally necessary—see how ordinary Americans interpreted these struggles.

Issues of the 20th Century

The United States in World War II

Overview

From 1940 to 1945, Americans underwent dramatic phases of orientation toward the outside world—in particular toward Europe, where a global war had begun in 1939, and toward Japan, which led continued aggressions against China. At the beginning of the decade of the 1940s, the great majority of the country was isolationist. In 1940, with the fall of France and the German air assault in the harrowing Battle of Britain, interventionism became stronger. In March 1941, the president and Congress passed the Lend Lease Bill, which gave all aid possible to remaining allies Britain and China (by June, aid extended to the Soviet Union). Still, the country remained adamant about not entering the war (after the earlier bitter experience of World War I, the citizenry was against involvement in the squabbles of the Old World). Then, on December 7, 1941, the United States suffered the sudden loss and devastation of most of its Pacific naval fleet due to the surprise Japanese air attack at Pearl Harbor, Hawaii. Within days, the country was at war in two combat theaters—the Japanese-controlled Pacific and the Nazi-controlled Europe. America instantly developed a united front for survival and, from 1942 to 1945, led the Allied fight to victory

In the process, the country would be changed in almost unimaginable ways. A centralized, planned economy emerged to determine prices, wages, supply, and demand. The federal government's size quadrupled. The budget and national debt each became larger in the 32 months of war than the grand totals of these

1

by all government agencies since the founding of the country. Steep graduated taxes and numerous gigantic war bonds rallies raised a sizable portion of the necessary money. Big government worked with big business (the antitrust laws were suspended) and with big labor (union recognition became easier in return for a nonstrike pledge). Industrial unions formed at a record pace, and big government led the home front to a miracle of production that gave the military a leading margin for victory by mid-1943.

War industries in urban areas of the West and North drew mass migrations, especially from the poor rural South. A sudden full-employment, high-wage war economy brought gains in income levels, especially for blue-collar workers. This made most Americans on the home front eager to sacrifice to serve the war effort overseas. Gasoline, tires, and certain foods deemed necessary to the military purposes were rationed. With a total of 16 million serving in the military, the remaining factory labor force needed minorities: blacks and women. Both made great gains in employment and income during the war.

The country's vast changes brought severe problems, the most serious of which was race relations. Hundreds of thousands of Southern African Americans migrated to cities in the North and West for work in defense plants and were stuffed into overcrowded ghettoes until the predictable happened—a series of race riots in 1943 in Detroit, Chicago, and other hubs of war production. In the military, African Americans were segregated and given largely noncombatant jobs. Protests to this occurred, and near the war's end, the generals experimented with integrated combat forces—a preview of what was to evolve in the late 1940s.

In what was later termed "the Good War," final victory came swiftly in 1945 with V-E Day in May and V-J Day following in August after two atomic bombs fell on Japan.

TIMELINE

1940   The New York World's Fair, called "The World of Tomorrow," opens in January for the second year running.

The national budget for home defense is upped from $1.3 to $1.8 billion.

The Office of Emergency Management (OEM) is instituted to plan a national defense economy.

President Roosevelt's speech in June announces a change from neutrality to a nonbelligerent policy to give aid to the Allies.

The Battle of Britain during summer stirs more Americans to sympathy with the Allies and brings a shift to interventionism.

Congress passes in September the first peacetime draft. One month later, 16.4 million potential draftees, all men between ages 18 and 35, are registered and 800,000 are drafted.

The president enacts the "destroyers for bases" exchange with Britain.

The Democrat Roosevelt wins a historic third term on November 5.

The president tells radio listeners that America should become "an arsenal for democracy."

The Office of Production Management (OPM) is instituted to speed defense production; existing auto factories are retooled to make planes, and new factories are constructed.

1941   The president introduces Allied war aim of the "Four Freedoms."

The January national budget of $17.4 billion marks $10.8 billion for defense, up from $1.8 billion.

The Lend-Lease Act passes in March making the United States the prime war supplier to the Allies.

The Atlantic Charter sets goals for a postwar world that incorporates FDR's Four Freedoms.

The Office of Price Administration (OPA) controls prices and rents and rations consumer items.

In June, the president issues Executive Order 8802, which outlaws discrimination in jobs in the government or the defense industry in reaction to A. Phillip Randolph's threat to march on Washington.

The president gives "Lend-Lease" to the Soviet Union in June.

Fair Employment Practices Commission (FEPC) oversees the government and defense sectors to ensure the equality of hiring and conditions for all workers.

The Revenue Act of 1941 calls for a steep tax levy to supply greatly increased monies for defense.

German submarines sink American merchant and war ships in the Battle of the Atlantic.

FDR announces open hostilities in the North Atlantic, and Congress revises the Neutrality Laws for the arming of U.S. ships and their entry into war zones while the public majority rejects war still.

On December 7, Japan attacks the U.S. Pacific fleet by surprise at Pearl Harbor, Hawaii. Americans react as one with anger and a fighting will to "Remember Pearl Harbor." The United States declares war on Japan and FDR refers to the attack as "a day that will live in infamy."

1942

In January, the National Budget calls for $52 billion for war, an increase of more than 50 percent.

The War Production Board (WPB) begins the conversion to a total war economy.

The president calls for the production of huge numbers of tanks, planes, and ships.

The Office of Civilian Defense (OCD) protects against attacks and employs volunteers to boost home morale.

The Office of Censorship opens all overseas mail and checks war news for publication or broadcast.

The WPB fulfills the president's war production goals by building a vast new government-subsidized defense economy, which seeds prosperity to replace the recent Depression.

Daylight Saving Time goes into effect nationally, and every clock in the United States is set back an hour for the duration of the war.

In February, the president issues Executive Order 9066, which demands the relocation of 120,000 Japanese (both aliens and civilians) from their West Coast homes to government relocation camps in the interior.

The National War Labor Board (NWLB) aims to negotiate labor–management disputes, prevent strikes in war industries, and stabilize wages and prices.

The Office of War Information (OWI) is instituted to shape home news of war; the mass media—movies, radio, and print—cooperate to clarify American battlefield positions and war goals.

The Fair Employment Practices Commission aims to prevent job discrimination in war industries, which makes more jobs available to females and African Americans.

The OPC freezes prices and wages and then rations gas to widespread complaints.

The Revenue Act of 1942 calls for a $9 billion tax increase, including 5 percent tax on all personal income over $624 annually. Now most all, along with the rich, will pay income tax.

The Congress on Racial Equality (CORE), founded by James Farmer in June, begins the earliest mass resistance to discrimination by promoting sit-ins at local segregated theaters and luncheon counters.

A war bond drive, the first of eight, goes on over the summer and fall and successfully raises billions from ordinary citizens to pay for the war.

Synthetic rubber is invented and relieves a dire shortage. Civilians get used to a host of other newly invented wartime substitutes including nylon and rayon for silk.

1943   The National Budget calls for a total of $108.9 billion with $100 billion for war (a 50 percent increase). This creates peak war production, a crucial factor in the eventual Allied victory. The expanded government will be the country's greatest employer, with the armed forces of 10 million.

The Office of War Mobilization (OWM) ensures the efficiency of the nation's total war effort, which results in a miracle boosting of the 1939 GNP of $90 billion to a 1945 level of $211 billion and the creation of 17 million new jobs.

The Current Tax Payment Act in June authorizes the first payroll withholding of taxes for all Americans who earn wages or salaries.

In the summer, cities experience race riots due to a massive new influx of African American defense workers who experience discrimination in housing and hiring; the worst violence is in Detroit.

In Los Angeles, the Zoot Suit Riots involve servicemen and Mexican American youth.

In *Korematsu v. U.S.,* the Supreme Court rules in December that the government's order for relocation of Japanese citizens of the United States is constitutional.

1944   The National Budget calls for a total of $70 billion, almost all for war (a decrease of 30 percent from the previous year).

The U.S. Supreme Court overturns the practice of white primaries in the South, and the victorious National Association for the Advancement of Colored People, with its Double V campaign of fighting fascism abroad and racism at home, grows to 450,000 members.

The G.I. Bill of Rights becomes law in June; it guarantees returning service persons a government-paid readjustment period and support for higher education after war's end.

General Dwight D. Eisenhower forms experimental integrated combat groups with African American volunteers, and the results convince the commander that the new units are better than segregated forces.

In the November election, FDR wins a fourth term, with Harry Truman as vice president.

The Women's Naval Corps (WAVES) admit African American women.

1945   The Yalta Conference of the Allied powers in February sets the stage for the final defeat of Germany and the construction of the postwar world with authorization for the new United Nations.

President Roosevelt dies on April 12, and the nation mourns a president who has guided the country through Depression and war; Harry S. Truman becomes president.

Germany surrenders on May 7. Allies celebrate Victory in Europe (V-E Day) on May 8.

The FEPC's budget is reduced by racist Southern members who see the commission as a source of social unrest.

Scientists secretly test the first atomic bomb at Alamogordo, New Mexico.

The July Potsdam Conference of the Allied powers is the first "Big Three" conference with Truman, who has decided to use the atomic bomb against Japan.

Hiroshima, Japan, is destroyed with one atomic bomb on August 6; Americans learn their government has developed and used this secret weapon that poses a threat to all existence.

Nagasaki, Japan, is destroyed with a second atomic bomb on August 9.

Allies celebrate on August 14 with the news of a Japanese surrender.

The Japanese formally surrender to Gen. Douglas MacArthur on September 12 aboard the battleship *Missouri* in Tokyo Bay while millions of Americans celebrate V-J Day, the end of World War II.

U.S. Entry into the Global Conflict

During 1940 and especially 1941, Americans reaped advantages due to the steadily improving economy brought about by their peacetime nation's foreign policy, which shifted from isolationism to interventionism and then to all-out aid to the Allies, short of war. A majority of Americans backed this trend because of their heightened awareness of the threat posed by the Nazis, who conquered Western Europe and threatened England in mid-1940. For homeland defense, Congress passed the nation's first peacetime draft, registering all male citizens between ages 18 and 35.

In 1940, the economy took a small upturn based on greater defense spending for domestic military preparedness and for foreign military aid to Allies on a strict cash-and-carry basis. An economic stimulus, this new spending boosted production, even causing some formerly closed factories to reopen. Many new workers came from the pool of the long unemployed. (The official unemployment rate was 14 percent at the start of 1940.)

There was a great increase in defense spending in 1941. Congress increased the military budget nearly tenfold to $10.8 billion. The economy expanded steadily and steeply upwards, production rose, the number of jobs increased, and wages went up. Congress passed the Lend-Lease Act on March 11, 1941, marking an additional $7 billion in aid to the Allies, especially Britain and China. The Soviet Union, which was attacked in June by their erstwhile ally Germany, requested and received Lend-Lease aid in continuous massive shipments of food and war materials. While steadfastly refusing to go to war, the country grew more prosperous by supplying the Allies in their war efforts.

The Peacetime Home Front

The government gave lucrative war contracts to domestic industries to increase production for war materiel to meet the needs of all the Allies. With such heightened military spending, the 1941 economy expanded to a record level. Tens of thousands of new jobs were created. Real wages (discounted for inflation) rose 10 percent in this single year. Many

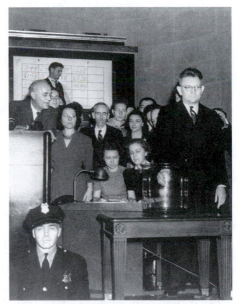

General Hershey draws the last capsule from the goldfish bowl during the first peacetime Selective Service lottery, October 15, 1940. (Library of Congress)

of the new, highly paid workers bought consumer goods in sizable quantities for the first time in a decade. In 1941, the auto industry, which had been in a slump during the 1930s Depression, had its best sales year since 1929. These new workers grew bolder. In the 18 months before the United States entered the war, the Congress of Industiral Unions added 1.5 million new members, and some 2.5 million workers went on strike over these months, seeking union recognition or higher wages.

Cities began to expand and prosper with war contracts. Industries attracted workers from near and far—men too old or too young for the draft; women, who over the war years began to fill jobs vacated by those who left for war; and the rural poor, both black and white, from the Midwest and South. California and Michigan were the greatest magnet states and had the highest number of war contracts.

Once out of the South, African Americans quickly learned that racism was a national problem, not just a Southern one. The North and West had their own forms of segregation, informal by custom. The aim was the same: to keep blacks separate and unequal. Racism led to inferior schools and job opportunities. In 1940, civil rights leader A. Phillip Randolph threatened a huge protest march on the nation's capital and successfully pressured FDR to issue the Fair Employment Practices Act. As a result, African Americans gained employment in the new federally funded defense industries on a relatively fair and equal basis. However, housing discrimination persisted, forcing Southern black newcomers into crowded ghettoes.

The Draft in Peacetime and War

Congress passed the first peacetime draft in September 1940, which helped to raise 800,000 new soldiers. Draftees and enlistees alike went through induction examinations to qualify for service. As millions were called up from 1940 to 1945, these exams produced a huge statistical profile of the physical and mental condition of America's male population. Some 40 percent of the draftees were rejected for physical reasons. Mental and psychological tests proved that roughly 12 percent lacked the education or mental facility to be in the military. The minimum education level was set at grade eight or lower; many were rejected as illiterate.

Beginning in 1941 with the Women's Army Auxiliary Corps (WAAC), women were included in the armed forces for the first time. The Army and the Navy accepted African Americans but assigned them supportive roles, mainly in service and supply units. They rarely saw combat. And the armed services were segregated. Blacks and whites had separate training, housing, mess, and assigned units of duty.

In all, 16 million Americans served in World War II. Only a small percentage experienced combat. Most were assigned to supply, transport, and office work—

in other words, the military bureaucracies. Those who served were destined to enter the most dangerous and destructive war of all time, due to the advances in weapons technology. The "miracle drugs"—sulfa and penicillin—developed in 1941 would save more of the wounded from death than in any previous war involving American forces.

Pearl Harbor and Its Immediate Aftermath

In 1940 and 1941, the peaceful build-up of the economy and the military, including the American efforts to supply material aid to harden the defenses of Allies, made people on the home front confident of the nation's capabilities. Then disaster struck. On December 7, 1941, Japan initiated a devastating, surprise attack on the U.S. Pacific fleet at Pearl Harbor, Hawaii. This united the country for the war effort.

The next day, December 8, President Franklin D. Roosevelt, speaking directly to the nation, made it official—following the attack, the United States was at war with Japan. Three days later, Germany and Italy joined Japan. Japan became the hated enemy, even more than Nazi Germany, because Americans had a preexisting racial bias, especially on the West Coast, where the prosperity of Japanese Americans was resented by some. That month, the government began planning a stunning attack on civil liberties. Three months later, 100,000 West Coast Japanese Americans, without being charged, were labeled potential traitors and were forcibly taken from their homes. They were denied any chance to prove their innocence in a court of law. Troops dispatched them to interior relocation camps. The length of their unlawful detention was indeterminate—for the duration of the war.

The America First Committee

World War II broke out in 1939 when the democracies Britain and France declared war on Nazi Germany for invading Poland; President Roosevelt and Congress officially declared the United States a neutral country. Isolationism remained the conventional wisdom even though technology had shrunk the width of the oceans, indeed the entire globe. It was believed that standing separate and in peace, alone in its ideals, and protected by its Neutrality Laws from allying with any side in the ongoing war in Europe, the United States would be strong enough to stand above and apart from the spreading war, even though it was a world power.

Formed in 1940, the America First Committee led the campaign to keep the United States on the path of isolationism, opposing entry into the war, and aiding U.S. allies in Europe. The foremost spokesman, Charles Lindbergh, was considered a national hero for flying across the Atlantic in 1927. In January 1941, America First supporter Montana senator Burton K. Wheeler vociferously opposed FDR's Lend-Lease proposal during debates on the floor (polls at the time indicated the proposal had 70 percent public support). By April Congress had approved Lend-Lease, agreeing to aid Great Britain and other enemies of the Axis nations.

Lindbergh maintained his opposition, noting in a speech on April 23, 1941, published by the America First Committee, "It is now obvious that England is losing the war. I believe this is realized even by the British government, but they have one last desperate plan remaining. They hope that they may be able to persuade us to send another American expeditionary force to Europe, and to share with England militarily, as well as financially, the fiasco of this war" (Lindbergh 1941). In a September 1941 speech in Des Moines, Iowa, Lindbergh undermined the credibility of the America Firsters when he said, "The three most important groups who have been pressing this country toward war are the British, the Jewish and the Roosevelt administration" (Berg 1998, 425–427). The press condemned the speech for its anti-Semitism, and Lindbergh's popular appeal waned. The America First Committee was dissolved four days after the Japanese attack on Pearl Harbor.

News of Pearl Harbor Attack Reaches the Public

The American people first learned of the Japanese attack on Pearl Harbor in a radio broadcast on a Sunday afternoon, December 7, at approximately 2:25 p.m. Eastern Standard Time. An Associated Press "flash" bulletin brought the unexpected news. Only one of the national radio networks, Mutual Broadcasting System, broke into its scheduled program, a professional football game, to announce the news of the start of war. Call-in listeners registered protests, thinking it likely to be of little consequence.

CBS and NBC waited until the scheduled 2:30 p.m. news slots. Over the next 30 minutes, the AP ticker broke more news, including that of a second attack on the fleet by Japanese fighter planes. Then the networks went over to an all-news format.

CBS's popular live broadcast of the New York Philharmonic's symphony began at three o'clock with an announcement of the attack. Just tuned in, most Americans heard it here for the first time. By late afternoon, the country's newspapers had special editions on the streets with more details.

The next day, the radio again brought news: On December 8, 1941, Americans tuned their radios to listen as FDR began an address to a special joint session of Congress with the words, "Yesterday, December 7, 1941—a date which will live in infamy—the United States of America was suddenly and deliberately attacked by naval and air forces of the Japanese empire." America was at war.

War's Impact: Fear and Vengeance

On the West Coast of the United States, the most immediate consequence of Pearl Harbor was a revival of the old fear of the "Yellow Peril." In the advent of an attack, the Hearst newspapers and many white citizens believed that Japanese American citizens and aliens were a potential fifth column—a group of unknown internal enemies.

At the beginning of the war, some 120,000 Japanese Americans lived on the West Coast, most of them in California. Many were fishermen, merchants, or small farmers. The latter had gained a reputation for "making the desert bloom" for their ability to grow high yields of vegetables and fruits on arid or less-than-promising land. Before the war, Japanese Americans grew 40 percent of California's produce.

Within 10 weeks of the Pearl Harbor attack, on February 19, 1942, FDR issued Executive Order 9066, whereby all Japanese Americans and immigrants from Japan living on the West Coast were evacuated, leaving behind their homes and businesses, and forcibly moved to the interior to live under guard in relocation centers. In Los Angeles, a thriving Little Tokyo disappeared, as thousands of Japanese Americans were deported from the city. A fearful breach in the history of American civil liberties, this relocation of some 120,000 American citizens of Japanese descent and Japanese nationals was a direct result of the American public's reaction to Pearl Harbor. The racist element was clear because Americans of German or Italian background were not rounded up in the same wholesale manner.

There were 10 major "relocation centers" in California, Arizona, Arkansas, Colorado, Idaho, Utah, and Wyoming. Conditions were prisonlike and harsh; hard work was the norm, and families lived behind barbed wire in barracks that offered little protection from the elements. In Tule Lake, California, the Topaz Relocation Center in the Utah desert, and Idaho's Camp Minidoka, winter temperatures were subzero, summers brutally hot. Arkansas internees were forced to work in the swampy Mississippi Delta in sweltering summer heat.

The traditional Japanese family structure, whereby first-generation immigrants (Issei) were traditionally respected as elders by the second-generation, American-born Nisei, was turned on its head in the camps, with only the Nisei allowed to hold leadership roles. In 1944, the U.S. Army began to accept enlistees from young Japanese Americans, and some 3,600 proved their loyalty by serving. A celebrated (and segregated) unit, the 100th Battalion, 442nd Regimental Combat Team, drawn primarily from Hawaii, was dubbed the "Purple Heart Battalion" because it was among the most courageous and most decorated in the Army. Their unit motto was "Go for Broke!" Its members received more than 18,000 individual decorations, including 9,486 Purple Hearts. While many of their families were living under guard in camps, members of this fighting battalion helped liberate Dachau, the Nazi concentration camp.

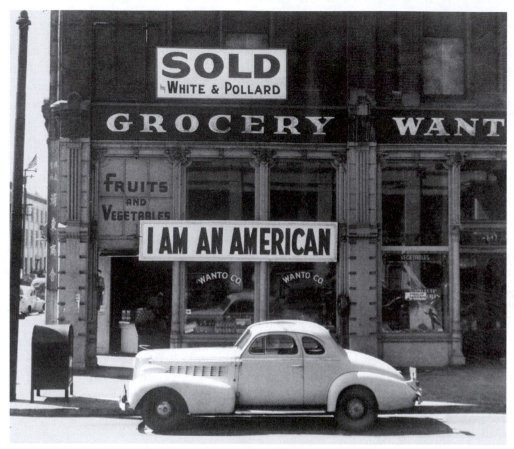

This store in Oakland, California, was closed following orders that all Japanese Americans evacuate to internment camps during World War II. The owner, a University of California graduate of Japanese descent, placed the "I am an American" sign on the storefront the day after Pearl Harbor was attacked by Japanese forces in December 1941. (National Archives)

Among these fighting men was future U.S. senator Daniel Inouye of Hawaii, who was 17 when Japan attacked Pearl Harbor. Inouye later enlisted and lost his right arm fighting in Italy. He was awarded the Bronze Star and the Distinguished Service Cross, but this was upgraded to the Medal of Honor in 2000 after a review. The files of Inouye and 20 other Asian American World War II veterans proved that these men had been denied this highest honor because of the prevailing climate of racial prejudice against Asian Pacific Americans during World War II.

The courts in the 1940s upheld the breach of civil liberties represented by these internment camps. However, in 1988, President Ronald Reagan signed an official apology to Japanese Americans for their internment during World War II in a measure that offered each surviving detainee $20,000 in reparations.

THE EVER-EXPANDING AMERICAN GOVERNMENT

During World War II, the U.S. federal government expanded its functions of overseeing the economy and society, growing larger than ever before in the country's history. The magnitude of the crisis of the war years was momentous—the country was fighting two wars in vastly separated theaters of combat against two powerful empires. Raising the armies, providing and shipping armaments, and feeding the home front were only some of the enormous tasks facing the country. During the war years from 1941 to 1945, there was a fourfold increase in the size of government in the United States, over an already enlarged government bureaucracy created during the Great Depression in the 1930s. The wartime national budget and debt were greater than all prior monies spent by the U.S. government since its beginnings in 1789.

Expansion of wartime government occurred most markedly in three areas: a more powerful presidency, a greater role for government in the overall economy, and a vast increase in the number of persons directly and indirectly employed by government. First, the government's executive branch and its many connected administrative branches increased enormously, as did the powers of the presidency itself in issuing executive orders and in managing secretive high security ventures like the Manhattan Project or war plans. With the added function of commander-in-chief during wartime under the U.S. Constitution, the country's president gained awesome additional power. What was later termed the "Imperial Presidency" had its beginnings in World War II, both with FDR and with his successor, Harry Truman.

As for the Great Depression's "alphabet agencies," the Agricultural Adjustment Act (AAA) and the Tennessee Valley Authority (TVA) were continued; the National Recovery Administration (NRA) and Works Progress Administration (WPA), eliminated. Other agencies proliferated under the president. The War Production Board (WPB) allotted and coordinated war resources by priorities. The National War Labor Board (NWLB) set conditions, pay, and work time for the country's union men and workers, and it enforced nonstrike agreements in critical defense industries. Under wartime executive orders, President Roosevelt mandated such sweeping and controversial changes as having all Japanese Americans on the West Coast removed from their homes to interior relocation camps to be held under guard indefinitely without charges. The Manhattan Project, the secret government project to develop, test, and ultimately use a new atomic weapon with the potential to destroy all mankind, was ultimately based on the final decisions of two men, FDR and Truman, both exercising the singular power of the American wartime leader.

With its increased wartime tax yield added to the enormous loaned sum from massive war bond sales to individuals and institutions, a giant government in Washington, from 1941 to 1945, had the power to grant lush war contracts to defense contractors. With supply needs so great, large corporations with production economies of scale won the largest of these contracts, which guaranteed cost-overrun profits. Many small or medium-sized firms lost out and went under or were absorbed. With antitrust laws suspended and any New Deal antibusiness antagonism forgotten, the largest American corporations got larger because of the largesse of the greatly expanded central government. America's corporations doubled their profits from the war. The Roosevelt administration directed and coordinated the entire wartime economy, eventually setting limits on prices, wages, and profits while steering resources and directing production nationwide.

Finally, during World War II, the U.S. government became the largest employer of Americans. The government payroll included some 16 million Americans who passed through the armed forces, a greatly expanded number of civil servants, the first Americans with Social Security pensions coming due, and a great number of civilians who were employed indirectly by defense industries because of government war contracts with their employers.

New Economic Policies:
The State Mobilizes Society for Total War

Out of a total population of 132 million Americans in the 1940 census, everyone who was roughly school age in 1917 had memories of two prior great national crises—World War I of April 6, 1917, to November 11, 1918, and the Great Depression, which lasted through the 1930s. Greatly enlarged government was necessary in both instances to provide the only adequate means of coping with the magnitude of the global crises. Economically, the country could no longer rely on a normal peacetime, free enterprise economy with only a minimum of government regulation. In each case, a large, strong central government arose to regulate the economy in a way similar to state capitalism, whereby the federal government became the greatly dominant customer, lender, and controller of production and resources to private industries. The 1917 War Industries Board and the 1933 National Recovery Administration provided this powerful function of overseeing and governing the entire U.S. economy in these crises. Only with the railroads during war and the vast Tennessee regional utilities project during the Depression did the government directly operate enterprises in the private sector. In the first instance, this was only temporary, and in the last instance, it was an experiment.

World War II necessitated "big government" in ways that dwarfed prior examples of enlargement of government. So massive were the global threats to the American way of life that only a massive government could wage war and manage huge corporations in an economy grown modern in vast and complex ways. The gross national product doubled and industries produced 24 hours a day, seven days a week under strict government regulation of production, profits, prices, wages, and hours for labor. Government, which had been the employer of last resort in the 1930s relief programs, became the employer of first resort during World War II, with millions of soldiers, civil servants, and wartime workers employed. World War II, not the New Deal, ended the Depression. The deficit spending theories of the economist Maynard Keynes proved the key to the return of mass prosperity for Americans in the war years. The huge government spending and borrowing for each year of war flabbergasted ordinary citizens. They also joined in common efforts to meet the increased costs through paying higher taxes and purchasing $50 billion in war bonds.

War Manpower Commission poster recruiting women into the defense industry, 1944. (Library of Congress)

Blue-collar Americans were keenly aware of the increased power and size of government in the early 1940s. Under the War Labor Board, FDR had received nonstrike pledges from unions in exchange for fair wages and conditions. The great majority complied. In a few instances, he did seize factories where a strike threatened wartime production, and the strikers were jailed and fined. As to government–labor relations, precedents from World War I and the Depression led to the official wartime encouragement of unions and fair wages, hours, and working conditions. By 1944, almost all workingmen looked with favor on big government's approval of unions. The Democrats especially favored the Wagner Act, which provided for easier plant elections for unions.

White-collar Americans in corporations and industries also favorably linked big business and big government agencies, with vast new agencies providing critical aid and direction to the wartime economy stimulated to its new Gulliver-like size. Defense industries depended on the War Manpower Commission to find the scarce workers nationwide to fill their labor needs. Vast migrations of poor white and black Americans moved from the South to fill new defense jobs in northern and western cities like Detroit, Pittsburgh, and Los Angeles.

Wartime Government Expands

The term "bureaucracy" refers to a large, white-collar administrative group, most often associated with government but also applicable to a large private corporate businesses or institutions. Both private and public bureaucracies usually have a top authority—a president or chief executive officer—and a significant layer of second-level officials, the cabinet. Under each of the cabinet heads are myriad layers of agencies or programs. Each is organized as a pyramid of authority so that a lower bureaucrat seeks approval at a higher level in a process involving much paperwork and a long wait for final approval. The typical bureaucrat, working in an agency or program, most often deals with individual clients as names on files identified by number. The client is faceless to the bureaucrat and vice versa.

In World War II, the size of the federal government increased fourfold. President Roosevelt frequently used the powerful executive branch to create new agencies to solve the unprecedented problems of fighting dual wars in separate theaters against the world's two most powerful empires, Germany and Japan. Most of the wartime agencies were headed and staffed by nonelected officials, and the important directors were presidential appointees.

New wartime agencies and programs were added to those already established in the government's New Deal programs. Some New Deal programs continued, like Social Security. This program provided the first pensions to qualified recipients enrolled when the program was mandated in 1935. The administration of this program involved growing numbers of civil servants to keep records on the lifetime earnings of millions of aging Americans to determine the monetary amount of their pensions. Numbers identified people, even more than names in many of these programs. Everyone was assigned a nine-digit Social Security number (SSN) upon reaching working age. In the process of annually totaling up an individual's lifetime income, the civil servants and the recipient often remained faceless and communicated by only letters and forms.

The Military's New Administrative Bureaucracies

Throughout the war, the American people became used to dealing with large nationwide bureaucracies involved with the many new wartime programs. In 1940, the country's first peacetime draft eventually required 16 million adult males aged 18 to 35 to register with their local draft boards. Lotteries were held, and by chance selection these boards chose the quota of men who at any one time would be draftees sent to basic training and off to war. The boards also handled deferments, such as those for conscientious objectors. In cities, towns, villages, and rural counties across America, draft boards constituted the first and one of the most complex of the wartime bureaucracies.

The armed forces themselves totaled at war's end 16 million men and women who had passed through the services. Overseeing this many service people required a myriad of bureaucracies—but most important was the service's central records departments, which kept millions of files updated with data on each and

The United States Constructs
the Largest Ever Office Building

The world's biggest office building was planned for Washington, D.C., and the decision was made to go ahead with construction in 1941, prior to the attack by Japan. Designed so huge as to be double the volume of New York's Empire State Building, it would house the entire War Department of some 40,000 people—from top-ranking heads of all the armed forces all the way down to civilians—on one site.

The Army was already in the process expanding to 1.4 million (from under 200,000) due to the new draft in effect, which created the imminent need for an expanded officer oversight staff to be housed all in a single building as mandated by the president. Thus, the need to construct it as quickly as humanly possible became the task of the head officer of the Army Corps of Engineers, Brig. Gen. Brehon Burke Somervell. Extremely capable, he spearheaded the project through every phase to get approval from Congress and the dense federal bureaucracy overseeing the layout, buildings, monuments, and parks of the capital. The final site was less than a mile south of the capital, and the unusual design for the building was a pentagonal (five sided) shape low in height. The architect G. Edwin Bergstrom drafted its clean, vertical neoclassical exterior look.

With Somervell setting the completion deadline for about 16 months, the chief contractor, John McShain, faced a near-impossible task. He quickly gathered a fine team with thousands of workers and began construction under around-the-clock shifts. McShain himself was under the push of Somervell's assistant, Col. Leslie R. Groves, who increased the pace of construction even more after the country entered the war in December 1941. After a year's work, a portion of the new structure—the Pentagon—was completed and occupied. In five months more, the job was finished.

A miracle had taken place—in 17 months, a heretofore-unimagined gargantuan office building had arisen ready as a central military headquarters to house all of the swelling city-sized group of desk workers required for the conduct of modern war. When completed, the building had used nearly 500,000 tons of concrete. The mix had required mountains of sand and gravel. The ever-pending deadline had even meant that the construction workers completed certain sections even before final plans from the architect and engineers were ready.

With the completion of this assignment, the war demanded the services of the two leading Army officers in charge; both went on to higher rank and prestigious assignments. Somervell went on to become a four-star general in charge of all war supply and logistics, a war post critical to victory. Just as important, his assistant, Groves, went on to be the general in charge of the secret Manhattan Project, pushing it to success in developing the first atomic bomb.

As to the future of the Pentagon, President Roosevelt intended from the first that this giant building was to be temporary headquarters used only to accommodate

Continued on next page

The United States Constructs the Largest Ever Office Building, Continued

the vastly enlarged wartime military. With peace, the country would downsize the military to traditional low peacetime levels, which would necessitate the evacuation of the proportionally shrunken War Department from the Pentagon. The National Archives, the president planned, would then occupy the building.

With the Cold War coming so soon after the end of World War, Roosevelt's intentions were not met; instead, for the first time in the country's history, a huge military presence became a permanent part of the peacetime capital. The Defense Department, so renamed soon after 1945, took up residence in the labyrinth-like interior of the building. The Pentagon became a world symbol of America's new military might.

---

every serviceman. Serial numbers—called dog tags by infantry soldiers—were the most important of all and were used for primary identification in most all circumstances, including the individual's death.

New Bureaucracies to Pay for War and Fight Inflation

The Roosevelt administration financed the war in two primary ways: taxes and loans. Each involved a vast new bureaucracy and greatly enhanced government. The United States' cost of waging the war between December 1941 and August 1945 came to $300 billion. New personal income tax and steeply progressive corporate taxes, in addition to the sale of war bonds, accounted for most of that amount. Borrowing through loans accounted for the rest. As an added benefit, the new taxes and war bond sales both took money out of the hands of newly prosperous citizenry in an economy with few available goods for sale, which helped to hold down inflation and prices for consumer goods.

Inflation was a problem throughout the war. At the end of 1942, after the first full year of war, the cost of living had risen 15 percent. The problem was a common one in wartime—the working population's overall income was rising, but fewer consumer goods were available for purchase. Increased taxes and war bond sales were the government's solution to soak up growing excess purchasing power.

Taxes

In 1941, Congress passed a law that required almost every working individual to pay a personal income tax for the first time (before this war, most were exempted).

This personal tax was withheld from the employee's paycheck. This was known as a pay-as-you-go plan for war costs. Thus the modern tax system came into being at this time.

Working- and middle-class Americans, because of their greater numbers, paid the most total taxes—this group of Americans overall paid a personal income tax for the first time. However, with a steeply progressive tax rate, the wealthiest individuals paid the highest tax rate (raised from low prewar levels). Large corporations also paid high taxes. By 1945, the total cost of war came to $300 billion; about 40 percent of this was financed by personal and corporate taxes.

War Bonds

Government borrowing would pay the other 60 percent. This involved sale of war bonds to the American public and to institutions. The public bond sales campaigns succeeded because the government used the new mass media of radio to blanket the country with news of bond drives and tied war bond sales to movies, comic books, cartoons, and other popular culture. The campaigns also boosted civilian morale at regular intervals during the war.

Of the total population of 132 million, the 90 percent of Americans who remained at home during the war had strong reasons for buying bonds during the sales campaigns. They showed support for the war by investing their own money to help pay for the needs of fellow Americans fighting and risking their lives abroad. War bonds became the means for Americans to be involved in helping those in the dangerous fight overseas. War bonds were also a way for Americans to take from their personal savings, lend money to the government to help pay for the soaring war costs, and, in the future, use the interest earned when the bonds came due to buy a home or car. Thus the patriotic buyer of bonds had both public and private motives for purchasing the bonds.

The government conducted eight bond drives in three-and-a-half years. Celebrities from popular culture, business, and other walks of life directly participated in the sales drives. Radio was

A U.S. propaganda poster encourages citizens to buy war bonds in order to protect the nation's children from the Nazi threat during World War II. (National Archives)

ideal for these marathon bond drives because they could continue until the
needed sum of money was raised. On September 21, 1943, the popular singer
Kate Smith, sold millions in a 16-hour radio bond drive. The public relished
Smith's version of "God Bless America." Hollywood sent its stars to pitch bonds;
among these were the comedic movie trio of Dorothy Lamour, Bob Hope, and
singer Bing Crosby.

New Bureaucracies For Taxes and Rationing

The IRS, the tax-collecting government branch, became for many Americans
the prime example of bureaucracy because its complex, changing rules were
often interpreted in a rigid, concrete way by its own tax collectors. (This strict,
rule-ridden aspect is also common to other bureaucracies.) Another wartime
bureaucracy geared to fight inflation through the nationwide system of rationing. Aiming to keep costs down, tens of thousands of locally run rationing
boards issued to the head of every local family monthly books of coupons for
the purchase of food and gas and other scarce consumer goods. Purchase of
items required a certain number of coupons. New bureaucracies such as these
needed to fight inflation and pay for war led the government to grow to enormous size.

Victory by Overwhelming Production with Broad Prosperity

Americans in businesses, factories, mining, and agriculture knew at war's end
that their part in the country's extraordinary wartime production had been as
essential to victory as that of the 16 million who served in the armed forces. The
American economy's growing strength underlay the rising dominance of its military. The United States supplied its own military needs and much of the needs
of its Allies during the two prewar and the four war years.

Americans working at home in the years 1941 to 1945 realized that the extraordinary demands of fighting a global war had necessitated the largest-ever U. S.
federal government to expand the national economy and spur production to
record levels. The gross national product rose dramatically until, by 1944, the
country produced more than the combined output of the enemy Axis countries.
The nation basked in a broader, more inclusive prosperity than that of the 1920s
before the 1929 stock market crash. Unemployment had virtually vanished; all
who wanted work had work. While the New Deal had eased the effects of the
Depression, World War II succeeded in eliminating it. In 1938, the U.S. unemployment rate had been 19 percent; by 1944, it had shrunk to 1.2 percent.
And millions who had not worked before had now entered the workforce.

Was this a lasting prosperity? No, maybe only temporary, many thought, because these war years had been the exception. After victory, when the millions

of soldiers returning to their jobs displaced the impermanent war workers, Americans assumed that the permanently unemployed would rise up again to pre-war levels of the 1930s because of the expected decline in productivity. War had activated the economy's excess productive capacity that had been idle in the Depression years. Peace could stop a great many machines and assembly lines, leaving vacated factories to again gather dust. The Depression could return. That was the anxiety among the masses of Americans as the war ended.

By what means could prosperity continue after victory for all Americans who had lived through World War II—those in the armed forces and at home? The answers were embedded in the success of the war years. The critical answer was the continued need for big government and for the strengthened and powerful presidency. If the peak World War II production levels could be maintained to protect against a powerful new threat to the nation, seen by many in 1945 as a Joseph Stalin–led communist expansion, then continued prosperity could be possible.

Also, if government raised the floodgates on the giant dam that had held back consumer spending throughout the war with measures like rationing, the public would likely become mass consumers of the goods scarce in war but plentiful again in peacetime. For instance, no new automobiles were made from 1942 to 1945. If the public's pent-up demand for such consumer goods as new 1946 model cars was to be met, then this could buoy up the economy. Eager buyers had sufficient money saved from wartime's government-generated jobs, decent wages with much overtime pay, and almost all consumers could draw upon earnings from war bonds.

Social Attitudes Favor Big Government

Big government would be the only source to regulate the greatly enlarged economy that had come into existence during the war. While many ordinary citizens worried about the rise of huge national deficits and unbalanced budgets (the president and Congress spent more during World War II than the total of all prior U.S. expenditures since 1789), the economists explained in ways often befuddling to the public that deficit spending was an essential tool to operate modern state finances. "Growing the economy" by this means created new wealth to pay back government lenders. The modern tax system and the IRS, with its awesome national bureaucracy, would continue raising yearly revenue in a most efficient way: by taking personal taxes from the paychecks of almost every working American.

As early as 1944, FDR and Congress planned for the coming transition to peace when they created what was soon termed the G.I. Bill, a package of benefits for the millions of veterans who would soon return home. The veterans would get unemployment payments for 52 weeks (a provision to reintegrate a larger work force), education at colleges paid by federal stipends (a provision to steer veterans toward learning for the future work force), and home loans at the lowest cost subsidized by the government (a provision to spur the new housing and construction industry). Here was a prime example of big government orchestrating the private business sector in ways beneficial to both—state capitalism with a mixed private–public economy.

However, in this type of economy, a great many Americans overlooked the critical role of big government and gave credit to businesses for beating the Axis almost solely by the free enterprise system alone. Conservatives especially had nostalgia, it seemed, for a long-gone time of small government with minimal regulation over industry and little responsibility for the social welfare of the people. While big government remained crucial to victory in war, a more conservative Congress eliminated many popular federal New Deal programs, such as the Works Progress Administration (WPA), but extended others, such as Social Security and the minimum wage law. Willing to provide a floor for the disadvantaged, Congress was clearly not inclined to take the path toward full social democracy that was chosen in the postwar years by many European democracies.

The majority of workers had the government's encouragement to organize unions within the capitalist system rather than organize a socialist party to radically reform this system. The War Labor Board (WLB) encouraged industry-wide unions, with skilled workers joining the traditionally conservative American Federation of Labor (AFL) and the more numerous unskilled workers joining the new Congress of Industrial Unions (CIO), the nationwide confederation that emerged after the Wagner Act of 1937 removed obstacles to such groups. The country in wartime functioned by the cooperation of big business and big labor under the overall direction of big government. This arrangement would continue after the war, but as unions renewed strikes to raise wages, and after inflation skyrocketed with the removal of wartime price controls, the conservative public turned strongly antiunion even in regions outside the South where this attitude was traditional.

Big government proved critical to providing nationwide solutions during the Depression and the war. Government needed to be immensely larger to meet the challenges of global war. The Roosevelt and Truman administrations set many precedents because enhanced federal government was critical to such projects as pooling all the scientific resources possible into the development of a usable atomic weapon, beginning with theories scratched on blackboards. At war's end, the people felt both awe and anxiety over the idea of a government grown so large as to often seem distant, impersonal, and filled with bureaucracy and red tape. But it seemed obvious that big government was here to stay.

WAR TRANSFORMS THE HOME FRONT

The overwhelming majority of citizens lived and worked on the home front during the war years. Out of a population of 132 million, 16 million Americans served

Women working in Douglas Aircraft's Long Beach, California, assembly plant during World War II complete final inspection of nose cones for A-20 attack bombers. (National Archives)

directly in war. The fighting primarily took young males, and a small number of young females joined the new armed forces women's auxiliaries. The pre-war industrial workforce was predominantly male and white, the very men now drafted and sent to war. One consequence was that their replacements and those hired for the many newly created jobs in the booming war economy were African Americans and women. Work gave individuals in each of these groups a newfound autonomy, self-confidence, security, and decent income as the government ensured good wages for defense workers. In many cases, married women with small children worked in defense plants that had government-sponsored day care centers.

Unions admitted African Americans in larger numbers, especially those in the new CIO, which was made up of unskilled and semiskilled workers. In 1935, the AFL, with its skilled workers, admitted its first all-black union, led by A. Phillip Randoph and made up of Pullman car porters on the railroads. Gains like these made urban African American blue-collar workers—most of whom, prior to the war, had been poor Southern sharecroppers—reasonably prosperous. Poor whites also gained defense jobs and improved their economic status.

Gains for minorities helped make the war years one of the few times in U.S. history when a real and provable redistribution of wealth occurred, with the wealthy moving slightly closer to the ascending lower class and the widening middle class. Greater per capita income on the home front in these years was of critical importance because it made possible mass purchasing of consumer goods that were no longer rationed, thus sustaining the healthy economy.

Mass migrations were another unusual consequence on the wartime home front. Millions of working people, both white and black, moved from the South to the North and West. The West Coast especially gained population as the government spawned booming defense businesses in California locations including Los Angeles (planes), the busy ports of San Francisco and Oakland, and the nearby boomtown of Richmond (merchant ships). These migrations gave a national scope to certain problems that had been considered regional issues before the war. Segregation and racism, for instance, were now no longer largely confined to the South. In 1943, a host of northern cities erupted in race riots because of black grievances and white antagonism.

National unity, however, prevailed over such strains. Most Americans at home believed they were engaged in "the Good Fight" on the side of imperiled democracies fighting against the new threat of mass totalitarian dictatorships. America had been attacked in 1941, and the public believed in this fight for survival. The war effort further integrated a diverse people as first-, second-, and third-generation immigrants worked in factories alongside old-stock Americans. Newcomers to the United States during the Great Immigration of the 1890s and their descendents were more assimilated during World War II than had been the case 20 years earlier, during World War I. One great difference between the two wars was that by the 1940s, government needed less propaganda to bring the people together in a common effort. Indeed, common sacrifices and benefits united the American people in the 1940s. Prosperity became widespread in the country by the mid-war years, and this was a welcome relief to those who had struggled throughout the Depression years. Amidst this newfound plenty, the public rushed to aid the fight, buying billions in personal war bonds. They also accepted rationing of scarce goods because of the will to sacrifice and because all—rich and poor—were required to sacrifice. Together, this national unity led to the miracle of production by which America alone produced more war material than all other nations combined. This was the greatest contribution of the home front.

Wartime Society and the State: The Growth of Boomtowns

Boomtowns were a phenomenon of the war. Federal war contracts were extended to local industries to convert assembly lines from civilian to defense production. The government also provided easy financing for this expansion and the building of new plants. Cost overrun contracts and guaranteed profit margins made for expansive optimistic business outlooks in many favorable urban locales, mostly in the West and in the North, where a manufacturing base existed.

In such boomtowns as Richmond, California, for instance, workers were needed to build aircraft carriers, the newest and most critical element of military strategy in World War II. In the wake of the attack on Pearl Harbor, the United States no longer had a two-ocean navy. The Japanese had destroyed the Pacific fleet, including eight battleships and 180 airplanes. Three aircraft carriers remained in the Pacific (they had been elsewhere when the attack came). To rebuild its Navy in the Pacific, the United States started the most massive program of shipbuilding the world had ever seen.

New workers streamed into the boomtowns attracted by high wages in the defense industries; while newfound prosperity was the reward, there were considerable problems and stresses for the communities absorbing this rapid influx of newcomers. Available housing was scarce and new building nonexistent because of higher wartime priorities. Trailers, barracks, even tents served as housing for the new war workers. Overcrowding was the rule.

Public services were overburdened. Schools were overflowing with the new arrivals; meanwhile, many teachers had left for war and new teachers were hard to attract because teachers' salaries were less than manufacturing wages. Some 1 million teens dropped out of school, many finding factory work. Others became antisocial and committed crimes, which raised the juvenile delinquency rate to new highs during the war. The youngest working teens had little protection, as existing child labor laws were eased. Day care centers were almost nonexistent to provide care for small children. Population overflow often led to ecological damage in local areas. Some communities allowed raw sewage to overflow into nearby rivers or lakes.

Union membership grew in many boomtowns, but the nationwide union organizations, the AFL and the new CIO, had ceded to the War Labor Board the power to set satisfactory wages, hours, and conditions in defense factories in exchange for a nonstrike pledge. Even so, 15,000 strikes occurred during the war, many of them bringing strife previously unknown to communities before the war made a boom in the local economy.

Social strife of another kind arose from the animosity that the longtime residents had for the newcomers. Poor white workers from the South were stigmatized as "Arkies" and "Oakies." Prejudice against black newcomers ran especially high as the local white population fought them for jobs and housing. During the summer of 1943 in many densely crowded boomtown black ghettoes, the angry residents warred with bigoted whites in a series of race riots. Detroit suffered the worst riot when white police shot 17 African Americans but only used tear gas to halt white looters or murderous gangs.

Entertainment was the normal release in boomtowns. Workers earned the highest paychecks in their lives yet were unable to buy consumer goods because these were scarce and available only on a limited basis through rationing; they frequented bars in large numbers, went to movies, and listened more intently than ever to war newscasts on the radio. Dance halls were popular, with the big band jazz sounds of swing music from Duke Ellington or Tommy Dorsey. Teens had their own entertainment—the jitterbug was the rage, and Frank Sinatra was the singing idol. He drew crowds of "bobby-soxers"—girls who screamed hysterically at his concerts.

With the end of war, a short, frenzied period was over for many of the boom-towns as the migrants moved away and output dwindled in the defense industries. Some boomtowns had a broader, more varied economic base that could absorb the newcomers on a lasting basis.

The Four Freedoms

Franklin Delano Roosevelt's State of the Union address to Congress in January 1941 introduced the concept of the "Four Freedoms": freedom of speech and of worship, and freedom from want and from fear (Roosevelt, 1941). The government used this concept to set a series of war aims for the Allied cause. African Americans and others who felt discrimination used its terms to point out how far the United States at home veered from its own ideals. Southern African Americans (some 9 to 10 million of the 13 million total African American population in the nation in 1945) experienced a segregated and inferior position that was in reality far removed from the nation's ideals of freedom and equality based in law. One in 10 Americans were black, but their plight in the states of the Old Confederacy went largely unnoticed by most white Americans who passed "the Negro problem" off as a regional problem of the South.

Social ideology in the South held to a belief in absolute white superiority and black inferiority. A Southern caste system developed over the 60 years prior to the 1940s, and this racism was institutionalized in a system of legal segregation of the races in matters political, economic, and social throughout the leading states of the Old Confederacy. Politically, African Americans were disenfranchised because of the poll tax and the All-White Party Primary, which restricted voting to whites only. Of approximately 4 million voting-age Southern African Americans in the 1940s, only about 5 percent actually voted; in Mississippi with African Americans making up 49 percent of its citizens, the race demagogue Theodore G. Bilbo was elected governor with a majority constituting of only 16 percent of potential voters. Economically, African Americans in the region were poor, rural sharecroppers with annual incomes below $250 per year; when they found work for wages in cities, their pay was generally 75 percent of what a white earned for doing the same work. Socially and in terms of education, the iron laws of segregation were in force—public facilities were separate: schools, parks, swimming pools, and drinking fountains. Black schools were far inferior to their "equal" white counterparts.

The Four Freedoms, as the goals of our fighting troops, represented a type of double standard for the military's one million African Americans who were put in segregated armed forces to fight the racism of the Axis powers and given "black" blood transfusions if wounded. Many Southern African Americans fighting for freedom abroad returned home to a region that made a mockery of the four freedoms—freedom of speech and worship and freedom from want and fear.

African Americans in the South lacked the freedom to vote because of chicanery and outright deadly threats and so had few if any political representatives to voice their cause and grievances on a state or national level. Newspapers rarely showed photos of African Americans except in cases of crime; few newspapers would give space to anything controversial about race. Thus, African Americans lacked anything but a phantom presence in the mainstream press. One of many social taboos in the region stigmatized a black who argued in public with a white.

African Americans in the South also could not worship freely because all Christian religious denominations, whether Baptist, Methodist, or Evangelical, were segregated, with the exception of Catholics, whose integrated worship was derided by most, and crossover services or worshippers were strictly forbidden. Segregation even prevailed in death, too, as African Americans had their own cemeteries.

Freedom from want was only a distant hope for many Southern African Americans. Work meant poverty for the many loan-extended tenants or croppers raising cotton and for those doing the work "unfit" for whites in all-African American turpentine mills or fertilizer factories. Want was a constant with this minority, even in medical care; they had access only to African American hospitals. Infant mortality rates for blacks were roughly three times the rate for whites; average life span was 50 years versus 60 for whites. Education was the biggest want—without good education, the cycle of poverty repeated each generation, and few were able to rise out of their origins. The South, even as the poorest region in the country, supported two systems of education because of the burden of segregation. The whole region in general and its African American population in particular had the lowest rates of education—in 1946, just $17 was spent per pupil per year compared to a national average of $80.26 per pupil per year—and also the highest rates of illiteracy.

Southern African Americans of the 1940s were rarely free of the fear of intimidation, threats, or deadly violence by lynching or by "disappearances" with no one knowing the fate of an abducted person. During the war, lynching continued, but at a greatly diminished rate—one lynching in 1945; however, in 1946, bigoted whites lynched six African Americans to put newly returned black veterans "back in their place." Most frightening of all for African Americans was the frequent sense of being without due protection of law because they had no representation in the police and justice systems. Subject to white judges and juries, many more black than white murder or rape suspects received the death penalty. Today, 21st-century DNA evidence has proven many convicts innocent of capital offenses; the number of innocents undergoing state executions in the South in the 1940s will never be known.

President Roosevelt concluded his 1941 "Four Freedoms" radio speech by making note of a long, ongoing evolution of human rights and freedom in America. Indeed, by 1945, there was evidence of more African Americans having gained the strength and confidence to confront racial injustices. Two million in all had experienced new, more cosmopolitan open ways of life—whether it was the one million who served overseas in the military or the one million who did integrated work for good pay in the urban defense industries, especially of the North and Far West. African Americans in large numbers could take pride in the achievements of their race, whether in the war or defense production. By 1945, if the reality of the Four Freedoms had slightly improved for some, the country was still a long way from Roosevelt's last ringing hope of human rights gaining victory everywhere for all people. A good start could be made at home for all African Americans in the post-1945 South.

Wartime Women's New Gender Role

A strong-muscled woman who rolled up her sleeves to get to work announced "We Can Do It!" in the War Production office's recruiting poster that urged women to replace in the country's factories and assembly lines the men who had gone to war. A 1943 popular song by Redd Evans and John Jacob Loeb titled "Rosie the Riveter" championed an assembly-line worker with the lines "She's making history, working for victory, Rosie the Riveter."

During the war years, the number of women in the workplace rose from 11 million to almost 20 million. About 6 million of these were white, middle-class women who were urged into the workplace by a government-led "Women at Work" campaign that enlisted the help of magazines like *McCall's* and *The Saturday Evening Post*. As the draft continued to call up American men, American women moved from agricultural and "pink-collar" jobs into higher paying jobs in airplane manufacturing, arsenals, and other heavy industry. Sybil Lewis, an African American riveter for the Los Angeles Lockheed Aircraft plant describes her experience as part of the Library of Congress Veterans History Project in the transcript of a presentation by Sheridan Harvey, Women's Studies Specialist, Humanities and Social Sciences Division, Library of Congress: "The women worked in pairs. I was the riveter and this big, strong, white girl from a cotton farm in Arkansas worked as the bucker. The riveter used a gun to shoot rivets through the metal and fasten it together. The bucker used a bucking bar on the other side of the metal to smooth out the rivets. Bucking was harder than shooting rivets. It required more muscle. Riveting required more skill." Still, women workers were paid 60 percent of a man's wage, on average, and considered replacements for "the real thing."

War and Minorities

Between June 3 and June 7, 1943, a series of clashes between military men and Mexican American youths, known as *pachucos* on the streets of East Los Angeles, drew nationwide attention. The *pachucos* were noted for wearing "zoot suits"—broad-shouldered long coats, high-waisted peg-legged pants, long dangling chains, and wide-brimmed hats. There were some 250,000 Mexicans in Los Angeles in the early 1940s, needed for labor to meet war demands. Adjusting to working-class life in a city where they weren't necessarily welcome had its tensions. Most of the "zoot suiters" were second-generation children of immigrants. Some were gang members, part of the wave of juvenile delinquency that affected the United States during the war years.

In May 1943, a violent confrontation occurred between hundreds of soldiers and civilians who had heard that a sailor had been stabbed by a group of young Mexican Americans leaving a dance. The resulting riots lasted into the wee hours of the morning, and the police arrested the Mexican Americans "for their own protection." In the following days, rioting servicemen attacked young Mexican American men, whether they were wearing zoot suits or not, along with other passers-by, including African Americans. At the worst, thousands of servicemen and civilians were involved. By June 8, 1943, hundreds of servicemen in groups of from 10 to 150 prowled downtown Los Angeles, mostly on foot and disorderly, carrying belts, knives, and tire irons, apparently searching for Mexican Americans. To restore order, much of Los Angeles was declared out of bounds to all Navy, Marine, Coast Guard, and Army personnel. In her column, First Lady Eleanor Roosevelt questioned the racial element of the riots. A commission appointed by Gov. Earl Warren found it to be "significant" that most of the persons mistreated during the recent incidents in Los Angeles were either persons of Mexican descent or African Americans. "In undertaking to deal with

U.S. armed forces personnel with wooden clubs on the street during a "Zoot Suit" riot, Los Angeles, California, 1943. (Library of Congress)

the cause of these outbreaks," the commission's report said, "the existence of race prejudice cannot be ignored."

American Society Views the Global War as the "Good Fight"

Americans referred to World War II as the "good fight" and, in the years after, increasingly as the "the last good war" fought by "the greatest generation." Why? When comparing the country's later wars in Korea, Vietnam, or Iraq and elsewhere, commentators and historians perceived World War II to be most clearly a just war. The United States had been a neutral that was attacked without warning by a powerful enemy, and its people had united in a fight to survive. To save their own values and way of life in America and to preserve the tradition of democratic nations in the world provided a great clarity of purpose. Americans gained an unprecedented unity from such aims and worked both at home and abroad in a great common effort toward eventual victory. In the popular mind, the war became a good fight to the very end as the peace-loving democracies battled the war-mongering totalitarian dictatorships. Increasing evidence of evil by the Nazis, revealed with the liberation of the concentration camps and the discovery of the deaths of millions, led most Americans to call for total victory. The American government demanded unconditional surrender of the Axis powers.

American military forces, however, pursued the "good fight" with sometimes morally dubious means, such as the deaths of countless helpless civilians in the repeated carpet bombings of German cities and later in the fire bombings of the wooden structures of Tokyo. The American president's decision to use atomic weapons against Japan was the most morally contested of the United States's military actions during the war. The United States had developed the weapon and set world precedent by using it not once but twice against Japan.

Historians and military strategists stated that the atomic bomb had been unnecessary for a variety of reasons. One was that Japan was already on the verge of surrender and would have done so without it. A later Cold War version of this argument stated that because the Soviets had newly entered the war against Japan, Truman, already wary of this ally, used the bomb to prevent a joint U.S.-Soviet occupation of the defeated country. Truman stated that the atomic bombs dropped on Hiroshima and Nagasaki saved the lives of an estimated one million American soldiers who might have died in a conventional invasion, and the weapon brought a quick end to the war. Japan's surrender elated Americans; the frightful means used to bring about that end did not disturb most of them—after all, Japan was the same nation that attacked America by surprise with overwhelming force at Pearl Harbor, unifying the country in this "good fight" for survival.

With victory in 1945, Americans saw the United States as the force of good in the world and believed their president had used atomic bombs responsibly. Some argued that the use of the two bombs was a kind of mission of mercy, ultimately saving more lives than would be lost in an extended war and occupation of Japan. Expediency was an especially convincing argument to Americans, who ignored the fact that the weapon used at Hiroshima and Nagasaki was a revolutionary leap into a new atomic age. In 1945, many took comfort in thinking that this new weapon would long be an American monopoly. They saw the United States as the single most powerful military nation ever existing in the world and believed that future presidents would use that awesome power to long safeguard the goals of peace and democracy secured in the "good fight."

The State and Society: National Unity

In 1945, Americans were the most united that they ever had been in many ways. On the wartime home front, all levels of society had made sacrifices for the common good to win the "good fight." Individual Americans from all classes had purchased war bonds in the eight nationwide campaigns. Similarly, all had shared in the rationing system and had mutually consented to restrictions on such necessities as gas, tires, women's stockings, meat, butter, and many other goods. All citizens, conservatives and liberals alike, felt a deep sadness when President Franklin D. Roosevelt died in early 1945. For a dozen years, he had led them through national crises, first the 1930s Depression and then the "good fight," which was nearing its end. Before Pearl Harbor, FDR had laid out the very goals of the Allies in his declaration of the Four Freedoms.

At home, common sacrifice had also brought a common reward. General prosperity had returned to the country and, certainly by comparison to the Depression, all generally enjoyed widespread employment, security, and the continued practice of time-consuming democratic politics throughout war. The 1944 presidential election had been hotly contested, with Roosevelt winning a fourth term by having the Democrats trim their sails away from any vestiges of domestic reform and toward the sole goal of victory. FDR, attuned to the conservative shift of the public mood, had named Truman his running mate and dropped the more liberal Henry Wallace, his prior vice president. Prosperity continuing and victory nearing were factors in this reelection. But more than anyone, FDR had evoked and sustained the national unity by getting the cooperation required of many groups. Labor, for instance, heeded closely their nonstrike pledge in defense industries. Corporate executives often went to work for the government as dollar-a-year men, foregoing any salary.

Roosevelt ordered all defense industries that earned government contracts to practice fair and equal employment, especially regarding jobs for African Americans from the South who had moved in search of work. Enforcing his order was a national Fair Employment Practices Commission. While the war did create greater national unity among white immigrants and older stock whites, racial harmony remained a greater challenge. In race relations, African Americans found the country as a whole to be hypocritical. Throughout the war, the NAACP had a Double-V Campaign to fight Hitler abroad and Jim Crow at home. Jim Crow was the catchall term for Southern legal segregation and Northern de facto segregation of the races. African American organizations called for integration of the races at home and in the military and noted that, lacking it, America itself was the exception in the eyes of blacks to the rhetoric of Four Freedoms or the "good fight."

Still, considering the deep ambiguities involved in America's later wars—for example, the Cold War's need for limited wars to defend a part of a country, as in South Korea or South Vietnam, without hope of total victory—the representation of World War II as "the good fight" has validity. Most of those who lived the war years sensed this, and even years afterward, the children and grandchildren of the war generation have accepted this portrayal.

The postwar years were noted for the rise in families and the baby boom. Both these trends had a start during the war. The newfound prosperity and the urgency of a departing serviceman made for a climate of increased wartime marriages, which also were unstable. Divorces in 1944 rose to 27 per 100 from 16 per 100 in 1940. In 1941, the last year prior to war, two million babies were born; in 1942 and 1943, a 33 percent increase in births occurred. War babies were bell ringers for the later boom. The divorce rate continued to be high after the war, but in time more settled marriages were norm.

In wartime, Americans tended to be more conservative about continued New Deal–type social reforms. The conservative trend would continue after the war's end but with an acceptance of government planning in the economy and of deficit spending to correct economic recessions. The trend was characterized by FDR in December 1943 when he announced "Dr. Win-the-War" had replaced "Dr. New Deal." With Truman replacing the more liberal Wallace as Roosevelt's running mate, Roosevelt nonetheless got a narrower margin of winning votes from the American people than in any of his prior campaigns. Still, the main core of the New Deal—such programs as Social Security, unemployment benefits, and the Tennessee Valley Authority (TVA)—had become the basis of the new American welfare state that had gained bipartisan acceptance.

War's End in 1945 Brings a New Demography

Over the course of four years, the war created a collective transformation of American society. The internal migration that took place during this time was the greatest in the country's history and made permanent shifts and continuing flows of migrants to other regions and to the cities. Witnessing the changes in demographics, Americans at war's end also experienced the social stresses and rewards that resulted from 27 million Americans leaving to go elsewhere during the war.

Among the more profound of these changes were the flow of people west, the decline of those in rural areas, the stressful changes in the South and in northern cities. The West was the fastest-growing region of the country during and after the war. California alone gained 1.4 million new wartime residents. Airplane manufacturing would remain a staple of the economy in Southern California, as would shipbuilding there and north in the San Francisco Bay area. Greater crop production was the result of better fertilizers and machinery and increasingly larger and more efficient farms; although farms lost 11 percent in population, they gained 15 percent in total production. Corporate farms had a precedent in such statistics.

The South was a curious instance; while losing total population, especially among poor whites and blacks, the area nevertheless got its first foothold in building up its cities and manufacturing base, both due to the allotment of rich defense contracts. The fastest-growing of all wartime states included Texas, Virginia, and Florida. Cities mushroomed, too. For example, Mobile, Alabama, grew 61 percent; this port was a noted boomtown. Here were the initial seeds of conservative politics and what was later to be termed the Sun Belt. The East lost population to the West during the war, a distant herald of the decline of liberalism.

Women constituted three out of five of the migrants during war. The number of females in the workforce doubled to 6 million. The most unprecedented gains were in manufacturing. This shift for women workers was in large part a temporary change. At war's end, most of their jobs were given over to returning male veterans. Many women returned to the more traditional roles of wives and mothers, although their adventure of wartime work and gain in economic independence would be a valuable precedent for these women.

The "Good Fight" and Race Relations at Home and in the Military

In 1940 and 1941, African Americans experienced a bold contradiction in terms of their country's ideals and realities regarding race. While opposing the various racist hierarchical theories of the Axis dictatorships of Germany, Italy, and Japan, Americans, in large part, advocated equality and opposed the enemy's racism; yet Americans also supported or sanctioned separating African Americans into their own segregated society based on feelings of white supremacy. In 1940 and throughout the war, African Americans endured the separation of the races at home and abroad in the armed forces. In response, African American adopted a more militant attitude against this sanctioned discrimination (often called Jim Crow laws) and made substantial gains in distinct areas. At home, African Americans gained jobs at a faster pace than ever before because of the severe labor needs of the booming defense industries, and because FDR ordered equal opportunity employment in 1941, even before Pearl Harbor.

Abroad, the American armed forces, in all branches, maintained segregation and for most of the war assigned African Americans to inferior noncombat roles. African American soldiers protested this treatment. Near the war's end, Gen. Dwight D. Eisenhower integrated some infantry groups by calling for volunteers among African American soldiers, noting that these units performed admirably well. The strategies of black protest organizations—NAACP, the new Congress for Racial Equality (CORE), and the March-on-Washington Committee (MOWC)— would give a lasting impetus to the growing successes of the civil rights movement in the postwar years.

In the two years prior to Pearl Harbor, the president and Congress steadily increased the military portion of the national budget, creating defense industry jobs, which African Americans sought in record numbers by a large internal migration from the South. Even with boom replacing Depression, many African Americans were still being passed over until A. Phillip Randolph threatened a massive all-black protest march on the nation's capital. FDR compromised by ordering fair and equal employment in any industry that gained a war contract from the government. During the remainder of the war, more than two million African Americans found unskilled and semiskilled jobs, and many joined CIO labor unions.

Race was thought by most Americans to be a distinctly Southern problem. With the nationwide dispersal of African Americans during World War II, the issue of race quickly became a national issue. In 1943, major cities such as Detroit and New York's Harlem had race riots ignited by rivalries for jobs, housing, and schools.

Race in the armed forces also caused disturbances. Northern-born blacks sent to basic training camps in the South resisted the segregation laws there and refused, for instance, to sit in the back of the bus. Change came slowly. America's first African American general, Benjamin O. Davis Sr., was appointed in 1940; its first African American pilots enlisted in 1942, led by Davis's son. African American officers were few. Integrated infantry units occurred on a trial basis only late in the war.

Civil rights organizations and strategies having success during the war included the long- standing NAACP, which won court fights against varied aspects of legal segregation. It sponsored the "Double V Campaign," which urged victory against Hitler *and* Jim Crow. CORE was a new organization that advocated nonviolent civil disobedience to peacefully integrate public facilities. A massive all-black protest in the nation's capital to highlight the gap between America's ideals and its reality was the effective new strategy of Randolph's organization.

The later 1950s and 1960s civil rights revolution had its seeds planted by these organizations during World War II.

Race and the Workplace

In 1940, A. Phillip Randolph, age 51, was president of the Brotherhood of Sleeping Car Porters (BSCP), the union that signed its first contract with the Pullman Company in 1937. In 1935, the BSCP was the first black union in the AFL. Randolph had led the long, hard fight for a black union since 1925. His achievement led African Americans to see Randolph as their most important leader in the struggle for economic equality during the start of the economic boom in wartime defense manufacturing in 1940 and 1941. Although he also championed the fight for civil rights, he had devoted his life to aiding his people to gain more and better jobs within the existing American economy. In doing so, he was adept at using militant tactics to force concessions from an employer.

Randolph organized the March-on-Washington Movement (MOWM) in 1940 and threatened massive, all-black protest in the nation's capital unless FDR issued an executive order forbidding discrimination in the employment of blacks in defense industries contracting with the government. In response, FDR issued an executive order and created a Fair Employment Practices Committee (FEPC) to execute the will of the government. Although without enforcement powers, the FEPC carried out the intention of the order. As a result, by 1944, two million blacks secured new jobs in the country's defense industries. With successes in advancing an agenda that emphasized equality in work and in war, Randolph became the most influential African American civil rights leader of the World War II era.

By organizing the BSCP and the MOWM, Randolph demonstrated success in all-black movements organizing, fighting, and winning difficult struggles. More than anything else, Randolph's victories were the first to inspire the ongoing civil rights struggle. He provided the early proof that the later long, agonizing struggle promised victory. After the war, he fought along with others to

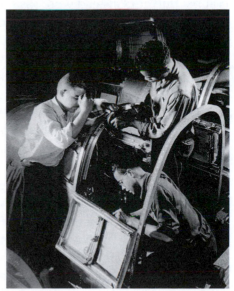

African American workers assemble the pilot's compartment in a large eastern aircraft factory, May 1942. (National Archives)

achieve significant milestones in that struggle. In 1948, he and Walter White of the NAACP were influential in President Harry S. Truman's landmark decision to integrate the U.S. armed forces. In 1963, Randolph saw the realization of his 1941 dream. The 1963 March on Washington numbered 200,000 and was the largest civil rights demonstration ever as well as the most famous. The Rev. Martin Luther King Jr. gave his "I Have a Dream" speech after the opening speech by the venerable, 75-year-old Randolph, who emphasized the need for greater economic opportunities for African Americans.

Social Inequality: Race and the Military

In 1940, African Americans were by far the largest racial minority in the country —10 percent, or roughly 13 million, in a population of 132 million Americans. With the draft in 1940, those eligible African American men signed the roster but were not called to the service in numbers proportional to their presence in their country. This underrepresentation was due to the white majority in the military resisting, as was true in prior wars, a large African American fighting force that might threaten the status quo. Throughout the war, African Americans in the military were segregated and discriminated against by the white majority. White and black soldiers fought in separate units in all branches of the service until near the war's end, when some experiments in integrated fighting occurred and were trial successes. African American servicemen were routinely denied combat duty and instead were assigned to menial service roles. Overall, this was a great affront to their dignity, and many servicemen demanded justice.

Powerful leaders, institutions, and groups also demanded that the American armed forces have racial justice to counter Hitler's virulent racism and be more in line with this country's ideals. FDR championed this cause as early as the 1940 election, when he promised that the segregated armed forces would have African American soldiers equal to 10 percent of the total armed forces, and with combat duties equal to that of whites. Lt. Benjamin O. Davis Sr. won promotion in the Army as the first African American general, which fulfilled another of these promises. Military leaders in all the services, unfortunately, did all possible to delay or resist entirely implementing these goals.

Thus, African Americans themselves fought a difficult uphill struggle during the war and ultimately began to get results, slowly at first and with a quickening near the end. The NAACP had its Double V campaign throughout the war— "Victory over Hitler. Victory over Jim Crow." Proud African American fighters militantly protested the Jim Crow armed forces. Support from a burgeoning active, crusading African American press also helped the cause; the country in the war years boasted over 300 African American newspapers that printed news for the black community that was uniformly left out of the white press.

The news was often disturbing. Many Southern basic training camps had large numbers of African American draftees from the North who suddenly were forced to conform to a state's legal segregation—sitting in the back of buses, drinking from "colored only" water fountains, and being subjected to local examples of white supremacist attitudes. Both the military and local police enforced the Jim Crow laws, often with brutality. In Little Rock, Arkansas, Sgt. Thomas Foster of the black 92nd Engineers Battalion was murdered—shot five times for questioning the harsh treatment of a fellow African American soldier by military police (MPs). Armed clashes occurred all over the world as African Americans resisted and refused to be the victims of this treatment. In Camp Stewart, Georgia, a gunfight between a large group of African American soldiers and MPs went on for five hours and left one dead and five wounded.

U.S. Army Leads in Early Racial Advances

The U.S. armed forces, mostly the Army, readily accepted certain racial minorities—Native Americans and Mexican Americans—into integrated fighting units. Both groups represented a relatively small proportion of the American population and in the service. Some 25,000 American Indians served in integrated units in the armed forces during the war. Most were enlistees, eager to fight. Most were assigned to low-level infantry units. Especially notable were the Navajo in the signal corps, who communicated in the Navajo language, which the Japanese were never able to translate. Ira Hayes, one of the iconic raisers of the American flag at Iwo Jima, was an American Indian. Some 350,000 Mexican Americans also served in integrated units. They won awards for bravery far beyond their numbers in the total U.S. population.

Integration was a more difficult challenge for African Americans, who at that point constituted 10 percent of the American population, or 13 million. Some 1.5 million served in the military. For them, progress toward military integration was achingly slow but ultimately gained momentum. The U.S. Army, with the largest number of African Americans in the segregated military, was the first of the service branches to make changes. In 1941, the Army put the black 758th Tank Battalion into combat. Once at the front, they performed bravely.

Integration was a more difficult challenge. The Army led here, as well. In 1941, the officer's candidate school was integrated. In 1944, the Army issued an edict forbidding discrimination in transportation and recreation—an order often overlooked until Lt. Jackie Robinson—soon to be the first player to break the color barrier in professional baseball—refused to sit in the back of the bus on his base in Texas and was court-martialed. He won; his victory gave pride and confidence to others.

The Battle of the Bulge in late 1944 became the unanticipated turning point in the Army's eventual backing of integrated fighting units. Caught by surprise when the Nazis began a massive, last-ditch counteroffensive against the American forces advancing on Berlin, General Eisenhower was caught with a dangerous shortage of manpower. He issued a request for African American volunteers to serve as privates in integrated units engaged in the desperate fighting. Thousands upon thousands volunteered and fought bravely, proving to the military brass that integration would ultimately be the wave for future combat. This request was the beginning of the end for the Jim Crow armed forces. Even so, until the end of the war (and on to 1948 when Truman by Executive Order integrated the services), whites and blacks fought in separate units.

Despite white resistance, African American veterans were proud of fighting for their principles as well as proud of their dutiful service in war in every service branch and war front. Veterans vehemently opposed returning to a civilian life of unquestioned segregation and assumptions of inferiority. Liberal Americans, too, pushed for change, seeing the shame as the South continued to lynch blacks while their nation battled against Hitler's goal of white racial supremacy.

Eleanor Roosevelt and the Tuskegee Airmen

The U.S. military was segregated during World War II, with African Americans limited to support jobs in the kitchen or motor pool. This changed in January 1941, when the Army chose the Tuskegee Institute in Tuskegee, Alabama, as the location for a program to create an all-black flying unit, the 99th Pursuit Squadron. Tuskegee, founded in 1881 by Booker T. Washington, had an existing Civilian Pilot Training Program directed by Charles Alfred Anderson, the first African American to earn a pilot's license.

First Lady Eleanor Roosevelt took a keen interest in Tuskegee and its flying school. She visited the institute in 1941 and, overriding the concerns of her Secret Service agents, took an hour-long flight with Anderson, the flight instructor. This flight convinced her that, despite racist popular attitudes of the time, African Americans could be capable pilots. Displaying a keen understanding of the symbolic power of the image, Eleanor Roosevelt brought a photograph of herself with Anderson back to the White House and urged her husband to put the 99th Squadron into combat. In May 1942, the Tuskegee-trained 99th Fighter Squadron became the first African Americans to fly combat missions. Throughout the war, Eleanor Roosevelt corresponded with Tuskegee airmen and faculty. In an August 1943 telegram in the collection of the Franklin D. Roosevelt Presidential Library and Museum, the institute's president, F. D. Patterson, wrote to Eleanor Roosevelt: "AM HAPPY MEN IN AVIATION NOW AT FRONT ARE JUSTIFYING IN FULL MEASURE THE GREAT CONFIDENCE YOU AND OTHERS EXPRESSED IN THEM."

Eleanor Roosevelt's faith in the Tuskegee Airmen was indeed justified. Their record was impeccable: in 1,500 missions in Europe and North Africa, the Tuskegee Airmen distinguished themselves as the only U.S. squadron during World War II that did not lose a single bomber to enemy fire. Their courage and achievement made an impact on the home front and helped to influence President Harry S. Truman in his decision to desegregate the U.S. military in 1948.

Tuskegee Airmen, Col. Benjamin O. Davis and Edward C. Gleed stand beside a plane during World War II. The Tuskegee Airmen were African American Air Corps officers who trained at the Tuskegee Army Airfield in Alabama, the only training facility for basic and advanced flight training open to black pilots during World War II. Davis was the first graduate of the program and the first African American general in the U.S. Air Force. Photograph by Toni Frissell. (Library of Congress)

African American Progress in the 1940s

In 1940, of 13 million African Americans, the majority still lived in the South. Mass migrations to the North and West started in 1940 and continued throughout the war years. Their ultimate destinations were the growing cities; there African Americans made gains but also faced white resistance and discrimination.

The NAACP was the one long-standing organization to fight against this discrimination, using legal means and enlightenment through education. The war years witnessed a coalescing and advancing but still nascent civil rights movement, especially involving the adoption of the tactic of direct action—marches, sit-ins, and nonviolent tactics developed by such newly emergent leaders as A. Phillip Randolph and the new CORE. In 1940, the NAACP totaled 45,000 members. All of this organization's successes at home during war are seeds for the later 1950s and 1960s civil rights movement.

New urban African Americans made considerable progress; among them was heightened job security and income and the rise of a broad-based black middle class, based on the increase of relatively prosperous African American blue-collar workers in industrial manufacturing. A half million African Americans became members of CIO unions, especially those of the auto and steel industries. About 1.5 million African Americans became skilled or partially skilled workers. The wages of the average African American worker in the war years increased from approximately $500 to $2,000; while this was still not at the same level as wages for white earners, the rate of increase was greater for blacks. Wartime industry employed 2 million blacks. In government, 200,000 more became new civil servants.

A change in life outlook came to many of these migrant African Americans. With the restrictive aspects of the Southern caste system left behind, many felt a sudden personal freedom. Hope came to many with the realization of more and better educational chances for themselves and their children. Still, the North and West presented a different set of problems: racism, de facto segregation (separation of the races by custom, not law), housing in crowded ghettoes due to white resistance to integrated neighborhoods.

White resistance to increasing numbers of blacks competing for jobs and scarce housing led to a series of race riots all over the United States, with such incidents reaching a peak in 1943. Beatings, deaths, arson, and looting took place in such places as Beaumont, Texas, and Mobile, Alabama. The worse riots occurred in the Northern cities, especially Detroit. There a dispute over hiring policies ignited days of pitched battles fueled by pent-up black resentment and fearful white resistance. Harlem, the capital of black America, also saw African Americans riot against injustice.

Wartime Changes in Minority Social Thought

In cities flooded by greater migrant numbers, a new African American political power arose. In close elections, the votes of this new minority were decisive. White politicians of both parties therefore became more aware and heedful of black political issues like civil rights. Electoral politics in presidential elections were often dependent on winning the state by taking its large city vote, where blacks had increased advantage. In 1944 in Harlem, the voters elected Adam Clayton Powell, the first African American congressman since Reconstruction.

During the war years, African American soldiers and civilians as well as the white majority became acutely aware that the world was predominantly made up of nonwhite peoples who were increasingly aware and critical of the racial injustices present in America. Japan's propaganda broadcast to people of color in Asia and South America emphasized the lynchings and riots in the United States. The white supremacy underlying Southern racism was often compared to the virulent Nazi variety and found to differ only in degree. Hitler's extremist views caused the horrific Holocaust of the Jews, which undermined race theories

The Harlem Riots of 1943

In the sultry summer of 1943, Harlem was tense. A widely aggrieved, largely African American citizenry faced a recently enhanced, aggressive, white police force. Police brutality increased. With this as the immediate cause, Harlem ignited in a riot. In this large, racially restricted neighborhood, the deeper, long-standing underlying causes included extreme crowding due to a flood of wartime migrants, higher-than-average rents and prices for everyday needs, and job discrimination in a war economy.

As a vast city within a city and a world-renowned African American capital, Harlem burst into a riot that signaled the country's race problem was even more serious in wartime than had been reported in the white press. Harlemites, foremost, experienced their country's hypocrisy when its war aims abroad ("the Good Fight" against racism and for democratic freedoms in Europe) were denied to African Americans at home. Contrary to what the Four Freedoms promised a postwar world, the city's blacks were second-class citizens at home. Northern de facto segregation, for example, resulted in publicly sanctioned all-white housing that constricted the expansion of a racial ghetto. The result was extreme crowding.

As defenders of their country, African Americans served in racially segregated armed forces, and thus were second-class soldiers. African Americans entering the services in Harlem were assigned to basic training camps in the severely and legally segregated states of the Old Confederacy. Letters home from these trainees, servicemen home awaiting assignment overseas, and veterans home on furlough, all told of humiliations endured. All of Harlem by this summer was aroused to indignation and anger about the mistreatment of its brave men in service. Police brutality provided the fuse.

On the evening of August 1, a rumor spread that a policeman shot an African American soldier in the back over a dispute about a woman at Harlem's Braddock Hotel. Soon an angry crowd of 3,000 was breaking windows and setting fires along 125th Street. The rumor turned out to be false, but by the end of the night-long riot, the clash had claimed 6 dead, 185 wounded, and 500 arrested.

in general. White America became more aware of the hindrance its racism represented to a world hoping to see America as a leader in the postwar world.

World War II released forces that would cause continued racial progress in the country. African American veterans—one million strong—helped gain the great war victory and had often fought back and won struggles for justice within the country's armed forces, and they would continue this more militant attitude toward civil rights in peacetime. African American soldiers back from war, if Southern, rarely returned to the South because they vowed never again to submit to the region's racial restrictions.

Stateside, A. Phillip Randolph had demonstrated success of more militant civil rights tactics, even before Pearl Harbor, with his threat of a massive march on Washington. CORE, founded in 1942, used sit-ins to integrate public facilities in wartime Detroit and Chicago (a tactic to be used again in the 1950s and 1960s civil rights struggles). The NAACP best captured the mood of blacks in this time with its slogan "Victory over Hitler. Victory over Jim Crow." Hitler met defeat, and in time so would Jim Crow. The World War II years were the seedbed for the later civil rights revolution.

WINNING THE WAR

Americans entered a two-front war in December 1941. Simultaneously in Asia and Europe, the country's as-yet weak military confronted formidable enemies in the midst of broad, fast-moving, successful offensives. After disabling the U.S. Pacific fleet, the American public witnessed Japanese forces overrun such American protectorates in the Pacific as Wake Island, Guam, and the Philippines. So far, this Asian enemy was invulnerable. The Germans, too, having launched their own surprise attack on their ally, the Soviet Union, had been relentlessly pushing back the retreating Soviet Army until the possibility loomed of a forthcoming surrender to Hitler.

Some Americans naturally wondered if their country had erred fatefully by delaying entry into the war. Was victory still possible? If so, the overall strategy on both fronts needed to proceed in three phases. First, the Allies must stop the enemy offensives. Second, the Allies had to start their own powerful counter-offensives. Lastly, especially as America's war productive capacities rose, the Allies needed to push to victory. In the Pacific, this meant closing in on the home islands of Japan; in Europe, this meant opening other fronts against the Germans to relieve pressure on the Soviets.

In the Pacific, the United States was fortunate because all three of its Hawaii-based aircraft carriers had been at sea and had survived the Pearl Harbor attack. Carriers were to prove the newest, most important aspect of sea battles in this war. The April 1942 Doolittle Raid, in which American B-25 bombers under the command of Col. James H. Doolittle launched a bold "hit and run" counterattack from an aircraft carrier, was the first raid on Japan. Although damage was slight, the implications—that Japan needed to defend the home islands against air attacks—proved decisively to be in America's favor. The Battle of Coral Sea, May 1942, was a standoff, but the American carrier-launched planes did damage enough to the Japanese carrier-based fleet that this halted the enemy's planned attack on Australia. At the Battle of Midway, in June 1942, the newly reconstituted U.S. fleet devastatingly defeated the larger enemy main fleet, with American carrier planes sinking 4 Japanese carriers and downing some 300 planes—the first major loss for the Japanese navy. The Americans had halted the Japanese offensive and thereafter had supremacy at sea. News of these sea battles in the Pacific enthused Americans, but most citizens were unfamiliar with the history and geography of the Far East and so instead focused on the European theater. The outlook there was glum. In September 1942, the triumphant Nazis attacked Stalingrad where the Soviets, in a ferocious five-month defense, turned the Germans back and eventually captured their large army.

Allied counteroffensives began after the theater turning-point battles of Midway and Stalingrad. In Europe, November 1942, British and American forces invaded North Africa, defeated the German army there, and continued this offensive by invading Sicily, then Italy. In Asia, the American land forces won Guadalcanal and began an "island-hopping" offensive toward the Japanese main cities.

By 1943, the United States had steadily mobilized its vast production capabilities for war and strengthened its military forces to defeat the Axis powers in the global conflict. The armed forces grew to 3.8 million by the start of 1943. By 1945, 16 million would have served. Throughout the war, all who served in the military realized that victory would be a long uphill struggle; they adopted a practical aim of "just get it done" (with little of the earlier idealism of World War I).

Americans on the home front in 1943 and thereafter enjoyed a full-employment economy. By 1945, the country was producing two times the war materiel of the combined Axis powers. Bigness in all sectors of the economy was the key to the production miracle: a giant government oversaw a centralized wartime economy of bigness in all sectors: business, labor, and agriculture.

By 1945, American production capacity allowed Allied forces both in Asia and Europe to push to victory. On D-Day, June 6, 1944, the Allies invaded Normandy and soon liberated France. V-E Day, May 8, 1945, came after Berlin fell to Soviet forces on May 2. American science marshaled for war produced the two A-bombs used on Japan, August 6 and 9, 1945, ending the war with V-J Day.

New Wartime Economic and Social Policy

Early War Footing

America's defense preparations in the prewar years were critical to its comeback in 1942 after the devastating surprise attack on the Pacific fleet on December 7, 1941. While America was officially neutral and then an intervening, nonwarring nation with Lend-Lease in March 1941, all throughout this time FDR did all possible to put the country on a war footing. For example, in the 18 months prior to December 1941, U.S. defense spending increased over tenfold to nearly $2 billion a month. In 1941, the economy produced 15 percent of all goods for war —U.S. self-defense and the defense of fighting Allies overseas. Most importantly, the fundamental government–business relationship was forged and significant businesses were retooled for war, which provided examples for the future. A partial but widespread war mobilization had already taken place so that after Pearl Harbor the process only had to be increased. Meanwhile, in the 18 months preceding Pearl Harbor, the U.S. Army increased by 800 percent and, although not war ready, was patterned to grow quickly after the first peacetime draft in 1940.

Record-Setting War Production

In 1942, only six months into the war and after suffering a string of defeats, the United States was only beginning to realize its hidden power. *Time* magazine editorialized on February 9, 1942, in a piece titled "Battle of Detroit," "Something is happening that Hitler does not yet understand. . . . It is the miracle of war production and its miracle worker is the automobile industry." In 1943, when the Big Three, FDR, Winston Churchill, and Joseph Stalin, met at the Teheran Conference, the Soviet leader boldly toasted American production that had helped win the war. The Allies were on the offensive by then largely because of the broadening flow of American-built arms and supply efforts. U.S. supply of its prodigious war goods was accomplished with the largest merchant marine fleet in history.

Victory in World War II ultimately came with the United States setting prodigious records. Its GNP had more than doubled from $91 to $210 billion in four years. The country had poured over $300 billion in, spurring the economy to unimagined heights. The total production figures were prodigious in all categories: 300,000 planes, 86,000 warships, and 88,000 tanks. The Navy by 1945 was larger than those of the Axis and Allies combined; the Army, nearly 12 million men at war's end; and the Air Force wielded the atomic bomb, which was another success of organized development and productivity for war.

What were the major reasons for the miracle of production in the years 1940 to 1945? One was that the country in its prewar years, 1940 and 1941, was able lay the basic foundations for the full-blown war economy after Pearl Harbor. Also, the government directed and controlled the national economy under strong war presidents—first Roosevelt, then Truman. Government war contracts flowed to businesses, especially large corporations, which responded with mass quantities at a good profit (corporate profits doubled in these years). Lastly, the American people sacrificed to make war records for manufacturing. Labor unions agreed to limit strikes and wage demands. Factories, in turn, ran 24 hours a day, seven days a week, all year long.

Government Control Spurs the Economy

Once war began in earnest in 1942, FDR increased the government's control and direction of the national economy primarily through the War Production Board

(WPB) headed by James F. Byrnes, who was nicknamed "the assistant president." State capitalism, in effect, was the system devised by the country to meet the unprecedented demands of war. War contracts flooded the economy, going mostly to the 100 largest corporations because of their efficiencies in size. By 1943, their profits bested those of 1929, which had been termed a miracle year. The real engine of corporate profits was the deficit spending the government pursued by flooding the economy with billions of dollars each month. The government contracts paid cost overruns and still guaranteed a set profit, which eliminated all risk. Antitrust laws were suspended. Corporations were assured their war facilities could be purchased inexpensively for postwar consumer production.

American corporations produced massively for the war under such favorable conditions. Henry Ford, whose Willow Run, Michigan, facilities made aircraft, notably the B-24 bombers; J. Edgar Kaiser, whose California and Oregon shipyards produced Liberty ships; and Howard Hughes, whose partnership with Kaiser produced the giant B-17 cargo planes that became legends in the public's mind—each symbolized the American "can do" spirit.

All Americans Contribute to Victory

Ordinary Americans supported the war in countless ways and across all age groups. Children eagerly participated in scrap drives for old tires, newspapers, and scrap metal. Older people had victory gardens to raise their own food so more farm crops could be sent overseas. Jobs increased by 17 million during these years, and soon a full-employment economy had many working overtime. With the 16 million serving in the military, women and African Americans staffed the assembly lines for the first time. First Lady Eleanor Roosevelt made a point of saving gasoline and rubber by riding a bicycle rather than driving the car. Friends and family on the home front sent packages to the GIs overseas, providing them with everything from homemade cookies to razor blades.

War, the State, and Society: The Atomic Age Begins

Stunned to learn after the fact of their government's secret use of the most powerfully destructive new weapon ever (one capable of destroying all human life), Americans were quick to realize that its immediate use might cause an unexpected sudden Japanese surrender. Before the bombs were used, the military's pending plan was to invade the Japanese home islands, a fight that some experts estimated would cost possibly one million American lives. Nearing Japan's homelands, the fighting had already been the deadliest yet; Iwo Jima was taken only with the enemy fighting to the last man. Even closer, Okinawa was taken with a stunning 50,000 American casualties.

Victory gardeners show off their vegetables. Americans planted over 20 million Victory Gardens in backyards, schools, and city parks across the United States to supplement vegetable production during World War II. (Library of Congress)

Hiroshima

Hiroshima lay in hot ruins on August 6, 1945. A B-29 bomber with the name *Enola Gay* dropped a single bomb, "Little Boy," with the unimaginable destructive power of 20,000 tons of dynamite on this city of 350,000. Dead instantly were 100,000 within a four-square-mile area left barren where the city was seconds before; another 100,000 would eventually die of radiation poisoning. The multiple mushroom cloud rose miles into the sky. The astonished crew of the returning bomber still saw it 350 miles away. Humans had entered the Atomic Age.

The American people learned of their country's momentous decision to use the atomic bomb after Hiroshima was already destroyed. When the bomb hit, it was 9:15 a.m. in Washington, D.C. Sixteen hours later, President Truman informed the public of the use of the world's first atomic bomb, a new weapon that encapsulated the universe's basic power. The force that lit the sun was fuel for this bomb.

The president spoke of the bomb being the great success of a secret, government-organized scientific project begun in 1940 that, in the end, cost $2 billion. More A-bombs were available, he told Japan's leaders. In an August 6, 1945, White House press release, a draft of which is in the collection at the Harry S. Truman Library, Truman announced the use of the A-bomb at Hiroshima, stating that if Japan did not accept unconditional surrender, "they may expect a rain of ruin from the air, the like of which has never been seen on this earth. . . ."

Earlier, at the July Potsdam Conference, Truman had secured Stalin's promise that the Soviet Union would enter the war against Japan. The atomic bomb was in its final development stage and still might be unfeasible. So Truman asked for and received Soviet military help against Japan. On July 16, during the Potsdam meeting, Truman got word that the Los Alamos scientists had tested the first A-bomb successfully at Alamogordo, New Mexico (the stationary test gave no indication if the bomb could be effective if dropped from a plane at high altitude). Truman mentioned vaguely to Stalin that the United States had a powerful new weapon. The Soviet leader was nonplussed (it was later discovered that a Soviet spy ring had infiltrated Los Alamos, the top-secret location where the bomb was being developed). Stalin suggested to Truman that he use it on Japan. On July 26, after the meeting's end, Truman issued the Potsdam Declaration, calling on the Japanese to surrender unconditionally or face "total destruction." The enemy declined. By August 6, Truman felt justified in a surprise first use of the A-bomb on Hiroshima. On August 8, Stalin declared war on Japan. The powerful Soviet army then speedily drove the enemy back out of Manchuria.

Like their president, many Americans hoped the A-bomb's impact would cause a quick Japanese surrender without the need for a costly Allied attack on the enemy's heartland islands. A few even thought, again like their leader, that the Soviets were proving a threat and an American A-bomb would keep them in check. A considerable number, though, immediately felt the use of such a weapon was barbaric and a disgrace to their country.

Nagasaki

On August 9, Nagasaki was in ruins from a second A-bomb ordered by Truman after he had waited three days without a Japanese surrender. This bomb, called "Fat Boy," killed nearly 60,000 instantaneously. Now came the long wait. Days passed. Americans waited for word from the Japanese, not knowing that the United States had only one more A-bomb left. Meanwhile, the Soviets had driven the Japanese from northern Korea. The American forces continued plans for the invasion.

On August 14, the Japanese finally surrendered and accepted conditions outlined in the Potsdam Declaration. They were allowed to retain their emperor. World War II was over. The word came at 1:49 a.m. in Washington, D.C. Victory celebrations began first on the West Coast, then spread eastward, with lights going on all across the country as cities, towns, and farms partied. The next day,

Truman declared a two-day holiday to mark the surrender (V-J Day, the official surrender ceremony, would come on September 2). Japan, the aggressor whose surprise attack had brought the United States into the war on December 7, 1941, was now vanquished.

Were Nuclear Weapons Necessary to Win the War?

Could rapid victory over Japan have been achieved by other means than the use of atomic weapons? American public opinion, while registering great pride in their nation's contribution to victory in 1945, shows a pang of conscience about the use of not just one but two atomic weapons on the helpless citizens of two Japanese cities. Was this necessary? The president and policymakers had one near-unified opinion at the time. Scientists on the Manhattan Project often had a different opinion as to the use of the bomb than did their political leaders. Historians have debated this question from various points of view, often finding fault with the motives of President Truman and his close circle of civilian and military advisers.

President Truman in his 1955 memoir left no doubt that he continued to feel fully justified for authorizing the atomic bombings. Ending the war at the earliest possible date had always been his goal, and the instant the new atomic bomb proved workable, this weapon would be used against enemies to bring about total unconditional surrender. Japan was the only enemy combatant left by August 1945, and little thought was given to the alternative of not using the weapon. He emphasized in his writing that saving huge numbers of lives, both American and Japanese, calculated to be lost in an pending land invasion of the heavily defended home islands of Japan was the main reason for his decision. As to the top policymakers, advisers, and experts, the later studies of historian Martin J. Sherwin give strong backing to these men never seriously considering another non-atomic option (Sherwin 1975).

Scientists critical to the project such as atomic physicists Albert Einstein and Robert J. Oppenheimer did object, however, to its being used against Japan. The scientists of the secret Manhattan Project believed Nazi Germany was near to having this bomb, and the Allies were in a deadly race to develop and use it against Hitler before the Fuhrer used it against the West. When Germany surrendered and showed no evidence of an imminent A-bomb, many scientists felt betrayed when Truman readily used it against a known nonnuclear enemy. Some scientists and later scholars suspected that a racist motivation underlay the decision to use this terrible weapon against the first modern non-European great power to rise to challenge the West. Scholars, however, have failed to find specific, convincing proof of an alleged official bias.

Notable scholars like Gar Alperovitz, in revisionist work like his 1965 *Atomic Diplomacy,* contended that Japan at the time was very near surrender due to secret diplomacy, and only the postwar status of the emperor remained to be negotiated (Alperovitz, 1985). Militarily, this argument maintained that Japan was no longer a dangerous enemy but instead was helpless against at-will American naval attacks on its vital interior shipping lanes and defenseless against bombing raids.

Why did the country not complete this pending diplomatic end to war and instead unnecessarily use the weapons? The revisionist school answers that the Soviet Union entering the war against Japan on August 8 (honoring a pledge sought by Truman at the June 1945 Potsdam Conference) had given Truman the real hidden reason for rushing to bomb Japan. As a tremendous show of unprecedented new military force, Truman had wanted to bring the Soviet Union in line to recognize postwar American military supremacy, especially after experiencing difficulties with the Soviets in the concurrent Allied occupation policies in Europe. Wanting to avoid a joint occupation of Japan with the Soviet Union, Truman subjected Japan to this bombing and surrender just in time to halt the Soviet army's advance down the Korean Peninsula.

Critical of Alperovitz and other revisionists like Gabriel Kolko, traditional historians agree the Soviet result was an added benefit but consider the prime motive was as stated originally by Truman—to end the war as soon as possible by whatever means necessary to save the maximum number of American lives. Thus, the use of the weapons served this stated purpose; Truman swore not one single night of his sleep was ever lost in rethinking his decision.

War, Society, and the State

Americans felt the new power of their nation when only two A-bombs caused the Japanese to surrender and, to widespread public relief, prevented the dreaded invasion of the Japanese home islands where American casualties were estimated would be extremely high. The total military and civilian deaths for the United States in World War II was about 418,000, compared to an estimated 23.6 million to 26.6 million for the Soviet Union and an estimated 7.5 million for Germany.

World War II was by far the deadliest in history. For the first time in warfare, mass bombings were a standard practice. Both the Axis and Allies practiced brutal total war. The atomic bomb, harnessing the power of the sun, devastated Hiroshima and Nagasaki, ended the war, and had the potential to end the world. The astounding toll in lives lost, both military and civilian, has been estimated at 50 million to upwards of 70 million.

The World's First Superpower

In 1939, eight nations had been world powers; in 1945, two had become supreme in victory; the others, including Britain, were nearly prostrate from the bombing of cities and factories, and the ruin of their economies. With a monopoly on the atomic bomb after having proved its incredible destructive power twice, America became the world's first superpower, and the Soviet Union was a distant second.

With World War II ended, the United States was the most powerful nation in the world, and in all history. It had a monopoly on the world's most destructive weapon, and its economy had no rival. The Axis powers were bombed wastelands; the other Allies were also badly damaged. The Soviet Union had lost 40 percent of its prewar industrial capacity. By contrast, the United States, with all its factories unharmed, had doubled its economy during the war. The United States alone among nations had the wealth after 1945 for capital investments and research. By 1947, the United States was producing a record 50 percent of the manufactured goods in the world.

America's New Cosmopolitan Perspectives

By comparison with almost all other modern industrialized nations, the American people realized their own good fortune, especially regarding their economy and prosperity. After winning a vast global war, Americans became more cosmopolitan. After 1945, the majority strongly favored internationalism.

Trygve Lie, secretary general of the United Nations, levels cement with a bricklayer's trowel as the cornerstone for the UN permanent headquarters is lowered into place during ceremonies in New York City, October 24, 1949. (Library of Congress)

Throughout the war, FDR was instrumental in supporting the idea of a post-war organization to provide collective security to preserve world peace. In San Francisco in 1945, a multinational conference wrote the charter for the new United Nations. The American public supported this new internationalism in peacetime foreign policy. The U.S. Senate voted in favor of the U.S. ratification of the United Nations charter and accession to the United Nations by an over-whelming vote (in contrast to the Senate's rejection of the League of Nations after World War I).

Americans and congressmen of prewar isolationist views had shifted to an interventionist sentiment largely because many had growing suspicions of Soviet territorial ambitions and the weakness of the European democracies immediately after the war. Even as citizens of the world's leading nation in 1945, Americans had their share of anxieties, both at home and abroad. Would the Depression return with the inevitable cutback in the expanded war economy and the return of those in the military? Could communist Soviet Union and capitalist America truly cooperate to bring peace? Or would the two become hostile rivals for world power and for ideological dominion? Would Europe get back on its feet again?

Americans in the New Global Economy

America had the only national economy in the world that was not greatly harmed by the war. By 1945, the prewar U.S. industry, banking, and infrastructure had greatly expanded to meet the massive production increase for war. The country's gross national product more than doubled between 1940 and 1945, reaching $211.9 billion. There were several reasons for this. The country began to produce war materiel for itself and the Allies for months before Pearl Harbor. Lend-Lease started in March 1941 and continued throughout the war, so the U.S. economy was producing for many of the military needs of both of its major Allies (Britain and the Soviet Union) as well as for its own needs in both the civilian and military sectors. The economy grew with large infusions of government defense contracts, which created 17 million new jobs. A full-employment economy was the end result.

Broad prosperity resulted from the general rise in salaries and wages; many newly entered the middle class. The country in these war years underwent its only absolute redistribution of wealth, which made possible mass purchasing power on a level heretofore not possible. With many consumer goods not available, or available in small quantities and at high prices, or rationed during the wartime years, ordinary Americans had saved and had money to spend at war's end.

With all its prewar economic rivals eliminated by the ruin of war, the United States was the world's one economic giant. Yet the United States was without any healthy trading partners unless it found a way to rebuild the capitalist economies of Allied Europe.

Ordinary Americans also had an underlying worry throughout the war that when peace came, the economy without defense contracts would shrink to the prewar levels of the Depression. The interrelationship between corporations and the U.S. military had matured in the war years and was the key to a long-term healthy economy capable of paying back the huge war debt.

BIOGRAPHIES

Father Charles Coughlin, 1891–1979

Radio Priest with a Pro-Fascist Message

Centered in Royal Oak, Michigan, at the Shrine of the Little Flower Church, Coughlin had broadcast his conservative Sunday sermons on his radio station since 1926. He was ardently isolationist in the late 1930s, then increasing pro-Fascist immediately before and after Pearl Harbor. In May 1942, government officials acting under the 1917 Espionage Act annulled the mailing rights to his magazine and curtailed his broadcasting. The Detroit archbishop forbade his extrapastoral duties under penalty of being defrocked. He was liable to being charged with sedition at the least and espionage at most for his outright pro-Fascism. Fervently anti-Communist and anti-Semitic, he saw Fascism as the antidote, praised Fascist dictators and gave voice to their propaganda material. He had praised the Christian Front, which had harassed Jews in New York City. After Pearl Harbor, he called for the United States to surrender. His declarations stopped in 1942 after many of his listeners had ceased to listen to him.

Iva Toguri D'Aquino, 1916–2006

American Known as "Tokyo Rose"

During World War II in the Pacific, an alluring voice of an American female regularly came over a Japanese propaganda radio broadcast, seductively calling on servicemen to surrender in the face of an overwhelming enemy force. Because her broadcast included interludes with current hit music from the States, many servicemen mocked her while enjoying the music. With her real identity unknown, she was nicknamed "Tokyo Rose" and became a living legend, widely known on the front lines as well as the home front. The voice of Tokyo Rose was one of more than a dozen females who broadcast in this way on Japanese radio, but servicemen designated the single nickname for the collective voices. After the war, the mythic name stuck to one woman, D'Aquino, an American-born citizen who had been stranded in Japan after the attack on Pearl Harbor.

She was employed by Japanese Radio to do one of the voices as "Orphan Ann." She married in Tokyo before the war ended. In 1948, she returned to her birthplace of Southern California, was arrested, and accused of treason. She was convicted in 1949 and sentenced to 10 years.

Gen. John L. DeWitt, 1880–1962

Command Officer Who Called for Japanese-American Internment

After the Japanese surprise attack on December 7, 1941, and with the West Coast engulfed in a hysteria churned by Hearst newspapers and other media, Gen. John DeWitt, who was in charge of security in the Western states, bent to that public mania and reported to Washington, D.C., that all enemy aliens should be

Correspondents interview Tokyo Rose (Iva Toguri) in September 1945. (National Archives)

rounded up and sent to relocation centers. In this he had backing from the U.S. War Department, where opinion was strong that all Japanese in the country were a potential fifth column, who had undying loyalty to the mother country. Seeing all Japanese Americans as potential spies and saboteurs, the War Department called for them to be relocated from the coast, the place of likely enemy invasion. However, specific evidence of spying or disloyalty was needed as a necessary rationale for the plan to take place. After suppressing FBI accounts that there was no specific security risk to report among this suspect minority, DeWitt charged that certain Japanese had been in communication with offshore enemy ships and were spying and already planning or carrying out acts of sabotage. Although the allegations were never verified, President Roosevelt in February 1942, issued Executive Order 9066, which authorized the plan put forth by DeWitt, who afterward designated a series of remote western locales for the building of the internment centers.

Sidney Hillman, 1887–1946

Labor Leader

The Lithuanian-born head of the Amalgamated Clothing Workers of America (ACWA) and cofounder (with John L. Lewis) of the CIO was a staunch supporter of FDR's New Deal. In 1940, Hillman supported FDR for president over Wendell Willkie, sensing that FDR's rearmament program would benefit labor. From 1940 to 1942, he served FDR as labor representative on the National Defense Advisory Commission and as associate director general of the Office of Production Management. He backed FDR's 1944 campaign with a CIO Political Action Committee and in 1945 helped found the World Federation of Trade Unions.

William O'Dwyer, 1890–1964

New York City Politician

Bill O'Dwyer was elected New York City mayor in 1945, succeeding the legendary three-term Fiorello La Guardia, who served twelve years to 1945. Born in County Mayo, he came to New York City at age 20. He had a typical rise to success: odd jobs, going to night school, and becoming a lawyer, then working for long while as a cop. Meanwhile, he rose in local Democratic political circles and became a crime-crushing county court judge who, in 1941, ran for mayor and lost to the incumbent, LaGuardia. In the war years, he enlisted and reached the rank of colonel as an investigator of fraud in wartime contracts and other war profiteering (much as Senator Truman had done in Congress). Scrupulously honest and successful, he mustered out as a brigadier general.

In 1945, with La Guardia retired, O'Dwyer won the mayor's office. A reformer and anticorruptionist, he cleaned up the Tammany Hall–tainted Democratic Party after its 15 years out of office. In 1945, his efforts were crucial to his city becoming home to the new United Nations.

Margaret Chase Smith, 1897–1995

Congresswoman, Supporter of Servicewomen

In April 1940, Congressman Clyde Smith, a Republican from Maine, died; his wife, Margaret Chase Smith, won a special election and served out the remainder of his term. She ran for reelection in September 1940, won, and went on to serve eight years in the House of Representatives as the victor in three more elections. While in the House, she served on two vital military committees, Naval Affairs and Armed Services. One of the few women in Congress at the time, Smith was a particularly strong backer of World War II as the first official opportunity for women to serve in the military—the Army's WACS, the Navy's WAVES, the Coast Guard's SPARS, a special women's unit of the Marines, and a vital all-services nurse corps. These first military women totaled 350,000 in all. After service, all were eligible for veterans' benefits. A special case were the roughly 1,000 civilian women flyers in the Air Force's WAFS and WASPS, whose jobs included serving as test pilots on new aircraft, flying them from factories to combat bases, and instructing male pilots in fighter flying and gunnery. These nonmilitary women had no veteran status and no benefits. Smith fought to improve the status of all military women. She was critical to the passage of the Women's Armed Services Integration Act of 1948, which gave women a regular, continuous status in the military and guaranteed them equal pay and allowances.

William Allen White, 1868–1944

Small-town Newspaper Editor, Adviser to FDR

The influential Republican owner of *The Emporia Gazette* in Kansas, William Allen White headed the Committee to Defend America by Aiding the Allies (also known as the White Committee). This group was created in May 1940 to set forth a middle path between isolationists and interventionists. A nationally known, Pulitzer-awarded newspaperman whose Kansas home was visited by presidents

Margaret Chase Smith, Republican of Maine, served as a U.S. representative from 1940 to 1949 and as a U.S. senator from 1949 to 1973. She was the first woman to be elected to both the U.S. House and U.S. Senate. She was also the first woman to be placed in nomination for the presidency at a major party convention in 1964. (Library of Congress)

who wanted to tap into middle America, White had FDR's ear and was a chief engineer of the Lend-Lease Act.

REFERENCES AND FURTHER READINGS

Alperovitz, Gar. 1985. *Atomic Diplomacy: Hiroshima and Potsdam: The Use of the Atomic Bomb and the American Confrontation with Soviet Power.* New York: Simon and Schuster.

Berg, A. Scott. 1998. *Lindbergh.* New York: Putnam.

Black, Allida. 1996. *Casting Her Own Shadow: Eleanor Roosevelt and the Shaping of Postwar Liberalism.* New York: Columbia University Press.

Blum, John M. 1976. *V Was for Victory: Politics and American Culture during World War II*. Orlando: Harcourt Brace Jovanovich.

Boyel, Paul. 1985. *By the Bomb's Early Light: American Thought and Culture at the Dawn of the Atomic Age*. New York: Pantheon.

Burns, James MacGregor. 1970. *Roosevelt: The Soldier of Freedom*. New York: Harcourt, Brace Jovanovich.

Cole, Wayne S. 1983. *Roosevelt and the Isolationists, 1932–1945*. Lincoln: University of Nebraska Press.

Diggins, John. 1988. *The Proud Decades: America in War and Peace, 1941–1960*. New York: W. W. Norton.

Doenecke, Justus D. 1997. *The Battle against Intervention, 1939–1941*. Malabar, FL: Krieger Publishing Company.

Doenecke, Justus D. 2000. *Storm on the Horizon: The Challenge to American Intervention, 1939–1941*. Lanham, MD: Rowman and Littlefield.

Ferraro, Vincent. "Documents Related to the Cold War." Mount Holyoke, Mass. www.mtholyoke.edu/acad/intrel/coldwar.htm. Accessed 8/7/07.

Goodwin, Doris Kearns. 1994. *No Ordinary Time: Franklin and Eleanor Roosevelt: The Home Front in World War II*. New York: Simon and Schuster.

Gordon, David. 2003. "America First: The Anti-War Movement, Charles Lindbergh and the Second World War, 1940–1941," paper presented at a joint meeting of the Historical Society and The New York Military Affairs Symposium, September 26, 2003. http://libraryautomation.com/nymas/americafirst.html. Accessed 8/7/07.

Hamby, Alonzo L. 1995. *Man of the People: A Life of Harry S. Truman*. New York: Oxford University Press.

Harry S. Truman Library and Museum, press release on dropping of the atom bomb. www.trumanlibrary.org/whistlestop/study_collections/bomb/small/mb10.htm. Accessed 8/7/07.

Hartmann, Susan M. 1982. *The Home Front and Beyond: American Women in the 40s*. Boston: G. K. Hall and Company.

Jonas, Manfred. 1966. *Isolationism in America, 1935–1941*. Ithaca, NY: Cornell University Press; paperback reprint: Imprint Publications, 1990.

Lash, Joseph. 1971. *Eleanor and Franklin*. New York: W. W. Norton & Company.

Lemann, Nicholas. 1991. *The Promised Land: The Great Black Migration and How It Changed America*. New York: Alfred A. Knopf.

Library of Congress. "On the Homefront." htttp://memory.loc.gov/learn/features/homefront/gallery.html. Accessed 8/7/07.

Library of Congress. "Rosie the Riveter: Real Women Workers in World War II." www.loc.gov/rr/program/journey/rosie.html. Accessed 8/7/07.

Lichtenstein, Nelson, Susan Strasser, Roy Rosenzweig, Stephen Brier, and Joshua Brown. 2000. *Who Built America?* Vol. 2, *From 1877 to Present.* New York: Worth Publishers.

Lindbergh, Charles. April 23, 1941 speech, published by America First Committee. www.ajcarchives.org/AJC_DATA/Files/THR-AF3.PDF. Accessed August 21, 2008.

Merton, Robert K. 1946. *Mass Persuasion: The Social Psychology of a War Bond Drive.* New York: H. Fertig.

O'Neill, William. 1993. *A Democracy at War: America's Fight at Home and Abroad during World War II.* Cambridge: Harvard University Press.

Polenberg, Richard. 1972. *War and Society.* Philadelphia: Lippincott Williams and Wilkins.

Rhodes, Richard. 1986. *The Making of the Atomic Bomb.* New York: Simon and Schuster.

Roosevelt, Franklin D. 1941. "The Four Freedoms." *Congressional Record,* 1941, Vol. 87, Pt. I.

Schoenheer, Steve. "Cold War Policies 1945–1991," University of California at San Diego. http://history.sandiego.edu/gen/20th/coldwar0.html. Accessed 8/7/07.

Sherwin, Martin. 1975. *A World Destroyed: The Atomic Bomb and the Grand Alliance.* New York: Vintage Books.

Terkel, Studs. 1984. *The Good War: An Oral History of World War II.* New York: New Press.

Time magazine, February 9, 1942 issue, "Battle of Detroit." www.time.com/time/magazine/article/0,9171,802251,00.html. Accessed April 20, 2008.

Vogel, Steve. 2007. *The Pentagon. A History.* New York: Random House.

Wynn, Neil A. 1976. *The Afro-Americans and the Second World War.* New York: Holmes and Meier.

From Hot War
to Cold War

OVERVIEW

The United States gained a momentous victory in World War II and emerged the most powerful country in the world with its predominant military anchored by its possession of the atomic bomb. The U.S. economy was the world's leader with no damage to the expanded wartime industrial capacity and the highest per capita wealth of any nation. All of the other major nations in the world—Allies as well as defeated enemies—had great loss of lives and damage to property; America in 1946 emerged with almost an embarrassment of good fortune.

World leadership by America, however, did not go uncontested after 1946. Having sacrificed millions of war dead, more than any other combatant, the Soviet Union worked to build a buffer zone in Eastern Europe to protect it from any future invasions from the West. (Germany had invaded the Soviet Union twice in the century.) As Stalin installed communist regimes in Eastern European nations liberated from the Nazis by the Red Army, the United States, led by President Harry S. Truman, found good reason to be wary of Stalin's new Soviet empire.

Truman articulated his new foreign policy of containment to halt what he perceived as Soviet aggression anywhere in the world in the 1947 Truman Doctrine. He gave millions of dollars in military aid to Greece and Turkey to fight communist insurgencies. Thus, the Cold War to defeat Communism formally began only two years after the 1945 defeat of Nazism. A former ally, the Soviet

Union had become the new enemy, and West Germany, Italy, and Japan, once enemies, became allies.

A conservative mood came over the United States in the immediate postwar period. The elections of 1946 brought Republican majorities to Congress for the first time since the advent of the New Deal in the early 1930s. Big business was in great favor; unions were in disfavor due to a wave of strikes in 1945 triggered by the skyrocketing cost of living. Big government was seen as necessary to continue the defense spending to business that had brought such prosperity in war. Defense spending continued, with some $16 billion targeted for aid to rebuild war-torn Western Europe, rebuild economies, and rearm these countries as allies in the new North Atlantic Treaty Organization, an U.S.-led defensive military alliance to counteract any Soviet expansion.

A domestic consequence of the new Cold War was growing public fear of a real or imagined network of communist conspirators here at home. The result was a series of such acts as the President's Federal Employee Loyalty Program and Congress's House Un-American Activities Committee (HUAC), designed to hunt for subversives. Both efforts accused Americans in ways that infringed on basic civil and constitutional rights. But fear of communists ruled media and politics and made precautions about individual liberties seem an unnecessary luxury to many. Certain high-profile examples seemed to confirm the fear. In 1948, Alger Hiss, the former assistant secretary of state, was accused of being a communist by a former friend, Whittaker Chambers, who in 1950 was convicted of perjury.

From 1945 to 1949, the average American family experienced a prosperity that was even greater than what the populace had last experienced in the boom 1920s. The pent-up consumer demand from the war years, when citizens had saved about $180 billion, was released in a frenzy of buying that signaled the advent of consumer capitalism. The middle class, already much expanded in the war, expanded even further, becoming the largest of any nation in the world. Their mass purchasing power went toward buying new homes in the suburbs, new model cars (1946 models were the first new models produced since 1942), new household appliances, and new fashionable clothes. College began to be a birthright for the generation of children born to this new middle class, which was greatly aided by higher education benefits for veterans in the G.I. Bill.

TIMELINE

1946   In March, Winston Churchill gives "Iron Curtain" speech in Fulton, Missouri.

In April, coal miners begin a strike, which creates a crisis in heating and energy.

Inflation peaks at 18 percent in late summer.

The Atomic Energy Commission is created in August.

Republicans win majorities in the House and Senate in November.

1947   The Truman Doctrine announced in March.

Also in March, Truman institutes the Federal Employee Loyalty Program.

The Taft Hartley Act passes over Truman's veto in June.

The Marshall Plan is proposed by General George Marshall in June.

The National Security Act (NSA) establishes the CIA, the Department of Defense (DoD), and the National Security Council (NSC).

The House Un-American Activities Committee (HUAC) investigates Hollywood.

1948   Soviets take over Czechoslovakia in February.

The Soviet blockade of Berlin and Allied airlift begins in June.

Alger Hiss testifies before the House Un-American Activities Committee (HUAC) in August.

In November's presidential election, Truman defeats Dewey.

1949   NATO is founded in April.

The Soviet blockade of Berlin and Allied airlift ends in May.

The Soviet Union explodes its first atomic bomb in August.

Communists under Mao gain victory in China in September.

POSTWAR TENSIONS

In the years after victory in World War II, the United States was by far the most fortunate major country in the world. With the fewest casualties suffered of any of the major combatants, America had not fought the war on home soil, leaving it alone among nations with its entire productive capacity intact and with a gross national product (GNP) that doubled in wartime.

Yet in a short time, the new president, Harry S. Truman, had become wary of his Soviet counterpart, Joseph Stalin, and suspicious of the growing Soviet control over a large sphere of satellite states in war-torn Eastern Europe. Eager to stay any additional Soviet takeovers—possibly in Italy or France, both of which had increasing support for the Communist Party—George F. Kennan, an American diplomat stationed in Moscow, circulated in 1946 a long internal telegram that suggested a new U.S. foreign policy to contain the Soviets as an enemy at any chosen point of expansion, at any time, anywhere on the globe.

In March 1947, the Truman Doctrine made manifest the theory by pledging $450 million in aid and arms to Greece and Turkey for their battles with communist rebels. Shortly afterward, *Foreign Affairs* magazine published "The Sources of Soviet Conduct," a seminal article signed by "X" that explained the necessity of a war of containment against a new enemy, the Soviet Union. George F. Kennan authored this framing document of the early Cold War, which essentially covered the points he had made in his earlier telegram. "The issue of Soviet-American relations is in essence a test of the overall worth of the United States as a nation among nations," he concludes. "To avoid destruction the United States need only measure up to its own best traditions and prove itself worthy of preservation as a great nation." ("The Sources of Soviet Conduct," by X, *Foreign Affairs,* July 1947, p. 6). As a result of this new policy, millions of dollars more would flow to threatened democracies in a program that bore a not-so-distant relationship to the World War II's Lend-Lease Act, by which the U.S. government subsidized its own businesses to aid Allies.

The American public wanted to maintain prosperity. A majority of people came to believe that wartime had proved two ways of doing this. First, through government spending to maintain internal productivity and jobs; and second, through continued spending for defense and foreign aid. Many Americans were against high government spending for social reform, an attitude bolstered by the growing public fear of communism.

The Cold War developed abroad over the period between 1945 and 1947. The tensions between Truman and Stalin caused a shift in the mood of many Americans. They grew cautious of major proposals for new social reforms and assumed more conservative attitudes about change in general. Opponents of additional New Deal-type reforms stigmatized proposals as "socialist," and convinced the shifting political majority that such reforms were a threat to the free enterprise system. By 1947, the conservative public grew ever more fearful of an enemy within American society and distrustful of almost any new domestic reform. The result was political stalemate.

If big government spending was welcome, business wished to be free of government planning. Portraying government as too intrusive, the new conservatives lauded a "free enterprise" economy (which economists, at best, termed a "mixed public-private" economy). Advertisers convinced the public that the wartime production miracle was caused by private enterprise, not overall government planning. Domestic postwar tensions caused by satisfying business demand to suddenly lift controls on prices and wages resulted in a chaotic transition that conservatives blamed on big government. In 1946, with skyrocketing inflation,

Marshall Plan shipment of cornmeal arrives in Reykjavik, Iceland. (U.S. Agency for International Development)

strong unions called a wave of strikes for wages equal to the increased cost of living.

Employers resisted, branding this call for cost-of-living raises as class-oriented strife caused by unions grown overly powerful during wartime. Employers demanded that the power of big unions be trimmed back so management could once again control work floor conditions. Corporate leaders targeted the CIO, charging that it wrongly aimed to continue the management-labor system maintained during the war years when the War Labor Board (WLB) had set wages and work floor conditions in favor of the unions to avoid strike issues. Corporate pressure aimed not to eliminate but to trim back that union power. With the Taft-Hartley Act in 1947, the Republican-led Congress lessened the power of the unions, eliminated the closed shop and sympathy strikes, and instituted an 80-day cooling-off period for strikes in key industries. Congress passed it over Truman's veto.

The Cold War was good for American business, and this containment of Soviet expansion became the cornerstone of American foreign policy for years to come.

The government also lent foreign aid to allies by extending massive monetary credit to the war-torn democracies to enable these free but nearly bankrupt countries to purchase American weapons. Thus, much postwar anticommunist foreign aid provided contracts or indirect credits to businesses and wartime defense industries. The Marshall Plan provided $16 billion to help the countries of Western Europe rebuild their free enterprise economies to ultimately create stable, prosperous trading partners for the United States. Big business benefited greatly from these key pillars of big government's new foreign policies. So did agricultural interests, which could now sell a growing postwar surplus of crops abroad.

While satisfying certain major domestic economic interests in the ways it fought the Cold War abroad, the Truman administration was not nearly as successful in gaining public or congressional approval of its domestic social reform program, The Fair Deal geared to extend the New Deal. Congress extended the time-proven FDR programs such as Social Security, unemployment insurance, the minimum wage, and others but voted down new proposals such as a national health plan, increased public housing, and federal funds for education and building schools, and it voted down renewing civil rights gains such as the wartime Fair Employment Practices Commission (FEPC).

Conservatives convinced the public that such proposals would open the door to socialism and ultimately the destruction of the country's time-honored free economy. Many of these national opponents of Truman's domestic initiatives in fact advocated the president's Cold War policies abroad. Many white southern Democrats opposed African American civil rights legislation as a destabilizing issue and a threat to the region's social traditions. They claimed that it would bring chaotic change only to the advantage of outside communist agitators. Thus the FEPC was eliminated as no longer necessary.

Encouraged by opinion-makers, business leaders, and conservative politicians, Americans fell prey to growing fear that there were hidden American communists or communist sympathizers who wanted to bring change and push the country in directions that were not in the best interests of the American people. The Cold War motto was "Trust the tried and true; beware, for change could be a wolf in sheep's clothing."

The State's Wartime Priorities
Replace Liberal Social Aims

During the war years from 1941 to 1945, the trend in domestic politics was already toward conservatism, especially among the Democrats. This shift toward conservatism became even more pronounced in the postwar years. The wartime reason was simple: the goal was survival, and the supreme and singular task was victory in the war. The booming war economy had relieved the president of the need to promote further New Deal-type work or welfare programs. President Roosevelt revoked the few such programs extending into the war years, such as the Civilian Conservation Corps (CCC). In fact, during a 1943 Christmas press conference, he told reporters that his domestic program should no longer be referred to as the "New Deal" because that was applicable only to the programs of the previous decade. He announced the retirement of "Dr. New Deal" and his replacement, "Dr. Win-the-War"—the former having dealt with problems internal to the patient, and the latter, as of December 7, 1941, with problems coming from outside the country.

Long-time New Dealers, such as Henry Wallace, were disappointed and suspected FDR was trimming his sails away from reform and toward a greater conservatism. Roosevelt, with his keen political instincts, knew that in Congress politics had shifted on many issues, so the true working majority more and more consisted of the alliance of conservative Southern Democrats and Republicans. Most of this group were for halting more reforms and were against gains by communists, unions, and blacks. Roosevelt did not agree, but he downplayed these issues to have the group's firm support for his war policies at home and abroad. This group also supported the expanding war economy—but only grudgingly supported overall government planning and control. They believed that, necessary as it might be for an emergency such as war, big government support for big business ought to continue in normal times but without the wartime overall government planning and control.

The 1944 Election: FDR Voters Turn Back Archconservative Dewey

In the 1944 presidential election, there was growing emphasis on this conservative trend by the Republicans and their candidate, Thomas Dewey, the popular governor of New York. Dewey dismissed his usual diplomatic side and attacked Roosevelt with emotional charges geared to appeal to the far right. He repeatedly stated that FDR had the support of communist groups. FDR rebutted this. Dewey charged that communists influenced the powerful CIO political action committee led by Sidney Hillman, the union leader and the president's friend and adviser. The committee was preparing to get out a massive labor vote for the incumbent. Dewey mocked and attacked Hillman as being under communist influences and attacked the president for often clearing matters with this adviser. "Clear it with Sidney," was the tagline in a Republican attack ad that ran constantly on the radio.

Dewey used quotes out of context, such as the 1937 comment from Winston Churchill, then back-bencher and not yet in power, who stated that the New Deal was waging a fierce attack on business due to set the world back to deep levels of the Great Depression.

Besides the Republican anticommunist, antiunion, and probusiness attacks, the Southern Democrats resented the Roosevelt administration's support for civil rights and job gains for blacks, and they threatened to cross party lines to vote for Dewey. These Southerners championed states' rights against the strong federal government involvement in matters like race relations.

FDR fought back hard with all the accumulated political savvy and acumen at his disposal. In November he won his fourth term by the closest popular vote margin since 1916: 53.5 percent for Roosevelt and 46 percent for Dewey. Even though the Republicans got the largest total of white votes in the South since Reconstruction, the threatened full revolt of Southern Democrats fizzled out.

Conservatives' Rising Votes Bring the Reactionary 80th Congress

The 1944 vote served as a bellwether of the political trends set to continue into the postwar years. While both parties downplayed any need for domestic reform (the Republicans more so than the Democrats), the two parties were together in favoring a bipartisan internationalist outlook in foreign policy. Several of the hidebound isolationists left in Congress, including the New York Republican Hamilton Fish, were voted out of office. Even in strongly anti-Roosevelt areas, the vote was for candidates favoring a foreign policy continuing this country's involvement in the world. Gone forever, it seemed, was that long American tradition of isolationism that had been strong as recently as 1940. As early as 1944, the United States was preparing the initial groundwork for the forthcoming bipartisan support for Cold War policy abroad.

Consequently, this meant that domestic reform received a lower priority and had less available expenditures. With the support of nearly half of the country's voters, Dewey's archconservative approach to domestic policies—antiunionism, anti-federal government control, and pro-big business—would certainly have a strong effect on the postwar era. In fact, in the 1946 midterm elections, the country voted in the noted 80th Congress, the first Congress with all-Republican control of both House and Senate since an archconservative Congress 20 years earlier. However, a sizable number of newly elected Republicans misread the mandate as a repudiation of the whole New Deal when in fact voters merely wanted a continuation of the existing social welfare state combined with an anticommunist foreign policy. Thus, two years later, the anticommunist, pro-New Dealer Truman defeated the smug Dewey.

Churchill's 1946 Speech Coins the Cold War Term "Iron Curtain"

After the World War II victory in the Asian and European fronts and its monopoly of the A-bomb, the United States became the dominant world power. The

Soviet Union was the only other superpower, but it lacked the bomb. Cooperation between these two powers during wartime had tipped the balance against Germany and led to the Allied victory. What was to be the nature of the postwar world? This became the great diplomatic question of the moment. The key question for the Truman administration was, how should the new internationalist United States exert its power in the world? Should America strive for a new postwar cooperation with the Soviets or for containment of Soviet expansion? In 1945 and 1946, the way was tentative, but by early 1947, it was clear that the president had decided on the anticommunist Truman Doctrine.

One of the initial influences for this decision came a year earlier, on March 5, 1946, when Churchill went to the American heartland at his friend Truman's request and delivered a landmark speech at little Westminster College in Fulton, Missouri, the president's home state. Soon referred to as the "Iron Curtain" speech, its actual title was "Sinews of Peace" (James 1974, 7285–7293). In this speech, Churchill proposed two ways for the West to prevent war with the Soviets. First, the East and West had to find a new unity and cooperate through the United Nations. Second, the West needed to contain Soviet expansion with an opposing united force of the United States, Britain, Canada (all would have the secret of the bomb).

Churchill advocated the latter because of his dramatic assessment of the current state of Europe: He said that an iron curtain had descended across the continent, from Stettin in the Baltic to Trieste in the Adriatic (James 1974, 00). The Soviets, he continued, sought an ever-expanding hegemony, not only in Europe but globally. America needed to use its overwhelming power to join with England in opposing this and present a strong barrier to stop the Moscow-led advance of communism, therefore preserving peace and preventing further totalitarianism.

The Soviets, he stated, are foremost a people whose leaders loathe weakness and admire strength, especially in the military. Therefore, he concluded, the traditional balance of power of the past was inadequate for the postwar period because any hesitation would tempt the Soviets to test the resolve of the West. A dominating military power backing a clear Western stance was the primary means to halt the Soviets without recourse to another world war. The work of the United Nations would be to further the secondary aim of eventually changing the Soviet stance to cooperation.

Society Committed to Containment

The Churchill speech became an important early template for the March 1947 Truman Doctrine, which initiated the new foreign policy of the United States in the Cold War. In short, this early Churchill speech had great future implications for the lives of ordinary Americans and their postwar society. The emphasis on military strength meant that the United States's defense spending would gain priority in future national budgets, with less and less money available for new domestic reforms beyond the New Deal. In place of reform, rising defense expenditures would spur a steadily expanding war economy, making jobs plentiful. With rising waters lifting all boats, people would feel little need for a greater New Deal-type welfare state. In domestic politics, future voters would be less liberal than in the 1930s because of the new military-based internationalist foreign policy.

Churchill's speech proposing such a stance created much controversy at the time. Many Americans found it difficult to see the Soviet Union, so recently a cooperative wartime ally, as an aggressive foreign antagonist. Others refused to think the recent war had failed to bring peace. Both criticism and agreement were vociferous in America after the speech. The most prominent critic was Truman's secretary of commerce, Henry Wallace, a traditional New Deal liberal. In September 1946, Wallace made a speech stating that the proposed Anglo-American pact would be divisive and would eventually lead to Britain's interests in the Near East inciting the Soviet Union to war, dragging this country into it. Wallace advocated that this country should lean neither toward Britain nor to the Soviet Union, and that the latter had its own rights to national security.

Protesters picket former vice president Henry Wallace as a "Red" at a campaign stop during his bid for the presidency in Tennessee, September 4, 1948. (Library of Congress)

Truman, who already leaned toward a strong anticommunist policy, responded angrily to this contradictory speech and dismissed Wallace from the cabinet. Wallace remained an example of an earlier New Dealer who had been bypassed by a Democratic Party grown more conservative, which even under FDR had begun trimming back its reform impulses in favor of an expanding war economy. In 1940, Wallace had been Roosevelt's vice president; in 1944, Roosevelt dropped him for the more moderate Truman. After being fired in 1946, Wallace went on to form a new third party, the Progressive Party. In the 1948 election, he got a pledge of support from Moscow and drew the support of the American Communist Party. So by 1948, the Democratic Party was devoid of the radicals who had supported it in the 1930s.

In March 1947, when Truman went to the conservative Republican-controlled 80th Congress and proposed his Truman Doctrine of giving aid to free countries fighting against outside influences—specifically, at the time, $400 million to imperiled Greece and Turkey—the congressmen gave him a standing ovation. From that point on, it was clear that America's new anticommunist foreign policy had strong bipartisan support. A revolutionary change from the traditional American policy of isolationism, this new internationalism was also unprecedented because it involved interventionism—in Greece and Turkey—without any direct threat to American security.

War and Society: The Birth of the Postwar Military Industrial State

The majority of Americans agreed to this newly evolving postwar society. A broad consensus formed among Republican and Democratic voters that anticommunism and high defense budgets were the top priorities for the country's foreign policy. That government borrowing and defense contracts were the means to a healthy economy became an accepted belief, and so the Keynesian economics of the war would become institutionalized during the Cold War.

However, during the war years, the federal government had been in charge of the overall planning and control of the economy. In the postwar period, the expanding war economy generally lacked that oversight of big government. The cost of living soared for ordinary people because the government was reluctant to reinstitute wage and price controls or to continue the high taxes or the war bond drives necessary to cut back inflation. Although many people chafed at such restraints and favored the advantages given to big business, many suffered as a result of rising everyday costs.

To buttress the Truman Doctrine, in 1947 the president and Congress passed the National Security Act, which authorized certain agencies as the central military network to gather secret intelligence. Among them were the CIA, which coordinated peacetime military and business affairs; the Defense Department

(DoD), renamed from the War Department; and the coordinating body and crisis-management agency for the president, the National Security Council (NSC). All of these agencies at times constituted a parallel secret government, as many of their decisions and actions were censored from public scrutiny. National security was invariably the reason—during the Cold War, keeping information from the enemy too often meant also keeping knowledge from a democratic public. When lacking crucial information, the democratic public was doomed to cast votes completely unaware of certain important solutions, problems, or issues.

On June 24, 1948, Truman signed a new peacetime draft law for the country, this one with no world war already under way, as was the case in 1916 and 1940. The Selective Service Act of 1948 mandated that males between the ages of 18 and 25 must register for the draft. About 250,000 males in the country were called up each year. During the Cold War, when an active, "hot" regional conflict was not occurring such as the looming Korean War (1950–1954), the active-duty soldiers, waiting in preparedness and receiving pay, served as a different kind of 1930s work project. This kept individuals temporarily out of the domestic job market yet allowed their Army earnings to become future consuming power. Thus, without raising taxes inordinately, the bipartisan policy of the country in the postwar period was to borrow from at-home and abroad to cover any present budget deficit and have an expanding economy strong enough to provide both guns and butter at all times.

The Churchill speech created the crucible for what followed in American society because it suggested containment of the Soviet Union through overwhelming strength. If the Soviet Union ever caught up militarily, then the United States must get stronger still; this implied a future arms race. In 1949, with the Soviet Union in possession of its own A-bomb, the United States immediately speeded up work on a much stronger hydrogen bomb. Americans began to live under the continuous pall of imminent all-out world destruction. The budget's defense costs for such an arms race would naturally leave less expendable monies for domestic reforms. This, too, was a lesser-known consequence traceable to the template for foreign policy implicit in the 1946 Churchill speech.

War and Society: Cold War Liberalism Emerges

In 1949, Americans were shocked at two foreign events: the unexpected announcement that the Soviets had an atomic bomb, and the communist victory in the world's most populous country, China. On the home front, Americans looking for scapegoats and found them readily at hand, due to recent revelations from the series of hearings held by the HUAC. Many Americans came to believe that such gains by communists abroad could only have been made with the aid of a conspiracy of communist spies and traitors within the American government and society dating back to the days of the New Deal.

The question became, why did we lose China? Many people believed it was because of traitors like Alger Hiss in the State Department, whose China experts had sold out the Nationalists. How did the Soviets gain the A-bomb? Many people believed that an atomic spy ring had stolen the secrets, which sped up the Soviet Union's progress and allowed it to catch up with America.

"Red" hysteria eventually swept the home front. Out of this came the makings of the Cold War liberal. Liberal groups of all sorts—Democrats, unions, African American civil rights groups, Hollywood, and others—began purges to isolate and remove known or suspected communists from their ranks. The Truman Democrats managed to isolate the Henry Wallace supporters, who remained stigmatized as Old New Deal Liberals, still soft on communism. Within the powerful United Automobile Workers (UAW) union, Walter Reuther led a purge of suspected communist members. This also took place throughout the ranks of the AFL and the CIO. The HUAC intimidated liberal Hollywood. Major studio heads readily blacklisted the Hollywood Ten—10 film actors, directors, and screenwriters accused of being communists who refused to testify before HUAC by taking the Fifth Amendment. The studios further vowed not hire any radicals in the future.

Curiously, the Cold War forced most American liberals to become more conservative and to recognize that the postwar public favored cautious reforms (in 1949, the new Democratic 81st Congress passed an expansion of Social Security and a raise of the minimum wage, both preexisting programs). Stigma readily attached to reforms that Americans now perceived as radical. For example, the American Medical Association successfully fought Truman's proposal for a national health program by calling it "socialized medicine."

American liberalism changed under the pressures of World War II and the Cold War so that its mainstream moved closer to conservatism. A bipartisan majority came to favor a strong anticommunist foreign policy abroad. At home, the Democratic liberal was prone to support an expanding Cold War economy without need for major reforms especially, ones easily tainted as radical or socialistic. As early as 1943, at a press conference in which he declared that "Dr. New Deal" had been replaced with "Dr. Win-the-War," FDR himself disavowed the old New Deal, noting that the country must plan for victory and develop strategies to help create an expanded economy. With economic growth, there would be no return of the Depression and, therefore, no longer any need for the radical reforms necessary only in the unusual context of the 1930s. The new Cold War liberal accepted this caution, especially given the booming economy, which was soon to get fresh infusions of defense spending after 1949 with the outbreak of the Korean War.

NATIONAL EFFORTS TO FIGHT THE COLD WAR

After victory in World War II, Americans learned that their country's wartime ally, Joseph Stalin, was aggressively securing territorial gains with the aim of creating a buffer zone of allied communist countries between Germany and the Soviet Union. This was done in a host of Eastern European countries that his Red Army had liberated from the Nazis on their drive toward Germany to defeat Hitler. With Soviet occupation forces on their land, these countries often held elections that the West saw as engineered by the Soviets—not free, as Stalin had promised they would be in various of the Big Three meetings held during the war. In Poland especially, the Soviets and the Polish communists had eliminated opposition parties; in other countries, coups had replaced elected leaders with Soviet-backed native communists.

Decree Demands Loyalty from Government Workers

After the Soviet threat abroad led President Truman by March 1947 to adopt an anticommunist policy of containing Soviet expansion globally, it was no wonder that Congress vowed to thwart any threat of an active conspiracy plot. Congress broadly targeted the whole American Communist Party (consisting of no more than 75,000 members). Suspects included not only all "card-carrying" party members but also persons called "fellow travelers" merely associated with this cause in the past. Congress sought proof of 100 percent Americanism for anyone suspected of disloyalty. The public had a fear of an internal enemy in the country and especially of Soviet spies or sympathizers within government. While some in government were or had been communists—an estimated 300, including Dexter White and Alger Hiss—the issue of loyalty was bent to partisan purpose.

In late 1946, President Truman set up a commission to draft a program to determine the loyalty of all government employees. He had done so largely because he feared his opponents would take the lead on the issue, especially with the Republicans in control of the newly elected 80th Congress. In March 1947, the President issued Executive Order 9835, which put into effect the Federal Employee Loyalty Program. Under its rules, a person could be removed from a federal position if reasonable grounds existed for believing a person was disloyal. The accused employee was allowed counsel but could neither confront the accuser nor demand evidence because this was classified material held by the Federal Bureau of Investigation (FBI), which was headed by the zealous J. Edgar Hoover. Over four years, this program caused approximately 3,000 government employees to resign, willingly or under pressure, and another 300 were fired. Those cleared in hearings nevertheless had records of their investigations remain on file permanently. Ironically, the public grew more, not less, fearful as the program seemed to provide ongoing evidence that an internal enemy did exist in the government, and possibly in other important areas of the country.

Domestic "Un-Americans" Hunted by Congressional Committee

Under New Jersey representative J. Parnell Thomas in the conservative 80th Congress, the HUAC would assume the task of ridding the country of any and all internal disloyal citizens. The HUAC's methods involved bringing forth known communists who were expected to witness for the state and name other persons suspected of being communists. The latter were then called to the stand and made to swear under oath, answering "Yes" or "No" to whether they were now or had ever been communists.

In 1947, the committee reported a series of findings that created sensational news for the public. Aided by the FBI, the investigators had revealed communist infiltration of writers, actors, and directors in Hollywood. The HUAC called suspects to answer questions; some took the Fifth Amendment, but studio heads nevertheless blacklisted them. The most famous were known as "the Hollywood Ten." Civil liberties were regularly breached in the hearings, and many were convicted of perjury for simply failing to cooperate. Many lives and careers were destroyed needlessly because many of the associations with communists had been from the earlier periods of the 1930s, or especially the 1940s, when the Soviet Union had been a valued ally.

Next, in 1948, the HUAC targeted the State Department, especially old New Dealers and liberals. Only weeks before that year's November presidential election, Alger Hiss, a former assistant secretary of state who had been at Yalta with FDR, found himself accused by Whittaker Chambers of having been a 1930s communist who had passed secret state documents to Chambers to give to the Soviet Union. The patrician Hiss denied ever knowing the rumpled Chambers, a

A spectator, seemingly unaware of being seated next to Whittaker Chambers, holds a newspaper with a headline reading "One of them still lying! Hiss and Chambers contradict each other under oath," at the House Un-American Activities Committee hearings in 1948. In testimony that transfixed the nation, Chambers accused Alger Hiss, a State Department official, of being a communist spy; Hiss vehemently denied the charges. (Library of Congress)

Time magazine editor, but a young California congressman, Richard Nixon, revealed in cross-examination that Hiss did know his accuser. He was charged with perjury. The first trial in 1949 would result in a hung jury. Hiss then sued for libel. The next trial found him guilty, and Hiss served five years.

The American Left Reacts to the Vicissitudes of Soviet Policy

In the late summer and fall of 1939, Americans confronted two shocking events: the alliance of Germany and the Soviet Union and, shortly thereafter, the outbreak of world war in Europe, with both countries attacking Poland. As the combined forces of Stalin and Hitler advanced during the next 22 months, on the American domestic front, Congress, often with the support of both conservatives and liberals, initiated attacks on potential subversives—American Nazis and especially communists. Conservatives relished investigations that brought charges against real or purported communists and convicted them often on the flimsiest of evidence. The pact embarrassed many liberals, who, in the 1930s, had defended the Soviets as part of a united front with the democracies against the newly risen fascist dictatorships. But in 1939, the Soviets had joined the enemy of liberals so that across the left, individual liberals praised the hunters of communist subversives and liberal organizations like the American Civil Liberties Union (ACLU), and the industrial unions purged their organizations of communists. On June 23, 1939, Hitler suddenly attacked the Soviet Union, and FDR welcomed a powerful new ally in the Soviets. Still, most liberals at home remained wary and rebuked the communists for wanting to forge another United Front. Most ordinary citizens retained their underlying antipathy to communism even while seeing the Soviet Union as a valuable new fighting partner.

Conservative congressional organizations that led the attacks against subversives after the Soviet-Nazi Pact were the HUAC and the administrators of the so-called Smith Act (after its sponsor), or the Alien Registration Act. The HUAC, referred to as the Dies Committee after its chairman, Martin Dies (Texas), by 1940 had become the most popular of all government committees largely because of Dies's way of playing to the public fear of a fifth column of Nazis or communists secretly forming to one day arise and overthrow the American government. Dies's primary target was communists; by 1939 he had already made public a list of 523 purported communists (this foreshadowed a tactic later used by Sen. Joseph McCarthy). In 1940, the Dies Committee investigated Earl Browder, head of the American Communist Party, for having three passports under different names. Because all charges were beyond the seven-year statute of limitations, the HUAC charged him with fraud for most recently applying under his proper name and failing to give his previous history. Convicted, he got four years in jail and a fine. In November 1940, Browder ran for president from his jail cell.

Groups Targeted as Subversives during the War

In June 1940, Congress passed the Smith Act. Government enforcement officials targeted all aliens—especially recent and older immigrants who were not yet naturalized citizens. The act set forth policies for stringent background checks on the political beliefs and acts of each alien. A sworn loyalty oath was required of the alien. Because the public fear was that immigrants, especially the many refugees fleeing Europe, might be subversives intending an internal revolution, the enforcers of the Smith Act had strong public backing. The act also had a broader reach; the act made it a federal crime for anyone to advocate the overthrow of the government or to be a member of a subversive organization. As with the Dies Committee, the Smith Act targeted communists more frequently than Nazis. Its enforcers went after Harry Bridges, the Australian-born head of the West Coast longshoremen, who was charged with being an illegal alien as well as a secret communist. In the long deportation fight that ensued, the government failed to muster the necessary proof.

By 1940, the federal government began to require loyalty oaths from all workers in defense plants. The two million remaining employees in the Works Project Administration (WPA), a program carried over from the 1930s New Deal, all now needed to vouch that they were not Nazis or communists. Within the Justice Department, the FBI's budget more than doubled during the time of the Soviet-Nazi Pact. Its director, J. Edgar Hoover, ardently joined the hunt for potential spies, using vast card indexes of suspects and illegal wire taps of phones. In 1940, the FBI uncovered a plot by 18 young pro-Nazis who were duly convicted. The public viewed it as the squashing of a secret conspiracy plot after the news media sensationalized the reporting of it.

On the other side of the democratic political spectrum, liberals were embarrassed and then increasingly angry at what seemed to be cynical opportunism from the communists in the 1939 pact. Walter Lippmann, the liberal columnist, praised the Dies Committee. Lewis Mumford, a noted liberal intellectual, called for the banning of both Nazi and communist parties. The ACLU, the organization foremost in guarding civil liberties, purged its board of communists (the only one was Helen Gurley Flynn, one of its founders). The head of the CIO, Phillip Murray, ordered all his local unions purged of communists. The New York State legislature mandated the removal of 64 professors from universities and colleges in New York City.

Even after June 23, 1941, when the Soviets again had become an anti-Nazi ally, Americans continued their historic distrust of communists, and America's liberals rejected their new appeals for common political efforts. In fact, in the summer of 1941, after the Soviet changeover, some liberals favored the liberal Newspaper Guild's purge of Stalinists or any like-minded members of the union. For the nearly two years that the Soviet-Nazi Pact was in effect, the American public grew extremely emotional about a potential fifth column; as a result, there was an early Red Scare that was a clear forerunner of the later HUAC investigations of the late 1940s and eventually the full-blown McCarthyism of the early 1950s.

Society's New Fears of Communism Cause Sociopolitical Realignment

The first post-World War II congressional elections were held in November 1946. In many ways, Americans were casting votes to signal their approval or disapproval of work done by the Truman administration in his roughly 18 months in office. A year before, in the fall of 1945 after V-E and V-J days, the public had given him an 87 percent job approval rating, higher even than the peak approval rating of his famous predecessor. In the year after the war, given the difficulties of converting to peacetime, the president's popularity had plummeted over 50 percent as he struggled with scarcities, strikes, and inflation. Markedly, the economy had remained strong; most people had money and security. Yet many were deeply disgruntled by the perception of one crisis after another. The scarcity of meat seemed to sum up a host of matters frustrating the public.

Controlling Congress for a dozen years throughout the New Deal and World War II, the Democrats for the first time seemed vulnerable to attacks by the opposing party. The Republicans, led by Sen. Robert Taft of Ohio, campaigned on the administration's failings: the skyrocketing cost of living and the still-unexplained shortages of many items, especially meat, because of lingering control of prices.

Most importantly, the Republicans used the Red Scare as a preeminent issue, claiming that Truman was appeasing the communists abroad by coddling them at home. The Democrats overall were soft on communism, was the charge introduced by Taft and slated to be a staple of politics for the following decades (also to be used by some Democrats against their opponents). The Democrats, Taft stated, had become a laughingstock and were unable to decide between Americanism and communism. The FBI's director, J. Edgar Hoover, lent his weight to the issue by warning that 100,000 communists existed in America. "Had Enough?" was the slogan of the minority Republican party.

The Republicans won both houses of Congress in a landslide. For the first time since the first election of FDR in 1932, the GOP would now control both houses of Congress by wide margins—in the House, 246 to 188; Senate, 51 to 45. The 80th Congress was to become famous as possibly the most ultraconservative Congress since the 1920s. The New Deal was over.

Conservative Tide Influences the State

The winners of congressional elections began to refer to Truman as the "accidental" president. Gov. Thomas Dewey of New York, who had won reelection by record numbers, seemed ideally positioned to defeat the now weak incumbent in the 1948 presidential election.

The 1946 election was a turning point in various ways in the fight against the Cold War at home. Early the next year, Truman moved, both at home and abroad, to counter the charge of being soft on communism. In March 1947, he instituted the Federal Employee Loyalty Program, whereby the FBI required every federal employee to submit to a background check and then sign an oath affirming their lifelong, noncommunist loyalty to the country. Nine days later, Truman went before Congress to state the aim of fighting communism abroad with aid to imperiled Greece and Turkey in what became known as The Truman Doctrine.

By the rules of Congress, the newly elected Republican legislators replaced Democrats as chairmen of committees. Congressman Parnell Thomas, thus, got backing as chair of the HUAC. With many new congressmen elected to office using Red Scare tactics, there was strong support for the HUAC, and Thomas presided over some of the committee's most dramatic hearings involving the Hollywood Ten and former State Department official Alger Hiss, who was accused by Whittaker Chambers of having been a communist spy in the 1930s. The victors in the 1946 election won by elevating anticommunism at home to a paramount issue. Thereafter the lesson was not lost on Truman.

Truman Calms Society's Anticommunist Hysteria

In the postwar 1940s, the American public was engulfed in a growing crusade against domestic communism. This laid the necessary foundations for the even greater Red Scare, which began October 1, 1949, when Mao and his huge army declared China a communist People's Republic. Immediately afterwards, Sen. Joseph McCarthy and others in the opposition party publicly declared that Truman had lost China because of disloyal advisers in the State Department. Communist gains abroad were closely tied to Americans' rising fear of a communist conspiracy at home.

As early as September 1948, President Truman reviled this fear as public hysteria and stated that Republicans pandered to it with endless spy hunts and loyalty investigations. Truman believed the Republicans did this to distract the public from objecting to Congress rebutting measures against inflation and for the New Deal. Truman claimed that a "Do Nothing" Congress was hiding behind this largely spurious charade of anticommunism. In November 1948, Truman won the presidency with the support of the loyal New Dealers, as well as strong support from the new anticommunist liberals. Domestic communists were isolated in their support for Henry Wallace's breakaway Progressive Party. During a June 1948 press conference, Truman again stated that the nation was becoming hysterical about a largely bogus threat of domestic Reds.

President Harry Truman holds up the front page of the Chicago Daily Tribune *issue that predicted his defeat in 1948. In the greatest upset in U.S. political history, Truman won the election with 49.5 percent of the vote. (Library of Congress)*

Society's Pattern: A Foreign Flare-up Brings Domestic Hunts for Subversives

A prime example of the pattern of containment of foreign communist expansion (whether a real or a perceived threat) was the 1948 Berlin Crisis. The Soviets for a year had blocked access to West Berlin; the Western Allies resisted this seeming Soviet expansion with a nonstop airlift. Such large-scale cooperation unified the West and led to such alliances as the formation in 1949 of NATO, an American and European mutual defense pact, as well as the formation of the independent nation of West Germany.

During the June 1948 to July 1949 Berlin crisis (the most dangerous period to date in the Cold War), Americans were closely following various crises of anticommunism at home: the HUAC trial of former FDR State Department adviser Alger Hiss and the indictment of the actor Charlie Chaplin, among the many charged as subversives.

In the fall of 1949, with the Communist takeover in China and the Soviet developing an atomic bomb, an American court convicted 11 leading members of the American Communist Party under the Smith Act of conspiring to overthrow the government of the United States. Each got a sentence of five years.

The feared spread of communism abroad was the seedbed for the frenzy of public support for accusations of subversives at home. Some Democrats became Cold War liberals or conservatives and denounced 1930s events or persons associated with radicalism, socialism, or communism, even though many liberals had joined with radicals in a common front to resist the fascist threat. By 1949, reactionary men like Hoover and the HUAC politicians were all too willing to make little or no distinction between old New Dealers, liberals, and communists.

THE COLD WAR AND DOMESTIC LIFE

The Cold War took place in a United States that had been transformed by World War II. In the 1940s, its population grew from 132 million to 150 million; the baby boom that began in 1946 accounted for a large portion of this increase. Individual Americans had more per capita wealth than ever before, and the United States' citizens encompassed the largest middle class of any comparable country in the world (wartime's steep, progressive taxes and full employment had created the first and only real redistribution of wealth in the country's history). At the end of the Depression, the middle-class population was relatively small, and only a few owned their own homes. By 1950, the middle class had become dominant, and a majority owned homes, usually in the new suburbs. Americans at home during the war had saved $180 billion. With a postwar flood of consumer goods unseen in wartime, the American populace went on a spending spree that buoyed the economy and maintained the general prosperity along with defense spending.

Education
The G.I. Bill, or the Servicemen's Readjustment Act, along with its implications and consequences for postwar America, is an example of the web of changes in domestic life during the Cold War. Passed in 1944, the bill covered the 16 million citizens who were veterans of the armed services. The government guaranteed them 52 weeks of unemployment pay while they looked for work or attended college, largely at government expense. Nothing down, low-interest, federally guaranteed home loans were also available to veterans and their families.

Women: Wives, Mothers, and Babies

The 16 million former servicemen divided into two groups: 10 million eventually returned to jobs and 6 million went to college. The consequences for both groups were similar; in both instances, women made way for the returning veterans. Although a postwar poll showed 70 percent of women preferred to keep their wartime jobs, societal pressures caused three million women, most of them married, to leave the work force. With colleges tightly crowded and young women urged to marry young because of a shortage of young males, the percentage of coeds plummeted down nearly a third from wartime levels.

Young women absorbed a barrage of propaganda in women's magazines, newspapers, radio programs, and the movies that spoke of the glories of being a wife, mother, and homemaker (a return to the "ideal woman" of the Victorian era). Early marriage became the norm and, of those coming of age, 95 percent married. By age 30, the average couple had 3.2 children.

Suburbia

The postwar housing shortage was soon solved by the building of huge suburbs, one of the first being Levittown on Long Island. Countless other married couples set a pattern of owning first homes. The American Dream became a new life in the suburbs. Never before had so many lived in such wholly new communities, with new schools, churches, and stores. While portrayed as ideal, these suburbs had a dulling sameness; the families were of the same age and income level and often had similar religious backgrounds. Cars became a necessity for husbands to commute into the city to work.

The Widening Middle Class, Growing Affluence, and Hidden Poor

As many factory owners converted back to producing consumer goods, they delighted in a market with seemingly endless demand following years of rationing and the lack of goods in wartime. Home appliances, especially washing machines and dryers, comprised a giant mass market. Automobiles sold at even a greater rate, with the first new models in four years unveiled at the showrooms in 1946. This was the beginning of an auto age of cheap gas and, eventually, multicar families, even jalopies for teenagers.

The country was fast becoming the modern America that is recognizable today, the affluent society that gave the title for the 1958 book by the economist John Kenneth Galbraith. Yet there also existed a separate America that had no share in the collective wealth. In his 1962 book *The Other America,* sociologist Michael Harrington, in contrast to Galbraith, pointed out that millions of Americans lived marginal lives limited by class, race, gender, and age discrimination. Included were those in forgotten family farms and small towns, in crumbling inner city neighborhoods, in old-age homes, in the cramped apartments of single mothers, and all the working poor who earned less than a living wage. Of the

Postwar Consumers, General Motors, and the Cadillac

The postwar economic boom and rise of mass consumption made the auto the single most important object of consumption. After sacrificing through 15 years of depression and war, postwar affluent Americans (many formerly of marginal status) wanted to reward themselves with a car that proved their newly attained higher social status. Historian Tom McCarthy, author of *Auto Mania,* writes that the immediate postwar decade after 1945 was the American auto's golden age.

The Cadillac was the single most desirable consumer item and status symbol in the postwar era of growing mass affluence. If you owned one, it signaled that you had the American Dream, or were near to having it. Even though the Cadillac was only 2 percent of all car registrations in the country, surveys showed that money was no object; nearly 50 percent of Americans named a new Cadillac as their first dream purchase. Thus, the Cadillac lent astounding prestige to all the cars of General Motors, the industry leader that was most focused on new models every year.

The entire auto market was, in fact, Cadillac centered. Other makers tried unsuccessfully to make their own competing high-cost, high-status autos. The postwar Cadillac, apropos of the country's new affluence, superseded the prewar Ford models as the country's iconic auto. New styling was one of the main reasons; in 1948, the Cadillac got its first tailfins, which created an instant shape of high distinction, never before associated with status of any sort. This revolutionary tailfin shape gave Americans the sense that the future held ever-growing prosperity, technological wonders, and progress.

millions of Americans left behind in the postwar boom, these mentioned were only some of the affected groups.

The Baby Boom and the New Demography

With the armed forces quickly demobilizing after World War II, the returning young servicemen married and began families. Starting a trend of younger marriages and bigger families than their Depression-era parents, these young couples began in 1946 what sociologists termed a "baby boom" that would last until 1964. This high fertility rate peaked in 1957 with 123 births per 1,000 women (totaling 4 million births). But the rate first rose with the increase of "war babies"; then the rate rose steeply in 1946 when births went to 3.4 million from 2.5 million in 1940. In 1950, the national population reached 151 million, an increase of 19 million from the 1940s decade.

A family of seven leaves the New Hope, Pennsylvania, train station after welcoming home their returning serviceman, ca. 1945. Many young men returning from war bought suburban homes and married during the decade following the conflict. (Hulton Archive)

This sharp postwar increase in births was unrivaled in the country's history. With wives by age 30 having an average of 3.2 children, the boom did its own part to fuel the growth of the economy. The demand of these families for affordable, larger housing started the growth of suburbs. Auto sales grew, too, because the husband and father needed a car to commute into his job in the city. Such labor-saving home appliances as washers, dryers, and dishwashers were part of this new and expanding market for families to help mothers care for large numbers of children. Toys, clothes, and children's medical and dental care were also in growing demand. The boom made for a child-centered society with an ethos calling for closeness in a big family.

The large baby boomer generation defined later American eras and events —the 1960s anti-Vietnam War protesters, Watergate, the 1970s me-decade, and the economic boom of the 1990s, when the generation was at its peak working and earning years. A massive retirement era was next for the generation that back in 1946 first began to grow its numbers.

Suburbanites as a New Social Group

Suburbs and the planned housing communities built outside the older cities had their inception in the postwar 1940s. Levittown on Long Island, which consisted of 17,500 homes newly built at a record pace of 150 homes a day in 1947, was the iconic first of countless such developments built across America. Built by the innovative construction firm of Abraham Levitt and Sons, this original suburb marked the beginning of revolutionary changes in the country: its geographic look, the differing urban and suburban demographics, and the environmental effect from increasing transportation needs.

Levitt understood that the immediate postwar housing shortage in cities created a huge market for good, affordable housing for the unprecedented number of newly married young couples. They could afford a modest down payment due to wartime savings and low-cost government housing loans. Veterans also had housing benefits under under the G.I. Bill. To supply this market, Levitt used assembly-line methods of housing construction that relied on many pre-fabricated elements and on-site assembly teams moving in sequence and doing only one task all day. For example, one team used heavy equipment to dig basements, another team followed to make the cement casings, a third came to pour the cement basement, and so on.

The Levittown homes all had the same floor plan with a choice of slight variations outside, but each was a small two-bedroom home. The homes all cost between $6,900 and $7,990 and were available to rent with an option to buy while the development was still under construction. One could expect a certain look: a tree planted near the sidewalk every 28 feet, streets laid out the same, parks with playgrounds, and shopping areas of uniform design.

Suburbia's Negatives: Race and the Environment

In time, these new automobile suburbs grew in clusters to circle the nation's cities, contrasting with the earlier outlying trolley car suburbs of small towns and villages. Built farther out, the new suburbs relied on automobiles. Soon new superhighways with commuter traffic jams were the norm. Pollution from the growing number of cars became common. The country's geography changed and the approach to cities was no longer farmland but interlocking housing developments, no longer a city shopping street but a circling, contorting super-highway. Smog was the most noticeable new environmental defect.

Meanwhile, in contrast to the new middle class that went to the suburbs and bought their first homes, those not as fortunate remained behind in the worn-down residential inner cities. All too often, these were minorities or the poor. Losing their promising young to the outward suburban migration, the cities saw their tax bases shrink while demand grew for city services. Many neighborhoods turned desperately poor and experienced a rising rate of crime, drugs, and violence.

Suburbs had housing covenants that prevented the sale of homes to African Americans (builders feared such sales would cause white flight and transform the new developments into all-black ghettoes). Government mortgage contracts also privileged this growing white population of new, more conservative, property-tax paying voters. For those in all-white ethnic city neighborhoods, the government also denied loans to African Americans on the basis that their owning homes in confirmed white-majority neighborhoods would cause social strife. The new demographics left the inner cities with more and more persons of color while the new suburbs held more and more whites who escaped the cities for a healthier, more spacious, green place to raise children and send them to better schools.

Family Life as Postwar Myth

In postwar America, the government and the media pushed a social campaign that idealized the family. From the dislocations and personal separations of war, the urge to return to family life was a part of the larger national impulse to return to normalcy. Family represented a microcosm of society; and a happy healthy, prosperous family was the aim, especially for the 16 million veterans. Family became the ideal—and this was widely and heavily trumpeted, beginning in 1946. Because the country's middle class broadened during and after the war, the illusion grew of a classless society that encompassed most families within this ideal and others within reach of it.

However, status anxiety overcame many who worried that their families might fall behind—especially so because advertisers gave this new middle class the general perception that, by not affording the latest consumer goods, persons would fall from their present status. One needed to continue the appearance of a comfortable status by selecting a yearly purchase and displaying "status symbols" in personal possessions. Ideally, the impression of rising mobility was the ongoing purchase of a greater status model than the one before it—for example, in the hierarchy of autos, going from Ford to Buick to Cadillac. All dreamed of this, yet, even members of families nearest the ideal had hidden misgivings and disappointments—some called it a "rat race." Yet, even though anxious about "keeping up with the Jones," most Americans achieved enough real prosperity to hold to the myth.

A myth about family that carried over from wartime conveyed the sense that the large number of married women who had met the government's call to work in factories had done so on a strictly temporary basis until the men returned to these jobs. When the veterans did return, the myth continued, the women workers, married or single, would be only too happy to give up their jobs and return to family life or, if single, to find a husband and have children. None would have the urge to work again. Such myth making was the subject of countless ads and articles in women's magazines.

Family roles of the husband, wife, and children also were idealized, with the husband returned to the provider role (in the 1930s Depression and World War II wives often had to become the sole support of the family). The man of the family knew best, this myth went; the wife and children were dependents who benefited from his greater worldliness and experience in financial matters and practical planning. As the undisputed family head, however, the postwar ideal held that he needed to learn to be less patriarchal, more a pal than a strict disciplinarian to his kids, and more a proponent of togetherness, not strict hierarchy, with wife and children. The family automobile with the husband as driver was the symbol of the power of his new role.

The new ideal American wife and mother would fulfill the two most desirable roles for a woman; ideally, she should marry young at age 20 and have three to four children, by age 30. Women got this or similar messages from every imaginable source in the culture—newspapers, magazines, radio, television, and ads of all sorts. Doctors and other experts portrayed the perfect, well-adjusted female as naturally selfless and a born nurturer, a wife devoted to her husband, children, and home.

The average woman gave birth to 3.2 children in the postwar period. Young mothers were icons of the time; one magazine, *Redbook,* devoted its content to this readership. Infants in ads were all cuddly, smiling, funny, and just plain adorable—in short, easy and fun to mother. The at-home parent, the mother, had the paramount responsibility to society of raising her children to be model citizens of the age.

Mrs. Earl Warren, first lady of California, sets an example for renewed female domesticity as she labels preserves, aided by her youngest son. (Library of Congress)

These various new 1940s social mores together served as early sources for the heralded conformity of the next decade. Summarily included were family "togetherness," similar lifestyles for the broadened middle class, and the myth of a new, comfortably prosperous "classless society." Finally, advertiser-induced mass consumption for similar private needs and desires created nebulous but real status-related "consumer communities" (for example, Buick or Ford owners). Ideally, the myth continued, all citizens wished to protect this "American Way of Life" against the reputed domestic threat of a conspiracy of communists coupled with the more real Soviet menace abroad.

Family Life as Postwar Reality

The myth of postwar family life ignored many facts. During the war, 95 percent of married women remained at home, primarily because of the lack of even minimal childcare centers until 1943. By that time, women constituted 35 percent of the workforce, a considerable number of them working in defense plants making their highest ever incomes. A total of 6 million women had newly gone to work in wartime, joining the 14 million women already working, many from the lower class as domestics and waitresses and in pink-collar jobs as low-paid shop girls, clerks, and telephone operators. Three million of the new workers left their jobs at war's end. Three million still needed to work, some to support a husband who was a disabled war veteran, and some now widows who were the sole support of their families. Demoted from factory jobs, these women took large pay cuts and joined other pink-collar workers. By 1949, a greater percentage of women were working than at the wartime peak, but at lower pay.

These low-paid women workers led family lives that, in reality, greatly contradicted the myth. The myth portrayed veterans as welcoming a return to marriage and family. Yet, for a time in 1945–1946, these men had the highest divorce rates ever seen in the United States. Readjustment to civilian life was often an ordeal, even with government-provided veterans' benefits.

The middle-class wife's role was not ideal either. The suburbs isolated her in a daytime ghetto of women and children only. Husbands commuted off to careers in the city, leaving early and returning home late. Many wives remembered their independence during the war years and found the new suburban life a step back. Few voiced such feelings because, in the induced mass perception of the nation's wives, so many other women seemed accepting and satisfied with the new life.

Expertise and the Family

In the immediate postwar years, Freudian thought came into vogue as reflected in expert views on children, the family, women, and human sexuality. Men and women, according to Freud, had proper and determinant gender roles in modern society. If a woman, for example, engaged in the aggressive world of male affairs and work, the effort, because it was against her nature, would cause a variety of psychological afflictions, the source of which would likely come from an errant upbringing dating from childhood or even infancy.

Permissiveness for Babies

In 1946, Dr. Benjamin Spock, a pediatrician and psychiatrist, published *The Common Sense Book of Baby and Childcare,* soon to be indispensable as a manual for the millions of new young mothers whose large families constituted the beginning baby boom. Dr. Spock, as influenced by Freud, held that older, stricter ways of child raising caused frustration, resentment, and, ultimately, a repression of feelings that could later in adulthood be the cause for problems like depression, anxiety, and various neuroses. Dr. Spock called for a new way to raise a child, in a permissive manner based on common sense and compassion. For instance, he advised feeding milk to an infant upon demand and not according to the strictly by-the-clock feeding times of prior years. The parents of the baby boom generation also took to heart other Dr. Spock standards, such as his suggestion that the father should be a friend to his children to minimize their fear of him. Dr. Spock promised those who followed his advice that the result would be a happy adult who would easily proceed to have a normal life, well adjusted to the norms of society. Later retitled *Baby and Child Care,* Dr. Spock's classic sold millions and shaped the generation that came of age in the 1960s (Spock, 1946).

The book reinforced two family life traits that took hold in the late 1940s: the primacy of the mother at home with children, and the heavily emphasized sense of family togetherness. Proper childcare in the new Spock manner was a full-time task for the mother, who consistently needed to be at home to provide complete nurturing for her family. Parlor-room board games, such as Scrabble and Monopoly, family picnics, outings, and vacations were only a few of the recommended ways for the family to become a sort of friendly team.

Favor for the Female Submissive Role

In 1947, another book of expertise, *Modern Woman: The Lost Sex,* conveyed advice to women about their proper role in society and the danger of taking on a role not fitted to the feminine sex. The authors, psychiatrist Marynia Farnham and sociologist Ferdinand Lundberg, claimed that a woman's nature and instincts were best fitted to the role of wife and mother. A woman working in a man's world was only fighting against her true nature at the price of frustration, which was likely to manifest in severe, possibly disabling neurosis. This type of woman, contended the authors, suffered from what Freud called penis envy—wrongly desiring the rewards of the man's role in life, one involving unwomanly power urges and competitive thrusts. The book also depicted an unmarried woman as being abnormal, a fate that should be avoided at all costs. The book recommended banning teachers who were "spinsters" (Lundberg and Farnham 1947). Americans agreed with the experts, and 90 percent of those in one poll believed a woman should not be single in life. Fearful of being left behind, nearly 90 percent of women who came of age at this time did marry, a task that was made more urgent by the widely publicized shortage of available males during and following the war.

Enlightenment on Male Sexuality

Another book appeared in 1948 that addressed a previously taboo side of American life. *Sexual Behavior in the Human Male* by Alfred Charles Kinsey, a zoologist at Indiana State University, was a factual study that contradicted the country's conventional wisdom and unscientific mores about normal sexuality. Through scientific research and statistics (from 18,500 men and women from all over the country giving interviews), Kinsey found evidence of deviant behavior in so many males as to make often hidden practices nearly the norm. Adultery and experimenting with homosexuality were found to be much more common than suspected by the general populace. A great dispute broke out, but many Americans wondered whether the new norm here, too, was a new permissiveness.

Why did Americans accept the advice of so many experts trained in Freudian theory in these years just after the war? One reason is that the sudden lifting of wartime restrictions created a libertine, permissive mood for some time. Combat veterans, who had overcome normal social restraints to survive by killing the enemy, were open to postwar society being less repressive. Wartime consumers, who for years endured the restrictions of nationwide rationing, experienced the sudden pleasure of consuming formerly forbidden products. These speculations might begin to provide the answer. The reason why so many new mothers relied on impersonal experts for childrearing advice, instead of on their own families, could lie in the millions of single-parent women who migrated in wartime from their place of family origin. In a new city for war work or living on a military base awaiting the return of a husband abroad in the service, child-rearing mothers would likely be more open to the advice of experts because their families no longer lived nearby. Many may have also felt this atomic age was so boldly new as to demand a new form of child raising to mold well-adjusted adults for an unknown future. Had the future norms been revealed in the Kinsey report? If so, this was disturbing to some and validating to others.

THE COLD WAR, MINORITIES, AND ETHNIC GROUPS

Although the legal rules of segregation did not apply outside the South, northern African Americans suffered from de facto or nonlegal, traditional segregation. In terms of housing and jobs, northern African Americans suffered discrimination because of white racism.

African Americans: New Outlook, Old Struggle

Lacking protection of their full civil rights, these new migrant African Americans were still second-class citizens after their country had won a war against global racism. During the war, the federal government banned discrimination in federal jobs and many African Americans enjoyed high-paying jobs in government-funded defense factories. When the war ended, the old guard of white Southern Democrats in Congress voted down the renewal of the wartime FEPC that maintained equal employment practices. African Americans experienced this as yet another betrayal of their equality as some postwar conservatives sought a return to the status quo. Cold War conservatives claimed that agitators from the Communist Party inspired the African American civil rights movement.

Congress repeatedly voted down civil rights legislation in this period; this was especially true for the 80th Congress (1946–1948), the first with Republican majorities in both houses in many years. Conservative Southern Democrats joined with the majority in defeating civil rights bills brought to Congress by the White House.

In the early years of the Cold War, 1946 to 1949, millions of African Americans had moved away from the South to the cities of the North and West. These new black migrants lived in segregated city neighborhoods and tended to vote (some for the first time in their adult lives) in concentrated power blocs that often resulted—especially in tight elections—in political gains and even the pioneering election of African American officials.

African Americans, however, had their lives permanently transformed by their experiences during World War II, whether at home or in the fighting services. With victory over enemies abroad, African Americans realized their fight against Jim Crow at home was ongoing; many refused to accept segregation at home in any of its forms.

From Reconstruction until the mid-1950s, Jim Crow laws segregated blacks from whites in all aspects of public life. Here, African American men march in the 1940s with a casket symbolizing the imminent dismantling and "death" of Jim Crow laws. (Library of Congress)

Pepsi-Cola Breaks the Color Barrier in Corporate America

A little-known aspect of civil rights history was made in the fall of 1947 when Pepsi-Cola became the first major American business to hire an all-black corporate-level, special marketing team with national responsibility for raising overall profits (Capparell 2007). The National Urban League and civil rights groups like the NAACP had pressured companies that sold to blacks to hire African Americans. Pepsi was one of the few companies in postwar America to go after this estimated $10 billion market because other major companies feared a white backlash.

Pepsi dared to be different. In 1947, the company hired Edward F. Boyd only months after Jackie Robinson's debut in the major leagues to be the Jackie Robinson of corporate America. He recruited 12 others for this Pepsi team. Working out of corporate headquarters with ample money for salaries, travel, and advertising, Boyd led his special sales department to greater African American sales while pioneering new strategies of niche marketing and advertising.

Boyd developed entire marketing strategies and pioneered ads with a new racial perception. Ads showed the rising middle class with black models having fun and enjoying their successes in settings on college campuses and in nice homes. His "Leaders in Their Fields" series became famous for profiling the success stories of then little-known blacks such as the diplomat Ralph Bunch. After a campaign in a particular area, sales of Pepsi usually increased by some 15 percent.

1948 Election: Victory Comes from the Urban Black Vote

President Harry Truman was a champion of African American civil rights, and he repeatedly presented proposals for equal opportunity in jobs, housing, and education that were shelved or vetoed by what he termed "the Do-Nothing 80th Congress." In addition to being a principled believer in this cause, Truman also wanted to retain the growing bloc of African American voters who had shifted en masse in the 1930s from the Republican Party to the Democratic Party. The president especially needed their votes to win the tight race forecast for the 1948 presidential election, where from the outset, the favorite was the Republican Dewey.

Building up to this election, the most noted civil rights leader of the time, A. Phillip Randolph, met with Truman and threatened to lead a giant march on Washington unless the president agreed to integrate the armed forces of the United States. Not willing to risk the political embarrassment, Truman issued an executive order integrating the armed forces, a courageous political decision. Truman's actions from 1948 onward were critical in eventually ensuring civil rights

African Americans wait in line to register to vote in 1948. It was the overwhelming support for Harry Truman by the black community that clinched his victory in 1948. (Library of Congress)

victory in the greater society. Once the practice became commonplace for a racist soldier to obey orders from an African American commanding officer, the pattern was set and continually reinforced for the transfer of this new race relationship to civil society. Years of protests in the 1950s and 1960s were necessary for this change, but the integration of the armed forces laid the critical foundation. The Korean War, from 1950 to 1954, was the first war fought with an integrated U.S. military.

Ethnics, WASPs, and Melted Americanism

In the postwar years, while African Americans began a long struggle for full social acceptance, the country's ethnic and religious minorities—Irish, Italians, and Jews—enjoyed their greatest acceptance to date by the white Anglo-Saxon Protestant (WASP) majority. One reason was that young war draftees or volunteers had been uprooted from ethnic neighborhoods and had experienced the common comradeship of war and the cosmopolitan views coming from knowledge of exotic foreign lands and cultures. More important to the growing acceptance of ethnic Americans was that this wartime generation was the third following the Great Immigration of the 1890s, when millions of immigrants—the grandparents of those fighting in the war—came to America from southern and eastern Europe. The third-generation grandchildren of these immigrants had deeply assimilated into American culture (after 1924, the Immigration Law reduced any new ethnic immigration to a trickle). Mass media furthered this image of common Americanism—a group with an Irishman, Italian, Jew, and a WASP—in war movies showing the common joys, tribulations, suffering, and friendship of these stock ethnic types in the foxholes, the fighter planes, and battle ships. Missing from this portrayal were citizens of color—African Americans, Asian Americans, Hispanic Americans, and Native Americans.

The Cold War Casts New Perspectives on Civil Rights Groups

White America after the war's end and the beginning of the East-West global rivalry had more reason than ever to improve its civil rights record, especially concerning African Americans. Recurring instances of the injustice and inequality suffered by African American citizens during the beginning Cold War (1946–1949) provided fodder for Soviet claims that American society oppressed its people of color and denied them their rights as citizens of a democracy. The United States, in short, was hypocritical to demand free elections and democracy in Eastern Europe when it denied its own African American citizens equal rights. Adopting a global foreign policy, some American leaders like Truman sought to erase these obstacles for African Americans and thus win the support of the peoples of color then fighting to overturn colonialism and declare new nations. East and West competed for the ideological allegiance of these new national liberation movements in Africa, and it was clear to some that the time was ripe to bring the full protection of the Constitution and the Bill of Rights to African Americans.

Coming back from the war or having worked the best jobs of their lives, African Americans felt newly empowered and were no longer willing to accept the prewar status quo in race relations. Race problems were many in 1946. Lynchings still occurred. Antilynching laws could not pass Congress because of the opposition of the conservative majority consisting of white Southern Democrats joining with Republicans on this issue. The right to vote was denied a majority of Southern blacks because of the poll tax; therefore, few were registered in the states of the Old Confederacy. Legal segregation, with separate public facilities like schools and parks for African Americans and whites, also prevailed in the Old South. In the North, African Americans were able to vote but suffered from inequality in jobs, housing, and schools. Finally, even after one million African Americans fought in the war, the armed forces still remained segregated.

Many African Americans were inspired to newly insist on their rights. The NAACP had grown tremendously during and after the war, going from a membership of 40,000 in 1940 to over half a million in 1950. Many new members lived in the South. The NAACP had won an earlier court victory outlawing the all-white Democratic primary in the South; thus, African American voters faced one less obstacle to voting. With the migration North and West, the increase in African American urban voters could be a decisive bloc of votes in a close election for president.

The President Boldly Declares for Equal Rights

In 1946, President Truman realized this failure of his country's democracy and set up a Commission on Civil Rights to investigate the problem and recommend solutions. The commission report, issued on October 29, 1947, was titled "To Secure These Rights." The report suggested these main resolves: that Congress pass new laws to outlaw lynching, ensure the equal right to vote, and end discrimination in jobs, schools, and housing. The members were forthright about the reasons for needing this new, modern legislation; besides moral necessity and economic benefit, the most important reason was international opinion—to let our allies and enemies witness the national will to bring our actions on race nearer to our democratic ideals. "The pervasive gap between our aims and what we actually do is creating a kind of moral dry rot which eats away at the emotional and rational bases of democratic beliefs," the report states. "There are times when the difference between what we preach about civil rights and what we practice is shockingly illustrated by individual outrages. There are times when the whole structure of our ideology is made ridiculous by individual instances. And there are certain continuing, quiet, omnipresent practices which do irreparable damage to our beliefs" (pp. 140–141).

The report included recent violent incidents against southern African Americans who were empowered by the war years to claim their rights. African American war veterans especially met violence as extreme racist whites feared those with recent military training might fight back against the traditional system of oppression. In February 1946 in Aiken, South Carolina, an African American sergeant, Isaac Woodward, was dragged off a bus by police and beaten so badly that he became blind in one eye. In July 1946 in Monroe, Georgia, two African American veterans and their wives were murdered by a white mob that fired a barrage of bullets into their car. No charges came out of instances such as these; individuals—and sometimes a whole community—knew who was responsible but steadfastly refused to say.

On February 2, 1948, Truman read Congress his civil rights message and requested legislation based on his commission report. A presidential proposal specifically on civil rights was unprecedented; his would be among the strongest ever after. "Not all groups are free to live and work where they please or to improve their conditions of life by their own efforts," the president stated. "Not all groups enjoy the full privilege of citizenship." The president told Congress that this was the role of the national government, not state government, and that only Congress could enact this pressing need for modern civil rights laws. To do so, Congress would be "demonstrating our continuing faith in a free way of life." ("Special Message to the Congress on Civil Rights," February 2, 1948, p. 2, http://www.trumanlibrary.org/publicpapers/index.php?pid=1380&st=&st1)

The legislation included the following points: reestablish of the FEPC; cease discrimination on buses, railroads, and planes engaged in interstate travel; and enact a law against poll taxes. The all-Republican 80th Congress joined by crossover Southern Democrats failed to enact this legislation. Most sensationally, Congress evaded passing an antilynching law. Some in Congress became indignant over this message; especially outraged were many southerners, for whom segregation had been an ingrained way of life for generations.

The President Integrates the Social Institution of the Armed Forces

On July 26, 1948, only months before the presidential election, Truman signed Executive Order 9981, which commanded the armed forces to implement a policy of integration without delay. Chiefs of the Army, Navy, Air Force, and Marines had all recommended that the president not take this step. Truman signed the order anyway, making a decision that possibly carried the greatest significance of all for the later integration of civilian society.

Once an African American infantry officer commanded whites, for instance, the southern race problem along with other pervasive racism would have to come to a working solution for the sake of mutual survival. The Korean War, which began in 1950, was the first the United States fought with integrated fighting units. In a short time, the whole issue was of little concern any longer to those who needed to rely on one another in the fighting. Such cooperative attitudes among the races in war carried over to help change attitudes on both sides regarding the integration of civilian society and the insurance of civil rights for those so long deprived of them. Without this early integration of the services, the civil rights struggle of the 1950s and 1960s would have met greater resistance than was to occur.

African American leaders, including A. Phillip Randolph, Grant Reynolds, and Morton White, the head of the NAACP, all applied political pressure on Truman to issue this executive order. With the world watching American race relations, these men pledged to organize a massive protest march on Washington and vowed that young African Americans selected in the draft would refuse en masse to answer the call of their country if Truman refused to issue the executive order. On June 26, 1948, Randolph announced the creation of The League for Non-Violent Civil Disobedience against Military Segregation. A month later, Truman signed the momentous order.

The 1948 Democratic Party Spurs Sociopolitical Realignments

In July 1948, at the Philadelphia Democratic Party convention and with the Party backing the incumbent, Harry S. Truman, as their nominee for president, the delegates had a floor fight as to whether to include a strong civil rights plank in their platform. Conservative southerners favored states rights and said "no" to a party plank that advocated new federal civil rights laws ensuring that African Americans would no longer be treated as second-class citizens. Thus, the initial plank was similar to the vague one in the platform at the previous party convention in 1944, when FDR was the nominee and eventual victor for a fourth term. Truman initially went along with the conservative southerners.

However, prior to approval, a floor fight ensued over the civil rights plank with Minneapolis, Minnesota, mayor Hubert Humphrey leading a group of supporters who sought to make the Democratic civil rights position rest on a plank consisting of the recommendations of the Truman Civil Rights Commission. Humphrey gave a powerful address calling on delegates to make this a fight for human rights and not states' rights. A floor vote favored Humphrey's stance over that of the conservative southerners, who then walked out and formed a breakaway Party termed the "Dixiecrats," with South Carolina senator Strom Thurmond as their candidate for president. Led by their own nominee for president, Henry Wallace, Truman's former secretary of commerce, the new Progressive Party took followers from the Democrat's left liberal wing while the other new party drew away the conservative wing. The strong civil rights plank would help the Democrats keep the now sizable northern African American urban vote from switching over to the Progressives. Truman finished his campaign with one of his last campaign stops in Harlem asking for the African American vote. Never before had a presidential candidate campaigned in Harlem.

The November 1948 election results made Truman the surprise winner against the highly favored Republican, Gov. Thomas Dewey of New York. The vote was so close that the overwhelming African American vote for Truman proved to be a decisive factor. His civil rights commission, message to Congress, executive order integrating the army, and the Democrats' strong civil rights party platform all solidified the support of the larger urban northern African American vote that was crucial to win a tight election. Truman had gambled that this new African American vote would go far enough to partially balance the loss of the southern wing. He was right.

Civil Rights Groups Seed the Future Social Revolution

By 1949, African Americans had made the critical first steps and had all the forces in place for the coming civil rights struggle of the 1950s and 1960s. The integration of the United States armed forces eased the way for integration of civilian society. Black and white comrades (often ethnics) bonded in new ways because mutual survival demanded cooperation and mutual protection, thus bringing a new respect for African Americans. Thus the integrated military continued for the next two decades as the crucial wedge to removing legal segregation in South and bringing greater equality and justice to African Americans in the North.

Politics and Early Civil Rights Activism

Northern urban African Americans flexed their newfound political muscle as a key factor in the Truman victory in 1948. In Truman, the nation's African Americans had the first president who broadly championed their principles and causes, even at the price of alienating the party's segregationist wing. During the 1930s New Deal, the nation's African Americans had crossed over to the Democrats en masse from their long loyalty to the GOP as the Party of Lincoln. In the 1940s, defense industry job opportunities kept their allegiance. Now Truman had solidified the African American vote. The Cold War rivalry was forcing the country to make stronger efforts to live up to its ideals and eliminate the castelike second-class citizenship for African Americans.

In the late 1940s, returning African American veterans and prospering northern African American migrants fought pressures to return to the status quo, and they had many helpful resources at hand. The NAACP had many new members in the South. The wartime made for postwar cadres of African Americans willing to join in the fight for civil rights. Proven tactics were available, from Ghandian ones of civil disobedience to marches on Washington, D.C., in massive numbers to protest a glaring inequality. A. Phillip Randolph used the threat of this tactic twice with great success—with FDR, who ordered fair employment in defense industries, and with Truman, who ordered the integration of the military. Remarkable civil rights leaders like Randolph had shown the way for younger emerging leaders.

Judicial Court Victories

NAACP lawyers (such as Thurgood Marshall, who would later be appointed to the Supreme Court) were continuing to win Supreme Court cases against legal segregation in the South. In October 1947, the Supreme Court ruled that buses engaged in interstate commerce had to seat customers without regard to race. In January 1948, the same court in a unanimous decision ordered the University of Oklahoma Law School to admit an African American student, citing an American citizen's right to equal protection under the law. Inroads like these held promise for the future, but the forces of reaction, especially among racists in the white South, were to remain strong as witnessed by the 1948 Democrat's breakaway white supremacist States Rights Party.

Sports Triumphs

Sports was the dominant symbol for postwar African American progress, especially in baseball and boxing. On December 19, 1947, Jackie Robinson broke the color barrier in major league baseball by signing with the Brooklyn Dodgers. Earlier during the war, then Lieutenant Robinson, faced with new integration orders on federal military bases in the South, refused to sit in the back of a bus on a Texas base and was court-martialed. He was vindicated. With the Dodgers in two World Series in 1948 and 1949, Robinson was named most valuable player (MVP) in 1949. In boxing, on March 1, 1949, Joe Louis retired after 11 years as the world's heavyweight champion. Nicknamed "The Brown Bomber," Louis had defended his title 25 times, losing only once to Max Schmelling, Hitler's example of the new Aryan. Harlem danced in the streets in the 1930s when Louis soundly won the rematch to take back his title. In a segregated country, Louis had achieved an African American version of the American Dream, rising up from a Southern sharecropper's son to first win the title in 1937. He held the title throughout the 1940s.

BIOGRAPHIES

Joan Barry, 1903–1989

Catalyst for Conservatives to Exile Charlie Chaplin

In the postwar years, Charlie Chaplin became increasingly disillusioned with the archconservative persecuting spirit growing in America. He would leave America for good in 1952, but the catalyst for this was the unending negative press resulting from false charges brought against him by Joan Barry.

Barry, a young actress, brought a paternity suit against the world-famous movie director-actor Chaplin, claiming he was the father of her newborn daughter, which he denied. With the case pending, the government charged Chaplin with a violation of the Mann Act, which forbade taking a female across states for immoral purposes. At his first trial, which took place in April 1944 in New York City,

Chaplin had admitted to an earlier affair with her and that she had once come to be with him in New York City. He was acquitted of violating the Mann Act. The gossip columnists were in a frenzy and denounced Chaplin as much for the charges as for his well-known leftist sympathies. They also defamed him because he continued to hold British citizenship despite paying taxes and living since 1913 in America. In December 1944, the paternity suit went to trial; his blood tests showed he could not be the father; a mistrial was declared, yet the judge still ordered him to pay large regular payments in child support. No matter the outcome, the American public opinion had convicted him and largely avoided his next movie, *Dr. Verdoux* in 1947, making it a failure. Soon afterward, he was charged with nonpayment of taxes. Feeling hounded, he soon left the country.

James Forrestal, 1892–1949

Devoted Military Cabinet Member

James Forrestal became the first cabinet member equivalent to the secretary of defense (the post was not immediately called such) in 1947, upon passage of the new National Security Act, which united under one post on the president's cabinet all the different branches of the armed forces. Forrestal was particularly well qualified; the former Wall Street investment banker had been a New Dealer, a personal aide to Roosevelt, and secretary of the Navy and then Army under Truman, who had appointed him to this new post. Caught in an intense rivalry between each of the services, formerly separate but now fighting over a reduced military budget, all against the background of a Soviet takeover of Czechoslovakia, Forrestal was under great stress. With Truman's victory in 1948, Forrestal was reappointed, even though there was protest from the military. With added tensions, Forrestal had a noticeable change of personality and became paranoid. Committed to Bethesda Naval Hospital, he leaped to his death from an upper-floor window on May 22, 1949.

James Forrestal was secretary of the navy from 1944 to 1947 and was the first U.S. secretary of defense, entering office in 1947 and resigning in 1949. As the secretary of defense, Forrestal guided the National Military Establishment at the dawn of the Cold War. (Library of Congress)

Ira Hayes, 1923–1955

Flag Raiser at Iwo Jima

The battle of Iwo Jima in March 1945 was a bitter desperate fight to capture a tiny barren, volcanic island near enough to the main Japanese islands for returning badly shot up American bombers to land. Japanese fighters, 22,000 strong, had all vowed to fight to the death, a claim made real, before Marines, at enormous cost—7,000 dead and some 25,000 wounded—won victory. Early in the fighting, war photographer Joe Rosenthal took the famous photo of six soldiers—including Ira Hayes, a Pima Indian from Arizona—raising the flag on the island's highest point, Mount Suribachi. Newspapers all over America ran the photo, making it an almost instant iconic image of victory. But the battle raged on for weeks as the dug-in enemy fought out of caves, and three of the flag raisers died. Hayes and the other two survivors, Rene Gagnon and John Bradley, were quickly shipped back home, greeted by tens of thousands as heroes of the flag raising. Their great public renown was used to bring out Americans to rally and invest in a giant ongoing government bond drive. As thousands of civilians cheered and the three reenacted the flag raising, Hayes felt undeserving, even guilty, for being hailed as a hero when he and his two buddies remembered many more courageous Marines who were more deserving and had given their lives. Yet, this trio of instant press celebrities was entertained lavishly; they met Hollywood stars, were applauded by a huge crowd in Times Square, and attracted more money to pay for the war. Drinking heavily and excused from any more combat duty, Hayes lived through the postwar days of forgotten glory and died of alcohol-related causes in 1955.

J. Robert Oppenheimer, 1904–1967

Atomic Physicist

Robert Oppenheimer was the most famous and accomplished American physicist of the1940s. He was the head of the secret Manhattan Project that developed the first atomic bomb in 1945, which caused him to be called "Father of the Bomb." When he saw the fireball in the first successful Trinity Test, he famously quoted an ancient Sanskrit poet, "I am become Death, the shatterer of worlds." Immediately after the war, he became chairman of the advisory group to the Atomic Energy Commission, which aimed to decide the future direction for the use of nuclear energy. In 1949, he and many other scientists opposed building the hydrogen bomb after the Soviet Union had exploded an atomic bomb. This, and his association for a limited period in mid-1930s with communist causes (although he had never been a member of the party), led to a hasty FBI accusation that he was a spy. His security clearance was denied and he was personally disgraced, even though he was the man who had done the most to end the war with Japan.

Dorothy Parker, 1893–1967

Writer

Dorothy Parker was among the most famous and important American short-story writers, poets, dramatists, wits, and critics of the first half of the 20th century. (Library of Congress)

Dorothy Parker was a noted writer of the 1940s, one of New York's Algonquin Round Table wits, contributor to *The New Yorker* magazine, and a successful screenwriter. Caught in the swiftly changing currents of history, like so many 1930s ultraliberals, Parker helped form an anti-Nazi League in 1936 and aided the legitimate left Loyalist Spanish government (backed by the Soviet Union) against the fascist leaning, Nazi-aided General Franco. Many isolationist conservatives of the time vehemently opposed her politics, and many of Hollywood's directors and producers despised the Screen Writers' Guild, of which Parker was a member, because they believed it was influenced by the Communist Party. By 1941, with America's immediate extension of Lend-Lease aid, the Soviet Union became an ally and remained so for the rest of the war. The liberal politics of the 1930s seemed suddenly benign, and Parker was, to a large degree, redeemed. With the advent of the Cold War era in 1947, Thomas Parnell, the new chair of the HUAC named Parker on a list of 300 persons he intended to question about their to loyalty to the United States. With that Parker was blackballed in Hollywood and rendered unemployable. The charges against her were based on innuendo, as she never was called to the stand and had no chance to defend herself. After the Hollywood Ten were convicted of contempt, the public was encouraged to assume that the others on the list of 300, even those never called, were to be presumed guilty.

Parnell Thomas, 1895–1970

HUAC Chairman

The chairman of the House Un-American Activities Committee since 1947, New Jersey Republican Thomas, in 1949, stood accused of having perpetuated a no-show employee's salary kickback fraud involving his own congressional office staff. The charge was that Thomas had pocketed his phantom employee's salary for his personal use. Wildly denying his guilt, he made excuses and accused liberals of concocting the charges against him. Out of excuses and out of luck, after 10 years in Congress, he pleaded guilty. It seemed to be his only choice. The charges against him came from his own long-time personal secretary, with whom the married Thomas had had a long affair. The press delighted in the blatant hypocrisy of this man who, as HUAC chairman, was known for his bruising, insinuating, no-excuses-accepted style of examining the Hollywood witnesses before his committee. Parnell especially disliked any witnesses who used an alias or seemed to hide disloyalty behind a veil of patriotism. Fined and sentenced to 18 months, he was pardoned in 1950 by President Truman.

Walter White, 1893–1955

Head of the NAACP

In 1949, Walter White was the respected leader of the NAACP. He was one of the leaders who had pressured President Truman into issuing the 1947 executive order integrating the armed forces. In 1949, he divorced his black wife and the mother of his children to marry Poppy Cannon, a white journalist and editor. The surprise interracial marriage created massive protest in the African American press and generated hate letters from African Americans. There was little significant reaction from whites at the time. Some saw this as a social attitude change because before the war, interracial marriage drew protests from whites but rarely from African Americans. White and his new wife left the country for a year to get away from the controversy. In his absence, the NAACP board tried to remove him as secretary of the organization, even though the NAACP was at the time winning civil rights battles against segregation and preparing further cases. One of the board's directors, Eleanor Roosevelt, rallied others against his removal. Instead, the directors cut back the power of his post.

REFERENCES AND FURTHER READINGS

Ballard, Jack Stokes. 1983. *The Shock of Peace: Military and Economic Demobilization after World War II*. Washington, DC: University Press of America.

Capparell, Stephanie. 2007. *The Real Pepsi Challenge: The Inspirational Story of Breaking the Color Barrier in American Business*. New York: Free Press (A Wall Street Journal Book).

Coontz, Stephanie. 1992. *The Way We Never Were: American Families and the Nostalgia Trap*. New York: Basic Books.

Fones-Wolf, Elizabeth A. 1994. *Selling Free Enterprise: The Business Assault on Labor and Liberalism, 1945–1960*. Urbana and Chicago: University of Illinois Press.

Freeland, Richard M. 1972. *The Truman Doctrine and the Origins of McCarthyism*. New York: Alfred A. Knopf.

Galbraith, John Kenneth. 1958. *The Affluent Society*. New York: Houghton Mifflin.

Goldman, Eric. 1961. *The Crucial Decade—and After, America, 1945–1960*. New York: Random House.

Hamby Alonzo L. 1973. *Beyond the New Deal: Harry S. Truman and American Liberalism*. New York: Columbia University Press.

Harrington, Michael. 1962. *The Other America*. New York: Simon and Schuster.

Harry S. Truman Library. http://www.trumanlibrary.org/library.htm. Includes text of *To Secure These Rights: The Report of the President's Commission on Civil Rights*. Accessed August 21, 2008.

Harry S. Truman primary documents and speeches online at PBS Web site for *American Experience* series film *Truman,* http://www.pbs.org/wgbh/amex/truman/index.html. Accessed August 21, 2008.

Hixson, Walter L. 1997. *Parting the Curtain: Propaganda, Culture and the Cold War, 1945–1961*. New York: St. Martin's.

Jackson, Kenneth T. 1985. *Crabgrass Frontier: The Suburbanization of the United States*. New York: Oxford University Press.

James, Robert Rhodes, ed. 1974. *Winston S. Churchill: His Complete Speeches, 1897–1963*. 8 vols. London: Chelsea.

Kinsey, Alfred. 1948. *Sexual Behavior in the Human Female*. New York: W. B. Saunders, 1948; reprinted by Indiana University Press.

Kinsey, Alfred. 1948. *Sexual Behavior in the Human Male*. New York: W. B. Saunders, 1948, reprinted by Indiana University Press.

Lundberg, Ferdinand, and Marynia F. Farnham. 1947. *Modern Women: The Lost Sex*. New York: Harper and Brothers.

McCarthy Tom. 2007. *Auto Mania: Cars, Consumers, and the Environment*. New Haven and London: Yale University Press.

McClure, Arthur F. 1969. *The Truman Administration and the Problems of Postwar Labor*. Rutherford, NJ: Fairleigh Dickinson University Press.

McCoy, Donald R. 1984. *The Presidency of Harry S. Truman*. Lawrence: University Press of Kansas.

McCoy, Donald R., and Richard T. Ruetten. 1973. *Quest and Response: Minority Rights and the Truman Administration*. Lawrence: University of Kansas Press.

Patterson, James. 1996. *Grand Expectations*. New York: Oxford University Press.

Reinhard, David W. 1983. *The Republican Right since 1945*. Lexington: University Press of Kentucky.

Spock, Dr. Benjamin. 1946. *The Common Sense Book of Baby and Child Care*. New York: Pocket Books.

Thorpe, Charles. 2006. *Oppenheimer: The Tragic Intellect*. Chicago: University of Chicago Press.

To Secure These Rights: The Report of the President's Commission on Civil Rights. 1947. New York: Simon and Schuster.

X (George F. Kennan). "The Sources of Soviet Conduct," *Foreign Affairs,* July 1947, online at http://www.foreignaffairs.org/19470701faessay25403/x/the-sources-of-soviet-conduct.html. Accessed August 7, 2007.

Yarnell, Allen. 1973. *Democrats and Progressives: The 1948 Election as a Test of Post War Liberalism*. Berkeley: University of California Press.

Labor and Work

OVERVIEW

Was America becoming a classless society? That's what American media, advertisers, and social scientists were wondering in the postwar 1940s, as the nation's workforce continued to expand, bringing affluence to all classes. The answer was no, but by 1949, the rapidly expanding economy and generally rising incomes made the reference easy to believe. Ironically, it implied that capitalism was achieving the idealistic goal long aspired to by its ideological antagonist, communist Russia. By comparison, the enemy nation was still burdened with the heavy weight of a lower class with scarce consumer goods (which was largely true due to Soviet resources going to a military buildup and civilian reconstruction in this most devastated of all the combatant nations).

American citizens remembered the 1930s and were astonished by some of the new trends in postwar society. Prosperity seemed the keynote. More people than ever were going to colleges and vocational schools and getting loans for new homes and thriving small businesses, all thanks to the G.I. Bill. Elite labor unions like the United Automobile Workers (UAW) and the United Steel Workers (USW) had negotiated contracts that gave their senior workers benefits, vacations, and guaranteed high wages (by contract automatically adjusted for cost of living increases). Never before could citizens remember blue-collar workers earning as much as the average middle-class worker, who was by then a salaried, mid-level manager in one of the giant new global corporations. Astonishing, too, large businesses were open to managing their operations with the orderly co-operation of unions so long as the latter did not insist on having a part in policy decisions. Unions were welcome! By 1949, more workers than ever were in unions. However, the majority remained nonunionized workers.

Labor unions had started the decade with flare and success—two powerful union affiliations were solidly in place, the longtime skilled workers' American Federation of Labor (AFL) and the five-year-old unskilled workers' Congress of Industrial Unions (CIO). Both had gains from the 1930s, in particular, the protection to organize and collectively bargain granted by the 1935 Wagner Act. By 1942, the government had set wartime labor–management policy with the National Labor Relations Board, which supported the peaceful growth of unions while getting from them a no-strike pledge matched by a no-lockout pledge from businesses. With the cost of living rising steadily during war, the unions eventually won a 15 percent across-the-board wage hike. Yet inflation and profits continued to rise until, in 1943, union strikes for higher wages came in a wave led by coal and railroad workers. Inflation was finally driven down due to rationing and its strict enforcement. This somewhat alleviated the need for a second round of wage hikes. As a counter to labor costs, management began to automate factories, and this eliminated well-paying factory jobs.

Turning antiliberal in many respects since the New Deal, Congress in 1943 reacted to the wartime strikes by passing, over the president's veto, the Smith-Connally Act, which provided a 30-day cooling-off period in vital war industries to protect against labor unrest. Strike leaders could be subject to fines and jail terms. By 1944, President Roosevelt would win a fourth term due to huge labor support and the political organizing of union leader Sidney Hillman's CIO Political Action Committee. PAC skirted the congressional act's prohibitions on union political contributions.

In 1946, the unions again confronted skyrocketing inflation and responded with a record number of strikes. The public blamed unions for rising prices and that year voted in the first Republican majority in many years to the 80th Congress. In 1947, the congressmen voted over President Truman's veto the Taft-Hartley Act, which tilted national labor policy to business once again. It deemed illegal the union shop, which required all new hires in a previously organized business to join the prevailing union. An 80-day cooling-off period was provided for strikes judged harmful to national interests. In 1948, labor support returned in such numbers to Truman that this became a vital factor in his come-from-behind victory.

By 1949, the more archly conservative Congress forced the CIO and AFL leadership to purge from membership all local union leaders suspected of ever having ties with communists. Communist allegations against organizers comprised one of the primary reasons for the failure of Operation Dixie, the CIO massive union campaign to unionize the many textile workers of the American South. This swan song for big labor ended further mass organizing of workers in America.

Moreover, the general trend signaled that the new fast-growing service sector —teachers and government and office workers—would provide the additional numbers to increase white-collar workers to a total surpassing blue-collar workers for the first time in the country's history (this change was to occur 10 years after 1946). Leading economists believed a new postindustrial society was forming based on such service industries as insurance, finance, and banking. The introduction of automation in factories was also permanently eliminating well-paying factory jobs.

Notably, many in the country constituted the working poor, those with jobs so low paying as to remain at or near poverty level. This group was forgotten and ignored in the talk of a classless society in the making. Also, the new service sector consisted of a secondary level of white-collar employees who were as lowly paid and lacking in job security as the nonunionized, unskilled blue-collar workers. Women still worked outside the home in large numbers in 1949, nearly as many as those in the war years but at much lesser pay and job security (many in what some referred to as the pink-collar job ghetto).

Ballyhooed at the time, of course, was the country's continued economic boom. Many marveled at the steady creation of new jobs, and this new prosperity and felt an underlying surprise and relief that the reverse had not come true, the feared postwar return to 1930s levels of production and joblessness. Federal spending continued to fuel prosperity, notably in the G.I. Bill, a social program as great in enrollee benefits as any in the New Deal. Then, by 1949, the government had refunded the military-industrial nexus to meet defense needs for the quickening arms race of the Cold War.

Generally the public credited business (not government) with the war and postwar economic miracles. This was due to a media emphasis on such dynamic businessmen as ship maker Edgar Kaiser and plane designer Howard Hughes, among others (politicians and public administrators were nondescript by comparison). The postwar public believed the big three automakers were responsible for fueling the nation's new growth. New cars were the public's favored consumer item, and the new makes and models available in postwar years made this even more the case. The construction industry was booming and, to public appearance, this was another economic pillar. Another pillar was the country's ever-expanding global corporate world, with the headquarters of many corporations' newly constructed all-glass skyscrapers in big cities across the country.

TIMELINE

1940	The number of organized workers totals 9 million, with most unions under either the AFL or the CIO, the latter led by

United Mine Workers' president, John L. Lewis, the most powerful and best-known labor leader in the country.

President Roosevelt wins his third term in office with strong labor support, although Lewis backed his opponent, Wendell Wilkie, the Republican. Lewis, as a result of Roosevelt's win, resigns the CIO Leadership.

1941   Unions protest the higher profits of defense industries with a total of strikes outnumbering those of any year since 1919; one of the most crucial was at North American Aviation in Los Angeles. Work stoppages result from 4,228 walkouts, involving 2.4 million workers.

1942   The National Labor Relations Act is passed with administrative authority residing variously in a War Labor Board (WLB) or National Defense Mediation Board (NDMB) designed to peacefully arbitrate all labor management disputes.

The War Production Board (WPB) is established to oversee the national war production effort with a tripartite cooperative pact of unions, business, and government. A mutual pledge by labor and business agrees to no strikes for no lockouts during the war.

The "Little Steel Formula" goes into effect, which ensures all workers get 15 percent more in wages than they earned on January 1, 1941.

1943   Inflation rises 29 percent over 30 months.

The United Mine Workers strikes for pay raises to exceed the 15 percent ceiling.

Congress passes the Smith-Connally Act to enable the president to postpone a strike with a 30-day cooling-off period and then levy fines or jail terms for leaders of strikes in vital industries. President Roosevelt vetoes it, but Congress wins passage with a two-thirds vote.

1944   President Roosevelt wins a fourth term helped by the CIO Political Action Committee.

1945   Inflation is down below 10 percent by war's end due to rationing and enforcement of price ceilings.

Factories cut back on employees due to slackening of war demand; unemployment rises along with public fears of a return to the Depression.

Inflation rises above 10 percent due to shortages claimed by employers.

1946 Corporate profits hit a record high, and inflation is more than 18 percent.

Unemployment approaches 3 million.

Powerful unions strike the major industries—coal, railroad, and automobile—with the goal to keep up with inflation. President Truman has removed wartime controls.

The Republicans gain a majority in the 80th Congress.

1947 Congress passes the Taft-Hartley Act that the unions view as strongly antilabor; President Truman agrees and tries in vain to veto it.

1948 Truman wins the election with critical support from labor.

1949 Unity eludes the national union movement, with many jurisdictional disputes between the CIO and the AFL. Both comply with the loyalty provisions of the Taft-Hartley Act and purge local unions of communists.

WARTIME LABOR OVERVIEW

In the years 1940 to 1945, the country witnessed a dramatic rise in organized labor. Union membership increased steadily along with the cumulative industrial and political power of the big worker affiliates such as the older AFL, comprised largely of skilled trade workers, and the 1938 CIO, comprising unskilled industry-wide workers. The 1940s decade began after five years during which the government had given protection to labor's right to organize and bargain collectively for better wages and conditions. The government had lent its weight to the protection of workers, viewing labor alone as a disadvantaged party in trying to organize against powerful employers. Thus, it sought to right the balance.

War and the Consolidation of Union Power

A month after Pearl Harbor, FDR created the National Labor Relations Board (NLRB) to reaffirm that the organizing and bargaining rights that labor had won

"Pledge to Victory. The war may be won or lost in this plant," War Production Board poster targeting factory labor. For the duration of World War II, Franklin Roosevelt obtained a no-strike pledge from labor and a no-lockout pledge from industry, in the interests of keeping war production on track. (National Archives)

in the late 1930s would continue for the duration of the war. At the same time, he won a no-strike pledge from labor and a no-lockout pledge from industry. Then, the president created the War Production Board (WPB), which had the primary aim of converting the economy from civilian to military production. So successful was this that the country, by 1945, would quadruple its output of goods. The great corporations benefited the most, and by war's end, their profits were the highest on record. The nation's huge increase in productivity meant a larger labor pool. Workers saw jobs multiply and union membership rise. Many businesses conducted union negotiations for the first time to prevent their workers from taking another job at a time of labor shortage.

Until mid-1943, labor accepted government control of wages even while the cost of living soared to 29 percent of what it had been prior to the war. Meanwhile, the NLRB had sought vainly to grant unions a 15 percent wage increase to cover the faster rising price inflation. In 1942 and especially early 1943, continuing inflation became critical and there occurred a series of strikes, the most serious in the coal and railroad industries. Beginning in mid-1943, the president, through gargantuan efforts, soon made good on his promise to dampen inflation through rationing and stricter enforcement. Lowered to single digits until war's end, it ceased being a great problem.

Congress and Restraint on Labor

By 1943, Congress, ruled by a conservative majority of Republicans and Southern Democrats, was antiunion. Over Roosevelt's veto, Congress passed the Smith-Connally Act, which empowered the president to protect war industries by postponing a strike for 30 days, seizing and operating an industry, and fining and jailing strikers. Attempting a blow at the growing political power of labor, the act forbade existing union contributions to political campaigns. With the wartime economic boom, Americans enjoyed the return of prosperity and the feeling of patriotic fervor; they reacted angrily to the unions striking during war, and Congress had played to this sentiment.

Labor Power and the Democrats

In November 1944, FRD campaigned for an unprecedented fourth term in office with huge support from labor, always one of the key components of his New Deal political alliance. The CIO's Political Action Committee (PAC) led by Sidney Hillman, a Roosevelt political adviser, was key to the president's narrow victory. For the first time in an election, FDR's opponent, New York governor Thomas Dewey, had introduced the accusation that Roosevelt had the support of communists and that communists had infiltrated the CIO.

By war's end, American labor had reached a zenith of organization. Its quick, dramatic rise to industrial and political power had not been without problems, the greatest of which was the lack of overall unity in the movement. The AFL and the CIO could not come together and fought countless jurisdictional disputes to the frustration of all, especially the public. Labor still awaited its greatest challenge—the sudden lifting in 1946 of all controls on prices and wages and the resulting skyrocketing of prices.

The New CIO and the War Labor Board

By 1940, the unskilled industrial workers had been organized for five years by the new CIO, headed by John L. Lewis. This was due to the 1935 Wagner Labor Relations Act, which authorized collective bargaining. Auto, steel, coal mining, and other industries had been organized at a bloody cost from corporate resistance. Success came with the use of new labor tactics, such as the 1937 sit-down strikes that resulted with unionization of General Motors by the United Auto Workers, an affiliate of the CIO. By 1940, the total number of organized workers in the country was approximately 9 million.

The 1941 Wave of Strikes

In 1941, the United States had the greatest strike year since 1919, the legendary peak of labor unrest. The union movement wanted to maintain its gains post–Wagner Act, but business was profiting from the government's Lend-Lease defense contracts, which subsidized companies for providing war material to the allied side. Prices were increasing as a result, and the cost of living inching upward. Unions wanted wage increases; the result was 4,228 walkout strikes involving 2.4 million workers. The government could not tolerate the manpower hours lost toward its preparedness mobilization drive; thus, it needed to halt the strikes. This was difficult because the Roosevelt administration had the full support of the union movement, especially the new CIO (with the exception of its president, John L. Lewis, who had resigned in 1940 after the third-term victory of Roosevelt, whom Lewis had opposed).

In the critical North American Aviation (NAA) strike in 1941, the administration showed its response as one of both fist and honey. The Southern California airplane manufacturer produced 25 percent of America's fighter planes, which were in short supply. Airplane workers in the region numbered 100,000 and were ripe for organization because their wages were approximately half those in other defense industries. Militant local branches of the UAW had begun to organize to strike, but the federal government could not afford the loss in manpower hours. Therefore, the National Defense Mediation Board (NDMB) enlisted national UAW and CIO officials to pressure the locals to abandon the strikes in favor of a mediated agreement. The locals voted down mediation. The president responded with a fist: an order to draft any striker not reporting for work after he nationalized the corporation. The union gave in. Later, the NDMB mandated the honey: that the corporation raise wages 50 percent to be in line with the industry and authorize payroll deductions for union dues.

War and Government Regulation of Labor

After the war began with the Pearl Harbor attack, the government needed to safeguard against inflation; on April 27, 1942, President Roosevelt gave his Stabilization Address, which called for a general freeze on prices, salaries, and wages. The latter was to be determined by the War Labor Board (WLB), which evolved from the prior government mediation agency. The WLB derived a policy for wartime wages to be set at the January 1, 1941, level plus 15 percent, which produced an hourly wage increase an average of 66 to 85 cents over the two years ending January 1, 1943. In July 1942, the WLB put its policy decision into effect during a strike involving the smaller steel companies; thus, the union wage increase became known as the "Little Steel Formula."

Unions were ecstatic about the formula initially, but they later became disgruntled when they realized this was intended to be a ceiling for wartime wages, essentially a wage freeze. Meanwhile, the administration proved ineffective in capping prices and the cost of living rose steadily beyond the 15 percent wage increase. At the beginning of the war, government mediators had secured a national union no-strike pledge coupled with a no-lockout pledge from the country's businesses. In 1942, the wartime unions began losing membership because the members desired increased wages beyond the government freeze. The WLB then moved to support unionization by demanding already unionized companies have a defense contract to have a union shop, which would mean the many new hires would be required to join the union within 15 days or leave the job.

The overall result was union growth from 9 million in 1940 to 14.3 million in 1945. The WLB, in effect, assured the unions of security in exchange for their patriotic pledge to not strike for higher wages. The no-strike pledge was honored to the war's end by most unions, except by the United Mine Workers, led by its maverick John L. Lewis.

The Emergence of John L. Lewis as CIO Leader

Wartime strikes were seen as nearly treasonous by the great majority of the public and especially by the military fighting overseas. Labor was unsuccessful in promoting its point of view in the media, especially in comparison to the public relations departments of the government and businesses. Striking workers got little understanding of their grievances in the press. Instead, the public stereotype of a unionized defense worker was a person who enjoyed safety and high pay at home while another man gave his life for little pay to defend his country. The public saw the defense workers as a mass of ingrates peppered with draft dodgers. When certain big unions dared strike in 1943 for higher wages, greed could be the only motive, many middle-class and fighting Americans believed.

The first to break the unions' wartime no-strike pledge was the UMW led by the fiery John L. Lewis, who, in 1942, singularly refused to sign the pledge. For some eight years, Lewis had been the focus of antiunion hatred in the country. A founding leader of the CIO in 1935, Lewis had been the spearhead for the great, first-time victories in the late 1930s of workers in mass industries such as auto and steel. Often, he had succeeded by such radical tactics as the sit-down, in which strikers refused to leave the factory to avoid the lock-out tactic used by management. Business said it was union expropriation of property; the moderate and conservative public agreed and feared social upheaval on a larger scale.

Yet the new CIO leader had wisely given $500,000 to the 1936 election campaign of President Roosevelt; thus, New Dealers backed his subsequent organization drives. Most importantly, union-backed Democratic governors defied precedent and refused to use the National Guard to remove strikers and favor management. General Motors thus conceded to its first labor contract after a CIO-UAW sit-down strike victory at the Flint, Michigan, plant in 1937. The auto industry organizing drive involved bloody conflicts adding up to near class warfare, and proponents for either side were fiercely passionate for or against the cause of unionizing unskilled labor.

Lewis came to be at loggerheads with the president, who he thought was taking for granted the support of the CIO. In 1940, Lewis called for the CIO to back the liberal Republican Wilkie. Instead, the CIO membership continued its support of Roosevelt, and Lewis resigned as the organization's founding leader. He remained the head of the UMW, the union of the nation's coal miners in an era when coal was the country's prime energy source as well as the essential component in the making of steel.

"Little Steel Formula" and the First Wartime Strike, 1943

After Pearl Harbor, President Roosevelt created the WLB to mediate grievances between labor and business. The unions vowed no strikes for the duration of the war; businesses, no lockouts. Industries that were already organized were required to write into their labor contracts a union shop clause requiring any new hire to join the union within 15 days. In 1942, the WLB worked out an across-the-board wage increase for labor called the "Little Steel Formula" by which workers would earn 15 percent more than the prevailing wage on January 1, 1941. Labor was pleased at the time but not after it became clear that the 15 percent was a one-time hike and essentially a wage freeze.

Government, meanwhile, was having little success in its mutual goal of a price freeze. By 1943, the cost of living was rising fast and, after taxes, business profits were 53 percent higher in wartime. The farming sector, aided by automation and the advent of the corporate farm, was on the way to doubling its gross income. Only labor seemed to be held back in this trend to general betterment.

By 1943, Lewis's miners had real grievances and pressured for increased wages. Their work was far more dangerous and poorly paid than almost all defense workers in factory jobs. Miners made $40 per week while a $100 was possible for other union workers. Injuries and deaths were a daily occurrence in the mines—so frequent that the press did not cover them unless the loss of lives was high. These miners were most galled by the gains of business and farming. These seemed to come at their expense.

Lewis agreed and was determined to bust out and get a wage settlement to break the chains of the Little Steel Formula. In April 1943, when the UMW contract ended with mine owners, Lewis led his 3,300 miners on strike. He demanded a 30 percent raise in weekly wages (a negotiating ploy), while his real goal was 13 percent more. The president was scheduled to go on the radio to ask Lewis to work with the WLB and the owners. Lewis put his men back to work shortly before the president's speech but refused to negotiate any settlement on a halfway basis. He set October 31, 1943, as the deadline for a contract.

In the interim, Congress passed, over Roosevelt's veto, the Smith-Connelly Act, which banned strikes in defense-related industries and decreed illegal (a federal offense) the organizing of a wartime strike. It mandated the declaring of a 30-day cooling-off period before a strike could begin. This action prevented a showdown strike by the UMW. Yet, by finessing the issue, Lewis was still to emerge triumphant as the labor leader who destroyed Little Steel and removed the onus on strikes by other unions seeking wage increases beyond the arbitrary freeze.

Lewis accomplished this by shifting the issue from a wage hike to payment for the time traveled from portal to coal face and back to portal. The United States was the only country not paying its coal miners to get from the shaft (via underground elevator) to the work area. Eventually getting the WLB to agree, Lewis skirted the 15 percent ceiling and got his miners near his original goal of a raise of $2 per day.

1944–1945: Labor Strikes over Layoffs and Inflation

By 1944, the Lewis's freeze-breaking contract had lessened the stigma unions felt for wartime work stoppages. Thereafter, organized labor underwent a series of wildcat strikes (unauthorized by union locals and lasting from a shift to a few days). The cause: The continuing rising cost of living. Businesses found ways to raise prices beyond mandated ceilings, therefore putting more of the weight unfairly on unions to control inflation.

Even the white-collar public, with its bias against unions, felt a common sympathy with the unions over their grievances about rising prices. More

Strikers of the Oil Workers International Local 456 CIO picket the Dearborn, Wyoming, bulk station at the Socony Vacuum Oil Company, September 23, 1945. (Bettmann/Corbis)

opinion makers also expressed some grudging sympathy for the grievances of labor.

By 1945, wartime factories were scaling back production and laying off workers, and many of those who remained no longer received the overtime that had been a primary means to cope with inflation. Unemployment was starting to rise and with it the prewar specter of the Depression returning with the billions of dollars in war contracts shrinking and millions of veterans taking back their jobs from war workers. Most workers imagined unemployment to be their fate in the near future with the return to peace.

Wartime Labor's Great Contributions and Sacrifices

Labor's contribution to the war effort deserved much more recognition from the American middle class that, conversely, granted excessive praise to business for making possible the miracle of mass production that supplied most of the war material for our military and allies. Businessmen were heroes while the arrogant John L. Lewis had aroused the ire of the public so as to water the seed of an already existing middle-class bias against unions. Labor's wage demands were blamed for rising inflation, a ruse that corporate publicity departments were only too willing to spread to a supportive media. Unions in general lacked the means to shape public opinion so the public would better understand their issues.

Blue-collar wartime contributions were heroic. The negative wartime strike issue was much overstated. Even with the major 1943 strikes of the coal miners and railroads added to all the wildcat strikes, the total loss of man-hours was miniscule, less than one. Unions had adhered to the no-strike pledge. From 1941 to 1945, war workers had endured overly long days and weeks to work the production lines that assembled every item of war material. Sharing the goal of victory with all of America, workers had agreed to speed-ups, double shifts, and most other factory means to hasten victory. Workers had purchased a large percentage of the war bonds sold to finance the war. Labor-management cooperation throughout the conflict had been consistently successful.

1945: Industrial Relations in Turmoil without Government

Labor, come peacetime, was certain to strike for higher wages and job security in the wake of the millions of workers (overwhelmingly women) being laid off in 1945. A year earlier, on Long Island at Brewster Aircraft, management had signaled a layoff for 4,000 workers. These employees then made America labor history by occupying the factory in a strike to continue work—in effect to deny management the right to render persons jobless and without income.

At the time, President Truman was speaking of the need for a full employment bill, and in testing the political climate for such legislation, the conservative Congress, where the voice of business spoke loudly, hinted of this being "creeping socialism." The government, however, did find additional war work for Brewster to retain its workers.

In the conversion to peacetime, labor-management relations were destined to remain largely in the private sphere, once federal controls were lifted from wages and prices. One exception was a strike or series of strikes in peacetime that the president might deem a danger to the general welfare of all citizens. Smart management during war had finally come to accept collective bargaining and unions. Businesses realized that organization of labor with satisfying wages, hours, and work conditions could well be a stabilizing factor in an industry. Such acceptance could pacify the unions and rid them of their prewar militancy. The aim was to give unions a limited yet important role in the free enterprise system while management retained all prerogatives as to major business decisions.

The test would come first as early as 1945. Walter Reuther of the United Automobile Workers (UAW) ordered a strike against Ford Motor Company, the weakest of the Big Three. Soon, in 1946, the country would experience its greatest strike year ever, as reconverting to peace proved near chaotic for the American government.

FORD MOTOR COMPANY TESTS THE CIO-UAW

Ford Motor Company in 1940 was the single nonunion holdout among the country's Big Three automakers. The UAW had organized other two, Chrysler and General Motors, in 1937 through a series a sit-down strikes and union certification elections by the respective workers. New Deal lawmakers had passed the prolabor 1935 Wagner Act, which eased challenges for the new CIO to organize an industry comprising the unskilled along with the skilled workers. Traditionally, the more elitist AFL had unionized exclusively the latter. The Ford Motor Company had long been a national citadel of fierce antiunionism and had defeated the earlier organizing effort of the UAW.

The Ford Motor Company, UAW, and Government

Ford was a special case for a number of reasons. The legendary Henry Ford, still head of the company, was regarded by a broad swath of the American public as a business lord who upheld the general welfare of his workers. After all, they remembered he had instituted the $5-a-day wage at a time when the shocked industry paid only a pittance of that to its workers. The public's image of the man and his company was of utmost importance; the company's publicity department

Henry Ford (right) with the head of the Ford Service Department, Harry Bennett, at Camp Legion on June 19, 1939. Bennett, who blended virulent anti-Semitism with super-patriotism, led the fight against unionization at Ford and converted Camp Legion into a veterans' facility in 1941. (Image from the collections of The Henry Ford, P.833.71965)

fed the myths regularly. Simple, honest, a man of his word, this was the Henry Ford tailored by the image-makers dealing with media and politicians in the city, state, and nation.

Harry Bennett, the head of Ford Services, was the other, shadow side of the living legend of Henry Ford. In 1940, Bennett was 48 years old, a small, dapper man who made certain his servicemen—ex-prisoners, boxers, toughs—took care of any of the dirty work of keeping all unions out of Ford factories, especially the giant River Rouge plant in Dearborn, a key to any union's organizing effort. Bennett's methods involved doing whatever was necessary—spying in factories, firings, and beatings by his thugs. He controlled local government, for example, with an ex-serviceman in 1940 placed as a compliant chief of police. His servicemen were also a private army that had beaten back the earlier 1930s union drive. Besides being ruthless, the suave, well-spoken Bennett maintained a good relationship with the governor of Michigan and the president. In all major decisions, Ford and Bennett both were involved, at times to the exclusion of Edsel Ford, the heir and sole son of the founder. Both had vowed a union would never come to Ford Motors.

The federal government in 1940 was a party to the ongoing Ford labor dispute. The National Labor Board, under petition from the UAW, had been doing fact-finding since 1937 for a hearing (under the Wagner law) to determine if the situation at Ford warranted holding a secret union certification election. Ford legal counsel had delayed and countersued the labor board at every instance until, in 1940, the Supreme Court had, on appeal, a pending case that affirmed the NLRB's process involving the company.

The UAW, meanwhile, was coming to the peak of its power, this time determined to unionize the last of the Big Three. Its Ford Organizing Committee was composed of the best possible men from the national union movement and key ex-Ford employees who had been fired for union activity. The Ford Drive came at time when this newly successful union was the most focused and unified it had ever been. A membership drive had been ongoing, and the growing list of in-plant members was kept secret and locked up until a ruling about the plant election was forthcoming from the Supreme Court. The allied CIO had pledged manpower and money to the UAW effort; every CIO member in the Detroit area had been urged to sign up one Ford worker. The secret list was growing.

The 1941 NLRB Ruling for a Plant Election

In late 1941, the highest court affirmed the law and thus the legitimacy of the NLRB procedure at Ford Motors. The company immediately obeyed, and throughout the River Rouge plant posted compliance notices that stated the workers were free to choose to organize a union without any management obstruction. Thousands flocked to sign up, and those already on the secret list openly wore union buttons. Stewards were elected in each department, and an eight-man union grievance committee was set up. Management turned suddenly very compliant, aware that any obstruction would be seen as a defiance of a court order. Regardless, Bennett aimed, at any cost, to keep the union from being a certified bargaining agent by democratic election. To that end, he fought cagily at first, then openly attacked against what was now designated UAW Union Local 600 of the Rouge plant.

But first, Ford notified the labor board of a refusal to voluntarily hold a plant election without a finalized hearing. This necessitated the completion of the fact-finding. It bought Bennett valuable time to break the union before the completed hearing would almost certainly require such an election.

Company Resistance and Call for Troops

Bennett began other strategies. He wooed the AFL in hopes of creating a time-saving jurisdictional rivalry between the two national union affiliates. Then he tried to control the election by running his own Ford Service men for election as union stewards. Not getting results, Bennett shifted his approach to an open attack in hopes of precipitating union violence. He dissolved the grievance committee through department transfers or dismissal of its members. He found pretext to demote or punish other union leaders. He succeeded in bullying the union to post formal notice of a pending walkout. The union did walk out and then used the strategy of encircling the River Rouge plant with so many strikers and sympathizers that no one could get in or out of the plant.

Inside the plant, Bennett had his private army of Ford Service fortified by a thousand newly imported Southern African American strikebreakers. His aim was to use this army to provoke violence on the part of the picketers outside so he could claim the plant was under siege by an out-of-control union mob. Bennett's ace was to get the governor or president to send soldiers to halt any further damage. The first step went as planned, and a local judge issued a temporary restraining order against the union picketers who had retaliated in their own defense to stop the Bennett insiders from standing on the roof hurtling objects down on them. All the while, the local police did nothing. Yet the pickets generally policed themselves and maintained order. In spring of 1941, the key question was when and how the Michigan governor in Lansing or the United States president in Washington, D.C., was going to react to the request for troops. Both parties to the dispute eagerly awaited the outcome.

Ford Strategy against the Government and Union

By 1940, the Ford Motor Company was generally considered the worst employer for autoworkers, not only because it was nonunionized but also because it offered lower than average wages for comparable work and had weak job security. The legend of the founder paying the unheard of high of $5 a day was long past. By 1940, the Ford worker earned a low yearly income because for two months all employees were temporarily laid off without pay while the plants were retooled to upgrade or restyle for the yearly new models. Then the company's mass production workers were hired back, which made them more like temporary workers without lasting job security.

Workers who were even vaguely associated with unions were never hired back and, with the least evidence, were permanently blackballed from the industry, losing all chance of holding any autoworker's job in the Detroit area. Ford servicemen moved secretly amidst workers at all times and kept dossiers on each for the least infractions. Thugs dealt with real troublemakers. Worker grievances had accumulated for 40 years, and witnesses were ready to testify before the Labor Board's fact-finding hearing. Ford and Bennett knew this would reveal a nightmarish underside to the public image of the revered 77-year-old founder and leader of the company—the man who invented the beloved Model T, created the assembly line for mass production, and instituted the highest pay scale for any workers in the world.

A full NRLB hearing would tarnish all this. With facts already having accumulated for more than three years, Ford could not allow the government fact finders to air such matters under public auspices. To prevent this from happening, Ford could choose either of two paths: the union had to be broken beforehand or the company, contrary to all public statements, would have to allow the plant election to forestall further hearings, even if a majority of Ford worker wanted to be represented by a union. If workers voted yes for a union, Bennett pledged he would negotiate forever and never concede a thing to a hated union. With or without a union, the message was that management would run the company no differently than in the past.

Bennett and Ford Service—Union Nemesis

Bennett had become his own legend; locally, Ford publicity portrayed him as a kind but principled and tough individual—a gun-slinging sheriff with a heart of gold. Taking pity on ex-prisoners and offering them jobs with Ford Service, he alone gave them their one chance to go straight and be on the right side of the law. Ford claimed he needed Bennett and his men to guard Ford and his family against the ever-present threat of a Lindberg-type kidnapping. Whenever Bennett needed to act the ruthless enforcer, Ford himself was often out of town or otherwise occupied with business so it was assumed that such action was not the great man's initiative. Bennett had been with the company a quarter century under the careful tutelage of Henry Ford himself, who reared him like a son and saw this employee as family.

Ford Service did its job cleverly, efficiently, and to the letter, according to precise orders from its head. The workforce Bennett hired was a carefully constructed balance of rival ethnic groups who spoke a mix of languages and were from different immigrant origins—an easily divided and intimidated group. For these reasons, it made them especially difficult to organize into a union. Assembly-line workers did their jobs in such a routine, repetitive, and simple way that a worker lacking full command of English was not at a disadvantage. African American workers numbered 10,000 of the 130,000 workforce in all plants. Management was ready to manipulate them to create racial frictions detrimental to union organizing. In short, Bennett had defended against all imagined possibilities.

Ford's All-out Resistance to the Election for a Union

Bennett had his own vulnerabilities. Certain matters lay beyond his control. His well-laid defenses could be overturned, as was the case on December 7, 1940, when a county judge upheld a municipal judge's ruling invalidating the long-standing Ford instituted law of no leafleting anywhere near the River Rouge plant. As a result, workers now received tens of thousands of UAW handbills and their newspaper, *Ford Facts*. Following this, the Supreme Court validated the NLRB, and Ford posted the compliance order, which opened the way for workers to openly join the as-yet-uncertified union (only an election would certify it). Under law, the UAW was now allowed to compete for membership. Thousands joined. Ford Service was never more understanding—even setting aside special smoking areas whereas before workers were not allowed to smoke on the job. Bennett went a long way toward frustrating the CIO membership drive when he invited the rival AFL to represent the workers. He gave these competing organizers the run of the plant.

Finally, Bennett began using underhanded tactics. He replaced a strike leader and used force against the Local 600 inside the plant. The union retaliated by

Young girl marches the picket line with her father at the Ford Motor Company's River Rouge plant in April 1941. His sign reads, "We'll walk until Hank talks." (Bettmann/Corbis)

using the ingenious method of an immediate defensive sit-down strike until the leader was ordered back to his original job. In other tactics, the union gained diverse members through radio broadcasts in all languages and by bringing in the head of the NAACP, Walter White, to quell anger aroused in African American workers.

Finally, Ford announced its refusal to voluntarily hold a plant election until forced to do so. It was a ruse to buy time. Bennett began all-out removals or job transfers. The union began a 10-day walkout, surrounding the plant the entire time with tens of thousands of supporters. Inside, with some 2,000 strikebreakers, Bennett sent a series of letters to government officials and the media claiming that Ford was illegally besieged by an alleged vast sit-down strike led by communists. Saboteurs were inside, he claimed, roaming the factory and damaging key machinery and tools. Because the city-issued restraining order was beyond the enforcement power of the outnumbered local police, Bennett asked for the immediate dispatch of state and federal troops to restore order.

Instead, labor law demanded a group of neutral observers go inside and make their own conclusions; one of them was Thomas Dewey. The report came back that the only leader and force inside was Bennett himself and an army of his own men. Damage was little. The CIO leaders offered to send in a delegation to take out any alleged union members. There were none.

Bennett had fallen ever so narrowly behind the times; his time-tested tactics were bringing no results. He ordered men to rush out exits and battle the strikers, certain now he could provoke the direly needed, violent overreaction by the strikers—the event necessary to discredit them and bring military aid.

Bennett wrote the president to say that vital military orders were disrupted; Roosevelt knew this was not true because Ford Motors only had a small defense contract in production. The CIO, meanwhile, had ensured their union workers that construction on the truly vital Ford factory for producing big bombers at Willow Run was continuing. The president was not about to aid Henry Ford, a man who had been a fierce isolationist and staunch opponent of the New Deal. Besides, Roosevelt was a labor man. Bennett's tactics all signified he must be getting desperate; yet, surely the governor knew what to do, didn't he?

The Governor, the NLRB, and the CIO-UAW Election Win, May 1941

The governor of Michigan, Murray D. Van Waggoner, hurried to Detroit with the aim of working with the two parties in this labor dispute to negotiate, find a middle ground, and come to a truce to end the walkout. He rebuffed Bennett's request that the state send an antiunion military force to aid the company. This governor was different from past compliant ones; he had been elected as a moderate Democratic with labor votes. With no choice left to him, Bennett agreed to sit with a Ford delegation and talk with Waggoner. Ford eventually conceded to a truce, granting key concessions to both labor and management. With that, the walkout ended after 10 days.

UAW Local 600 of the River Rouge plant gained two key concessions. First, the grievance committee was reinstated only with five stewards (not eight as previously). And, second, and of inestimable importance, Ford agreed to hold a NLRB-supervised secret election to determine if autoworkers in the River Rouge plant and two other Detroit-area plants wanted a union to represent them. If a majority voted in the affirmative, then the union and management would negotiate a collective bargaining contract.

With that, Ford gained the end of the walkout and the resumption of assembly-line production. Also, Bennett's one nonnegotiable demand was met—the NLRB agreed to a temporary halt in its hearings. Recently relocated to Detroit, the Board was about to begin its open, public testimony. Sessions were bound to get wide press coverage likely to harm the image of the founder and his company.

The historic union election was held May 21, 1941. Votes from three plants totalled over 80,000. The vote for a union was 97 percent, with the AFL getting 25 percent and the CIO 72 percent. Only 3 percent in all voted down a union. The UAW announced now it was ready to negotiate; Henry Ford and Bennett complied, but before doing so, the two along with other Ford representatives denounced the Wagner Act. Yet, they stated that the company would abide by this law and do its best to negotiate—even initially, after being forced against its will to submit to a communist-like directive against private property. In early June, the negotiations began, with company spokesman Bennett seeming to set a course of frustrating delaying tactics.

CIO Negotiates Ford's First Union Contract, June 1941

Outside pressure quickly came to bear on Bennett as the NLRB reopened its Ford hearings. The board's fact finders had cold, hard evidence about past abuses by Ford Service. The company's history of grievances went back years. All this was now about to be laid open. Numerous witnesses for the Board were already waiting to give public testimony under oath. The testimony in the hearing's first three days was sensational and headlined in Detroit papers. It was enough for the company; more of the same would put too much in jeopardy.

On June 21, a contract was ready and negotiations were quickly completed. The union felt the contract was a bonanza; its officials felt elated to have defeated the last of the Big Three and then gained a seeming golden contract. Certain concessions were standard for contracts at other auto companies but highly unusual for Ford. Among the Ford concessions was the new requirement that company guards, who until then had passed as fellow workers, were required to wear uniforms. In major ways, the contract was common to the trade—guarantees of seniority rules, overtime pay, paid leaves, and no layoffs until actual average hours per week fell below a certain preset average in a week. The contract weakened the company's inside power arm, Ford Service. Workers gained previously unknown job security. Overall they enjoyed the enhanced status finally of being equal to other unionized autoworkers in the industry.

Ford dealt with wages largely in an oral pledge that was rather innocently accepted by the union. The company vowed to immediately bring its own wages up to scale for all commensurate jobs in the industry. In fact, Ford would equal the highest rate paid by any of its major rivals. The reason the union was so trusting about wages was likely because Ford made two major unprecedented concessions in the written contract: the "closed shop," which meant that all future hires must join the union, and the "sign-off," whereby the company would automatically have the payroll department deduct union dues. What's more, the company had volunteered the concessions—which startled not only the grateful union but also the other rival automakers, which had not to date conceded these points. Then, as a capstone, Ford asked to stamp "union label" on all its future products. These gave what the UAW saw as a model contract for the industry.

In molding this generous contract, the company had in mind its own future agenda. The wily Ford and Bennett had made the industry-leading concessions to eliminate future issues at Ford likely to ignite costly strikes. This cleverly left the other auto-making competitors vulnerable in this regard. By seeming such a forward-looking employer, the company reaped public relations benefits—rejuvenating in the public mind the iconic founder who once granted joyous workers the $5 day—much to the disgust of his then rivals.

What Ford Motor Company gained from this contract far exceeded the publicity value of the unusual concessions. What really mattered had been accomplished—the good name of the company was spared being dragged in the mud as the election and contract put an end to the NLRB hearings. Not so evident to the public was one other company gain: the contract removed all obstacles to the company getting lucrative armaments contracts in the immediate future as well as likely war contracts in due time. Finally, Bennett assured Ford that, with or without a union, he could find ways for the company to do largely as it had done in the past regarding labor relations.

Company Strategy I:
Compliance to Co-opt the New UAW

Bennett determined to manipulate the new UAW union to company advantage in all possible circumstances. The company interest was uppermost in his mind; ideally, the company would go on dealing with its workforce mostly in the old time-tested, nonunion way. Bennett tried three different strategies to do so, one after the other—first, co-opting the union, second, buying off the union's local and national officials, and third, openly resisting or delaying contract enforcement with the union, for instance, prolonging the handling of ongoing grievances. From 1942 on, Bennett's aim was to bait the union into a strike during wartime to bring public criticism to the UAW and sympathy for Ford for having to halt vital wartime production.

After the contract was in effect in June 1941, workers in the plants first elected their own officials and shop stewards. Seeing this as a chance to bore within and capture the union, Bennett put former Ford Service men to work on the assembly lines and ensured that many were put up for election on the union slates. In a move proving both impulsive and foolish, Bennett failed to realize fully that workers truly wanted leaders to honestly represent their interests. In this rigged election effort, the UAW also quickly learned that Ford was still as hidebound traditional as ever and was in a bad faith in dealing with the new union.

For the rest of 1941 and early 1942, after Pearl Harbor, Bennett and Ford management went all-out to overcome this initial bad impression. To win the union over, Ford wooed all union representatives, especially those on the national level of the UAW and CIO. On the plant level, Ford dealt warmly and cooperatively with officials and shop stewards and offered mutual help to settle the problems of workers. While Ford played the good cop, Bennett played the bad one. On occasion, Bennett would hint that the two prize concessions—the union shop and the sign-off—could just as easily be taken away by the company. Thus, he hoped to cause fear so the union would be cautious, tame, and nonconfrontational—in effect become a "company union."

On the national level, the UAW resisted the blandishments of Ford management; Local 600 of the all-important River Rouge plant was steadfast, insisting that the concessions were final. Its Detroit leaders remained firm in wanting management to follow the letter of the contract. Locally, the union built an impressive headquarters. Union policies geared to the national patriotic mood followed after Pearl Harbor and the national UAW was the first major union to take a no-strike pledge during war. The public approved.

Company Strategy II:
Provoke UAW to Unpopular Wartime Strike

For roughly two years after May 1942, Ford Motors set in place its third strategy against the new union—to press and resist the union on every point to provoke a wartime strike likely to bring public criticism of the union. One provocation was for Ford management to long delay the settling of worker grievances that were coming in on a regular daily basis. Nothing was being cleared up—the grievance committee of union stewards confronted only empty promises, endless delays. Worker frustrations mounted.

Ford had orally pledged to bring up to industry standards the wages of its workers in each category. Yet, management initiated no surveys to determine the wage gaps needing to be closed and instead acted helpless to find the right remedy for this. In fact, during this time, the company actually lowered wages for anyone receiving an interplant transfer in Detroit. Only after the union appealed to the government in 1944 did such workers get their due in back pay. Some workers felt their union ought to be doing more, especially because Bennett was steadily making the new Plant Protection group into another Ford Service, with patrols looking for workers guilty of breaking petty rules and then penalizing the workers, just as in the past.

Lead by its own small group of fiery members, the union workers of certain departments dealt with grievances through a series of defensive sit-downs led by stewards. Other Ford policies led to worker reactions. The union favored hiring African Americans and letting them learn while working alongside experienced plant workers. Ford instead kept African Americans segregated in certain departments. In 1943, a group of these new African American UAW members rose up in rage and rioted for a short while before all was quelled. In 1944 at the River Rouge plant, however, with anger peaking from unsettled grievances, a white group from one department stormed into a management labor relations office, trashed it, and then barricaded their workplace—stopping work for 10,000 others for the day. All 26 involved were fired with union approval because their actions lacked any union authorization.

Possibly what spared Ford a larger strike during the war years was the mutually agreed appointment of an impartial umpire (a common practice with other companies but new to Ford) to deal with the most pressing unsettled grievances. Management used a delaying tactic even in this umpire's selection, and after vetoing candidate after candidate for five months, they finally agreed on a university law professor.

The other automakers viewed Ford as having the least progressive and most ineffective labor policies in the industry (the contract concessions aside). Yet even with constant strife on the factory floors, the company contributed through its unionized plants to the country's wartime economic miracle—producing tanks, planes, jeeps, and many more items in huge quantities. Continuing to fulfill its flow of lucrative government military contracts, the company achieved record wartime profits.

POSTWAR LABOR

During wartime and in the postwar period, Americans enjoyed growing, broad-based national prosperity. With the wartime focus on victory and the postwar focus on the continued health of the economy, Congress had turned conservative. Americans were less inclined toward continued social reforms and more wary of blue-collar union demands. Americans tended to see the country's corporations (not government planning and control) as responsible for the production miracle during war.

Corporate executives recognized unions as legitimate bargaining agents for their members' wages, hours, and benefits, and they acknowledged that unions expected wage gains. What concerned these executives was the meteoric rise of the militant industrial unions under the CIO, whose leaders were demanding a share of decision-making on the floor of the factory. The CIO's growing political power was another concern for the top businesses. These businesses had clout (having gone from Depression era scapegoats to World War II production miracle-makers in the mind of the public), and in 1946, corporate profits were at a record high. Their goal was to get the government to remove all remaining controls on prices. By mid-1946, the last controls were lifted.

Companies' Prices Surge at War's End

The results in 1945 and 1946 were predictable—an inflationary cycle of rising prices set in—and, for most Americans, workers especially, the cost of living rose at a far greater pace than wages or salaries. At the end of the war, the runaway rise in consumer prices was 31 percent. The inflation rate for the year 1946 was a stunning 18.2 percent. In 1946, in March the price of dozen eggs and a pound of butter was 48 cents and 55 cents, respectively; by December, these rose to 70 cents for eggs and 92 cents for butter. Basic everyday commodities were reaching alarming costs, and a housing shortage meant high rents and home prices.

Labor's Reaction: 1945–1946 Wave of Strikes

In the immediate postwar years, labor wanted to conserve its wartime gains. Yet, workers were met with a variety of shocks. Before the war's end, plants cut back on overtime; with victory, manufacturers reduced production from wartime

Grocery clerk writes up a bill for a shopper, 1948. Inflation soared following the end of the war. (Library of Congress)

levels. This led to vast layoffs. Ten days after V-J Day, 1.8 million workers joined the unemployed. In March 1946, postwar unemployment reached a peak of 2.7 million. Despite this, the overall economy remained healthy and growing with no danger of the return of Depression. But at the time, one could not be certain this would last.

In 1945 and 1946, unions reacted with a wave of strikes fighting for increased wages to meet the skyrocketing cost of living. Major strikes shook the country —against General Motors, soft coal operators, steel, and the railroads. The year 1946 had more strikers, 4.75 million, than any prior year.

Public and 80th Congress Blame Labor

A large majority of the public thought unions (not employers) were at fault for these strikes. The white-collar public was angry at various continued wartime scarcities of desired consumer goods and tended to blame strikes for the lower output and higher prices for these commodities. Many consumers grew angry and impatient with unions and felt that union demands had grown excessive, their leaders greedy and power hungry. Newspapers mostly mirrored these sentiments, some even suggesting communist influence in the unrest of the unions.

The 1947 Taft-Hartley Act against Unions

The 80th Congress with its conservative majority reacted in 1947 by passing the Taft-Hartley Act, which went a long way toward tipping the balance back to business from the government support for labor during the late 1930s and during the war. The act did not aim to destroy unions (as was the case after World War I) but instead sought to make labor an important but subordinate part of the emerging system of corporate state capitalism whereby government-aided corporations controlled labor and limited union power. The act, for example, aimed to bar the closed shop, by which all hirers had to be union. In strikes relating to national defense or safety (instead of temporarily nationalizing the affected business), the president now had the power to order strikers back to work for an 80-day cooling-off period, during which the union and the corporate officials would continue negotiations for a contract.

Truman, Leader of Liberals, and Unions, Purged of Communists

President Truman vetoed the Taft-Hartley Act; Congress passed it over his veto. Truman bellowed at what he portrayed as a forced labor bill. The result was dramatic; the president, who had alienated the union movement in prior instances by, for example, threatening to draft railroad workers unless they ended their strike, with his veto won back labor support, which would prove crucial to his election in 1948.

By remaining in the Democratic Party as one vital part of Truman's New Deal coalition, liberal, noncommunist labor forfeited its own postwar vision of realigning the American political system. In the 1940s' final years, the AFL and CIO began purging their locals of communists. The Taft-Hartley Act had stipulated that loyalty provisions applied to all unions. The unions in America continued their growth in organizing and bargaining until reaching a peak in 1955; nevertheless, the Taft-Hartley Act probably prevented the full organization of textile workers in the largely nonunion South.

The Great UAW–General Motors Strike, 1945–1946

In March 1946, the UAW branch, led by the quickly rising 38-year-old Walter Reuther, signed a contract with General Motors to boost autoworker's wages by 18.5 cents. The hike met the recommendation by a fact-finding panel set up by

Truman. Begun in December 1945, the 113-day strike was the first major strike of the new peacetime period. In the talks, the innovative Reuther introduced a novel negotiating issue—he argued that pay increases ought to be directly and proportionately linked to GM's profits, and he also demanded GM open its books to an arbitration panel constituted by the still-existent wartime Office of Price Control. A stunned GM management refused, but two years later, the GM president Charles Wilson would reconsider this.

The factors causing Reuther to target GM were many and varied; GM was the most prosperous of the Big Three automakers, having made giant profits from war contracts. But GM had also made stunning savings in labor costs, due to its vast workforce being held to the wartime ceiling of the one-time 15 percent wage hike. At war's end, however, GM instantly lost $2 billion in contracts. This meant a scaling back of production, which caused a layoff of 140,000 UMW workers. In a further cost reduction, GM realized an across-the-board 25 percent pay reduction for all workers due to the elimination of wartime overtime pay. All these factors combined made Reuther fear for the very survival of the UAW unless he could safeguard the organization with a successful strike. GM was vulnerable, he felt, because it was in the process of converting its more than 100 plants back to peacetime auto production. A strike would halt this, and GM would see its competitors gain great advantage. In October, the two sides evaluated one another and GM finally made an offer of a 10-cents-per-hour hike; the UAW board flatly refused it.

The strike began in December with 195,000 UMW workers in 95 plants walking off the job. Wilson and the other top GM corporate executives strongly believed that the government needed to withdraw any remaining wartime controls over prices, and that the union movement had no right to make corporate price setting a part of collective bargaining. With ads in major newspapers and spokesmen addressing local business gatherings around the country, GM argued that union and government interference in management decisions was socialism. Such interference undercut the key role of management's sole decision-making powers in the private enterprise system. It warned the national economy was at a vital fork in the road to the future.

Nationwide, in the initial months of 1946, a wave of new strikes hit other large industries, including steel, which left 1.6 million new strikers in addition to the nearly 200,000 in Detroit. With the GM strike dragging on and the will of the UMW strikers near the breaking point, the president intervened forcefully to end it. A government panel injected a new perspective into the GM–UAW standoff: since January 1941, the cost of living had increased 33 percent while wages had remained constant. On this basis, the panel recommended a wage hike of nearly 20 cents per hour without a need for the company to raise prices. GM held to an offer of one cent less. Reuther wavered, Truman pressed him, and the epic strike was settled in March 1946.

In the two months after the settlement, the government gave in to GM and allowed three separate price increases. The result was that the autoworkers, even with their new wage hike, were left vulnerable to inflation again cutting into their income and consumer purchasing power. This lessened the country's overall capability to buy new cars.

Truman Poses Nationalization to Stop Railroad Strike

In 1946, President Truman saw this epic strike year's first major labor conflicts in auto and steel come to an end without his having sacrificed his substantial backing from the labor movement. Two years earlier, when as senator he was selected vice president, Truman was fully vetted and given the approval of labor, especially by Sidney Hillman, who was the head of the CIO political action committee that had greatly contributed to Roosevelt winning his fourth term in office. In the initial months of his presidency, Truman seemed a fine choice and won good approval ratings from the union movement. In fact, in the auto and steel strikes, the corporations thought the president was biased in labor's favor. Soon Truman would show another side.

In the spring of 1946, the country's railroad system was in the throes of a pending strike between the rail carriers and the 20 unions representing all its workers. A group of arbitrators had worked for weeks to finally get an agreement favorable to 18 of the unions. But the 2 most powerful, the Brotherhood of Locomotive Engineers and the Brotherhood of Railroad Trainmen, rejected the offer and set a strike deadline. Both defiant unions were headed by old political friends of the president. With union heads called into the White House three days before the deadline, Truman vehemently stated that he could never stand idly by and let them bring a halt to the nation's economy and business. Come to an agreement within 48 hours or Truman would have government seize the railroads. Negotiations continued; the deadline was extended five days. Still, there was no contract. On the morning of May 24, 1946, the rails went quiet with the strike call.

Truman was furious, reported the June 3, 1946, issue of *Time* magazine. He announced to his cabinet two intentions. First, he was going to Congress to ask for the authority to draft the railway strikers into the military, regardless of each one's age or family size. If this measure passed, this would be the most extreme ever government antiunion measure. Second, he planned to give a speech that evening on radio. Upon reading it, his advisers reacted with shock because its language was infused with rage (for example, he suggested that good Americans should "hang a few traitors" such as the top heads of the railroad unions and John L. Lewis). His staff softened the language before Truman made a radio speech to 25 million listeners the next day. Truman started his speech, "The crisis of Pearl

Harbor was the result of action by a foreign enemy. The crisis tonight is caused by a group of men within our country." As he continued, *Time* reported, Truman used such forceful statements as "This is no contest between labor and management. This is a contest between a small group of men and the government," with the nation's welfare at stake.

Meanwhile, at the capital's Statler Hotel, the president's top labor adviser, John Steelman, was forcefully negotiating with the heads of the two holdout unions. Midway through Truman's address to a joint session of Congress the day after his radio speech, he got word that Steelman had convinced the men to sign a contract. The strike is over, Truman announced to rousing applause by congressmen of all parties. He went on to ask for the draft legislation for those striking in violation of the greatest good of the people. The House passed it, but in the Senate, the archconservative Republican Robert Taft persuaded other members it was unconstitutional while in private terming it fascist.

The labor movement instantly voiced fierce opposition to this would-be friendly president proposing draft legislation for strikers. The powerful railroad unions vowed to defeat him in 1948. The CIO's Political Action Committee, so essential to the Democratic victory in 1944, held a New York rally where speakers branded Truman a labor hater. His hasty action had cut his political career short was the widespread opinion of varied labor commentators.

Truman Fights John L. Lewis and Risks Losing Labor

Just prior to the railroad work stoppage and just after the settlements in the auto and steel industries, Truman dealt with yet another of the cascade of major war's end strikes as the arrogant Lewis took his coal miners out of the pits for the fourth time in two years. Lewis brought forth a new issue with the mine operators. He demanded a union health and welfare fund financed by the operators paying a royalty on each ton of mined coal. When he met rejection, he called his miners out in April 1946.

That spring, with the pits idle, the nation's supply of coal dropped dangerously low, which caused the economy to slow with worrisome side effects. Coal supplied almost 100 percent of America's fuel for its electrical stations and steel foundries. As the nation's coal supply ran low, Ford Motors laid off some 50,000 workers. Twenty eastern states ordered dim outs and New Jersey declared a state of emergency. As all but 5 percent of railroad locomotives ran on coal, the nation's carriers could be forced to cease operations if the coal strike was not settled quickly. The carriers did lay off over 100,000 workers. Many people believed Lewis was holding the American public hostage until the operators met his demands. Some saw a national economic disaster as imminent.

The American white-collar public had long viewed Lewis as the most hated labor leader, if not most hated single individual, in America. The press and gov-

Miners checking in at the lamp house upon completion of the morning shift, Kopperston Mines, West Virginia, August 1946. (National Archives)

ernment had long been his antagonists. Millions of veterans still bitterly resented his breaking the wartime no-strike pledge, imagining his only motive then was greed. Lewis even had many enemies among the labor movement because he most recently fought bitterly and split from the AFL, and prior to that from the CIO, which he had founded and led in the late 1930s to a position of power. He and his UMW were loners within labor but, to his men, he was a heroic figure always fighting to safeguard the miners' safety welfare and family security, even if the rest of the country paid the price.

Ever since his days in the Senate, Truman detested Lewis. This latest strike tested Truman. Lewis caught him off guard by ordering his men back to work for a two-week cooling-off period. This resulted just as the public was becoming so furious as to demand the government take severe action against him. Truman responded with a government takeover of the mines and placed Secretary of the Interior Julius Krug in charge of daily operations. Krug ordered the miners back to work. All refused. Never easily replaceable, coal miners had special knowledge and skills. Nine days later, the administration gave in. With the new contract, operators paid the UMW five cents per ton for the union's welfare and retirement fund. The mines were not immediately returned to the owners.

In the fall, Lewis demanded that Krug reopen negotiations in mid-contract. The union leader demanded more monies for his miners' new welfare fund and for vacations with pay. Krug refused. Lewis ordered his miners out despite the existing contract's no-strike clause. Truman this time was determined to have a showdown and fight Lewis to the end, no matter the consequences for his political future. Instead of a private labor–management negotiation, the president felt passionately that this was a bold uprising against the government and the rule of law. His role was to protect the public. It would be him or Lewis in this fight, Truman warned his closest advisers.

The prior court injunction against labor, invalidated in appeals court, had pertained only to the private sector, Truman reasoned. Now, with matters in the public sector, the government, as employer, could use it against an illegal strike. He ordered his attorney general to file for such an injunction. The federal judge granted it. While the president avoided any direct involvement in the case, his close advisers pursued it. Lewis was found in contempt, and his UMW fined $3.5 million, a huge sum for the time. Legal tactics, instead of the usual political tug-of-war, had thrown Lewis off target. He ordered his miners back to work. Truman had triumphed, but at what cost? Possibly the loss of the presidency in 1948, should Truman choose to run.

Labor Gains Enemies and an Ally in the New ADA

At the beginning of 1948, the political backdrop had changed radically for America's labor unions. Internationally, the Truman Doctrine and the Marshall Plan were in effect and the Cold War was a fact. Both won support from anticommunist liberals but leftists saw these as imperialistic. At home, the Red Scare had begun. Truman instituted a loyalty oath for government employees. HUAC had begun hearings to question the Hollywood Ten about any prior associations with the Communist Party. The American public was keenly aware that present or past associations with communists were likely to be destructive for an individual or institution. An opportunistic politician could gain from even the hint of an opponent having such an association. For instance, in the November 1946 congressional midterm elections, Republicans had swept both houses by deftly portraying the Democrats as tainted with a communist influence from the CIO, which had known radical local chapters and organizers. That year's massive wave of strikes, conservatives also implied, had been partially inspired by the communists in the union movement.

The notorious Republican 80th Congress (1946–1948) had been strongly antiunion—foremost, by passing the 1947 Taft-Hartley Act over Truman's veto. Big labor, the AFL and CIO, had pressured to muster votes enough to sustain the veto but failed. They were taken aback to learn of their dire lack of allies in Congress. Big labor was now running scared and vowed to work hard for a prolabor president and prolabor representatives in Congress in the coming 1948 election. Labor was not greatly enthusiastic about Truman, yet by his veto, he'd redeemed himself to a degree with labor. The prospect of a Republican president and Congress could be disastrous for labor. Still, the communists within the union movement, especially certain CIO locals, remained a problem because labor's critics would capitalize on this once again.

The turning point came in January 1947 when a group of very prominent veteran New Dealers in Washington, including such notable persons as John Kenneth Galbraith and Chester Bowles, formed the Americans for Democratic Action (ADA). Later, Eleanor Roosevelt herself would endorse the group's statement of politics. Essentially, this was the founding charter, so to speak, of Cold War liberalism, which meant followers were anticommunist in foreign affairs and were for the continuation of New Deal–type social welfare programs in domestic affairs. Crucial in their official statement was their complete disassociation with any communists or those linked in any way to such organizations.

Thus, the ADA made itself a ready haven for the many liberal unions while the more radical ones were drawn to the new Progressive Party, a breakaway remnant from the Democratic Party, led in 1948 by their presidential candidate, Henry Wallace. Wallace and his equivalent Progressive Citizens of America (PCA) welcomed those in the breakaway leftist unions and benefited from their campaign foot soldiers, monies, and ideology. The liberal ADA, meanwhile, gained powerful union leaders such as Walter Reuther, of UAW, and David Dubinsky, of the International Ladies Garment Workers Union.

Labor Gives Critical Boost to Truman in the 1948 Election

In the winter of 1947–1948, big labor knew their many campaign workers, political unity, and funds all had to be at peak levels to avoid the election of Thomas Dewey, who in their view was a reactionary. Even so, in his enigmatic perverseness, Lewis endorsed Dewey, as did the head of The Brotherhood of Locomotive Engineers, who never forgave Truman for threatening his strikers with the draft back in 1946. Labor in general rebuked Dewey. Big labor, now backed almost exclusively from ADA-type unions, enjoyed greater public appeal. It benefited from Wallace being a magnet drawing off radical unions possibly controversial in the election. This left Truman as the candidate of liberal labor.

The CIO's powerful PAC, which had first entered politics in 1944 and put Roosevelt over the top, went to work in the same fashion for Truman. It fielded nearly a quarter million union campaign workers who focused on registering new voters (among these were Southern African Americans who had moved to big cities). The other large affiliate of big labor, the AFL, was studiously neutral in past presidential races, decided too much was at stake in 1948 and formed Labor's League for Political Education (LLPE). While not openly endorsing Truman, the League's implicit goal was to get campaign manpower and money for

Truman. The huge effort of the unions to have its campaign workers get out the vote was the critical factor in the dramatic come-from-behind victory by Truman, who said it was labor that did it.

General Motors and a Key Change in Labor Relations

In 1948, with the auto contract again open to negotiation, GM president Charles Wilson made Reuther a startling offer consisting of two novel and dramatic conditions: first, the company would grant an automatic wage increase geared to the general price index for consumers, and second, the company would grant a two-wage improvement factor based on gains in company productivity. Wilson reasoned correctly that the new contract would be copied throughout the automotive industry, thus eliminating wage competition and costly confrontational strikes. With such an ongoing arrangement, the danger of government's permanent interference in private management's decisions would be eliminated. Thus, GM was free to set long-range planning.

The impact of the sensational 1948 UMW-GM Pact was far-reaching. In this was the seed for the next 25 years of labor-management relations. In each industry, the corporate leader would set the template for a wage and benefits contract with the complementary major unions. In exchange for guaranteed high wages and security, the major unions agreed to maintain discipline on the shop floor and ensure worker obedience to proper grievance procedures. Dispensing with earlier militancy or a wish for broad social or political changes, the country's major unions thus made a crucial accommodation to the capitalist system—labor accepted an important but secondary role in the newly evolved economy led by big business and big government.

WHITE-COLLAR WORK

The postwar economic boom led to profound changes in the composition and compensation of the nation's workforce (white-collar jobs rose dramatically; blue-collar jobs meant relative affluence). Correspondingly, there was a rethinking of the meaning of social status and comparative income. Many thought America was becoming a classless society in the years after 1945. Evaluating the income gain of those industrial unions that were so militant as recently as 1946, CIO President Phillip Murray opined that America had become a country with no classes. The dream of a classless society with abundance for all seemed near. Unions helped raise working class people into the middle class. This vision provoked many questions: Was the country middle class? If so, what was the criterion? Was the class issue solved? How? Which Americans were not in the middle class?

White-collar Workers: More and Higher Salaried

The postwar boom created a rapidly expanding economy with a demand for more highly paid white-collar workers, professionals, managers, and businessmen. Higher education was democratized for the first time with the G.I. Bill paying the tuition of millions of veterans and fulfilling the growing need for these salaried personnel. Everyone was in college at the time, it seemed; most were the first ones in their families to do so. Children of old main stock families mixed freely with ethnic families in an homogenization of adult white males that had first begun in the wartime draft and military units.

Blue-collar Workers: Big Labor Is Middle Class

The privileged blue-collar workers represented by such powerful unions as the UAW and the USW were on a par with these new white-collar workers with regard to their eventual earning power. Workers like these enjoyed an ever-rising standard of living and actually became part of the affluent American society in no small part because employers like General Motors in 1948 suggested that the contract with the UAW have an automatic cost of living adjustment (COLA) geared to an inflation index. Guaranteed high wages combined with an enviable benefits package made blue collar-workers equal in affluence to many white-collar workers.

Advertisers Target the Growing Middle Class

The largest primary sector workforce, adult white males of both the blue- and white-collar classes were united in their affluence and rising incomes. Mass media and advertisers especially played to this new hybrid middle-class group. If both a GM worker and an IBM middle manager could buy a high-end Buick Road Master then, in terms of consumer power, both were classless or equally well off—or so claimed a pandering media eager to please its advertisers. Such mass affluence was also a patriotic claim; during the Cold War, Russian workers lacked any such affluence and their society was not "classless."

Service Sector Spreads and Still Struggles

Simultaneously, the American economy expanded its relatively low-paying service sector so greatly in these years that this secondary white-collar work world mushroomed in size. Millions of workers took jobs as relatively low-paid teachers, government and office workers, hospital staff, and other service jobs. So great was the growth of this particular sector that dozens of years after 1946,

Jeannette Poirier looking at photographs in a file cabinet drawer at the Washington office of the Overseas Branch of the U.S. Office of War Information, 1945. World War II sparked the entrance of women into the workplace and following the war they were usually hired as clerical or service workers on low salaries. (Library of Congress)

the country counted more white- than blue-collar workers. In 1940, among all workers, not even one in three were counted as white collar.

Although all of these new jobs were white collar and salaried, they constituted a secondary sector of work because these workers fell considerably below the middle-class standard of the highly compensated white- and blue-collar males. Jobs for new workers, including typists, telephone operators, clerical, sales persons, and others, were often boring, repetitive work, lacking prestige and without creativity. Most of the new workers were women; the telephone company AT&T employed 500,000 women as clerical or service workers with low salaries. By contrast, the company's highly paid unionized crafts unit was all male with high middle-class incomes. By 1950, 20 million women had jobs outside the home.

Nonunion Blue Collar: Job Loss and Low Pay

Meanwhile, as the service sector grew, the manual labor sector declined in the overall job picture in postwar America. Automated machinery had greatly lowered the numbers needed for factory and farm worker. The blue-collar sector of the workforce was declining. Yet, in terms of total numbers, there was slight increase to 22 million in 1950. Earning low wages and lacking job security or benefits, many of these blue-collar workers were in nonunion plants such as the vast textile industry of the South. Divided from the highly paid union workers, these blue-collar workers were invisible to those who claimed a new classless society had been born. At best, these jobs were near the bottom tier, and below them was a sector of casual, often seasonal employment—ranch and farm help, cab drivers, and short-order cooks.

Society's Postwar Wealth Distribution

After 1945, the country's wealth was not redistributed, but because the economic pie was growing larger, the standard of living rose for all proportionately, which gave the myth of a classless country. New fault lines of separation were coming into being: the advantaged included white males, premium blue-collar union workers, suburbanites, and the educated young; the disadvantaged included males of color, blue-collar nonunion workers, inner-city dwellers, the poorly educated young, and the old.

American Middle Class, Old and New

America's new economic class—the salaried middle class—greatly expanded during World War II and contrasted with the old middle class of small farmers, independent businessmen, shop owners, and professionals in private practice. The nucleus for this new middle class began with the midlevel, often desk-bound employees of the war-expanded giant bureaucracies of government and corporations. The old middle class were independent owners of property that produced some type of profit. Farmers and the small-town people of this type often lived and worked within a small local setting, rarely moving elsewhere.

The modern salaried middle class first became significant in the 19th century with the advent of the railroads, and of large nation-spanning, personally owned corporations aided by government subsidies, and by institutional and private investments. The employees of these corporations consisted primarily of hourly wage–earning blue-collar workers and a new salaried group consisting of accountants, clerks, salesmen, and others. This salaried group consisted of an estimated 6 percent of all employees by 1870.

With the 20th century, the larger public-owned corporation required so much capital investment that ownership was by a vast, impersonal stockholder group with top management often split off from any meaningful ownership. These giant, impersonal corporations employed greater and greater numbers of mid-level salaried employees who composed a new portion of the middle class, distinct from the older one of independent businessmen and farmers. By contrast to that older one, the new salaried group had little independence and lacked ownership or property holdings. This new salaried group also did not include entrepreneurs.

By the 1920s, the dependant salaried worker surpassed the older go-it-alone businessman of the traditional middle class. By 1940, white-collar workers were greatly outnumbered by the working or blue-collar class, which constituted over 60 percent of the total workforce.

War greatly expanded the already wide, white-collar, midlevel support sector below the top administrators of the expanding bureaucracies in government and corporations. White-collar administrative groups even emerged in the major trade union alliances like the AFL-CIO. Women entered the wartime workforce most dramatically in the manufacturing industries, but they also enhanced the salaried sector until this group gained the momentum to become the dominant employee strata in the United States.

The continued postwar economic boom brought ever new and broadened areas of white-collar salaried employment. One example was the entire new industry of television with all its subsidiary aspects of manufacturing, wholesale and retail sales, broadcast ad sales, and programming.

Wartime Bureaucracies Widen the White-collar Group

The war years were a time of epic dramatic growth for the white-collar group. The military, which had the largest numbers serving in the service sector, foreshadowed the emerging, altered postwar class configuration of American society. A total of 16 million served in the country's armed forces at some time during the war, but of this total, only 1.5 million were actually in a combat zone. Behind the lines, a blue-collar equivalent served the military as supply and liaison persons. But the greatest percentage of noncombat personnel were the more numerous white-collar equivalent who handled the mountainous paperwork involved with the administration of this vast manpower reserve spread all over the globe. The so-called white-collar salaried military personnel constituted more than 40 percent of the men at war. The GIs in combat units resented these behind-the-lines types because of their relative safety. The GI "grunts" also resented the salaried men for arranging special deals for themselves, like getting better food or special furloughs.

The wartime federal government created more sudden, dramatic growth for the new salaried middle class. Government employment had expanded with many unprecedented, new departments to administer affairs on the home front. These included a giant force of office workers administering such affairs as the complex nationwide freeze on wages, prices, and salaries; the rationing of scarce commodities; and the drafting of people to serve in the military, to mention just a few such activities. The Office of Price Administration (OPA), for example, numbered 75,000 white-collar workers at war's end, plus another 200,000 volunteers all throughout the country.

Bureaucracies in other areas also extended from Washington to the grassroots level. For example, the rationing system covered all the daily nutrition needs of all citizens; the government regularly issued rationing books depending on such factors as the size of the family, the commuting needs of defense workers, and the varying availability of the average person's countless daily necessities. The Selective Service Act of 1940 put in place another tremendous wartime white-collar bureaucracy that extended from Washington to every state, and from states

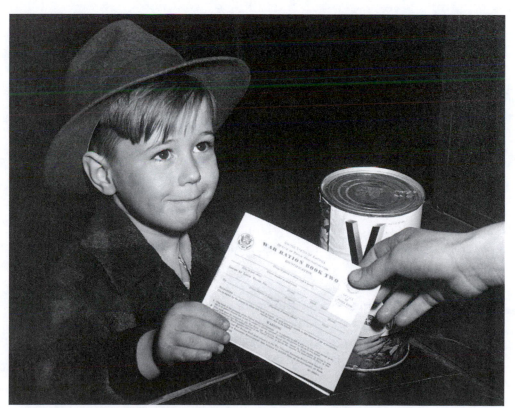

An eager schoolboy gets his first experience in using War Ration Book Two in February 1943. During World War II, children learned about point rationing at school and in real-life experience. (National Archives)

down to the rural county and city neighborhood level—a task that enlisted both salaried and volunteers by the hundreds of thousands.

If the war spurred the pivotal growth of this new salaried middle class, the postwar boom continued the same social dynamic. With the constant growth of this new middle class, the total of all white-collar workers 10 years after 1946 would exceed the total number of blue-collar workers in the country. Everywhere their numbers were growing: the late 1940s housing boom spurred the real estate, banking, and insurance industries; the auto boom spurred the credit firms, oil, tire, steel, and coal companies. Huge new department store chains with sales and support staffs grew to keep up with the continued fervid rise in postwar consumption. College graduates (more than at any other time in United States because of the G.I. Bill) filled the ranks of the new salaried class that would become legendary—the most broadly-based middle class ever to emerge in the country's history. This was the starting point for the force behind most political, social, and economic developments from the late 1940s to mid-1970s. This was an era when rising prosperity was the national norm.

New Postwar Middle Class Shapes Its Own Lifestyle

This new salaried middle class had certain distinguishing traits—most importantly, the desire to always be distinct from blue-collar workers, of whom the highest paid in the major unions often had a greater income than a salaried man in a suit. The mid-level employee thus frequently leaned toward the style and opinions of the top executives in their firms. Lacking any group security such as a union contract, the average salaried person was anxiety prone about the certain matters: the income was satisfactory but the job was without guarantees as to duration (beyond day-to-day) or income level (salary cuts often came with drop-offs in the volume of business). The middling corporate manager also expected to move frequently and often with little advance notice, depending on the needs of his employer. This made for anxiety in a family that always needed to be ready for a possible family move, ready to change houses, schools, social life, and friends.

Suburbs

A certain standardization became the norm for the new middle class; a move to a similar kind of suburb in another city was a welcome matter. The new and the old abodes often shared similar social rites and rituals, including welcome wagons and bridge clubs, and consumer status objects such as desired makes of cars and appliances. Status anxiety reached almost panic levels at times, however, with the syndrome of "keeping up with the Joneses" or, essentially, wanting desperately to avoid seeming to fall behind the others if one was unable to purchase the endlessly more stylish, supposedly better and improved models that others—who must be "getting ahead"—possessed.

Cocktails

At the very least, the new middle class must maintain a style of life that markedly differed from the working class, from which many had arisen by getting a college education. In general, the middling style decreed that one prefer mixed drink "cocktails" over beer, suits and never bib overalls; speech and vocabulary must indicate exposure to upper levels of society and not a seemingly crass, cursing manner associated with workers. Make it clear you use a pencil (not a shovel) and work inside in a warm office (not outside exposed to the elements).

Conformity

Conformity seemed the safest way to maintain a job; no getting out of line for long without good reason. The military hierarchy of the early 1940s transferred readily over to the new corporate hierarchies with executives, divisions, branches, and local offices. What the new middling individual desired most was security, which was often difficult given the ephemeral aspects inherent in being salaried, such as the lack of real job tenure. The best way to get security was, as in the military, to be disciplined, dutiful, and subservient, especially to those above. The old middle-class sense of independence and speaking your mind were not the work mores best for the new middle class.

Seeking security, valuing conformity, and cherishing a first home and new possessions, many of this new middle class were inclined to fear the hidden domestic menace of communism. Many supported those in government who sought to reveal its presence, especially in the CIO industrial unions. Many backed the red hunts of the HUAC and, later, Sen. Joseph McCarthy.

Consumerism

This new middle class exerted tremendous broad influence in the area of specific mass tastes, such as the most viewed programs on television, the newest and most powerful national media to date. Their great numbers and suitable incomes made up a great river of purchasing power that determined American styles—everything from gargantuan cars to Dior's New Look in fashion for women. This new class was prone to be upwardly influenced and more educated, and they expressed cultural tastes that the critic Dwight Macdonald would term "mid-brow culture" that embraced neither high-brow opera nor low-brow Grand Ole Opry but simply a good Broadway musical like *Oklahoma* or *South Pacific*.

THE GROWTH OF CORPORATIONS

The World War II production miracle occurred because of government cooperation and extensive funding of the largest of the large corporations like General

Motors, Ford, United States Steel, and others. In January 1942, the president established the WPB, which directed the initial conversion to a war economy and thereafter the overall coordination and orientation of the production in the vast business sector. By war's end, the result was a gross national product so expanded that the country was producing more than the combined total of all its allies and enemies.

Wartime Big Government Nurtures Big Business

The national government was clearly at the head of this effort to direct business through the wartime federal agencies such as the essential NLRB, which mediated labor-industrial disputes; the war Manpower Commission; and the Office of War Mobilization, among others. During the five years following mid-1941, the government gained the cooperation of business in a variety of ways. For example, the government war contracts had cost overrun and guaranteed profit provisions, and businesses received antitrust and tax exemptions.

Corporations ranking in the top 100 won the lion's share of this huge federal expenditure and, as a result, grew even larger by expanding and diversifying their products. In the five years following mid-1941, the top 100 corporations received more than two-thirds of the government contracts totaling the then-stunning sum of $175 billion. Steel, aircraft, chemical, and airplane industries were all giant beneficiaries along with autos, with General Motors getting 8 percent of all awarded contracts, the highest of any corporation in the country. Many small businesses, unable to compete by scale or efficiency, went out of business, outbid by their largest competitors. Significantly, for the future, the war established a government-corporate codependency based on meeting the needs of the military in states of national emergency.

Postwar Government Still Benefits "Free Enterprise" Big Business

With the war's end, the mass media had established in the public's mind that private business, and not government, had been the heroes of the home front's victorious production miracle. A corporate executive like Henry Kaiser who launched thousands of new Liberty supply ships using novel mass production methods became known as Sir Launch-a-Lot. By 1945, the public image was of can-do corporations performing the at home heroics; largely ignored was the truly Herculean effort of government in terms of planning and controlling the overall national economy.

The public did understand that government spending expanded the economy and made for more jobs and therefore should be continued in the postwar era but with corporations freer of government planning. Conservatives reigned in

Ford Motor Company rolls out the 1949 models at its auto show in 1948. (Library of Congress)

Congress. They held that wartime union gains ought to be cut back so management would again control unions but as subordinate partners in a system of new corporate state capitalism.

In the postwar, the economy continued expanding due to wartime's high personal savings and the pent-up consumer demand to purchase commodities newly on the market after wartime bans and rationing. Large corporations again reaped the largest benefits with the auto industry's Big Three companies reintroducing models in 1946 after none had been produced from 1942 on, when auto factories had converted to the mass production of tanks and airplanes. Autos were one of the pillars of the postwar consumer economy and more than anything represented the symbolic nexus of the ongoing boom. The UAW was the country's most powerful union, and its contracts were copied industrywide upon initial agreement with one automaker. The banner sales year for autos had been 1929, but sales of 1949 surpassed it with 5 million buyers of new cars.

Constantly rising family incomes along with installment buying made new car purchases possible, and the car culture took over America. New yearly models, the ads persuaded, made last year's models obsolete although changes were often only cosmetic. Eventually in the 1950s, to make way for so many cars,

President Eisenhower initiated the largest public works system ever by starting to build the interstate highway system. Military defense needs also justified fast national transport in the event of a communist invasion or attack.

Housing construction also was a pillar of the postwar consumer economy. Corporations such as Levitt & Sons constructed the new suburbs using techniques acquired in building housing on wartime bases with government contracts. The government provided guaranteed home mortgages with no down payment, and low-interest, to millions of veterans under the G.I. Bill, which made possible mass purchasing of hundreds of thousands of first homes in the new suburbs.

In turn, demand grew for more autos as the two-car family became the norm in suburbia with one for the commuting husband and the other for the wife at home. Such car congestion soon resulted in a new ecological danger—urban smog.

1940–1941: FDR Turns to Big Business for Preparedness

In 1940, President Roosevelt steered his administration's prime goal to a peace-time preparedness for a war that he felt was almost certain to involve America at some point. The president's new aim of a defense buildup required that he set aside any continued reform aims. For the sake of raising up 1940s national defense, he curtailed the 1930s New Deal, with the exception of Social Security and the best of the prior era's social welfare programs. But to build military preparedness, the president needed the cooperation of big business. Executives of the corporations were the most capable of partial changeover to producing a military line of goods to fulfill America's early (pre-Lend-Lease) government defense contracts.

The president now needed to welcome the leaders of Wall Street and big business that only recently in his late 1930s New Deal's trust-busting phase he had branded the enemies, "the economic royalists," who had built the monopolies seen as the prime obstacles to recovery. Now, with a mass military buildup needed quickly, Roosevelt knew that the efficiency of scale and speed could only come from the nation's largest corporations. His new pro–big business approach also had a precedent in his early 1930s New Deal under the National Industrial Recovery Act, which encouraged the giant businesses to cooperate on pricing, profits, and wages with all of their other competitors in each industry. This policy accepted those who played by the government rules and punished offenders only (government acceptance of the efficiencies of big business went back to the New Nationalism espoused by cousin and third party candidate Theodore Roosevelt during the 1912 presidential race).

Franklin D. Roosevelt did a fine job of opening up his administration to select business leaders, much to the dismay of some of his long-time liberal New Dealers. Even for the sake of the new 1940s National Defense aim, these old-time reform fighters against business regretted seeing the end of the New Deal as they had known it. In July 1940, the president appointed two prominent Republican interventionists to his cabinet in key roles: Henry Stimson as secretary of war and Frank Knox as secretary of the Navy.

Succeeding in attracting the best executive talent, he offered top administrative posts to "dollar-a-year" executives who continued their private salaries yet only accepted one dollar in government pay. In spring 1941, Lend-Lease began and brought defense spending and production to new levels. The head of this new program was the president of United States Steel, Edward R. Stettinius. A defense production boom ensued, although with resistance from Detroit's automakers, especially Ford, because 1941 had been the first banner sales year for autos since 1929 (this was evidence mass production benefited from the 1940–1941 increase in mass consumption due to the growth of industrial unions, higher wages, and disappearing joblessness).

Government Regulation of Unions

In 1940 and 1941, many large manufacturing corporations faced a wave of strikes and consented to recognition of mostly CIO industrial unions; the result was a 1.6 million rise in union membership. Even Ford Motors, the one nonunion holdout from the Great Detroit Strikes of 1937, accepted unionization by the UAW in 1941. The result was that in most major industries, one or a few businesses dominated and most all had contracts with the same major union, a situation that made eventual wartime government planning easier than dealing with the confusion of many smaller units.

A combination of big corporations, the military, and conservatives made it clear to the president that industrial strikes were too costly in hampering defense production and such work stoppages needed to be severely restricted. In January 1941, Roosevelt gave an address in which he unequivocally stated that nothing would be tolerated that blocks the speed and efficiency of defense production. The CIO top officials consented; the AFL called off work stoppages at defense sites.

Also, in 1941, the president set up the NDMB with an equal number of representatives from labor, business, and government to bring fair arbitration to bear on all labor management disputes. So satisfying was the aim that CIO head Phillip Murray agreed to be a board member and cooperated to squash unauthorized wildcat strikes by radical locals.

A New Wartime Centrally Planned, Government-operated Economy

After Pearl Harbor and for the next four years, the government exerted central planning and control over the entire economy. Because of the need to quickly overcome chronic shortages and to supply massive manpower needs and raw materials, the government could not rely on the pace of work and scarcity pricing of a free market economy. Thus, administration officials had decided early for a planned government economy with strict controls on everything: wages, prices, and salaries. This included the rationing of all consumer goods. Civilian and military production both had to proceed in rough overall balance, with the military taking 47 percent of all production at the peak of war.

The armed services portion of this huge system worked with the military procurement branch giving all production requirements to the WPB, which then selected the corporations to get war contracts to meet production. The WPA chairman was Donald Nelson, a vice president of Sears, and the next in command was Charles Wilson, the president of General Electric. Controlling the very powerful WPA, dollar-a-year men like these and many other executives organized the system to be most favorable to the largest corporations. The government suspended all antitrust laws, paid for the construction cost of expanded or new defense factories, and guaranteed handsome profits with cost overrun plus profit contracts.

Wartime Production Miracle with Lasting Effects on the Economy

This system produced the wartime production miracle that virtually won the war for the Allies, but the system also produced costly failures and corruption. The legendary Howard Hughes, a supposed airplane design genius, received many war contracts worth millions from alleged bribery but never managed to get a plane into the war. The national idol Henry Ford was another who increased his private fortune by millions in contracts granted to produce a state-of-the-art bomber at his new huge Willow Run plant where the government built a town for new workers and the world's largest factory. Failing for most of the term of the war, Ford, the great mass manufacturer, finally got a few bombers in the air before war's end. To ensure that the defense contractors produced war material up to specification, Congress ran an oversight committee headed by Sen. Harry Truman. On frequent occasions, Truman found corporations trying to increase profits with substandard goods for the armed forces. The Anaconda Copper Company, for instance, secretly made an inferior alloy for the specified metal; it got a fine and received damning headlines for war profiteering.

Government planning like this over four years produced even greater centralization in the economy. By 1945, the top 100 American firms had gained 70 percent of the market for civilian and military services and goods, up from 30 percent in 1940. Corporate monopolies got bigger; the small businesses struggled or failed. The military procurement branch, ignoring the smaller manufacturers, continued closer ties with the largest military supply corporations. The military became essential to the economy.

1946: The Employment Act with Support for the Economy

The American public overwhelmingly came to one common conclusion about the overall economic pattern of the wartime years on the home front: that only government spending in such a massive way could dissolve the high Depression-era unemployment still existing at the beginning of 1940. As the government gave more and more defense contracts to industry for preparedness and later, after lend-lease, to aid Allies, the country's jobless rate steadily dropped. After Pearl Harbor in December 1941, the government increased war contracts to industries soon to produce at record levels, which created a full employment economy and unprecedented private sector income and savings.

At war's end, Americans' common hope was to continue to perpetuate broad affluence. Although not necessarily familiar with the new deficit spending theories of the British economist John Maynard Keynes, following the war many in the public had come to realize that the magic formula was for Washington to spend to counter a business recession. This would expand the economy and, thus, generate more federal tax income without necessarily adjusting rates.

A dramatic change in federal fiscal policy came in the immediate postwar years when the government maintained high tax and spending levels for domestic programs and for increased international aid and military programs to combat the Soviets in the early Cold War. Validating the theory and recent public experience, the Employment Act of 1946 was passed by Congress to ensure that the federal government did everything possible to ensure "maximum" production, employment, and consumption. This fiscal policy would be the keystone to the next 25 years of continued growth and prosperity in the country.

The wartime public's huge savings combined with pent-up demand created a sudden tide of consumer spending once the country's economy could again produce for this greatly expanded home economy. The government's continued high taxes and spending directly aided businesses, especially the large corporations, in this reconversion. The postwar boom resulted from the continuation of two government policies: high taxation and peak spending to corporations. This sustained peak employment due to peak production for both growing civilian and military markets. The postwar economy was based on a core of big government (vastly expanded from the prewar period) and big business (the top corporations in each leading industry) and, secondarily, big labor (the AFL and CIO major craft and industrial unions constituting a peak combined membership of 35 percent of all laborers in 1953).

1947: A Military Industrial State Sustains a Growing Economy

The government also continued orders to corporate military contractors to build up defenses against the perceived growing threat of communists in the Cold War. The United States first formally acknowledged this threat with the 1947 Truman Doctrine, which promised military aid to friendly countries fighting for democracy against an internal or external threat from the Soviets. In 1948, Congress passed a new Selective Service Act, a year after the 1940 law had been allowed to expire. In 1950, only five years after the end of World War II, the Korean War began and the newest draft enlisted 800,000 in 16 months' time. By this time, the federal budget allocated about 50 percent for the military.

Both Cold War liberals and conservatives could agree on this one thing: that the spending was necessary for the protection of the country and its values. The pump was primed by this Cold War spending and the result was full production and full employment. In the Korean War, the country was so rich it could afford both guns and butter—easily fulfilling both consumer and military demands and still growing to the satisfaction of the public.

Big government spent a large percentage of its gross tax revenue for contracting with top corporations to supply the military in the Cold War. Five years after the arrival of peace in 1945, the military spending portion of the annual national budget had risen to about 50 percent after an immediate postwar drop. These massive government expenditures created waves of new high-paying union jobs in military preparedness industries such as airplane manufacturing, electronics, and many others.

The Cold War's increasing tensions spurred the military spending. In 1949, the Soviet Union exploded its first atomic bomb. The United States responded with a go-ahead to develop the hydrogen bomb. The superpowers' nuclear arms race was on, with each side producing seemingly endless new competing models of missiles and warheads. Competition also reigned in conventional weapons. The corporate–military defense nexus absorbed multimillions as the United States assumed growing global commitments and vowed to contain communism by force anywhere on the world. This meant the country paid daily to maintain its military forces in NATO and around the world in a state of continuous and immediate preparedness. The cost would be billions of dollars to constantly update military hardware and to maintain the largest standing armed forces in peacetime in the nation's history.

The Middle Class: Ever-expanding and Ever-consuming

The ever-expanding middle-class sector of the economy evolved from both salaried and wage earners' production in both the defense and civilian sectors of the growing national economy. Highly paid blue-collar and most white-collar

Rush of buyers waiting to inspect a model of a popular-priced ($7,990) two-bedroom house being mass-produced on Long Island, New York, in early 1949. (Library of Congress)

workers constituted this dominant and growing class in America. Defense industries contributed greatly to increasing national consumption by paying their union workers a continually rising wage adjusted to the gains in the consumer price index along with fringe health and welfare benefits.

Producers for the civilian market sold record volumes of goods for a variety of factors: the expanding middle-class, the rise of television as the greatest marketing tool ever invented, and the built-in calculated obsolescence of products based on yearly changes in models, many of which involved only superfluous changes in style. With new models appearing regularly, advertising played on middle-class status anxieties of keeping up with the Joneses and not appearing to fall behind by not owning this year's model.

The system that evolved in the postwar years drove the economy for the next 25 years of the country's record continuous prosperity. The system had a variety of serious flaws, the most obvious was that it depended on almost continuous war preparedness, approaching a near garrison state. Waste was built in, with still usable older models forsaken to the dump for the newer, more fashionable models. The corporate-union private welfare states, excluding the other two-thirds of nonunion workers, might well have impeded any powerful push for national health care.

Also, manpower shortages in wartime and war's technological spin-offs in peacetime led to many advances in factory machinery. One in particular was very important in speeding the country to a postindustrial society—automated machinery to replace manpower. This also posed an ominous threat to the future of unions. Automation, just begun in these years, was the wave of the future, and it eventually minimized the need for many blue-collar workers in farming and automobile manufacturing. The UAW would suffer long term as a result. Many once-powerful unions, like the West Coast Longshoremen's Union, when faced with the fait accompli of container ship automation, saw no recourse but for their once-militant leader, Harry Bridges, to negotiate a contract that grand-fathered existing members while allowing automated machinery to gradually supplant manpower, thus diminishing the ultimate size and power of his once-feared union. In adopting wide-scale automation, corporations would eventually undercut a foundation of the postwar boom—the vast aggregate of highly paid union members who provided the power of mass consumption to sustain a large portion of the economy.

Biographies

Fred Allen Hartley, 1902–1969

Cosponsor of the Antiunion 1947 Taft-Hartley Act

In 1946, the Republican Party won their first majority in Congress since 1928. Hartley (R-N.J.) had been one of few representatives of his party with continuous service bridging the two dates. In 1950, he ended his service with ten terms in office. In all that time, he is best known for being a cosponsor with Senator Taft (R-Ohio) of the bill that bears both their names. Congressional majorities passed it over President Truman's veto; it was known thereafter as a stringent antiunion law, modifying and restricting the 1935 prolabor Wagner Act, often termed labor's Magna Carta. The provision most objectionable to unions was Section 14(b), which allowed states to pass so-called right-to-work laws. All southern states and many western and midwest states did so, thus allowing newly hired workers refrain from joining the existing union. This endangered the closed-shop arrangement that required all new workers to join the union to continue employment, a right previously won by unions in hard fights.

John Maynard Keynes, 1883–1946

British Economist and Macroeconomic Theorist

The theories of Keynes proved successful in leading the United States to the economic miracle of massive wartime production, ensuring victory for the Allies. Propounded in the 1930s, his theories propelled capitalist states to start massive government spending to raise a modern economy out of an economic slump. During the war years, the United States raised the amount of spending to a height that ended the Depression, proving the real success of a Keynesian economy. In such an economy, labor benefited enormously because this theory was based on full employment and production. The United States reaffirmed this type of economy as early as 1946, when Congress passed the Full Employment Act, ensuring continued public spending for both military and civilian consumer needs to create full production and jobs for all. The Keynesian Revolution brought mass prosperity and an expanding economy to America for the next 25 years.

Fiorello Henry LaGuardia, 1882–1947

Congressman and Three-term New York Mayor

LaGuardia was one of the most famous politicians of his day. Throughout his public service, he remained a backer of labor. A life-long reformer and early supporter of the New Deal, he was a co-sponsor of the 1932 Norris–LaGuardia Act, which greatly lessened the use of injunctions against workers on strike. He ran successfully for his third and final four-year term, 1940–45, again as a fusion candidate with the union-backed American Labor Party ticket (begun with his organizational help in 1936) while nominally being a highly untraditional, liberal Republican. New York City workers who had been unemployed in the 1930s remembered his tireless and successful efforts in getting more wartime contracts so full employment and production returned to the city during the conflict. LaGuardia was renowned for

For over three decades during the first half of the 20th century, Fiorello La Guardia played a unique and important role in American politics, first as a congressman and then as mayor of New York City. (Library of Congress)

settling strikes in the city. His more conservative critics claimed he favored organized labor; some irresponsibly called him a "communist." He ignored them and remained a proud populist, the only mayor at the time who completed 12 years in office.

Bernard Melzer, 1914–2006

Labor Law Expert

Melzer became one of the country's top experts in labor law, starting in 1946 when a wave of strikes brought about by worker unrest over inflation caused a peacetime need to interpret further the major labor laws already on the books from the 1930s but largely ignored during wartime with its unique mutual union–management accords. In 1946, after assisting with the draft charter of the United Nations and acting as a prosecutor at the Nuremberg war crimes trials, Melzer became a law professor at the University of Chicago. From that point on, he quickly made his name by interpreting and clarifying laws relating to workers, based on the 1935 National Labor Relations Act and, in 1947, the restrictive Taft-Hartley Act. His writings and advocacy helped clarify such complicated issues as federal-state jurisdiction in labor law, the general legality of union boycotts against suppliers of the primary, and strike-targeted company matters.

Phillip Murray, 1886–1952

Labor Leader and President of the CIO throughout the 1940s

Phillip Murray worked his way up the union hierarchy through the United Mine Workers union led by John L. Lewis, who befriended and mentored Murray. Murray achieved the gargantuan task of unionizing the steel industry in 1937, became president of the new independent Congress of Industrial Organizations in 1940, and continued in that office until his death in 1952. Lewis and Murray had a breach in 1942, with Murray supporting Roosevelt, the war effort, and the union's no-strike pledge. Lewis resisted these, leading to the UMW break from the CIO. During this rocky decade, Murray propelled the union movement to steady membership and wage gains and fought for racial equality and against the 1947 Taft-Hartley Act. He also called for the removal of any local leaders who refused to sign the anticommunist oath (although eventually he had to do so against some who jeopardized his own cause).

Gunnar Myrdal, 1898–1987

Swedish Economist and Analyst of American Race Inequality

In 1944, Gunnar Myrdal published a book, *The American Dilemma,* which was the culmination of a Carnegie Foundation study he headed on the American race problem. His prime message was that the country's racism would indefinitely thwart the realization of the nation's ideals. He predicted that the country's African American workers would be caught up in an endless cycle of the lowest wages and poverty, a condition geared to depress the general wage levels in areas with concentrations of African American workers. Unionization of these workers was a solution but the postwar Operation Dixie, the powerful union effort to organize the American South, met with steadfast, bitter opposition from the area's employers and white supremacists. In place of unionization, Myrdal stated, the federal government's efforts to improve working conditions and provide a minimum wage would only lessen the available jobs for African Americans and bring pressure for increased automation. Ironically, this "solution" made matters worse for the working poor among Southern African Americans.

Walter Reuther, 1907–1970

Humanitarian, Leader of UAW, and CIO President

Walter Reuther was a life-long labor leader, famed for heading a UAW union local that in 1937 won the first organizing campaign in the auto industry by using the sit-down strike against General Motors. In 1946, he became head of the UAW and was the person responsible for winning the cost-of-living allowances clause in a contract with General Motors in 1948. This ensured that union autoworkers got a yearly wage increase tied to inflation. Then he built up the pension and health benefits of his membership, almost single-handedly bringing an elite group of blue-collar workers into the comfortable middle class. In 1955, he became president of the CIO and continued the fight for similar gains for other unions. He was also instrumental in bringing about the powerful AFL-CIO merger.

Walter Reuther was a union organizer who rose to head one of the country's largest unions, the United Automobile Workers. A Socialist in the 1930s, he became prominent in the anticommunist Left of the labor movement. (Library of Congress)

REFERENCES AND FURTHER READINGS

Anderson, Karen T. 1982. "Last Hired, First Fired: Black Women Workers during World War II," *Journal of American History,* 69:82–97.

Barnard, John. 1983. *Walter Reuther and the Rise of the Auto Workers.* New York: Little, Brown and Company.

Bernstein, Irving. 1969. *Turbulent Years: A History of the American Worker, 1933–1941.* Boston: Houghton Mifflin.

"The Decision," *Time* magazine, June 3, 1946. http://www.time.com/time/magazine/article/0,9171,797791–2,00.html. Accessed August 21, 2008.

Dubofsky, Melvin, and Warren Van Tine. 1977. *John L. Lewis: A Biography.* Urbana: University of Illinois Press.

Foster, James C. 1975. *The Union Politic: The CIO Political Action Committee.* Columbia: University of Missouri Press.

Gregory, Chester W. 1974. *Women in Defense Work during World War II: An Analysis of the Labor Problem and Women's Rights.* New York: Exposition Press.

Lichtenstein, Nelson. 1983. *Labor's War at Home: The CIO in World War II.* Cambridge and New York: Cambridge University Press.

McClure, Arthur F. 1969. *The Truman Administration and the Problems of Postwar Labor.* Rutherford, NJ: Fairleigh Dickinson University Press.

Meier, August, and Elliott Rudwick. 1979. *Black Detroit and the Rise of the UAW.* Oxford: Oxford University Press.

Milton, David. 1982. *The Politics of U.S. Labor.* New York: Monthly Review Press.

Seidman, Joel. 1953. *American Labor from Detroit to Reconversion.* Chicago: University of Chicago Press.

Sward, Keith. 1948. *The Legend of Henry Ford.* New York: Rinehart.

Education

In the 1940s, the change in education was so profound that this became a primary factor in altering the class structure. In turn, this caused a transformation in society that lasted over the next 25 years. In the postwar years, 1945–1949, Americans in greater numbers than ever experienced some college learning or received a degree. This resulted mostly from the G.I. Bill, which offered all 16 million veterans a free college education, with living expenses paid by the federal government. This established a strong precedent as aid from Washington, D.C., went directly to veterans who then paid fees to local institutions of education countrywide. A college education increasingly became a standard for professional success in society, and more so in the future.

The level of education is the strongest indicator of social class in the country. Thus, the G.I. Bill acted as an upward elevator to a middle-class lifestyle for veterans. Many of these had been born to families that had little realistic expectation of that type of social mobility being a possibility for them or any of their offspring, especially in the era of the 1930s Great Depression. Broadening the country's middle class through education was only one way the G.I. Bill aided veterans; the bill also provided for low-interest small business and home loans with nothing down and low monthly payments. The federal government had singled out the 16 million veterans, mostly young white males, for special rewards in return for their service to the country. As a result, white males of the generation that had served in the war would gain new social status and professional and political leadership roles that lasted decades. Meanwhile, a majority of adults—the lower class in general but also the middle-class wives of these men and African American veterans—were left relatively lacking in power and opportunities.

From 1900 to 1940, the country held out various educational standards to a young person wishing to be successful. Finishing grade school was all that was necessary in 1900. Getting a high school diploma was an expectation arising in the 1930s. By 1940, a majority got as far as completing some years of high school before going on to the labor market or entering the armed forces. By this time, young women finished high school at a greater rate than opposite sex peers. Few of either sex went on to college.

What a difference the last half of the decade meant for the society of the country. In short, the postwar national education policy began the vast change in the social fabric of the country, laid the foundations for the vast middle class, and changed gender roles essential to a new consumer-based capitalism. This new capitalism was defended and safeguarded by higher taxes for the support of the military and related industries to safeguard the newfound well-being and relative security of this generation from any threats, namely that of communism.

Universities and colleges throughout the decade experienced a dismal period, 1940–1945, followed by a dizzyingly successful period, 1945–1949. Continuing the trend of the 1930s, higher education up to 1945 suffered falling enrollments and financial difficulties due to the national draft taking college age students. Therefore, these institutions were deeply grateful for any aid monies coming from the federal government for such endeavors as certificate programs or on-campus Officer Training Schools. The war's emergency situation overcame the otherwise strong local opposition to any federal interference in solely local prerogatives and initiatives in this area.

A democratizing trend in educational opportunity started in the 1940s, and yet a large proportion of the population—African Americans, women, the poor, and many in the South—were left behind with far less than equal educations. African Americans totaled 1.3 million of the veterans, yet the institutions of 17 middle-border and southern states had two systems of public schools, one for whites and another for blacks, equal by law but grossly unequal in reality. Altogether, these states maintained some 100 black colleges but none had professional schools for law or medicine. In the North, de facto segregation, by local custom, meant administrative quotas limited African American enrollees. Women veterans attended college but often dropped out to marry and have children. In short, the G.I. Bill was admirably race neutral, but the United States was divided by race.

Forgotten and left behind, this sizable lower social strata lacked any future hope of raising education levels largely due to race, poverty, and the impoverished southern schools. In 1944, Gunnar Myrdal, Swedish sociologist, wrote in his book *The American Dilemma* that the country ran the risk of perpetuating an endless cycle of poverty unless the country's realities came closer to its ideals—for instance universal versus segregated public education.

Higher education in the crucial area of science fell below the standards set by the best colleges in the world, including those in Britain and prewar Germany. One major reason was that the American public often confused scientific advances with technological advances. Yet, scientists in basic research needed to discover new theories from which derived concrete applications or technology. Europe had produced a great number of pure scientists, and—fortunately for the United States—many had fled Nazism or fascism and had come to the United States as émigrés in the late 1930s; for example, Albert Einstein, Enrico Fermi, and many more. With the Manhattan Project, the United States began with a given, atomic theory, and made possible the applied technology in the form of the workable atomic bomb, which would have been impossible to achieve without the work of basic theoretical scientists.

The World War II wonder drug, sulfa, the first of the world's antibiotics, was also first developed in Europe by Nazi scientists in the early 1930s. However, the organization and money for its manufacture and distribution was made possible through this country's pharmaceutical firms' skills in secondary research, investments, and organization. The result was dramatic—hundreds of thousands of U.S combat personnel were saved from death because, for the first time in any war, there was a drug, sulfa, to prevent deadly infection in wounds. In the Pacific Theater, this may have tipped the balance of war against a sulfa-deprived Japan, a country even more lacking in basic science than the United States.

TIMELINE

1940   Education levels of the populace: 50 percent have had some grade school and the other 50 percent have some high school; of those finishing high school, roughly 15 percent go on to college.

Sulfa-based chemical compounds are the first medical wonder drug used widely to cure deadly diseases such as those caused by strep germs. From 1942 to 1945, this drug will keep U.S. casualties extremely low by preventing wounds from becoming infected.

1941   Public colleges see declining enrollments and diminished endowments for this and the prior year, continuing a trend from the 1930s. Private colleges survive better because their endowments are not endangered by lower tax yields.

President Roosevelt sets up the Office of Scientific Research and Development out of which develops the top-secret Manhattan Project to develop the atomic bomb.

1942   Wartime federal aid to higher education occurs as grants go to colleges for such things as Officer Training School and individual training in specialties. IQ tests are required to find those best suited to become specialists. This aid is a prelude to the later G.I. Bill.

High schools suffer a great loss in qualified teachers who leave either for war or for more pay in war industries. Teacher credentials are waived to gain replacements. These schools receive no federal aid and have long been considered the exclusive domain of state and local governments.

1943   Penicillin, the next and better wonder drug after sulfa, sees its first use in North Africa. It will supplant sulfa in the postwar period.

One million students drop out of high school.

1944   College enrollment due to federal aid decreases as those monies are gradually withdrawn when students attending college are called up for military duty.

The high wartime success rate of those selected by IQ tests to attend college for specialist training in the military—in many cases soldiers who could not ordinarily afford to go to college—leads lawmakers to support broad opportunity for higher education for all returning veterans. This idea spurs the drafting of the G.I. Bill.

The G.I. Bill passes; it provides education and other benefits to returning veterans; as written, it is race and gender neutral.

Gunnar Myrdal, the Swedish sociologist, states in his *The American Dilemma* that racism is a self-perpetuating cycle that keeps the United States from realizing its ideals.

1945   Higher education institutions, which have benefited from government aid in wartime, wish to continue the relationship with research grants in many areas, primarily for the military.

A Harvard report, "General Education in a Free Society," advocates a new liberal education as a required area for all majors. Curriculums had become very pragmatic and career-oriented in war years.

Two-billion-dollar investment in the Manhattan Project brings results with the production of the two bombs dropped on Japan on August 7 and 9 to end the war.

1946   G.I. Bill's provisions in effect for 16 million veterans provide college tuition aid and living expenses (wife and family included) for any veteran. Vocational schools up their enrollments due to the bill's aid (proportionally more African American veterans choose this path). Veterans totaling 1.5 million are in college, and the numbers will increase over the next seven years, democratizing higher education.

Segregation, both legal and de facto, decrease the opportunities for 1.3 million African American veterans to take full advantage of the G.I. Bill.

The Computer Age begins with the giant ENIAC computer at the University of Pennsylvania.

DDT is introduced as a "miracle" pesticide (later, the effects are found to be devastating to the ecological life cycle of birds and animals).

1947   The Truman Doctrine begins the Cold War (for the next 40 years this confrontation will create a need for federal aid for research in higher education, in some instances causing the university aim of free inquiry to conflict with secret research).

1948   Truman's Fair Deal aims to further broad education goals but has only slight success.

The G.I. Bill extends to those in future service to the military in the Cold War due to the new draft bill, the second in peacetime.

Congress, led by Republicans and Southern Democrats, votes down Truman's bill, which would have given federal courts jurisdiction in all lynching cases.

Truman segregates the U.S. armed forces by an Executive Order.

1949   Educational levels of the populace: some 60 percent finish high school. College graduates double the percentage of 1940 and continue to rise. A college diploma becomes the best means to upward social mobility for a working-class person. Income for middle-class families rises markedly.

Expenditures for the G.I. Bill benefits make up 30 percent of the national welfare budget. The national economy, in turn, has expanded greatly due to the bill's successful results.

WAR AND EDUCATION

The military was a growing influence, and then a determining force, in shaping U.S. education on all levels from 1940 to V-J Day in 1945. From 1940 to 1941, the government's own defense preparedness and then military assistance to democratic allies meant that federal contracts were flowing in greater volume to industries that, in the late 1930s, ran at far less than maximum production levels. Starting the 1940s, with defense production increasing along with jobs, the military was bound to impact all institutions of learning in the nation.

Education Weakened by War Boom Economy

Professors and teachers, in 1940 and 1941, were either leaving education or were eager to do so, students were even dropping out—because many could gain solid, high-paying jobs for the first time since the 1929 stock market crash. Continuing a 1930s trend, public colleges lost enrollment and nearly depleted their endowments with little state monies available. College presidents and administrators adapted education in a number of ways. B.A. degrees could be completed in three years, and medical and law degrees required a year less than usual to complete. Colleges offered correspondence courses, and the curriculum reverted to a traditional one, favoring such practical degrees as engineering. Electives, which had previously expanded the liberal arts, were eliminated. Whenever possible, new courses were added to appeal to military needs.

After the country declared war, military expansion and economic growth rose so greatly as to affect high schools in the most drastic ways. Nearly 350,000 teachers left education for the military or for more pay in war industries; inexperienced teachers replaced those who left. Boomtown schools that were overcrowded with the children of migrants faced teacher shortages. Many high schools soon dispensed with the need for teacher credentials or issued emergency credentials for the replacements. A vocational curriculum was in place. Few teachers, however, were inspiring in this area. The government offered a limited number of scholarships to students who showed promise in technical areas that were calculated to be useful to the military.

Students also dropped out of high school to work in the booming economy; in 1943, one million students left high school. The result was overcrowded classrooms, inept teachers, and a drop in standards. Secondary schools' national achievement levels, already low from the 1930s, continued during the war. The draft data, gathered from tests and examinations given millions of young Americans during the war, indicated embarrassingly substandard national results. The military turned away hundreds of thousands of physically fit young men who lacked the ability to read or write; these were labeled as 4-F status. Many others were functionally illiterate although they had a high school education. Others had not finished grade school.

Once the war started, colleges suffered a drop in enrollments; they welcomed whatever federal aid was offered to them. Once this aid began, colleges later had difficulty dispensing with it. The war made for an overwhelming military presence on the country's campuses. Linked to military needs, federal aid went to institutions of higher education, especially the large and prestigious ones. The aid had two forms: first, the Army sent thousands of promising high school graduates to get one or two years of specific college courses before going to Officer Training Schools, and second, the Navy and other services also sent draftees to college for a limited period to study particular specialties. All received training certificates, not diplomas, for their limited time. While on the campus, these students wore their military uniforms, so their presence in great numbers was unmistakable to others.

Federal Aid to Colleges for Military Goals

Colleges were very grateful for the sizable government sums given for wartime military programs. Such programs were some of the seeds for the 1944 G.I. Bill that offered free education and expenses to all veterans of the war. The bill was the precedent for the future when the norm became federal aid to higher education.

Colleges leaped at the wartime opportunity to begin programs that caused the military to draw more trainees. The University of Chicago set up a new Institute for Military Studies. During the war, Harvard was proud to have become a leading institution of military studies and research. Its scientists contributed to the discovery of napalm, the fiery foam dropped from planes primarily to destroy jungle foliage cover. Humans, both civilian and combatants, were also vulnerable to the flesh-burning adhesive substance. The wartime curriculums of such colleges were distinctly utilitarian. Anti-intellectual, some would say; a *New York Times* poll found that 80 percent of colleges did not offer a course in American history during this time.

In 1944, colleges had a shock—the military was pulling all servicemen out of the training certificate programs and sending them directly into active duty to join the forces already fighting the war. It was precipitous and necessary due to the increased manpower needs arising from wartime casualties and enemy forces that became more desperate to stave off certain defeat.

This loss in enrollment made the colleges value the prior government aid all the more; colleges were grateful for the smaller amount that was still forthcoming

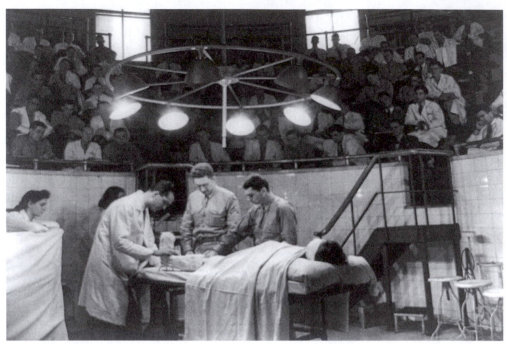

Fellow students watching two U.S. Army medical students attempt a diagnosis of a leg injury under the charge of a surgeon at Bellevue Hospital, affiliate of New York University Medical School, as part of the U.S. Army's specialized training course, 1944. (Library of Congress)

for the draftees who remained in medical, dental, and engineering programs. These programs were streamlined and condensed to speed graduation. The federally funded program that sustained many colleges provided management training for companies that were retooling to military production, and later reconverting to peacetime production again.

Educational Deficiencies Revealed in the Draft

In 1940, the first peacetime draft in the country's history went into effect. Many of those called up at this time had induction test results that showed the physical and mental scars the 1930s had left on the young population. Fifty percent of the draftees had ended their education at some point in elementary school (grades one through eight). Although almost all had a grade school education, examiners found that hundreds of thousands of draftees were illiterate, or functionally so; these draftees were declared 4-F. Examiners also found that many of them lacked any purpose in life, a sure sign of an upbringing in the Depression when hope and self-determination had become luxuries for many. The average mental age, they determined, was 14.

Only 15 percent of draftees had ever enrolled in college. These usually were not the ones with highest intelligence but those who could afford it, the sons and daughters of the wealthy. Of those who had no chance to go to college, it is estimated that 50 percent had better than average intelligence. Higher education had long been a privilege of the few (not the right of the many). It was so in the 1930s and, for the most part, throughout the war.

College Education and 1930s Society

The effects of the Depression continued into the 1940s as state and city colleges and universities often faced depleted endowments, cut back local or state public budgets, and declining enrollments. Administrators in public higher education frequently found themselves in such dire circumstances that they were in great need of aid from almost any source.

Private institutions of higher education, on the other hand, had fared reasonably well in the Depression decade. Their large endowments had continued to grow. The wealthy continued family traditions of sending their children to certain Ivy League or Seven Sisters colleges. American higher education then provided an elite class and status distinction in a society that, as a whole, proclaimed to be egalitarian.

By 1940, a different attitude about college had developed among the less educated in general, and even among college graduates themselves—it was simply not worth it. Everyone seemed to know someone with a college degree who was on relief or working as a longshoreman, teamster, or in a similar blue-collar job. There was truth in this contention—in a 1930s poll of the Harvard class of 1911, one in eight was on relief or forced to live with relatives.

High School Education and 1930s Society

The nation's high schools by 1940 had experienced a much different situation. Student enrollments were bursting; the 1930s had made high schools the only remaining refuge for many of the destitute, jobless young. Yet, most high schools received their funds from local property taxes, and the share of taxes going to schools steadily declined, which left these institutions poorer than ever, and with the most students ever.

Most of these students were there not so much to learn but to pass time. What is more, some high schools had distinct advantages for their many poor students —namely, heated spaces and free lunches. In 1935, 20 million Americans were on relief, and of that number, 40 percent were aged 16 or under. Poor families had more children. With crowded living quarters, many were sent off not so much to get an education but just to be out of the way. The physical effects of poverty often made learning difficult—for instance, in New York City in 1937, the health department found that 20 percent of all schoolchildren were mal-nourished. In some coal mining areas, it was 90 percent of children.

Teachers in the 1930s—even though overwhelmed by social problems—were some of the most dedicated professionals in the country. The historian William Manchester writes that the teachers of that time in Chicago were some of the era's true heroes and even martyrs. Rather than close schools and leave a half million students without any chance for education, the teachers proposed to re-ceive pay for only 5 of the 12 months of 1932. To get by, many teachers mort-gaged and eventually lost their own houses to bank foreclosure. Did the adult public appreciate them? No. The general public envied teachers for having "depression-proof" jobs and approved of teachers getting cuts in pay to lessen local taxes. This was true all over America.

War Emergency Allows Federal Monies to Colleges

In the past, strong local opposition always existed to federal aid to education; since 1937, Congress had annually voted down a bill providing government aid nationally to education. However, the government in the war emergency made inroads. Large amounts of the federal taxpayer money went to cities and states to aid education. Secondary schools had select areas of study for which students could qualify for government scholarships. Higher educational institutions pro-vided a variety of programs for the military. Many college programs were pos-sible only at government expense. The colleges were the biggest beneficiaries of this new, tradition-bending, government largesse, suddenly made necessary by the exigencies of war.

In another new development resulting from war, intelligence testing was used to determine those best qualified to go to college. In late 1943, the military began cutting back on its college training programs, but it retained a minimal program of college preparation for candidates to the Officers Training Program. The military called on the College Entrance Examinations Board to determine the applicants with the best minds to send on to college. Merit, not wealth, was suddenly a determinant in going to college.

War reversed the old conventional wisdom about college in other ways. In-telligence testing aside, the earlier broad training programs proved that a wide spectrum of youth were capable of succeeding at the college level. This proved, in a democratic sense, all could claim a legitimate right to higher education. But because most lacked the funds, federal aid became necessary to realize equal opportunity in higher education. In the past, without this aid, the best minds of a generation had often gone to waste for lack of money while many dullards had gone to college solely because of family wealth.

Higher education officials, having realized the benefits of federal aid, became strong advocates for continuing it. This caused wartime rethinking of the pur-

Harvard enrollment hits a new high, Cambridge, Massachusetts, 1946. (Library of Congress)

pose and role of a college in a free society. The idea, overlooked by the pressing needs of war, was that the role of a college was to be an island of independent, critical, and reflective learning. The individual aim was to further rational thought. A growing number of rational thinkers ensured progress for humanity in the world. Objectivity and positivism were prized goals. Yet this idea was fading. The new idea coming into prominence held that the purpose of college was to aid the government and society in pragmatically solving the immediate problems of war. In doing so, colleges willingly accepted their greater dependence and reliance on government.

The government, in turn, realized that colleges could solve the government's problems. During war, the relationship of the federal government to higher education was determined largely by the military. This involved a pattern whereby the Army or Navy chose the students and their courses and then paid their tuition. Government control of the overall curriculum was kept to the discretion of the college.

The war created a circumstance at home that initiated a trend toward big changes in the country's higher education. One such change was the beginning of the democratization of college: it was a right, not a privilege, to attend.

Colleges welcomed the extra enrollments along with the necessary federal aid to education. College also became a problem-solving institution for both the military and industry.

World War II gave America's institutions of higher learning a new mission. In June 1944, the government passed the G.I. Bill, which gave a new urge to the democratizing already under way in education. When the bill passed, the first of the war veterans already were returning home. The bill's aim was to provide a package of benefits to ease the transition to peacetime. The education benefit was extremely generous, offering a free college education with living expenses to any of the 11 million active veterans due to return home upon victory. In all, 16 million qualified. Colleges approved of the general provisions: federal education aid, a democratic student spectrum, and little government control. The bill instantly wedded colleges closely to government. In the long view, it shaped American education for decades into the future.

1945 Harvard Report and Liberal Arts Education in Colleges

Benchmark change also came in the overall philosophy governing education not only in the colleges but also on all levels leading up to it. This would shape American schooling for the future. The change originated in 1945, when Harvard University published the seminal report "General Education in a Free Society." The report called for a new "liberal education" to mold a "well-rounded" person. The aim was to give the individual an abiding knowledge of how his or her own culture's values, traditions, and beliefs have evolved. These were to come through a study of Western civilization and American history. A citizen educated in this way from grade school to high school and possibly college, the report held, would be the ideal participant in the ongoing life of this country's democracy. All individuals had the right to enjoy a life of the mind and immersion in cultural pursuits beyond their daily jobs. Whether or not one went on to college, this should be the educational right of each individual.

Such an education in the liberal arts had never before been attempted with such breadth, covering the entire nation, and with such depth, covering education from the first grade to the senior year of college. High schools had previously divided their curriculums in two parts: the vocational and the liberal arts. The new thinking was the two should be combined. Then, in college, every beginning student should be required to take some courses in each of three fields: science, social science and the humanities. After finishing these requirements in this new liberal arts core curriculum, the student would specialize in a chosen major field of study.

The 1945 Harvard report created a change in the college curriculum so graduates would benefit from a deeper understanding of and broader participation

American's Wartime Ignorance of Foreign Cultures and Geography: The Islamic World

Upon entering the global war after Pearl Harbor, the American armed forces were soon engaged in widespread fighting in the Pacific and European Theaters and in remote geographic places—in the Pacific islands, then North African and Middle Eastern tribal and colonial domains. The great majority of persons at home knew little or nothing in about these places. However, the entertainment world of music and the movies had supplied a false, romantic, mythic representation that sufficed for "knowledge" of these places. The American school system for the 1930s and wartime 1940s had not included education about foreign geography or cultures in the curriculum. Only very curious adults were likely to brief themselves on the prior histories of the areas of combat.

Young recruits were in the same predicament, as demonstrated in the first massive United States engagement in Europe—the invasion of North Africa and the thrust eastward toward Egypt. All of this area and the Near East made up the Islamic World and constituted some 70 million believers, mostly Arab speakers and a composite of Arabs and other ethnicities, Persian, Kurd, Berber, Druise, and others. Muslims were split between two groups of believers, the majority Sunni and minority Shia.

The War Department gave a 50-odd page pamphlet of background and guidelines to the invading forces because they realized these young men had, at best, a "movies sense" of the area—the so-called exotic East of minarets, bazaars, bearded sheiks, and veiled woman. Do not expect this, the pamphlet stated. Expect facts like the following: Muslims felt inherently superior to those of any other religions. The culture had no racial divides and, ironically, although not democratic, the relationships amongst superiors and inferiors (like servants) was quite co-equal (War Department 1943).

So not to offend or antagonize the locals (some 25 million Muslims in North Africa alone), guidelines included these "don'ts": never offer alcohol; never enter a mosque; never gaze at, converse with, or remove the veil from a Muslim woman.

American fighting men had their own reactions from their experience during the ongoing campaign. Arabs was the term GIs used for everyone. They disliked the desert climate; it was torrid and the fine sand lodged as grit on everyone. Compared to the United States, the GIs felt the region lacked general hygiene, and its men took advantage of women, for example, by having them carry the heavier burden. If men seemed overly friendly with one another, on the other hand, the handbook explained, in the Muslim culture, two males holding hands simply were friends, nothing more.

GIs found the region had little to their personal liking. The locals often appeared indifferent to both warring Axis and Allies. The Allies had no great sense of gratitude from locals for being liberated from the Nazis; a major reason for this was, of course, that Muslims saw the war as merely another inter-Christian rivalry with an Allied victory likely, which would mean a return to the disliked status of being a European colony.

in the ongoing life of democracy in America. The democratizing trend set in motion by war was to extend far ahead beyond the 1940s decade.

Postwar and Education

American society, anticipating the end of the war, granted a handsome benefit package to "our boys" as a show of their gratitude to the returning armed forces men and women. The package singled out only these mostly young and over-whelmingly white male veterans (excluding any other age and gender stratum of non-veteran society) to be the beneficiaries. It was to be a uniquely generous, one-of-a-kind, broad and varied social welfare package, and it was more expensive than any earlier 1930s New Deal program. The conservative political majority of the time meant this G.I. Bill to be exclusively for those deemed deserving, the postwar military. They opposed broadening this group to any domestic civilian group.

Equally as deserving as the 16 million service veterans, it was argued, were the millions of workers at home responsible for the manufacturing miracle that produced the war material necessary for these servicemen to outfight the enemy. Victory in the end was in equal part due to the effort of stateside war workers and active-duty servicemen, yet only the latter earned postwar benefits. That lawmakers passed a restricted bill was likely due to their political sense that a wider bill would have caused many veterans to react angrily because of their feeling that stateside workers had grown prosperous without risking their lives. Thus, legislators wished to benefit the servicemen who, while overseas, had the feeling of being left behind by their peers on the home front. The bill, however, was more than a "catch-up" package that guaranteed jobs for all vets. In actuality, it was a "go-ahead" package that allowed veterans who used the benefits to become better educated, better housed, and better employed in the future than their nonveteran peers.

The G.I. Bill's Wide Coverage Brings Results

The bill's design appealed to conservatives and liberals alike, the former because it kept overall government control to a minimum. For instance, the bill did not provide jobs but paid opportunities for the individual to gain training or education to obtain a better job. The bill overall was progressive legislation—the first significant revival of prewar New Deal type programs—and this appealed to liberals. Conservatives approved that the beneficiaries were limited only to those completing duty in the military; liberals wanted a broader spectrum of beneficiaries to ensure a new postwar society. As it was, the bill helped many working-class veterans achieve their 1930s and wartime American Dream of gaining an education and moving into the middle class (still a minority of society during the 1930s and war) with a good job and first home. In short time, it gave America a majority middle class but left behind others who lacked the privilege of this special GI Generation.

The bill, approved by Congress and signed by the president in June 1944, had the formal title Serviceman's Readjustment Act, otherwise known as the G.I. Bill of Rights, or simply the G.I. Bill. Its provisions had three key elements: education, job training, and home ownership. The first consideration, in the transition period of the readjustment of the soldier from war to peace, was to provide the veteran with subsistence living for a year. The government did this by offering various options. One was job training or a college education with living expenses extending to four years. Another option was a farm or small business loan guaranteed up to 50 percent. Otherwise, veterans received un-employment of $20 per week for one year. The bill's aim was for veterans to eventually obtain a job (earned by training or education) and to secure a first home. The government made the home benefit possible by offering guaranteed loans that required no down payment and had historically low mortgage pay-ments. The government also paid comprehensive medical costs for all veterans. This medical coverage has continued into the 21st century as the one national-ized low-cost public health program in America, but it is limited to ex-servicemen

A new crop of ex-soldier students acquires school supplies on January 28, 1945. Books and notebooks, as well as tuition and other fees, up to a total of $500 for an ordinary school year, were furnished to World War II veterans under the G.I. Bill of Rights. (UPI/ Bettmann/Corbis)

(along with a select group of elected national political officeholders who voted themselves the benefit).

The results in education were immediately dramatic. By 1946, 1.5 million veterans were in college taking advantage of the G.I. Bill. In the period 1945 to 1952, more than 8 million veterans took advantage of the educational or vocational benefits. In this relatively brief period, veterans achieved higher education levels than their nonveteran peers. No longer working class but with a college diploma welcoming them into the middle class, many never looked back and had little concern for any left behind in a lower status level.

Educational and Social Criticism of the G.I. Bill

The G.I. Bill represented a return to normalcy, with male leadership in family, work, and politics restored to 16 million veterans, almost all of whom were white males. Although the bill did have the approval of the great majority, it had its critics, especially regarding the status of the country's institutions of higher education. With college increasingly being democratized and made a right of the many, educators complained of such matters as falling academic standards and fast-tracked, hollowed-out courses and degrees (George Bush Sr., a wealthy veteran, finished Yale in three years on the G.I. Bill which had no means test to exclude those who could afford college without federal help). Another complaint was grade inflation because professors were reluctant to fail veterans for fear of losing the government payment to their college. Higher education, many complained, was increasingly intermeshed into a dependence on the government's military-related allotments.

Intellectuals criticized the very nature of the country's sudden, new middle class. In college, most of the vets were older and were focused mostly on some job-promising major and interested in little else—in a word, dull and anti-intellectual. Coming out of backgrounds of dire want in the 1930s and war years, these vets, once established in the middle class, were obsessed with being secure and projecting the appropriate status through calculated consumption and "keeping up appearances." The military had instilled a crude commonality that carried over into a barracks-like contentment with general levels of affluence, conformity in thinking, and a strong dislike of outside nonconformist critics of their new life styles.

Underlying their new status, many veterans had a status anxiety about the possibility of losing out one day and sliding back to the want of their origins. Any threat—such as communism—that could possibly cause this, veterans felt must be fought to protect their newly earned position, status, and possessions. Meanwhile, their need was to maintain the new status quo—expressed with operative mottoes such as "don't make waves."

Education Plan to Prevent Veterans' Backlash

In 1943, when the tide of war began to turn in favor of the Allies, the American people gave thought to possible victory and the shape of the postwar era. While the war had brought the return of widespread prosperity, many feared and anticipated the postwar would bring a return of the Depression. Peace would mean 16 million returning vets displacing millions of war workers who were destined to be surplus labor, the mass of the unemployed. This would happen once production was cut back from peak war levels to modest peacetime markets.

Society's fear (before the G.I. Bill) was that at war's end, many returning veterans would be jobless and idle. A group of veterans long unemployed could become discontented, those citizens knowledgeable of history knew, and they might protest their condition in violent ways, since all had military training. Within the living memory of many Americans in mid–World War II was the 1933 incident of the Bonus Army, composed of thousands of World War I vets who had marched on Washington peaceably demanding early payment of their veteran's pensions. The Army, under the president's orders, had dispersed them in violent fashion after many had camped in a tent city on the Anacostia Flats in the nation's capital. No one wanted this to occur again.

Fascist enemies of the Allies in World War II, Germany and Italy, had histories of postwar disgruntled veterans forming into powerful street militias and overthrowing democratic governments in favor of militaristic dictators Hitler and Mussolini. Americans had little fear this could happen here. But it was best to have a postwar plan for a smooth demobilization and reintegration of the soldiers back into civilian society.

As early as October 1943, President Roosevelt said he was especially concerned with the problem of the returning soldiers. All would need retraining and jobs. Official Washington shared this as a top priority. Both political parties had this as an important item on their future legislative agendas.

Government Aid to Vocational Schools

The idea that shaped what eventually evolved as the G.I. Bill was that the program would buffer the economy from the sudden onslaught of veterans needing jobs instantly. Enrolling veterans in higher or vocational education would be one way of holding them out of the job market while they gained skills and knowledge for better jobs. College would do so for up to four years, time for the national economy to grow and better absorb these veterans into it.

Education in various forms served this function in the postwar period. First, because 50 percent of all veterans had not finished high school, many went on to get a high school degree with school costs and living expenses paid by the government. Within a year after the war, 1.5 million veterans had started college.

Veterans and the "52–20 Club"

In another important way, the G.I. Bill was designed to allow veterans to gradually phase back into civilian life. This was due to the provision giving a year's unemployment payments to veterans who were looking for work, a benefit for those who chose not to take the college or vocational school option. The veterans called this benefit the "52–20 Club" because they would each earn $20 weekly for 52 weeks.

Vocational schools that dispensed training for high-paying skilled and semi-skilled jobs were the most popular choice of veterans. With training of this sort, previously available only through limited programs like union apprenticeships, the postwar era began a new vogue of the independent vocational school open to all and offering training in a range of areas. The Culinary Institute of America was started at this time by 13 veterans to train chefs and restaurant workers; it would go on to become one of the most famous vocational schools. Veterans in such schools had their costs paid by the government, and veterans such as the institute's founders had their start-up small business loan, guaranteed to 50 percent, granted by the government.

The Surging Postwar Economy Reabsorbs Veterans

Peace in the postwar era would not bring a return to the 1930s levels of unemployment. Instead, the economy began to boom in an unexpected manner because consumers spent wartime savings that were bursting their banking accounts. The boom was aided secondarily by the G.I. Bill's provisions to slowly reintegrate the veterans back into the economy.

During the war, with its civilian contribution by a dominant blue-collar class, few would have predicted a postwar rise in prosperity, let alone foresee the growth of a new middle-class majority that cherished the new right to a college education for their children. Society as a whole in the postwar underwent a closing of the income gap between the middle and the working class. Some highly skilled workers earned a premium wage amounting to more than the salary of a corporate manager. All made up this new middle class.

The postwar American Dream, for all those serving in the military and the many more at home working in war industries, was for security and prosperity, that had been lacking in the long years of the Depression and war. Everyone's hope for the postwar was for personal security to be assured by education leading to a good job then to a home and prosperity; the home's growing worth and equity were comparable to interest-paid bank savings. The 16 million qualified veterans including 350,000 women were also assured of these opportunities. Nonveterans in society did not have assurances of these opportunities, but many realized them just the same because of the broader educational opportunity made possible amid the rising tide of general prosperity.

Postwar society left many outside this prosperity. Together these comprised millions—the old, rural poor, migrants, uninsured long-term ill, and children of one-parent families. These persons were left behind and largely forgotten. The euphoric majority that enjoyed the ongoing relief of continued good times did not look back or look down for fear of seeing the specter of poverty once haunting many of their own lives.

Roosevelt's 1944 Second Bill of Rights

If President Roosevelt had his way, society as a whole would have been included in the postwar benefits, not just veterans. During January 1944, in his State of the Union message, the president set forth what he termed the "Second Bill of Rights" for all citizens beginning in the postwar period. "Dr. Win-the-War" brought back "Dr. New Deal" in this speech as he aimed to set a new foundation for society after the war. Security and prosperity for all was the basis of his plan; he outlined the provisions for this.

All people were to be guaranteed certain new rights: the right to a job with meaning and enough pay to provide food, clothing, and play; the right to adequate housing; and the right to social welfare protections against joblessness, illness, and job injury. Most importantly, all had the right to educational opportunity according to the limits of individual potential. Lastly, no business monopoly should erase freedom of enterprise for the individual or the smaller aspiring business. Americans widely praised his speech outlining the promise of a new postvictory United States of America.

Congress, not the president, ultimately provided the substance to this outline and narrowed its scope to a Bill of Rights—not for all—but for veterans. As such, the wartime Congress's conservative majority (Republicans and Southern Democrats) drafted the bill to exclude all nonveterans, even the equally worthy war workers at home.

The president settled for the compromise and got credit for his role in initiating a bill for returning veterans. The bill excluded the rest of society, some of whom expected him to expand benefits to others in the postwar era. In November 1944, he won his fourth consecutive term in office, but he died in April 1945 before completing the term. His successor, Harry S. Truman, tried but lacked the political muscle of Roosevelt to push through his Fair Deal, which would have gone a long way toward fulfilling the promise of a Second Bill of Rights for all. As it was, the G.I. Bill became a microcosm of what might have been for all of American society. If Roosevelt had lived to serve his full term, he might have broadened coverage.

The G.I. Bill's Immediate Results for the Postwar

In the postwar years to 1949, Americans gained proof that many individuals could overcome class barriers by government-subsidized education for a broad group. Education, Americans had long known, was the key to upward social mobility. In this period, education itself passed over a divide to become a key building block for a truly modern future country and a superpower in the world.

High school diplomas became more important. By 1949, some 60 percent of college-age young people were finishing their secondary education, compared to 50 percent in 1940. College graduates doubled from 432,000 in 1940 to nearly 1 million in 1949. A college degree was the ultimate emblem of belonging in the new middle-class society.

After the war, it was easier for nonveterans to go to college. Amid the general prosperity, the medium family income rose faster than the cost of going to college for the years from 1945 to 1955. Thus, for the first time, an increased number of young people could afford to go to college. Some did with the help of a part-time job; others worked and went to college off and on until getting a degree.

Veterans who took advantage of the educational or vocational benefits of the G.I. Bill numbered 8 million by 1952. Those going to college had all costs paid by the government, without a means test. Each veteran had the equivalent of a "full ride" scholarship, with tuition and all living expenses paid. The education benefits made veterans the catalysts in opening education up to the many.

Social Welfare Legislation at Its Best

The G.I. Bill proved to be the country's single most expensive piece of social welfare legislation. The education proviso was important, yet far from the most costly, of the benefits. Its cost came to 125 percent that of the total money spent on World War II. By 1949, it made up 30 percent of the national welfare budget.

Veteran's benefits continued through later wars, such as the Korean War from 1950 to 1954. The 1944 version—the first and most generous of all—became the gold standard template for later war's G.I. Bills. Korean veterans received almost similar benefits, but the benefits package continued to narrow for every war after that one.

Nonetheless, the World War II G.I. Bill paid for itself many times over because its recipients helped expand the economy greatly in the 25 years of continued prosperity, beginning in 1945. With a larger economic base, the government collected more taxes to reinvest in the economy to keep it expanding, and to give added job and educational opportunities to all.

The bill, in the collective sense, created an aggregate workforce of greater skills and education. This promised greater per capita output, adding up to a greater gross national product. With greater per capita output came greater pay, which produced a proliferation of consumers with greater and greater buying power. The result was the richest consumer society the world had ever known.

With a society so rich, the country sent an increasingly greater percentage of its baby boom children to college in the postwar 1940s, 1950s, and especially the 1960s. Four times the number of students in 1940 were in college in 1968, a total of 6 million.

With the democratizing of college, whole new categories of young people were newly in attendance. They became a critical force for dissent against the mores, values, and political beliefs of their parents' generation. From sheer numbers alone, one might have been able to foresee a youth rebellion with the first of the postwar population bulge entering college.

SCIENCE AND TECHNOLOGY

Throughout the war, average American citizens did not have a clear understanding of the basic difference between science and technology. Americans talked about both of these categories in an interchangeable manner. The distinction between them, however, is very important. In short, science is abstract theory and technology is concrete application of theory. All technology has a theoretical basis. Thus, only with a great advance in theory is technology able to open up a new area of inventions. American scientists had been inventors but not usually great theorists. Europeans, however, had excelled in both areas. Scientific and mathematical education in prewar America gave six times the money to advance technology as opposed to science.

The Manhattan Project

Atomic theory had been developed in elite European universities in the prewar period, and the results indicated that a real possibility existed for a sustained nuclear chain reaction. The problem from then on was an engineering one— how to make it real. The race was on to invent the atomic bomb. European scientists such as Einstein and others who fled fascism for refuge in America were crucial to this country's successful effort over four years to produce the final product. The government provided the up-to-date research laboratory in Los Alamos, New Mexico. With the aid of these émigré scientists, the United States had organized a community of scientists with the mission of inventing the bomb

The "Trinity" explosion on July 16, 1945, the first atomic bomb test, was the result of the Manhattan Project's work, which was conducted primarily at Los Alamos National Laboratory in New Mexico. (National Archives)

to win the war against Germany. In so doing, for the first time in its history the United States became an international center for theoretical as well as applied science.

American Fascination with Technology

In addition to the secret Manhattan Project, American colleges in wartime focused on technology. The government gave wartime contracts to science departments doing research for practical results. Basic theoretical science was largely ignored, and this country made few if any advances in this area during the war. With the focus on advanced technological discoveries, college science departments became dependent on the government granting them large cost-overrun contracts. The government, in turn, began to see higher education as a laboratory for solving practical problems of warfare.

Wartime America began to make more and faster technological advances during the continuing global struggle. Ingenious inventions such as radar made the public more enamored of science as did clever inventions like those of national idol Thomas Edison. The object of science, in the layperson's mind, was producing new, practical devices for use in war; the atomic bomb, oddly enough, fit this category.

Even so, in the immediate prewar period, the country did not fully realize the ways scientists could contribute to the war effort. British policy was to make every effort to keep their scientific community engaged on the home front; scientists were exempt from the armed forces. The United States took the opposite approach. After the peacetime draft of 1940 and after Pearl Harbor in December 1941, and in the early years of the war (1942–1943), thousands of men with scientific backgrounds were drafted, and their expertise was wasted.

The war years also proved that, contrary to popular belief, America was lacking in new and better war technology. All of the other countries in the conflict, with the exceptions of Japan and Italy, led the United States in this area. In fact, at the beginning of the war, American forces used surplus rifles and materiel from World War I. The United States played catch-up in many areas throughout the remainder of the war. Soviet tanks, for instance, remained vastly superior to those of the U.S. Army, and German rocket science led the world.

The country did excel at the sheer volume of production of the material necessities of war, if not always in the superior quality of the product. The miracle of production would win the war, Americans eventually sensed. But the people did not always get the information that an American weapon might not be top quality. The mass media was not eager to emphasize this.

Contributions of British and European Refugee Scientists

Mass media shamelessly led the America public into believing certain critical wartime devices were solely American inventions, even when British scientists were the first to lay out the groundwork. This pretense of giving no mention to the Allies was also prominent in a popular form of entertainment, the comics, where American heroes were portrayed as winning the war single-handedly against all odds.

The instances of overlooking British and European accomplishments are many. Britain had broken both the Japanese and German codes before Pearl Harbor. (The overpowered American naval forces in the Pacific won early victories only because American code-reading gave advance warning of Japanese plans.) In 1941, with the English isle still under severe threat, the government transferred much scientific information to America. Included in this was the basic groundwork for the proximity fuse (which allowed a bomb exploding above the target to do more damage than one hitting the ground), and for radar and solid fuel. Americans tended to take full credit for these vital and ingenious inventions rather than acknowledging they had been developed from earlier work.

The most important instance of European scientists having done the necessary basic theoretical groundwork for an American invention was, of course, the development of the atomic bomb. During the prewar, German theoretical physicists used formulas to learn of the possibility of a chain nuclear reaction. Albert Einstein, a German Jew, came to this country with that knowledge. His personal letter to President Roosevelt urged this country to start a project to develop the bomb before the Germans did it. Roosevelt agreed and set things in motion.

A Brain Trust of Atomic Physicists

In June 1941, six months before Pearl Harbor, the president had set up the Office of Scientific Research and Development (OSRD) headed by Vannevar Bush. Gathering émigré scientists and those from this country's industry and universities, Bush organized the special top-secret Manhattan Project, a concentrated brain trust of the best available allied researchers, especially physicists to develop the bomb, if indeed one was possible (theory indicated so but would practice prove it?). The sum of $2 billion went into the gamble.

The American public learned the result of the gamble on August 7, 1945, when President Truman announced that a day earlier, an Air Force bomber had dropped an atomic bomb on the Japanese city of Hiroshima, and that this bomb had a destructive power greater than anything ever known—comparable to 20,000 tons of dynamite exploding at one time. The public learned that scientists had harnessed the universe's basic energy. On August 9, a second bomb was dropped on Nagasaki. Six days later, on August 14, the president announced that the Japanese had surrendered. Throughout the country, Americans greeted the news with elation and wild happiness—in Times Square, a huge crowd gathered and *Life* photographer Alfred Eisenstadt snapped the famous iconic photo: a sailor, kissing a nurse he held in a dramatic embrace.

Human Life Sciences Favored by Americans

Prior to World War II, the American public had a positive view of science and scientists. The field was linked, in the popular view, to the new life-saving advances in medicine; to revolutionary ways to vitalize life (the discovery of the importance of vitamins for nutrition, for example); and to practical uses derived from theory (for example, the X-ray resulting from the discovery of radiation).

Medical science in the country by the early 1940s was advanced, and yet the cross section of young male draftees showed the lower class had poor medical care and a high incidence of malnutrition from bad diet during the dire 1930s. Nationwide, hospitals and medical schools for African Americans were fewer, inferior, and segregated (even blood banks were separate for African Americans). Many medical advances remained unavailable to African American facilities and patients while whites had full access (ironically, an African American medical scientist discovered plasma, a blood concentrate that improved blood supplies to the wounded during the war. This saved many combat soldiers' lives.).

Individual scientists were held in high regard in the popular mind. Hollywood produced a movie on the life of Louis Pasteur, who discovered the need to heat milk to destroy disease-causing germs in raw milk. His theory brought results, and these diseases decreased. Germ theory was not known at the time of the American Civil War (1861–1865) and was still relatively new in 1940. Popular books of the prewar years included *Microbe Hunters*. Biology and chemistry were leading fields of science at this time.

However, the American public knew science had a destructive aspect. For instance, they remembered well the mass indiscriminate death caused in World War I by the poisonous gas German chemists had devised. Their armies had used it on the Allies, who in defense had retaliated with the same measures. By 1940, this had been banned as a weapon of war (in part because the army using it could not ensure that the wind would not reverse and cause the gas to kill those who used it).

1930s America Lags Behind Europe in Theoretical Physics

The science of the interwar years had shifted to physics; one dimension was an exploration of the outer universe based on Einstein's theories of relativity, and the other dimension was an exploration of the hidden subatomic world. Americans found this a much more complex field of science. In both the cosmic and atomic dimensions, abstract theories seemed to defy common sense. At times, science seemed downright irrational to the usually pragmatic American, even if the theories proved accurate.

Europeans led the way in these theoretical explorations; universities there were more inclined to allow a brilliant scientist to forego immediate results and instead formulate imaginative answers to some of the as yet unsolved mysteries of life. The aim was a sustainable theory, able to stand up to various proofs. Pure science, it was called; here the elite British and German universities were the foremost in the field of the new physics.

American physicists usually needed to study abroad or keep abreast of developments in the European arena to be at the top in their fields. The United States did produce scientists such as Robert Oppenheimer, who headed the Los Alamos facility and was a professor at the University of California at Berkeley. However, for the most part, American higher education was not oriented to scientific theory in the prewar era, nor did it make advances in pure science during the war.

The Soviet Union's A-Bomb and Atomic Spies

The American people heard President Truman say on the radio in 1949 that the Soviet Union had tested its first atomic bomb, catching up to this country in 4 years rather than the estimated 10 years most experts had expected it would take. Immediately afterward, the president gave the order for America to develop an even more powerful weapon of destruction—the hydrogen bomb. A new corner had been turned.

Worldwide peaceful use of atomic energy under the aegis of the United Nations held out as a hope after the war soon ceased to be a possibility. In its place would be the fearfully real prospect of two bitter enemy superpowers engaged in a never-ending arms race in nuclear weapons. Each would gain the power to destroy the human species in a war. The government, the military, and the media kept Americans in a state of fearful anticipation that the enemy was benefiting from spies stealing secrets or that their scientists were making unknown breakthroughs to the disadvantage of the United States.

In this atmosphere, the American public seemed to be of two minds about the new group of nuclear physicists. They had the suspicion, then the proof, that certain of them had been spies giving atomic secrets to the Soviets. Also they had to give an almost blind trust to the loyal scientists to maintain American supremacy. Americans were captive to the mysterious physicists for their own national survival. The public gave willingly of its tax monies to support all branches of science in America, especially physics. Pure science got greater government support.

The New Nuclear Age and Military Scientific Research

Most Americans could not help but feel a certain revulsion for this new nuclear world that had suddenly enveloped them with the announcement of the bombing of Hiroshima on August 7, 1945. One man, the president, had made the decision to use this devastating weapon. The consequence changed the very tenor of human lives forever. No votes had been cast on the issue, no pros and cons given in democratic debate until after the fact. The country remained in total ignorance for 24 hours after the epic bombing of August 6, 1945, which was among the most momentous of all decisions in human history.

Immediately after the second atomic bomb destroyed Nagasaki and the Japanese surrendered, Americans were glad the decision had ended the war. Yet, in a short time, many realized that their sense of the future would never be the same. If there were a next war, commentators said, it would never again be like World War II. A next war could be over in minutes, with no winners or losers.

Education took on a new and different meaning. After 1945, a large sector of the public favored government-funded university research for military purposes. The traditional view of the university as an island of dissent protected from the exigencies of the world at large was a luxury of the past. Despite the Harvard Report leading the way in instilling a new curriculum of the liberal arts, American higher education was divided between science and liberal arts.

In the public view of science, the focus had shifted from life-affirming medicine to what seemed to many as life-denying nuclear physics. With the exception of Einstein, few physicists were familiar to the public. Science now had an evil side—even medicine during the war had led the Nazis to grotesque experiments on helpless captives in the concentration camps.

Lessons and Benefits from War

In 1944, a Rockefeller Foundation Report stated that the country had virtually ceased the essential training of basic scientists during the war and, as a result, this field was a vacuum. The need was to educate the current generation to be the most scientifically learned in the country's history. By end of the 1940s, educators set forth a plan to give more science and mathematics training to students.

Postwar American education did produce more pure scientists. But what still constituted scientific progress for most Americans was the array of novel technologies developed for war and now available for use in peacetime. In terms of medical advances, Americans were grateful, foremost, for the arrival of penicillin. A war-tested medicine (1943 saw the first broad use of penicillin on the wounded in North Africa), it was capable of saving countless lives. The first killer of bacteria, it was termed a miracle drug. Blood plasma was another miracle; it gave greater hope than ever to those who needed blood transfusions. Victims of venereal disease had new drugs that postponed death and brought cures. In World War II, these combined advances meant that 3 percent of the wounded died, half the number of wounded who died in World War I.

As a result, the health of Americans at home began to improve. Individual life expectancy began to rise. The nation's infant mortality rate decreased by 30 percent. Largely because of spin-offs in wartime medical advances, Americans at home enjoyed the best health for generations to come.

The Computer Age entered its promising infancy during the war. The British code-breakers used mathematical formulas to process so much information that

The world's first all-purpose electronic computer, a 30-ton behemoth of steel, wire, and tubes known as the Electronic Numerical Integrator & Computer (ENIAC), is shown in an undated photo. ENIAC was launched at the University of Pennsylvania in February 1946. (National Archives)

they invented some machines to aid their computing. Machine advances here were seen as capable of giving a giant assist to sorting data accumulating in government, businesses, and unions. A new industry of data processing was born here. In 1946, the University of Pennsylvania spent $500,000 developing the huge ENIAC computer, a digital model that could process data rapidly but had no memory.

Wartime Wonders: A Negative Side

Some of the wartime breakthroughs had immediate advantages but not as evident downsides. Storage of radioactive fuel, for instance, led to human illness. Nuclear power could be used for good or great evil. Another instance was the miracle pesticide, DDT. Discovered in wartime, it could save crops by killing insects and wipe out malaria by eliminating mosquitoes. Soon, it was widely adopted by farmers and health officials at home. But a terrible downside emerged over time, and the noxious pesticide filtered into the lifecycle of many living species and caused widespread death. This was the subject of the breakthrough ecological book, Rachel Carson's *Silent Spring*. In time, DDT was taken off the market.

Corporations developed and produced breakthrough products often at little expense because of generous wartime government contracts. The government granted corporations the right to privately own and manufacture for commercial use many of the products developed during wartime. Plants built by the government to manufacture such products were sold at little cost to private industry. For instance, by 1946, the radar industry had grown sixfold from 1940, to a worth of $3 billion, largely due to wartime government subsidies. The consequence was that the media and the public tended to give private business credit for this growth when government subsidies had been the prime mover.

Wonders to Transform Ordinary Lives

The media alerted the American people repeatedly of a wonderful new postwar transformation in their way of life. A new modern world was to replace the one of old. The key elements were to be new synthetic materials like plastic and a whole host of wondrous new electrical appliances. Commercial air travel was widely available. The Wurlitzer jukebox became a wonder of colorful design soon after the war. Plastics were used in sleek new modern furniture, kitchens, and cars. A hidden downside was that manmade plastic lasted forever and was not biodegradable like natural things.

The postwar home was electrified; the consumer could purchase a whole array of novel labor-saving housewares. The list was extensive but included such items as water heaters, huge refrigerators, dishwashers, washing machines, and dryers. Electrical power plants ran cheaply then, but with growing massive usage, these became major polluters. The fuel to power some plants was nuclear until a fault in design caused a disaster.

Commercial air travel became available inexpensively to the great mass of Americans, thanks to wartime aeronautical advances. Large planes mass-produced during the war were easily converted to peacetime use. Airline companies began scheduling the planes on set routes. Flight technology allowed ordinary citizens the chance to travel far distances for the first time, greatly expanding the domestic and foreign travel industries.

America grouped all of these advances under science and technology. But the truth was the country, while constantly putting new wonder technologies on the postwar market, was still playing catch-up to Europe in the development of pure science, which seemed to advance at its own pace, not affected one way or the other by war. Pure science would, in due time, bring such breakthroughs as the discovery of DNA, the basic component of human life.

EDUCATIONAL OPPORTUNITIES

Education made remarkable advances in the 1940s. By 1949, more students were finishing high school and job training in vocational schools. General Educational Development (GED) exams, developed in 1942 by the American Council on Education for the military to measure high school–equivalent academic skills, were introduced in 1947 to allow civilians who had not completed high school to prove they had the necessary skills to continue to higher education or succeed in the workplace.

Thanks to the G.I. Bill, 16 million veterans serving in World War II were offered tuition and living expenses to attend college or vocational school. The G.I. Bill democratized education. In the 1930s, a high school diploma was the norm. From the 1940s on, college education became the standard. College enrollments were rising. There were 1.5 million veterans in college in 1946, and this number increased steadily over the next seven years.

The G.I. Bill aided the goals of higher education disproportionately among whites (in contrast to many minority veterans, still without a good job or home ownership). Thanks to this benefit for veterans, a majority of families owned their own homes, a record for the country. Because of higher job earnings and overall financial worth (much future family worth was based on rising equity in homes whose original ownership was subsidized by the government), America was transformed into a country with a middle-class majority for the first time in its history.

Education Forms White Male Leaders

Notwithstanding these gains, the G.I. Bill gave unfair advantage to the 14.5 million white war veterans over the 1.3 million African American veterans and the roughly 350,000 female veterans. For the next 25 years, the white male recipients of the bill's benefits became society's leaders in all spheres of life—politics, business, finance, charities, culture, and the family. Their values and mores were formed in their coming-of-age years during the 1930s, when society was still largely patriarchal (starting in the early 1940s, and during the war, many women became breadwinners). By 1945, the country experienced a return to prewar normalcy but enhanced by broad prosperity.

African-American Veterans and the G.I. Bill

Beneficial as it was to returning service personnel, the G.I. Bill had inequalities for African American veterans. The bill left many African Americans further behind than before the war, especially when it came to its two major benefits—a free college education and low-cost home ownership. The bill as legislation was a benchmark in that the wording was truly colorblind; any African American veteran had the right to freely choose anywhere to own a first home or attend a college. The reality was that the United States had a rigorously segregated society in which African Americans were second-class citizens. In the postwar years, many whites in the North as well as the South wanted the country to remain this way. Their attitudes undermined the potential of this race-free social welfare legislation, the first of its kind, the most extensive, and the farthest reaching in the country's history.

As to education, the G.I. Bill offered most African American veterans their first affordable chance for a college education. But few of them could take advantage of it. One reason is that the South had maintained an entirely separate school system for African Americans, from grade school through college. That system was markedly inferior to the parallel white system. Having received poor primary and secondary educations, a large number of African Americans proved to be illiterate as draftees and qualified as 4-F, although otherwise fit. As a result, the Army developed a special wartime program that taught 150,000 African Americans to read and write.

When it came to the education benefit in the bill, African Americans faced very real limitations. In the South, the vast majority of colleges and universities were legally set aside for African Americans; a small number (about 100 in all) were segregated African American colleges: Tuskegee, Howard, and Emory, among others. But all of these colleges struggled for funds, and few had graduate programs. Most offered careers in "teaching and preaching." The separate African American system of schools and churches held jobs in these professions.

G. W. McLaurin sits at a segregated desk outside of a classroom at the University of Oklahoma in 1948. Originally denied entrance to the university, he successfully sued to enroll. After being admitted, McLaurin challenged the new state law that segregated public facilities. In McLaurin v. Oklahoma State Regents *(1950) the Supreme Court ruled that once a college or university accepted a member of a minority race, the institution had to treat that individual as it did members of the majority. (Library of Congress)*

A considerable number of African American veterans went to these historically black colleges on the G.I. Bill.

The North had de facto segregation, a separation of the races by tradition or custom rather than the law. While nominally integrated, northern institutions of higher education had set quotas for the numbers of African Americans admitted to each class (many also had quotas for Jews, Catholics, and ethnics in general). Lacking the proper college preparation due to poor early schooling and discrimination, a certain number of African Americans in both sections of the country failed to qualify for the opportunity to go to college. Others felt then, as before the war, that college was a waste of time for an African American because segregated society offered few rewards in terms of higher paying middle-class jobs. So, while the bill may have offered a chance for these veterans to be the bulk of a new African American middle class, American society of the time defeated that promise. The Swedish sociologist Gunnar Myrdal, in his 1944

Man clips a hedge, woman and child on the porch, Greenbelt, Maryland, July 1946. Greenbelt was one of the nation's first publicly funded, planned communities and it was segregated. (Library of Congress)

classic *The American Dilemma,* described the country's historic race problem as one of a yawning gap between stated ideals and practice.

As regards the G.I. Bill, that yawning gap was maintained through the machinations of Rep. John Elliot Rankin, the Democrat who controlled all legislation pertaining to veterans. In 1944, he and his fellow committee members shaped the legislation that became the G.I. Bill. Rankin had backing from the American Legion, a segregated veterans' organization. (The Veterans Administration [VA], which was slated to administer the emerging bill, maintained segregated hospitals.) Rankin and his congressional supporters tailored the planned administration of the bill according to a states' rights agenda. They defeated the proposal for federal control and monitoring of the dispersal of veterans' benefits. The bill they passed favored local control. After the G.I. Bill went into effect, the VA went along with Rankin and agreed with local administrators who denied benefits to blacks except for tuition for historically black colleges. Local banks denied home loans to blacks, even though the government guaranteed them at no risk to the bank. Ironically, the bill, although colorblind, perpetuated the system of south-

Varying Historical Views on the Impact of the G.I. Bill Impact

Historians are of two different schools when analyzing the impact of the World War II G.I. Bill on overall race relations in America, particularly in the key area of education. One school includes historian Suzanne Mettler, who in *Soldiers to Citizens: The G.I. Bill and the Making of the Greatest Generation,* takes the position that this law was a turning point. She emphasizes how the bill transcended race both in intent and practice. It was fair and resulted in greater social mobility for all, she argues, especially in terms of the vocational and educational opportunities.

Historian Ira Katznelson of the other prominent school argues that the future result was a negative one in *When Affirmative Action Was White.* The bill increased the existing gap in influence, power, and income between the races. The so-called Greatest Generation comprised mostly powerful white males who were boosted up by the bill to lifelong positions of leadership and dominance in all areas of society. African Americans, women, and minorities would be under their sway for years to come.

Historian Edward Humes's *Over Here: How the G.I. Bill Transformed the American Dream* assumes a middle position, conceding parts of both of the prior arguments but finding the matter more complex than either. Humes believes that because of a segregated society, the bill did not have the socially transforming power for African Americans, yet it did help whites to overcome existing class barriers en masse.

ern segregation and did little to make marked advances in the northern system of de facto racial separation.

Still, the bill written as race neutral held the promise of a potential civil rights revolution in the country. But the time was not yet ripe.

While the college option was taken up by only 12 percent of African American veterans, compared to 28 percent of whites, an impressive 90 percent of those who enrolled in the historic black colleges in the South went on to complete college degrees. Many became ministers or teachers and were able to influence others in the fight for civil rights from these leadership positions. The 1944 G.I. Bill benefited these veterans, and created a critical mass of leaders for the coming struggle to end legal segregation in the United States. Although the bill failed to create a new strong African American middle class, its education benefits in particular did create this leadership core of educated veterans.

By the end of the 1940s, nearly half of the country's 1.3 million African American World War II veterans had taken advantage of at least one of the multiple benefits of the G.I. Bill, compared to 43 percent, or about 6.5 million, of the white veterans. When it came to the education benefit, most African Americans chose vocational school over college. They learned job skills that gave them real hope that they could gain higher-paying jobs in the growing ranks of the nation's skilled and semiskilled workforce.

But many of those who acquired the necessary skills or training still found barriers to obtaining jobs. In the South, this was due to the administrative re-strictions calling for local job counseling that rightist leaders had built into the law. In the South, local Veterans Administration career counselors often steered newly skilled African American workers toward unskilled positions like janitorial work, even when blue-collar skilled jobs were open. In the North, the unions of nearly all skilled workers often maintained quotas (relying heavily on nepotism) in their apprenticeship programs and thus offered only very limited opportuni-ties for African American veterans schooled on the G.I. Bill. Exceptions included those who had joined unions while working in wartime defense plants and those who had the on-the-job training and experience to be rehired in the post-war period.

The Cost of Universal Public Education

Universal public education has long been America's ideal goal, along with uni-versal suffrage. During the decade of the 1940s, with the country suddenly hav-ing global involvement and concerns, the complexity of the issues of war and peace became manifest to most Americans. During the decade of the 1940s, es-pecially the postwar period, public education was more widespread during the first 12 grades. Students remained in school longer than at any previous time in the country's history. After 1945, this school enrollment was on a steep upward curve, with the first of the babies of the boom old enough to begin entering grade schools by 1949. The new suburbs required new schools. In short, the nation's public school system, based on the total numbers enrolled, was the nation's largest public endeavor.

And it was getting larger still. One's educational level bore a close relation-ship to one's status in society. The more education, the greater status one had in terms of work and social class. Education was the ladder of upward social mobility in the country. By the late 1940s, a high school degree was becoming the required minimum for many jobs. College and universities had more enrollees than ever and, like high schools, were overcrowded due to the G.I. Bill. More students than ever were graduating college.

In the postwar period and after, the costs of local public schools through grade 12 were rising steadily, with monies needed for the construction of new buildings, equipment, books, and study materials, and especially for the salaries of the vastly increased numbers of teachers needed for the expansion of the sys-tem. Teacher's salaries were usually the largest item in local school budgets.

Local school systems were supported by local property taxes relative to the total assessed value of a town, city, or rural district. In general, these taxes paid some 50 percent of the total cost; state taxes provided locales with another 40 percent, leaving some 10 percent to be made up by other means. Education was the well-guarded preserve of local and state authorities. Although the federal government might offer aid in the form of grants for special programs, any hint of control from Washington was unwelcome.

A great paradox gripped this educational system. Americans were devoted to public education but were reluctant to pay for it in full. A high quality education required fine, well-trained teachers. Attracting good teachers meant paying decent salaries. Yet most locales kept salaries low.

Educating multitudes also called for new facilities. Yet local school boards kept expansion at a minimum, leading to overcrowded schools with daily shifts of students. Local school taxes were the only taxes in the country submitted directly to voters for a "yes" or "no" vote on local bond issues; those without school-age children might be less likely to favor increased taxes. Often a request for higher taxes to support schools was voted down. A plea to raise taxes was rarely a popular stance for a politician to take. In the overall picture, adult citizens tended to stint education while spending much more on such personal consumer satisfactions as appliances, home furnishings, clothing, entertainment, liquor, cigarettes, cosmetics, and automobiles.

Even more troubling for the educational needs of the country was the fact that an individual's opportunity for a good education varied widely according to region, state, city or rural area, and race. Of all regions in the nation, the South suffered the lowest yields from local and state property taxes because each of its 17 states had low property valuations and low incomes. Unlike the rest of the country, Southern states used their tax yields to maintain two separate public school systems (for African Americans and for whites). The result was a national disgrace. For both races (but especially for African Americans), this region offered inferior educational opportunities throughout the 1940s. Low average family income in the region also led to some of nation's highest rates for non-schooling, dropouts, and illiteracy.

In the northwest during the postwar years, the mass migration of the middle class to the suburbs was beginning to create another problem. With the departure of their more affluent residents to the growing suburbs, the inner cities had shrinking tax bases and lower yields from local school taxes. As a result, inner city schools began to suffer, with decrepit buildings, overcrowding, unqualified teachers, ill-equipped students, gangs, and violence.

One obvious answer was federal intervention and funding for local school systems. Local opposition to this approach was widespread, and relied upon the fact that the U.S Constitution does not give the federal government authority over education.

MEDICINE, RESEARCH, AND BUSINESS

The first decade beginning the era of modern medicine was the 1940s. This was due solely to the world's full acceptance of the earlier 1933 discovery by German scientists of sulfa, human history's first antibiotic. In the United States, sulfa's use on an experimental basis in the late 1930s grew more widespread in the 1940s, bringing mass public acceptance, both at home and in war. The first of the miracle drugs, sulfa caused patients to survive a host of diseases previously believed to have no known cure. Medicine's most important discovery in centuries, sulfa was a wholly chemically derived drug that could destroy the root cause of the family of diseases caused by bacteria; diseases combatted with sulfa were the world's greatest human killers—diphtheria, pneumonia, plague, meningitis, and cholera as well as countless lethal childhood diseases.

Miracle Drug Saves American War Wounded

Sulfa alone began the revolution in antibiotic medicine (with penicillin soon following after it), which brought major consequences for mankind. Sulfa's first trials with masses of human beings came during the war, especially in the Pacific Theater, where soldiers were more prone to infection and disease. In all previous American wars, the toll of the wounded who died of infections was equal or nearly so to those killed instantly by the enemy. In World War II, America's relatively low overall numbers of dead in combat was the least of all countries at war largely because of the early discovery that sulfa prevented the spread and cured infection due to wounds. Sulfa drugs were also the cure for such common fighting men's diseases as diarrhea (from bad water), meningitis (from crowded quarters), and gonorrhea (from sexual activity). Given that the Japanese were not as advanced in the mass production or use of sulfa as the Americans, a primary reason for America's victory was the widespread military use of this first wonder drug. Every G.I. had sulfa tablets in his medicine kit.

Medical Profession Adapts to Modern Methods

Medical school education changed drastically due the chemically produced sulfa and the forthcoming newer antibiotics. The latter also were produced in research laboratories by teams of scientists financed by the new, growing, factory-like drug companies. Medical students as a result now graduated high in their class after mastering a curriculum of new scientific cures, their chemical compositions, and their effects on the human body. The new doctor would soon be a master of curative technique, a decision maker for the patient regarding the right prescription for complex drugs. Pharmacy sales also changed due to the new, high-priced drugs produced by a few corporations (not as previously on a trial-and-error basis by patent medicine companies and individual druggists themselves); these newest drugs all required doctors' written prescriptions, whereas previously all medicines had been sold over the counter, except for narcotics.

Postwar Society Adjusts to a New Antibiotic Era

In the postwar, the newest antibiotics caused demographic, economic, governmental, and ecological changes. The latest wave of sulfa drugs and the advent of penicillin spared many newborns and young children from previously deadly diseases. The postwar boom in babies was due in part to an overall decline in the country's infant mortality rate. At the other end of the age spectrum, the new era of modern medicines overcame such diseases as pneumonia that often were fatal to older citizens. The results were an overall population increase and a longer life span for citizens.

Economically, the pharmaceutical companies made up a new growth industry of the postwar boom. New industries such as this grew the economy to absorb both male war workers and veterans. New pharmaceuticals soon entirely supplanted the prewar patent medicine companies (not organized on an industrial scientific research basis). The government helped the process along by ensuring changes in the laws relating to the making of medicines. A new legal structure for companies discovering new antibiotics or other modern medicines was put into practice. Accordingly, corporations that discovered a new drug received a monopoly on sales for a set term, allegedly as a monetary return for the high cost of scientific research leading to a breakthrough. Profits were generally high in this new industry.

The Federal Drug Administration soon began an expanded new branch to oversee the new industry. Officials of the FDA made regulations requiring substantial testing of a new medicine in an effort at early detection of any harmful side effects. In the end, every new drug required government approval before release for sale to the public.

Sulfa was the first of the antibiotics to have unforeseen, unplanned massive effects on the food consumed by humans, especially Americans. During the war, the government contracted for such huge quantities of sulfa drugs (in midwar, over 4 tons stood ready for use with orders for up to 100,000 tons). In 1946, after the advent of newer antibiotics, the problem was to find a use for the huge surplus inventory of sulfa. Thereafter, veterinarians in the country began using sulfa to cure farm animals suffering from bacteria-caused diseases. Then farmers injected their livestock to make them immune to diseases. Crop farmers began widespread spraying to kill bacteria and pests. Overall, the result was that nearly every American soon had some trace of sulfa in their bodies. This was so even with persons who had never taken it to treat an illness.

Overused in this manner, sulfa eventually became ineffective because certain strains of diseases adapted and built up a resistance so the drug no longer had effect. Fortunately, a newer form of antibiotic or other medicines were newly coming onto the market to solve the problem. Yet, this was a warning against massive overuse of some other "miracle" drug.

Unknown Wonder Drug Saves the President's Son

In November 1936, two medical researchers at Johns Hopkins University, Perrin Long and Eleanor Bliss, announced that they had found in their lab experiments that sulfa was a cure for strep infections. The two told a group of doctors about the remarkable curative powers of sulfa in cases of large internal infections. They stated it was even effective against the strep caused by a type of childhood meningitis (an illness previously fatal in all but 2 of 100 cases). This country's doctors had a 20-year bias against any synthesized chemicals ever being capable of curing organic human tissues. This first report then was only the beginning. The drug was still highly experimental.

However, in December 1936, an event occurred in this country that rocketed this little-known drug to mass public awareness and headlines here and elsewhere in the world. The president's son, Franklin Delano Roosevelt Jr., had been in Boston hospital because of a severe sinus infection that had turned into a strep infection that threatened to enter his blood stream, which would mean almost certain death. His physician, Dr. George Loring Tobey, the best in the field, was aware of the research of Long and Bliss, and he had just recently conducted the first test uses of sulfa on a few patients. He took the risk of using the new experimental drug as a last resort cure on the young Roosevelt. Within 10 days, the patient had returned to normal. The *New York Times* broke the story with a bold, front-page headline about a new wonder drug saving him. Newspapers everywhere picked up the story and soon the medicine's name was a household word. All over the country, huge numbers of people were demanding its wider use.

America Adopts the First Wonder Drug

In the United States in 1940, sulfa signaled a new modern era in medicine. It had been in wide public use since mid-1937. This happened only a relatively short time after its discovery by German chemists in 1933. Bayer had been the German corporation that first sold the drug with great profits under the prescription name Prontosi. But, due to legal problems over the trademark, Americans gained entry into the field.

Such prominent American pharmaceutical companies as Merck, Lilly, Parke, Davis, and others started manufacturing and selling their own brands of sulfa medicines. By 1940, because it was easy to make and inexpensive to buy, the

Medical Care Prior to Antibiotics: Pluses and Minuses

With the dramatic advent of the era of antibiotics, Americans changed their attitudes toward medicine. Antibiotics would mean certain losses and gains. Prior to sulfa, the patient understood that doctors worked against the odds because there was no cure for the bacteria-caused killer diseases—flu, strep, bronchitis, pneumonia. These swept the country every fall and winter and regularly took thousands of lives. Doctors who were general practitioners often worked out of their own homes and made house calls to their patients. They were primarily caregivers who would diagnose disease and relieve symptoms. They would often be there at a bedside standing vigil and hoping for the patient's own resistance to be strong enough to restore health.

Public health programs, prior to sulfa, were the most effective way to guard against these yearly epidemics. Cities, towns, and local officials took great precautions to ensure the public health by enforcing regulations to ensure safe drinking water and proper sewage treatment. Campaigns for public vaccinations against certain diseases took place across the country. Quarantines of infected persons kept disease from spreading to the general populace. The concern for public health reached its zenith in many areas in the 1930s. In the 1940s, after cures were found for once-deadly diseases, many public programs were disbanded or left vastly underfunded.

public had grown accustomed to its ready availability from family doctors. This new wonder drug sulfa now cured diseases that only a few years before had been fatal.

By 1941, the top 10 drug-making corporations in the country had manufactured some 1,700 tons of sulfa. A sulfa boom was ongoing, fueled by four years of media stories of miracle cures and patients being rescued from the jaw of death. Researchers found sulfa cured other, different diseases. Most importantly, doctors found it effective against the perennial killer, pneumonia. Leading medical journals published research that added more validity to the reports. American drug manufacturers began making their own patented, chemical compounds using sulfa, a generic that in its pure form could not be patented. By 1938, the country's hospitals were using it like common aspirin (such matters as correct dosages and toxic effects were left to the future).

Wonder Drug's Slow Use in War, 1939–1941

With world war beginning in Europe in 1939, government and military officials questioned what use the new wonder drug may have with such problems as deadly infections from war wounds. In World War I, wounded soldiers died from infection in almost equal numbers to those killed on the battlefield; in the American Civil War, many more had died from infected wounds than had been killed on the battlefield. In World War I, American combat deaths also included 50,000 deaths from pneumonia. Meningitis killed two of every three infected soldiers. Gonorrhea had no ready cure and meant a soldier was absent from the front for three months while undergoing treatment.

In the first years of the world war, 1939 to 1941, the non-American combatants were slow to test sulfa in battlefield conditions. Germany was slowed because of the Fuhrer's dislike of the use of animals in lab tests, and rumors persisted of its toxic effects. England, too, was slow to make use of sulfa for soldiers with infected battle wounds (in World War I a total of some two million English soldiers were wounded, and for every five, two got complications from infections and either died or were disabled for life). One reason was that the country's military brass was generally conservative and wary about any possible negative effects that the mass use of sulfa might have on fighting forces. Japan was the combatant least aware of the new wonder drug.

Pearl Harbor: Drug's Dramatic Result on the Wounded

On December 7, 1941, during the attack on Pearl Harbor, Honolulu's Tripler General Hospital filled with hundreds of wounded from the bomb-blasted ships and those burned from the flaming oil-slicked waters. Stretchers on the lawn bore the overflow of casualties. Every civilian doctor and nurse in the area had been commandeered for duty. The gathered group divided into surgical teams to begin immediately treating and operating on the patients. In the next 11 straight hours, the teams performed hundreds of operations on these wounded and hoped that infections would not complicate and likely kill many, as was the case in World War I.

A New Yorker, Dr. John J. Moorhead, chanced to be in Honolulu. The day before the attack, he was a guest speaker before a local doctors' convention and had talked about his specialty, trauma surgery and the newest treatment for wounds. With the attack ongoing, he was made an officer in the Medical Corps; Moorhead lead the teams in giving the wounded the latest treatment consisting of the following: cleaning the wound, scraping away flesh until finding a healthy layer, constricting the bleeding, packing the cavity with sulfa, lightly bandaging it for three days, and then, ensured of no infection, stitching up the wound. Every four hours during the interim, the patient took a sulfa pill. Fortunately, Tripler had a large supply of sulfa on hand. This was the first mass test in battlefield conditions of the new drug's ability to stop wounds and burns from developing into infections that had been nearly always fatal in the past.

Among all the casualties, certain ones were the most likely to develop infected wounds. These included young fly boys who had been eating breakfast at the base mess hall when it was bombed. These survivors bled from cavities filled with bits of food, dirt, shrapnel and other small debris. After giving the special treatment, doctors closely watched for infection, especially the deadliest, gangrene. Those who did develop infection were put in an isolated ward where doctors cleaned and repacked sulfa into the wound and prescribed a higher dosage of sulfa pills by mouth.

The doctors also used sulfa treatment on the burn patients who had leaped overboard and floated in the burning oil slicks on the water. Those in the water for long periods had the severest burns. The treatment involved cleaning and scraping away all the burned flesh and then sprinkling sulfa in powdered form over the healthy tissue. Under battlefield conditions and used with all these wounded, the new sulfa drug would either prove itself a striking success or a failure.

The results proved dramatic. Suffering under a death sentence from a wound infected with gangrene, patients survived—a medical wonder in comparison to the past. Aside from the wounded who died almost immediately of trauma, those patients who had sulfa treatment for infected wounds did not suffer a single death. The commanders of the military ordered that sulfa be in the medical kits of all persons entering the armed forces after Pearl Harbor.

American Battlefield Tests Yield More Uses for Sulfa

By 1943, almost every American and British soldier either carried the drug or was within range of its medical use. Instructions in the field were to sprinkle any wound immediately with sulfa and start taking the pills. In the Pacific Theater, especially, sulfa may have given the Allies a necessary edge over the Japanese who lacked it and thus lost hundreds of thousands of their wounded fighters. Americans, on the other hand, had found that deaths from infected wounds almost ceased to be a major medical problem. Thereby, Americans held a manpower advantage over the enemy.

This new wonder drug also proved effective against a number of other often fatal diseases traditionally affecting soldiers. Dysentery had long been a problem, especially in warm, humid climates like the South Pacific. At Guadalcanal and again in New Guinea, early in the war, epidemics of dystenery broke out amidst Allied fighters. Thousands of lives stood to be lost, but sulfa treatments again proved dramatically effective. The drug restored their health and kept forces in the field at near full strength.

Military medical researchers used large numbers of soldiers in experiments, primarily to find the full spectrum of diseases curable by sulfa and, secondarily to find if the drug had preventative capabilities against diseases. Meningitis had

A casualty from front-line fighting during the Battle of Guadalcanal is cared for before being taken through the jungle and down river to a hospital. (Library of Congress)

spread previously in killer epidemics in the ideal breeding grounds of crowded Army basic training camps. By winter 1942 at Army camps in the Southeastern United States, serious epidemics raged among men in basic training. Military doctors found sulfa could cure it.

Doctors now asked if sulfa could prevent meningitis. The army camps provided ideal conditions for mass medical tests. Doctors knew certain persons were carriers of meningitis while never themselves becoming ill. Researchers tested whether giving sulfa to carriers would reduce the chance of an outbreak or lessen the severity of one happening on a base. Using one large test group with some treated carriers and another control group without them, the researchers found that sulfa was highly effective in preventing the disease from spreading beyond the first outbreak. By 1943, after numerous tests (also conducted by the Navy and Air Force) the drug was used widely for this purpose. As a result, the British and the United States cut the disease's death rate back to between 15 and 10 percent. Meanwhile, other combatants had 65 percent death rates for those with meningitis during World War II.

Sulfa cures also occurred for many diseases infecting the lungs—flu, pneumonia, and bronchitis (these had killed 50,000 Americans during World War I). In World War II, the loss from these was nearly insignificant due to sulfa treatment. With sulfa so effective against the diseases most deadly to soldiers, the American military use of it quickly became widespread. It was certainly conducive to the country's low combat death rate. Most importantly in the Pacific Theater, this one factor clearly gave the Americans a significant advantage against the Japanese.

Sulfa in War; Penicillin in the Postwar

Sulfa reigned as the wonder drug until the end of the war. Then it was steadily replaced by penicillin, the newer, better antibiotic, as advertised by the new industrial scientific drug companies. A compound made from a mold, this latest antibiotic matched sulfa in curing the same diseases, but it did so faster and with fewer side effects. In addition, it was effective against some sulfa-resistant diseases, like anthrax.

After sulfa and penicillin, there was a seeming cornucopia of more specialized antibiotics, capable of treating an ever-growing number of number of diseases, including tuberculosis. In 1944, the Rutgers University microbiologist Selman Waksman discovered streptomycin, the newest antibiotic. It tested effective against tuberculosis, and doctors now had their first cure. Earlier there existed only a preventative vaccine and, of course, the long rest cure, which was often futile. However, the tuberculosis bacteria soon developed a resistance to the new drug. This was overcome by using streptomycin in varying combination with other new drug strains.

Penicillin had been developed to the point of testable medical application by a team of British microbiologists working at Oxford University. They had followed up on an original research paper in 1926 by Alexander Fleming who discovered it and suggested its bacteria-killing properties. In 1941, the Oxford team stabilized penicillin in a substance sufficient for medical use. Animal test results had proved it to be the best antibiotic, but it was too difficult and expensive to manufacture on a large scale in war-torn England. But American pharmaceuticals accepted the challenge. By D-Day 1944, the troops had been supplied with a good quantity of penicillin.

By war's end, the companies were producing ever-greater quantities for civilian as well as military use. By 1945, penicillin use outpaced that of sulfa. This was very timely because sulfa no longer cured certain diseases that had evolved sulfa-resistant strains of bacteria. By 1945, a strain of strep resistant to sulfa was becoming alarmingly prevalent. This was also the case in the treatment of venereal diseases such as gonorrhea. The sulfa cure rates for it among British troops had dropped from an initial 90 percent to below 25 percent.

Americans Learn Sulfa Saves Churchill

The fame of sulfa as a wonder drug likely peaked in December 1943 when British prime minister Winston Churchill came down with pneumonia at Gen. Dwight D. Eisenhower's villa in Tunis, a city in Tunisia, North Africa, distant from any modern medical care. Churchill's condition became alarmingly desperate as he lay near death with his lungs filling with fluid. The British sulfa derivative, M&B, did not seem to be taking effect. Then the sulfa did start working, and within a few short days, the world leader was back to near normal. When he returned to London, he told a pack of reporters what a close call it was and how only this wonderful drug saved him. World headlines repeated the miracle-making qualities of sulfa. But although this drug was only ten years old, its wonders already were taken for granted by the public.

Cautionary Lessons after the Introduction of the First Wonder Drug

With the postwar wave of new antibiotics, sulfa settled into a middling range of cures (it is still prescribed today for such things as urinary tract infections and a particular type of AIDs-related pneumonia). Yet, sulfa proved essential to the future of antibiotics in many ways. First, it clearly erased the bias against chemical medicines capable of curing human diseases. Second, it proved the theory of a "magic bullet" medicine capable of targeting specific diseases in a relatively safe way for the patient. Three, it led to pharmaceuticals expanding to have large medical laboratories to research specific diseases and target chemical compounds to cure them. If successful, the drug corporation then advertised and marketed a new chemical compound as medicine. This built the foundation of a powerful pharmaceutical industry. Lastly, readily publicizing new discoveries in antibiotics, such companies led the public to expect or even demand miracle cures. Unfortunately, the demand often led to overuse and the inevitable growth of strains of antibiotic-resistant bacteria.

The cautionary tale resulting from the cycle of sulfa and other antibiotic drugs is that the public should not demand and get instant mass use of a drug not yet fully tested. Otherwise, the result can be overuse, which creates long-term, undiscovered side effects. One side effect suffered by Pearl Harbor wounded was severe liver damage due to too much sulfa intake. For the wave of miracle drugs following sulfa, the pattern remained oddly similar—with overuse of a new drug, diseases evolved strains resistant to the new cure. For newer drugs in the future, there is a cautionary lesson to be learned from the story of sulfa: moderate use can preserve the long-term effectiveness of new wonder drugs.

BIOGRAPHIES

Norman Borlaug, 1914–2007

Agronomist and Inventor

As the head of the Rockefeller-sponsored Cooperative Mexican Agricultural Program, Iowa-born Borlaug is credited with starting the "Green Revolution," for which he received the Nobel Prize in 1970. The seminal project was launched in Mexico in 1944. His results there led to surprising gains in food production through a novel combination of innovative seed hybrids, irrigation schemes, and fertilizer use. Fifteen years later, Mexican food production had increased 100 percent and Borlaug was well on the way to being the man best known for countering staggering global population growth with his successes in the war on hunger.

Dr. Norman Borlaug, an Iowa native, shows some of the wheat he helped develop for which he won the Nobel Peace Prize, Toluca, Mexico. (Bettmann/Corbis)

Enrico Fermi, 1901–1954

Physicist and Inventor

An émigré Italian scientist, Fermi, had fled the European totalitarian regimes for America in the 1930s, like many other brilliant men in his field. While he and his partner, the Hungarian Leo Szilard, were still both technically enemy aliens, they both taught at Columbia University, where they devised a nuclear reactor, and sketched out a model. In 1942, their work continued at the University of Chicago and was incorporated into the new Manhattan Project. On December 2, 1942, in a laboratory under the football stadium, they successfully field tested the model and proved that a "chain reaction" had taken place. The nuclear age dawned with this actual proof of a chain reaction, an indispensable first step in the process of harnessing nuclear energy.

George Gamow, 1904–1968

Inventor, Physicist, and Cosmologist

A Russian émigré scientist who came to the United States in 1934, Gamow and his student, Ralph Alpher, published a landmark paper, "The Origin of Chemical

As a U.S. brigadier general, Leslie Groves assumed control of the Manhattan Project in 1942 and successfully orchestrated the creation of the first atomic bomb, effectively ending World War II in 1945 and beginning the atomic age. (National Archives)

Elements," in 1948. The paper provided the theoretical underpinning for the "Big Bang" origin of the cosmos (a theory first proposed in the 1920s). A proof of that origin was their theory of an expanding universe. Since then, most astronomers, cosmologists, and physicists accept this as the dominant explanation for the origins of the universe.

Leslie R. Groves, 1896–1970

Head of the Manhattan Project

General Groves was a fitting military choice in 1942 to be the U.S. Army's coordinator of ongoing nuclear weapons research. He named the vast new secret effort the Manhattan Project. Eventually, the project encompassed some 35 installations in 13 states and at least a dozen university science departments. More than 100,000 workers were involved, but only a few at the very top had overall knowledge of this effort to burst the atom and create the world's first nuclear bomb. Physicist J. Robert Oppenheimer led the project's highest-level research scientists at the top-secret Los Alamos National Laboratory in the New Mexico desert. In 1945, a test nuclear bomb exploded, the initial step toward the use of the two bombs dropped on Hiroshima and Nagasaki, Japan, ending the war in the Pacific.

Willard Libby, 1908–1980

Inventor and Scientist

A physical chemist, Libby went to work on the Manhattan Project in 1942. After the war, in 1947, while a professor at the University of Chicago, he made the discovery for which he was most famous—radiocarbon dating. Prior to that time, scientists, archeologists, and anthropologists had no positive means of determining the age of an ancient artifact or fossil. The discovery provided dates for hitherto unknown periods in human history and created a revolution in the study of humankind.

George Papanicolaou, 1883–1962

Inventor and Physiologist

A Greek scientist who immigrated to the United States in 1913, Papanicolaou spent his medical career at New York's Cornell Medical School. In 1927, he found evidence of growing cancer cells in a vaginal smear. Sixteen years later in 1943, he published the breakthrough paper, "Diagnosis of Uterine Cancer by the Vaginal Smear." He outlined the use of a diagnostic test to help doctors detect cervical cancer at an early stage and save women's lives, called the "Pap smear." After some years of convincing the medical profession, mass screenings became the norm, which led to a notable decline in this form of cancer, then second only to breast cancer as a killer of women.

John von Neumann, 1903–1957

Mathematician and Inventor

Termed a genius by his peers, von Neumann was one of the men (including Albert Einstein) who were invited to be the initial faculty at The Institute of Advanced Study at Princeton. A Hungarian-born numbers prodigy, von Neumann was a member of the Manhattan Project and made contributions in many areas of science and math. He was best known as the inventor of game theory. In his 1944 book, *Game Theory and Economic Behavior,* he coined the term "game theory," which soon gained wide use in many fields as a readily usable system of logic that allowed users to conceive of everything from finances to diplomacy as games bound by rules, which allowed the players to progressively narrow possibilities, and forecast results.

REFERENCES AND FURTHER READINGS

Adler, Mortimer J., and Milton Mayer. 1950. *The Revolution in Education*. Chicago: University of Chicago Press.

Curti, Merle. 1960. *Social Ideas of American Educators*. New Jersey: Littlefield, Adams.

Griswold A. Whitney. 1959. *Liberal Education and the Democratic Ideal*. New Haven: Yale University Press.

Hager, Thomas. 2006. *The Demon under the Microscope*. New York: Harmony Books, 2006.

Humes, Edward. 2006. *Over There: How the G.I. Bill Transformed the American Dream*. New York: Harcourt.

Hutchins, Robert Maynard. 1936. *Higher Learning in America*. New Haven: Yale University Press.

Kandel Isaac. 1949. *The Impact of War upon American Education*. Chapel Hill: University of North Carolina Press.

Katznelson, Ira. 2005. *When Affirmative Action Was White: An Untold History of Racial Discrimination in Twentieth-Century America*. New York: W. W. Norton.

Kevles, Daniel J. 1977. *The Physicists*. New York: Knopf.

Mettler, Suzanne. 2005. *Soldiers to Citizens: The G.I. Bill and the Making of the Greatest Generation*. New York: Oxford University Press.

Oren, Michael B. 2006. *Power, Faith and Fantasy: America in the Middle East, 1776 to the Present*. New York: W. W. Norton.

Polenberg, Richard. 1972. *War and Society: The United States 1941–1945*. New York: J. P. Lippincott.

Rhodes, Richard. 1986. *The Making of the Atomic Bomb*. New York: Simon and Schuster.

Sirjamaki, John. 1947. *The American Family in the Twentieth Century*. Boston: Houghton Mifflin.

Van Doren, Mark. 1943. *Liberal Education*. New York: Holt.

U.S. Army. 1943. *Instructions for American Servicemen in Iraq during World War II*. Chicago: University of Chicago Press (facsimile ed., 2007).

Domestic Life: Age, Gender, and Family

OVERVIEW

Domestic life of the 1940s can be reviewed reasonably well by examining five categories—youth, women, men, family, and religion—and within each category studying the home front during three timeframes: 1940–1942, the prewar years; 1942–1945, the war years; and 1946–1949, the postwar years. The war years especially transformed virtually all aspects of domesticity, creating unforeseen radical changes in all these categories.

Youth was generally defined for boys as being under 18 years of age and thus not yet eligible to be drafted; for girls there was no strict age definition because females were not included in the draft. Rather, a girl's youth ended when she left school. Teen boys were more likely, especially during the war years, to drop out of high school and work in the high-wage war industries. Teen girls stayed in school in greater numbers than boys, and more girls completed 12 years of schooling. During the war years, four million teens worked. For the first time, the country developed a distinct teen subculture, with its own music, slang, and style of dress, especially among girls. In the postwar boom, teens enjoyed even larger incomes or allowances and further evolved the teen culture into what would in the next decade be characterized by rock 'n' roll.

With a little time to go before the call to war, male teens committed crimes at a considerably higher rate than the national crime rate (this decreased during the war). Many adults were concerned by this rise in juvenile delinquency.

A small number of minority male teens rebelled by wearing the baggy zoot suits and causing riots in various big cities. Young single women also had a rise in illegitimate births, and some ran away to hang around military bases and experiment with a fast lifestyle.

Women in the decade proved to be incredibly capable and flexible beginning in the prewar period. They were simply grateful that the men folk in their families had finally found steady, well-paying blue-collar jobs after the widespread unemployment of the 1930s economic depression. When the war began and millions of men became part of the military, the labor shortage at home caused industry to recruit the single women, wives, and mothers for the jobs in factories. While a minority of women (most did not work but stayed at home or at military bases to wait for their husbands), the blue-collar women were uniquely adventurous and capable—most had to move some distance to find work, and many were single mothers. For the first time, they had to cope with all of the family responsibilities while living far away from home and friends.

However difficult, most women cherished their new autonomy and strength. Women created networks among themselves and gave mutual help in matters like commuting and childcare (the government provided childcare in only a few locations). While later displaced in their jobs by men and again relegated to the home, the work experiences of these women during the war planted a seed that later grew into the women's movement.

Men on the home front during the war fell into a variety of categories. Some were too old for the war and others had such family deferments as, for example, being an only son or the sole support for an aging parent. The largest number of men at home worked in industries vital to the war effort (for example, coal and the railroads). Millions had work deferments. With take-home pay high and few goods available because of shortages and rationing, men spent large sums of money on entertainment: nightclubs, horse races, gambling, drinking. Saturday night and all day Sunday were the times for having fun because war work was six days a week. In the postwar 1940s, the home front workers, concerned at first at being displaced by veterans and again being unemployed as during the 1930s, were instead absorbed into the hugely expanding boom economy.

As for the wartime family, the society upheld this grand myth of togetherness while the reality was very different—never before had the American family been so scattered and fragmented with its individuals having feelings of being rootless and lonely. Total war, which involved the entire civilian population working in conjunction with the overseas military, gave society a single major focus, which was a first-time experience for many families who were accustomed to a greater degree of autonomy from society. Social aberrations emerged with a rise in alcoholism (greater among women), quick marriages that would not last, and, according to the later Kinsey Report, a rise in adultery among married women. However, after 1946, when the divorce rate spiked, adults remarried a second time much more successfully and thrived as part of a family-oriented postwar boom.

Churches saw a continuing steep rise in membership during the entire decade of the 1940s. The main reason was that many people, understandably, had anxiety over so many large questions: the aftermath of victory in war, the long-term consequences of living in a nuclear age, and the threat of the new Cold War. Old time religion was the answer for many, and the postwar era saw a great rise in what some have called the American consensus religion, in which all Christian denominations seemed united in a vague sense of belief and of faith, without great heed for intellectual trappings or theology. The late 1940s saw a great rise in largely Protestant evangelicalism, a revival of personal spirituality by being "reborn" and telling others of your newfound faith.

TIMELINE

1940   Economy begins a steady, decade-long rise, fueled by defense contracts (to 1945) with teens and unemployed men finding more work than during the 1930s.

Pop music centers on big band swing music.

Divorce rate is 16 percent of all marriages.

1941   Military draft instituted with mandatory registration beginning with 18- and 19-year-olds on up to males age 36. It is the first peacetime draft in nation's history.

On December 7, Pearl Harbor is attacked by Japan; the United States subsequently declares war against Japan. Germany and Italy declare war on the United States.

1942   The first draft initially calls for teens born in 1923 and 1924 on up to 36-year-olds, born in 1906. Eligible males working in vital defense industries get deferments for the duration of the war. Draft's top age limit later upped to 37.

Four million teens work in war industries through the end of the war; many drop out of school at age 16 or 17 to work before being drafted.

The auto industry makes a conversion to the production of war materiel and ceases production of all cars. Americans must drive pre-1942 models.

Frank Sinatra is a new "bobby-soxer" crooning idol; at New York's Paramount Theater, his live singing creates the first instance of young girls screaming and fainting.

1943   There is a mini baby boom this and the previous year (some experts use this year as the start of the boom); births then taper off for the rest of the war.

Young male Mexicans in zoot suits riot in Los Angeles.

Women enter the workforce in record numbers and enter higher-paying factory jobs in a significant way. Many one-parent families populate new war-industry boomtowns.

The juvenile delinquency rate goes up.

1944   Big bands are broken up because of war's restrictions on train travel and hotel reservations; teen music of lead male "crooners" moves more into vogue. Overseas, many GIs still listen to swing, the music more in vogue upon leaving for war.

The number of women working outside the home peaks at 20 million.

Divorce rate is 27 percent, an increase of 11 percent since 1940.

1945   Teen subculture, the first in the nation's history, becomes full-blown in the war years, with crooners, jive music, and new dances such as the jitterbug.

The nuclear age begins for Americans. Children born after V-J Day (Victory in Japan) are the first generation to live every day with nuclear weapons and potential world destruction.

The military draft ends.

1946   New car models are produced for the first time since 1942. Teens use the older jalopies.

Many women are replaced by male veterans in factory work.

Dior's "New Look" becomes the vogue in women's fashion.

The movie *The Best Years of Our Lives* deals with the problems experienced by returning veterans and their families.

1947   The Cold War formally begins with the president instituting his Truman Doctrine.

1948   Military draft reinstituted for an indefinite period (the second in history, in peacetime, and in this decade) for readiness in the Cold War.

A three-year rise in mass consumption continues with the wartime boom. The government spending on the welfare of veterans is a great aid to this. The G.I. Bill is the largest social welfare program to date in the country's history.

1949   Families of the baby boom (from 1946 on, according to most experts) and suburban living increase in great numbers.

The divorce rate is 23 percent, down 4 percent since 1944.

The average family size is 3.6 persons.

America becomes the world's first and largest mass consumption society.

The country has 10 million television sets, and sales continue.

YOUTH

In the 1940s, youth in their teen years experienced both increased wealth and neglect. As the war production got fully under way, employment needs for the growing defense industries became so great that the government removed prior restrictions on child labor for those aged 13 and older; the result was 4 million teens (mostly boys) who worked in factories during the war. Many dropped out of schools, left the farms for the cities, or ran away to take these jobs—the first jobs available to many boys who had grown up in the Great Depression, when the rule had been mass unemployment. The war had brought full employment and general prosperity.

Teen Culture

Many teens lived in single-parent homes (a war widow or left-behind spouse) in a new city or town, where high paying work was available to women in new or converted factories producing wartime goods. The teen girls in these families stayed in school in greater numbers than boys. Most were given an allowance for necessities like school clothes but also for some discretionary items like a record player to listen to songs first heard on radio, the era's popular mass media. With discretionary income, both boys and girls bought according to their own tastes; thus, teens created for the first time in America a separate subculture shaped solely for this age group.

Juvenile Delinquency

Wartime relocations affected teens in significant ways. Often uprooted and living in a new, unknown city, in crowded housing, teens attended new schools without old friends, perhaps with a single mother who worked long hours. As a result, teens were often ill adjusted, lonely, and neglected. Older boys often had a "damn the devil" attitude, feeling a precious few years might be their last prior to the draft and the dangers of war. Some young girls were not willing to risk falling for boys their own age, who often had uncertain futures. Instead, they chose to project their longings onto one of their idolized crooners, such as Frank Sinatra.

Many of the boys rebelled. Hanging out on street corners, they got into trouble frequently. The crime rate for teens rose during the war. Overall, the national crime rate decreased in the war years largely because the aggressive, testosterone-fueled young men in their 20s were in the war overseas.

Girls also contributed to the rising wartime juvenile delinquency rate. Some became runaways and went to live near army training camps and many young men looking for a good time. Sexual activity increased for teen females during the war. The number of teen mothers giving birth to illegitimate children also grew in the war years.

Minority Teens and Racism

Minorities outside the dominant white culture, Chicano and African American male teens in this period rebelled by becoming "zoot suiters" or "zooters," and many joined gangs. Zoot suits had an overly long jacket with billowing pants and pinched cuffs along with a distinctive square-nosed, raised-heel shoe. Rebelliously flaunting an excess of fabric at a time when middle-class men sacrificed by giving up vests in their three-piece suits and doing without cuffs in pants, the zoot suit provoked antagonism from "decent" folk.

Los Angeles was one place that experienced such conflict in 1943 when the "zoot suit riot" erupted. The city's ghetto had expanded as Mexican pickers in the fields found jobs in the city's new defense industries, leaving their male teen offspring to idle away time. The riot started when groups of servicemen from a nearby base roved in cars around the East Los Angeles' Mexican barrio and beat up any Mexican teen wearing a zoot suit. White civilians approved and the police pretended not to see. This melee had started with the rumor that a zooter gang of Mexicans (also called pachucos) had beaten up a serviceman at a dance club. Military officials finally ended it after a few days by restricting servicemen to their base. Long-standing widespread white racism against Mexicans had prolonged the riot.

On the East Coast, African American teen zoot suiters in Harlem were the earliest precursor to both the postwar African American hipsters and the mostly white beatniks. Associated with jazz, these early wartime African American rebel teens dressed as zooters to outrage and defy conventional patriotism about the war among their elders. How did one fight Germany and Japan's racism when

Zoot suiters line up outside of jail en route to court after being attacked by some drunken and xenophobic sailors, June 9, 1943. (Library of Congress)

America itself was permeated with white racism directed at Mexicans and African Americans, whose minority teens were soon expected to join the fight? "With an outrageous outfit" is how, these rebellious teen outsiders seemed to be saying.

Teens in the Postwar Period

After the war's end, the teen generation relished the first prolonged boom time of their lives. Their parents had money saved during the war to consume the new readily available goods, which often included an older car for a teen-aged son. Other teen sons had postwar jobs and bought their own new late-1940s' cars. Soon a youth car culture sprang up with hot rods, drive-ins, and just cruising around with tanks full of no-longer-rationed gas.

The girls readily adopted media urgings to marry, have a family, and own a home in the new suburbs. Returning servicemen made for good prospective husbands, given their more mature ways. They also had assured income from the government G.I. Bill and increased chances of going to college with the promise of a long business career. This meant lifetime security for young women who had been teens during the war. The buying power of these new families (baby clothes, appliances, furniture) added force to the expanding economy.

Jobless 1930s Affects 1940s Teens

Beginning in 1940, youths aged 13 to 19 formed a group that since childhood had lived in a post-1929 crash and depression world of scarcity, insecurity, and anxiety about the future. During their brief lives, they had only one president, Franklin D. Roosevelt, who first came into office in 1932; a year later, the country's economy hit the depths with the jobless rate rising to one out of every three workers. Many adults who still had jobs were working part time, barely able to pay for necessities. In the first 100 days of 1933, Roosevelt inaugurated his New Deal, which evolved in various phases until the end of the 1930s but never succeeded in relieving the country of the great burden of mass unemployment. Beginning in 1940, there were still four million jobless, even though some preparedness defense contracts were beginning to produce jobs.

In 1940, families continued to struggle to get on by being frugal, and young adults often continued to live with their parents so everyone could earn some of the family income. Schooling was often too great a sacrifice; in 1940, only 50 percent had gone to high school. During the Depression, young persons postponed marriage or, if they did marry, often lived with the husband's or the wife's family and postponed having children. By the end of the decade, marriage and birth rates had both fallen. Women and girls often had an easier time finding work because the employer could pay them less than a male worker. Many had what were called Depression-proof jobs doing women's work—teaching, social work, social work, and civil service. Many wives supported the family because the traditional breadwinner, the husband, was unable to find work and often ashamed to admit this. He often felt like a failure and a poor example to his sons; in turn, they saw little if any hope of ever rising up out of their station in life. Three of four single women, mostly young daughters living at home, had to work but they did so for very little pay.

Up to 1940, America's young people rarely differentiated their own consumer needs from their family's need for necessities. Personal indulgence by a young person was frowned upon by the adult world. Youth did have their own tastes in music; they enjoyed swing music by the big bands, and the radio gave this free. At parties, if one friend had a record player, all could jitterbug to the same tunes.

1940–1941, Peacetime Jobs and the Draft

In 1940 and 1941, the situation in the country's economy changed for the good when third-term president Roosevelt directed big manufacturers to produce armaments for growing national defense needs and, by 1941, for military aid to the Allies fighting Germany and Japan. Billions of dollars in military preparedness contracts soon spiked production to new levels and created new jobs. Fathers began returning to jobs; now for the first time in their lives, young people had a sense of hope for more family income and possibly jobs again for young males.

Pearl Harbor and Teens

The Japanese attack on Pearl Harbor, December 7, 1941, created massive call-ups for the draft. Among those reporting were all young males aged 18 and 19. (The draft included men through the age of 35.) Most of these late-teen draftees qualified and were sent to American training bases. It was the first time away from home for many. It also was the first time most of these teens mixed with so many other different Americans—old stock, recent immigrant, older immigrants. Their provinciality would slowly give way to a growing worldliness. This worldliness was even more pronounced once the new trainees were dispatched to foreign lands.

The wartime boom brought prosperity to teens who remained on the home front; they were allowed to work from age 13 on. Many dropped out of high school to go to work, some worked while awaiting the draft. Because of these wartime jobs, for the first time in this country's history, this age group had the independent spending power to indulge their tastes in popular culture, creating a true teen subculture separate from the older generations.

In 1940, the president and Congress instituted the first peacetime draft requiring all young males, age 18 and over to register at their local draft boards. Young men grumbled about this, complaining it was unnecessary because the country, at the time, was dominantly isolationist and opposed to America entering a foreign war. Youth were often influenced by their elders, who told them that the prior Great War of 1917 to 1919 had not been worth the price America had paid then to save Europe—a folly that should not be repeated. The majority opinion held that America should not go to war but should serve instead as an arsenal of democracy.

Because peace, preparedness, and production meant jobs, many young males saw this situation as being very much in their personal best interest, as well as the nation's best interest. Most had paid scant attention to the aggressions of Germany and Japan because, they believed, they posed no direct military threat to America. The peoples and lands involved in this war seemed far away to most Americans and the strife escaped most of them because their education was limited to American affairs. What did interest them was the novel prospect of jobs.

Bobby-Soxers Are the First Teen Culture

The 1930s Swing Generation did have their own youthful style: their dance was the jitterbug; music, the big bands; and in girls' fashions, it was convertible raincoats, two-tone saddle shoes, cardigan sweaters, and long socks. In the early

1940s, a new youth generation known for their change to short socks—"bobby-soxers"—supplanted the earlier pop tastes. Fashonable dress was a parka, loafers, and baggy sweater—a precursor to blue jeans worn with a man's white shirt hanging out. Their preference in music was for individual male singers, "crooners" was the nickname, such as 25-year-old Frank Sinatra (who was not drafted because he was rated 4F due to a pierced eardrum). He looked high school age and had the distinction of becoming the first teenage singing idol.

Sinatra became the first great sex symbol for teen girls at a time when their boy peers were moving up to draft age and being sent off to war. Left behind, often pining for love, girls were the dominant tastemakers in the evolving youth culture that, by 1943, became the first actual teen subculture. These girls were of the first generation to have money to indulge their tastes: to buy records, go to live concerts, and even splurge on bobbles such as rings of jet black to symbolize a GI friend (real or imagined) gone overseas. These peculiarities set this group apart, and the older generation took notice; they disapproved of the antics of the "bobby-soxers" who began flocking to live concerts by the new male crooners.

A line of teenage girls, holding Song Hits *magazine, waiting for singer Frank Sinatra to arrive at the Paramount Theatre in New York, 1945. (Library of Congress)*

Frank Sinatra, the First Teen Idol

It happened on December 30, 1942. Frank Sinatra, a singer who accompanied Harry James and other big bands, gave a solo concert at New York's Paramount Theater. Midway through the performance, a girl in one of the rows closest to the stage fainted and fell to the floor. It was later determined she had been dieting and had missed lunch. The girl next to her screamed, thinking she was dead. Sinatra kept singing. Within minutes, all the girls present began shrieking, moaning, screaming, and fainting. Most Sinatra concerts during this period caused the same reaction. Girls wept and tried to tear off pieces of his clothing for souvenirs. To disapproving parents, this was something new on the American scene—teens seemingly as a category rebelling against their parents.

Sinatra quickly became known as "The Voice." His solo appearances replaced the swing bands he had once fronted. Swing was the music loved by the first American fighting men who went overseas. When they came back in 1945, many of the big bands had broken up or been overtaken by something called progressive jazz. The new jazz singers were unknowns at the time of Pearl Harbor.

Postwar Teen Culture

Male teens of the 1940s comprised two broad categories: those who had turned 18 and were draft age during the war years (born from 1924 to 1927) and those born after 1927 and those who reached the draft age of 18 after the war, from 1946 to 1950. Girls were the dominant sex among wartime teens (they were not included in the draft). So they were the prime instigators of the country's first teen subculture, the "bobby-soxers." All teens were referred to as "youth" during the first half of the decade. The distinctive term "teenagers" did not come into use until 1946, when it was coined in the *New York Times*. The teen subculture mixed girls with boys in a normal peacetime fashion in the late 1940s; therefore, the influence of the young males began to show in the subtly changing subculture.

After 1946, cars become the status symbol for high school boys (they got drivers' licenses at age 16 more frequently than girls did). Many American men were eager to buy new model cars (produced again in 1946 after a three-year hiatus), and their high school sons borrowed the family car for dates. Drive-in restaurants and movies soon became teen gathering places. California set trends for much of this evolving subculture. The drive-in movies became "passion pits" where teen couples engaged in sexual explorations in the dark in front of the giant screens. Teen males also bought pre-1942 "hot rods" cheaply and customized them to give an individual look to a mass-produced older model.

Musical tastes of this young set became more inclusive; the crooners still captured audiences on records, radio, and in live concerts. Youthful jazz tastes turned further away from swing (the music of parents) and began to embrace progressive jazz and the new sound of bebop coming from Charlie Parker and others. New songs were still heard first on the radio, but their lyrics often were composed by regional unknowns (not the well-known traditional songwriters of Tin Pan Alley), sung by newcomers, recorded in independent studios, and made popular by a local radio station's disk jockey repeatedly playing a new favorite. Record sales often followed if the song became a teen hit. In this opening up of the music business, the way was cleared for the "race music" of African Americans singing blues and rhythm and blues on their own record labels. In this way, the early 1950s crossover white-black phenomenon of teen rock 'n' roll was made possible. In a way, it was youth affirming the early beginnings of the civil rights movement.

The late-1940s teen culture had another distinction. These young people would be the first to live their entire adult lives in the new nuclear age, where all human life could vanish in an atomic war. The United States had dropped two atomic bombs on Hiroshima and Nagasaki in 1946. But when the Soviet Union tested its first A-bomb in 1949, fearful Americans understood this weapon of unfathomable destruction could be as easily used against them as by them. Youth of the era in the greatest numbers soon adopted the anxieties and trends that riddled mainstream society—becoming security conscious, cautious, and conformist in reaction to the government-induced mass fear of internal subversion or external attack by the communists. As voters, they supported increasing the portion of the budget devoted to the military.

In general, almost all teens of this decade, by 1946, felt a deep yearning for security, having passed almost all the early years of their lives either in the Great Depression or World War II. Most saw the means to this desired security in the developing postwar culture of prosperity, materialism, consumerism, and anti-communism. They welcomed such trends and believed these trends gave personal meaning to their lives.

As early as this, however, some of the prominent figures of a coming culture of protest were rebellious in their late teens. Allen Ginsberg, in 1945, was expelled from Columbia University for tracing a forbidden word in the dust on a window. By the early 1950s, the rebellious teens became the Beats, intensely critical of this postwar culture supported by the vast majority, whom they saw as blind two-dimensional sheep lost in a kind of Orwellian 1984 of their own making (Orwell's dystopian book was first published in 1949).

Postwar Baby Boom and Pregnant Single Teens

During the postwar 1940s, with so many veterans home and marrying or dating, the country's sexual mores became more relaxed as witnessed by data in the Kinsey Report; for married couples, the result was the start of the baby boom.

Some teen and single women also experimented sexually. However, this was an era when little or no contraception was available, and should the woman become pregnant and want an abortion, it was of course illegal.

However, abortion at the time was a class matter. A single pregnant woman from a wealthy family had a much better chance of finding a good doctor to perform an abortion than one from a poorer family. Rich teen girls did not have the same problem as their high school peers from homes of lesser means. Cheap abortions were available; yet the danger of going to a secret "back-alley" doctor was high, and girls risked death.

A pregnant unmarried teen-aged mother had limited choices. One was what was termed a "shotgun wedding" in which the girl's father pressured his daughter's boyfriend to marry her before the arrival of the child, making the baby legitimate. An "illegitimate" child was the terminology of the time used for an infant born out of wedlock—something that shamed the mother and her family. At the time, with many families rising newly into the middle class and seeking acceptance from their new neighbors in the suburbs, a daughter in this predicament could blight their hopes of being the model family seen so often in advertisements.

The unwed mother-to-be had the choice of telling the child's father and hoping he would do the honorable thing by marrying her and taking responsibility for the child. Sometimes this did happen. But the double standard of the time made some others less than honorable: men would be praised for sexual conquests while their lovers would be ostracized if they became pregnant or were rumored to be active with a number of men. Indeed, some men refused to take responsibility for various reasons; at other times, the mother was too embarrassed even to tell the father.

An unwed mother had another but risky choice: tell her family and hope they would accept the child and help her raise the child as a single mother. At the time, this option was the slimmest of all. An exception was made among some African American families, who would accept the new child, usually after the daughter had gone away from home to have the baby.

Homes for unwed mothers were what these single women opted for most often at the time. Under enormous pressure from church, family, and society, the women disappeared, went away to a home, gave birth, and then surrendered the child for adoption under the condition the mother would never know the whereabouts or even the name of her child. Some 1.5 million women gave up their children for adoption between the 1940s and 1973, according to an oral history of their stories (Fessler 2006).

WOMEN

In the 1940s, women on the home front went through a number of phases. During the prewar years of 1940 to 1941, the government contracted with defense industries for preparedness and lend-lease materials. New jobs resulting from increased production meant that the male heads of families often needed to move to secure these opportunities in new boomtowns. During the war, 1942 to 1945, the country sent a total of 16 million men and women overseas (about 350,000 were servicewomen), which left a vast labor shortage; married women were then given the opportunity to migrate with their families to boomtowns. Then expanding factories called for female workers to help fill well-paid, blue-collar jobs. During the war, however, the majority of married women did not work. They moved to army bases to wait for their husbands to return. In the third post-war phase, returning veterans replaced women in factories, and the displaced women were told by society and government that their true place was in the home caring for their families. For many, this meant still another migration to a new life in the postwar suburbs.

New Wartime Horizons

There were constants in the working women's lives during the 1940s: migration, adaptability, the difficulty of being both sole breadwinner and mother. On and off military bases, the women waiting had the underlying fear of becoming war widows with fatherless children.

In the positive sense, wartime 1940s women experienced a whole new sense of independence, often of necessity because they moved from the familiar to an unknown place, handled all their finances, and planned for their futures. In the boomtowns, whether those housing military bases or defense industries, women met other newly arrived women from all over the country. They had common problems and formed networks of female friends to help one another solve these unusual new wartime challenges. Single mothers working in factories, for instance, often had long difficult commutes and worked six-day weeks with overtime. These mothers needed other women to help with day care, transportation, and babysitting (the government only occasionally provided child care). Strong bonds grew among these women.

Women migrating to other regions gained a sometimes startling new awareness of different laws and mores within a new place, especially northerners coming for the first time to the South where the races were legally separated in all public facilities. Grace Paley, the noted American short story writer, tells a story from her own experience of the firsthand shock of being hit with the color line after coming from the Bronx to the South with her first husband, who was assigned to a training camp there before going overseas. With husbands gone overseas, Paley speaks of the growth of a special comradeship among the women on base. Paley credits the long-remembered positive memory of this as influencing the northern support for the civil rights movement in the 1950s and the feminist cause in the 1960s.

Evelyn and Lillian Buxkeurple work on a practice bombshell at the Naval Air Base in Corpus Christi, Texas, in August 1942. (National Archives)

Postwar Prospects

In the postwar 1940s, while factory women were being replaced by returning veterans, polls showed a large majority chose to continue in those jobs. Those who left did so not through personal choice but to meet the expectations of a society that wished to return to normalcy after the end of the fighting. Women, especially married women, continued to work outside the home in greater numbers than during the war, except at much lower-paying jobs in the growing pink-collar job ghetto of typists and telephone operators in the expanding service sector of the new state-corporate society. Always seeming to be able to make the best of a difficult situation, postwar women took on two jobs: working at a job outside the home as well as inside the home, caring for the family. Working women actually retained more personal satisfaction in their lives than the isolated suburban wives, whose duties were limited to home and family care; in the suburbs, generally only the husbands worked. Frustration at a lack of personal fulfillment on the part of these suburban wives later fueled the women's liberation movement of the 1960s. The experience women had of nearly equal work status and autonomy during World War II and joining in common cause with other women from around the country during the war set a precedent for their daughters' later crusade for equal rights.

Female Life Compared with the 1930s

The women of the 1940s carried over lessons learned in the 1930s. Women in both decades faced different constrictions but they adapted and coped well, often adopting variations on earlier methods. In the 1930s with Depression-caused food scarcity, women developed scrimping to a fine art; in wartime, with government-caused scarcity, housewives used rationing and currency to squeeze their food budgets. The wartime housewife had few actual money worries even though she faced a scarcity of life's necessities. This set her apart from the same role in the Depression. Married women in the 1940s worked as single parents (with husbands in the military overseas) in high-paying factories, but this tradition of married women working outside the home began in 1930s when wives had stepped in because their husbands couldn't find work. Infant care and child rearing were difficult in both decades. A mother in the 1930s usually had others to help at home, which was often overcrowded with in-laws and other relatives out of work and at home. During the war, the mother working in a defense plant 48 hours per week was a single parent raising a family in a new strange place without day care. Her children were often "latchkey kids," who were sometimes prone to getting into trouble in the idle hours after school.

Wartime single women, in general, saw increased earnings due to higher productivity; they frequently felt economically secure enough to risk early marriage to a soldier going overseas and even to have a child. The rate of wartime babies rose in 1942 and 1943 then, fell for the next two years; in 1946, the birth rate spiked dramatically, which began the famous unpredicted, and unprecedentedly high birth rates that continued for years. Marriage rates and birth rates rose slightly during war and greatly in the late 1940s due largely to the return of prosperity.

Lack of prosperity during the Depression created the opposite circumstances; women postponed marriage until the prospective groom had enough savings for them to manage household duties together. While late marriage was sanctioned, Depression-era mores dictated no children—a young couple could not afford them. Children were seen as an economic burden.

Yet, these 1930s trends gave women new, unexpected freedoms that carried over into the war years. Putting off marriage, a young woman could feel fine being single, even it led to eventual spinsterhood. Pioneer career women served as models for females devoted to public service and politics. Frances Perkins, the Secretary of Labor, was one such model, and the most striking example to women was Eleanor Roosevelt. A new type of childless marriage evolved in the 1930s, which also proved a way for a woman to get more freedom as part of a

Women's Fashions Change with Wartime Austerity

Women's fashion changed during the war. The American fashion industry shifted its focus away from war-torn Paris, the traditional fashion center, and substituted American designs featuring sportswear. Because fabric was rationed, skirts and jackets were short. Women turned to separates as a way of expanding their wardrobes. Leather was reserved for use by the military, so shoe manufacturers turned to snakeskin, mesh, and other substitutes. Shoe heels were limited to one inch, and shoes were only allowed in six colors. Shoes with cork wedges were popular. After 1943, stockings were not available. Women painted a line down the back of their legs, simulating stockings, or used tan to color their legs. White ankle socks also became popular. Following the "Rosie the Riveter" style, women dressed down and took on a more casual look, especially on college campuses. Women returned to sewing at home, and altering or recycling clothing. They used new patterns to transform men's suits into women's clothing and women's dresses into children's garments. *Vogue* magazine gave tips on how to "Mend & Make Do." In 1947, with the war over, Dior's "new look" brought back feminine, small-waisted dresses with long skirts made with yards of fabric. This seemed luxurious after the limitations of the war years. The new look was romantic and feminine, the opposite of Rosie.

couple. Husband and wife both had the private time to develop personal talents while sharing or alternating the workload. Single women coping alone or married women without children were models for single women in wartime.

Married Women and Wartime Work

From 1942 to 1945, married women worked for the first time in large numbers outside of the home. It was a precedent but for only a temporary duration. In 1945, many women gave up what had been their first high-paying factory jobs and returned to their traditional role as homemakers. This resumption of the traditional female role was a critical decision for this generation of women. Americans, in general, approved. In one poll, seven of eight thought homemaking was women's rightful role.

Middle-class married women, especially, had done war work out of economic necessity and found relief in turning away from work and returning to the home. A poll shortly after war's end found that 76 percent of women felt no great loss in leaving war work. A telling 24 percent, however, did find the work meaningful, and many of these yearned for equal job opportunity with males. It was not feasible at the time.

Nearly 70 percent of married women chose to remain as full-time home-makers throughout the war. Although the government and industry began an all-out campaign to tap one of the last remaining unused pools of labor, only one in three of the country's married women answered their country's call to enter factories and help boost war production.

Nevertheless, Americans bound to tradition insisted that a married woman's place was in the home. Contrary to the smiling Rosie happily holding her riveting gun, the first women to reverse gender roles and take on factory work met with ridicule from their male co-workers. Some of them were subjected to rumors that they were having affairs, especially those who worked on the night shift. With a scarcity of government day care centers, those who were working mothers left their children unsupervised at times, and if these children got in trouble, many traditionalists blamed the mother who was made to feel guilty for taking up the offer of a high-paying job, most often out of economic necessity. The force of tradition remained hard set against this trend.

Nonetheless, from 1942 to 1944, 72 percent of all women hired were married. By 1944, for the first time in the country's history, married women outnumbered single women at work. In that year, the total of all working women was just short of 20 million, a record for the time. Nearly 12 million (including a small percentage of married women) had been working in 1940, two years before the wartime surge. Some 8 million married women did war work; many had worked while single, but for most, it was the first chance to work at high-paid factory jobs traditionally held by men.

The Postwar Push for the Traditional Woman

Late in 1944, with veterans soon expected to return, the media began a campaign that urged women leave their wartime work. The women's magazines, a powerful force, reminded women that in its original 1942 campaign to recruit married women, the government had stated their help was needed only until the end of hostilities. With victory imminent, the magazines advised women that taking an early leave was wise. Home duties were pressing, and they were particularly urged to care for their children, to make up for the lost love and attention during their months and years of work. The "back to the nest" campaign used guilt as a motivator.

Meanwhile, the divorce rate divorce increased to 27 percent in 1944 from 16 percent in 1940. Although the reasons for breakups were numerous, including whirlwind marriages to furloughed strangers, many social conservatives liked to blame it solely on women working.

Many others were grateful to these women for doing their part for the war, but they had limited patience with a woman who insisted on keeping her job instead of giving it to a returning veteran. Americans in large numbers welcomed the prospect of the women returning home to restore the traditional family. After working in this temporary national emergency, some even believed women had undergone few changes. This ran contrary to the latter 1960s feminist revolt of their daughters, who rebelled against the homemaking suburban life styles that their own mothers had ultimately chosen after the war. Rosie the Riveter became mythic later, not at the time.

Women Fuel Mass Consumption

In World War II, the government mobilized the entire population for the fight— no aspect of society was left without changes in these years. Women's work roles certainly underwent changes during the war. But these changes were not of a lasting nature in the postwar. There was no radical restructuring of gender and work, no second wave of feminism, although some women, and particualry black women for whom the war provided hitherto impossible work opportunities, continued to relish the wages and independence of a job and continued to work. But other women (and men!) welcomed, although sometimes in a stoic way, their return to the traditional expectations for women at home and at work.

Joseph Tannenbaum rations canned foods to his customers in his New York City grocery store, December 28, 1942. (Library of Congress)

Easter 1947:
American Women Adopt Dior's New Look

In 1946, the Parisian clothes designer Christian Dior introduced a New Look with dresses of yards of fabric and long mid-calf skirts. Extravagantly made, Dior's new wardrobe aimed to replace the sparely made wartime styles of short skirts and no-frills blouses that adhered to fabric limits imposed due to scarcity. The wartime style showing women's legs appealed to men who disliked the newly proposed style. Women wavered; some protested that Paris ought not to assume its pre-war role of dictating fashion to American women; others objected to the expense required for an entirely new wardrobe to keep in style. In the end, come Easter 1947, women used money or expanded credit to chose Dior.

Women during war had proved they could do what had been considered men's work. But the majority seemed willing to return to the homemaking role.

During wartime, women did greatly expand one of their important roles—that of consumer. Absent their husbands, married women, both working and non-working, assumed the role of the one decisive primary consumer in the family—taking command of purchases traditionally made by men. With money and a scarcity of goods, women enjoyed just window-shopping, but they also consumed and were a primary reason the rate of domestic consumption doubled during wartime. Women bought in a panic, as in 1942, when a sudden goods shortage hit along with rumors of worse still to come. Black markets were familiar to many women who were willing to pay more under the table, for instance, for a pair of nylons. This was so even if such illegal purchases undercut a quite just and fair rationing system. Women became the major buyers and were the target of most advertising.

In the postwar, women proved the engine of consumer choice (the pattern was often that his wife's preference became a man's choice). Women continued to be powerful consumers in their own right, even when their choice did not at first meet with men's approval.

Women Forced to Return to Low-paying Traditional Jobs

A certain number of women (some married but mostly single) had traditionally worked outside the home in low-paying jobs before the war. After the elimination of higher-paying factory jobs and the exodus of many women from the workplace in 1945, the working women who remained found themselves in jobs that reverted to earlier gender patterns. More women than ever filled the low-paying jobs considered "women's work" such as switchboard operators. With the emergency labor shortage of war over, the jobs in defense and war industries disappeared, and women were crowded into low paid repetitive jobs.

Throughout the 1940s, few women were in the upper level professional jobs—as doctors, lawyers, mid-level managers—because they faced male-made barriers for entering graduate schools and being hired. Men tended to frown upon career women and expressed the attitude that women would work only temporarily in high-level jobs before leaving for marriage and family.

As to pay, women traditionally received 60 percent of what men earned for doing the same work. This held true for the newly hired women welders and riveters doing war work. Their record income was due to these jobs linking to the highest wages ever paid to women, so it was good money, even if 40 percent less than a male counterpart.

Even during World War II, only a minority of women worked in factories while the majority of women continued doing the traditional women's jobs. Men rationalized that females had innate traits that made them more suited for repetitive work. The war made this even more emphatic, when males doing any work of this sort gave it up to women. By 1945, for instance, the typing, secretarial, and clerical jobs had a female contingent of near 100 percent while back in 1942, males still held nearly 50 percent of these jobs. Many women also replaced men as store salespersons and as bank tellers. Women could be paid less, and men could find higher-paying jobs elsewhere. Working women were locked in what was termed a pink-collar ghetto in the postwar—salaried jobs but without security or protection from sudden termination.

MEN

In the 1940s, men on the home front fell into four categories: those too young for war (under age 18 as of 1942); those too old for war (the draft limit moved up from age 36 to 37 as of 1942); those termed 4F and disqualified from serving; and the many who had partial deferments from the draft (including married men and fathers) and those with full deferments.

Men in Vital War Work

Millions of men had full deferments from the draft because of their work in defense factories or other industries deemed vital to the nation's economy. This was by far the largest group of deferments. These men, for example, included workers in defense factories, farmers, coal miners (coal was the era's primary energy source fueling electrical plants and firing hearths for the making of steel), railroad workers, and electrical workers.

Work Experience Changes

Men working at home front jobs vital to the war had a variety of unprecedented experiences. In the many northern and western war industry locations, men worked alongside women for the first time doing heavy-duty factory work such as welding and riveting. Races, ethnics, classes, and regions mixed in wartime blue-collar work—northern white ethnic men and women labored for the first time along with newly arrived southerners, mostly rural whites and African Americans. Industrial unions, to the surprise of many of these workers, had the full acceptance of management for the first time and enjoyed government support.

Traditional white male workers experienced numerous troubling changes during the war. Due to the need to fill expanded employment needs in the area, outsiders suddenly moved into hometowns or local neighborhoods. With no new housing to assist this influx, the old housing suddenly was overcrowded and turned into slums. While the government mandated in its defense contracts that whites and African Americans would work together, northern white neighborhoods exhibited racism. De facto segregation kept African Americans in their own neighborhoods. In 1943, race riots broke out in Detroit, Cleveland, and Harlem because of tensions between whites and African Americans over housing and jobs.

War, Prosperity, and Entertainment

Defense workers enjoyed the first prosperous period in most of their lifetimes. Jobs provided record high personal income from high wages and from overtime pay. Those workers who had long commutes to work were given government preference in the form of "A" ration stamps for gas for their pre-1942 cars (no autos were manufactured between 1943 and 1946). Most of these workers had time for enjoyment and fun only on Saturday nights and Sundays, because of their otherwise demanding jobs with long daily hours and six-day workweeks.

With limited consumer goods and rationing for those goods that were available, men had only their own entertainment for expendable income. Bars, casinos, illegal gambling establishments earned peak profits during the war. Liquor in certain areas and at certain times ran out due to war scarcity, which prompted periodic revivals of bootlegging (once common during the 1920s Prohibition years). Black marketers broke or hedged around the laws limiting consumer goods so that almost any otherwise law-abiding citizen knew that, for a price, almost anything was still obtainable. Average Americans (mostly rogue males) spent more and more on the black market in 1944 and 1945, much to the dismay of the government regulators asking for common sacrifice from all on the home front.

Stigma for Some War Workers

The general public often referred to males in defense jobs as "draft dodgers" who sought the deferments to avoid war. Yet, the government, realizing in total war these civilian makers of arms and supplies were equal in importance to the fighting men on the front lines, did everything possible to hold these workers in the factories with the national labor scarcity. Absenteeism became a growing problem as victory seemed nearer. The government tried to combat this with posters on factory walls. One poster, for example, shows a close-up of a man fishing in a rowboat with the slogans, "In the 'Service' They're DESERTERS. Don't be a PRODUCTION SLACKER." The government's goal was for civilian workers to remain focused on steady, efficient production to bring the war to a quicker end. War workers themselves were not necessarily super patriots. Many viewed their work as simply getting the job done.

By war's end, many of these male war workers feared that war veterans replacing them would again mean mass unemployment and a return to the

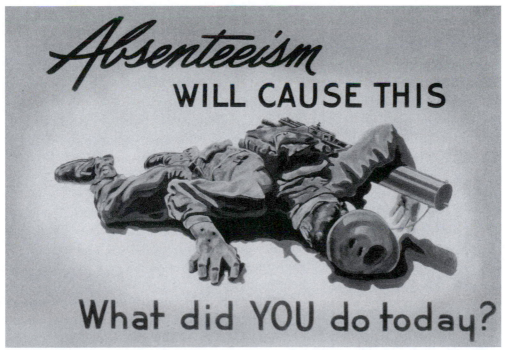

Poster produced by the War Production Board: "Absenteeism Will Cause This. What did You do today?" (National Archives)

Depression. However, while postwar dislocations did take place, these one-time war workers eventually found good jobs and a continuity of the comfortable living the war had first afforded them. The postwar boom absorbed them in high-paying union jobs while many returning veterans had broader avenues of upward mobility because of the G.I. Bill, which made a college degree possible.

The Draft Calls Up the Depression-Bred Male

Men in the decade that began in 1940, whether blue or white collar, shared a common experience of enduring family hardship during the 1930s. The Depression experience created a mutual bond. American society then was more hierarchical; imagine a pyramid: the rich were the very tip, beneath them to a line about a third down was the middle class, the bottom nearly two-thirds was the working class, and the extremely poor were at the bottom. Blue-collar family members were the majority of society, and they experienced the greatest unemployment; the smaller middle class had only recently expanded with the rise of white-collar work service, professional and clerical work. The rich were largely industrialists, financiers, and a few whose fortunes from the late-19th century survived the 1929 crash.

In Suzanne Mettler's *Soldiers to Citizens,* based on her series of interviews and surveys with surviving veterans, she found that those answering the 1940s draft shared common experiences from their Depression-era upbringing: 44 percent had a father out of work; 25 percent had a working mother who often was the sole breadwinner; and 77 percent had worked at any job available. Many of these young men had to cut short their educations and often suffered dietary deficiencies.

Draft call-ups from 1940 on and voluntary enlistments required physical and mental testing to qualify. The early rejection rate was a surprising 30 percent. Men aged 30 to 36 had a 40 percent rejection rate. This spoke to the damage done to individuals due to the years of stress and deprivation of the 1930s. Sixteen million Americans registered for the draft in 1940 (draft age was 21 to 36 from 1940 to 1942, and was changed in late 1943 to ages 18 through 37). In addition to the 16 million who served, millions of others were termed 4F and rejected for the military. Of the total rejected, 17 percent were rejected for mental reasons, 14 percent because of illiteracy or failure on an IQ test, and the rest for physical reasons. Many had ailments due to gross overweight caused by the fatty and sweet foods customarily eaten by the poor.

All men during the wartime 1940s carried memories of the 1930s, whether these were the 16 million men in the military or their 15 million and more counterparts working on the domestic front producing massive amount of armaments, food, and consumer goods. If from a family in the predominant blue-collar class, the father's memories may have been of disgrace at losing his factory job and being stuck at home unable to find work while his wife became the working head of family. The children had to contribute to helping the family by their own meager earnings. Lack of work often left fathers of the 1930s feeling emasculated; the 1930s-era sons became closer to their mothers. Even through the prosperous 1940s, the blue-collar family's constant fear of falling into greater poverty due to an outside force undermined the family's peace of mind.

Prosperity Washes Over Prior Deprivation

In time, the war would bring prosperity to the country's wage earners and greatly expand the numbers of the salaried middle-class in the next decades. In 1940, however, this latter class was still relatively small. These families expended great effort to maintain their status, frequently with the same methods as the wage-earning family, by scrimping and doing without. The salaried took pay cuts to retain jobs but customarily did not make that public because others would then know the truth behind appearances. They struggled to keep up appearances and had a fear of circumstances beyond their control that would cast their family back down into the working class from which many had only recently risen.

After 1940 with the boom in war production, rich heads of corporations felt less constrained than they had during the Depression by prolabor legislation or a public sense of their responsibility for the economic collapse. In the 1930s, businessmen were the scapegoats for not having seen the 1929 debacle and for opposing social reforms. Aware of so many poor and unemployed, the wealthy heads of family had played down their wealth by, for instance, dry-docking their yachts and shutting down their big summer houses. Shortly after the start of war, the largest heads of corporations were again making profits, with the welcome generous subsidies and necessary oversight from government.

Postwar Males on the Path to Full Employment

For the generation's males, the pivotal year was 1946. The economy then did not sink back into depression. The widespread prediction had been that when the government cut back on the record spending of the war years, the economy would constrict, leaving unemployment at the 1930s level and displacing wartime workers to give up their jobs to returning veterans. Postwar economic disaster did not occur though: the United States had learned one important lesson for the home front during the war—government spending made for general prosperity. Thus, in 1944, the conservative Congress passed the G.I. Bill to ensure that returning veterans had financial security to remain consumers while finding a job. Part of this bill guaranteed veterans $20 a week for one year as they looked for work, hence the term the "52/20 club." The government's low-cost veterans' mortgages in turn spurred the country's construction, banking, and real estate industries, which made jobs in these fields available.

This male generation was the first to abide by the deficit spending theories of the famous English economist, John Maynard Keynes. For example, the massive wartime government contracts to industries created huge numbers of new jobs at higher earnings so that as the economy expanded, so did government tax totals on industrial profits and personal earnings. This generation realized that the government had not risked nearly the deficit required to have spent the economy out of depression. The government did spend during the war, and most American males, whether war veterans or defense workers, supported the government in maintaining high spending levels in the postwar late 1940s. As a result, the high prosperity level continued and even rose higher in peacetime.

Postwar Younger Men Become Mostly Middle Class

The wartime boom, and most especially the high levels of consumer goods available during the conversion to a peacetime economy, turned America's pyramidal social hierarchy on it's head. In the 1930s, a majority of families were of the working class, whereas by the end of the 1940s, a majority of Americans saw themselves as "middle class" (based on earnings and accompanying lifestyles of both high-paid wage earnings and a growing salaried class). The war had been a leveler of prewar class distinctions. Most male heads of family in the postwar counted themselves as broadly middle class, albeit the new language of class increasingly bespoke a language of consumption rather than the collar of the worker.

Competition among males in this broad middle class frequently had to do with displaying subtle gradations of symbols of status within that class. The Buick Roadmaster, for instance, had four portals on each side of the hood; the less-expensive models had progressively fewer portals. Ads of the late 1940s urged the individual to rise up in status within the middle class. Ads assumed continued prosperity and projected a brighter future for all if one kept up with the Joneses. Ads telling of the rewards of still higher social mobility for those already comfortable stood in bold contrast to the negative 1930s ads that emphasized the fear of falling back into the working class or from there down further into the most meager poverty.

What postwar veterans and young men had most in common was the opportunity to take advantage of the economic abundance—the first many had experienced—rather than return to the traumas of hard times. In rebellion against the Depression adage of doing without, the postwar male generation instead had its motto: Don't do without. Men took readily to accumulating debt and adopting new installment and easy credit plans to buy on time. Marry now, make babies now; it's affordable. New, better-paying jobs and war savings fueled the avalanche of mass consumer buying in 1946, 1947, and 1948. Government ex-

Advertisement for Swann Hats, ca. 1946. Ads in the late 1940s encouraged postwar consumerism, urging men to aspire to higher social mobility. (Lake County Museum/ Corbis)

penditures for veterans' benefits ensured the further growth of this middle class. This was also due to the government meeting the rising costs of the military's needs in the growing rivalry of the Cold War.

Wartime Males and a Trend to Conservative Attitudes

The postwar male world was characterized by various conservative trends in the country. Foremost, society again became firmly patriarchal. Veterans took back the high-paying factory jobs from women, and men reasserted themselves as heads of family.

In corporations and business, the top levels of ownership and management traditionally continued to be an elite of white males. College education was a determinant for achieving this top rank. In this regard, more men qualified because the G.I. Bill made college degrees possible for many men from nonprivileged backgrounds. Men were being trained to continue future leadership in business and politics.

America's political leadership and decision makers were nearly exclusively male in the 1940s, as was traditional even after women gained the vote in 1919. The exceptions to this were few and included Jeanette Rankin, who had cast the only vote against both world wars, and Margaret Chase Smith of Maine, who in defense of civil liberties questioned some of the harsher, more groundless charges of anticommunism against individuals.

Home-front political conservatism had been on the rise during the decade of the 1940s. Beginning with the 1942 congressional elections, a new working majority consisting of rightist Democrats voting with Republicans proved more conservative than their predecessors. Politicians were less prone to social reform and more interested in growing the war economy to bring military victory and continue the prosperity at home. The rising income across the classes made calls for reform less urgent. Corporate businesses were profitable, and unions were more subdued in their demands. America's voting majority was in favor of this conservative trend primarily because of the reward of boom prosperity and full employment. Roosevelt adapted as well by choosing the safe Harry Truman over the very liberal Henry Wallace as his running mate in 1944. The FDR-Truman ticket won.

The United States had war goals that the public also seemingly saw as safe and modestly pragmatic. The war effort was conservative in aiming to defend and preserve the country's traditional democracy and freedoms against the foreign threat of aggressive, revolutionary totalitarian fascism and military dictatorship. Some of the millions overseas expressed the fight simply as one for national survival, apple pie, and Mom. The war was less to advance the new than to return the status quo in former democracies that had fallen under fascist occupation. Americans had no soaring Wilsonian hopes to change the world in a major way but wanted simply to survive, and then continue wartime global involvement and institute collective security to preserve other democracies and preserve the peace of the world.

Cold War Males and Greater Conservatism

With the beginning of the Cold War, the wartime struggle to preserve democracies and peace for the world was increasingly seen as under threat from worldwide communism. Political leaders and the media constantly warned the public American males—so many of whom were veterans who had just experienced and won a long, brutal, grueling war—that the Soviets were a militaristic, dictatorial totalitarian threat similar to the recently vanquished Axis powers. Only a strong in-place military would prevent another war. A top priority was preparedness so the country would not again find itself in an uphill fight as in 1942.

Once again, America's postwar foreign policy had a seemingly cautious, safe military aim—to defend and protect recently restored Western democracy and freedom against a new revolutionary threat of the overthrow of capitalism. Domestic policy similarly remained conservative—maintain the prosperity level of the war and grow the economy even more by government spending on the vast, new global military defense perimeter against communism. An economy growing ever larger would enrich all income levels and again reduce the need for postwar social reform.

A defense strategy of worldwide containment of communism required a new, growing military budget. High military leadership required large military outlays to build foreign bases, maintain a large peacetime standing army (the peacetime draft for males returned in 1947), and provide armaments for allies in alliances like the NATO. Military preparedness was the watchword at home as the nation's defense came to rely on ready nuclear weapons.

The postwar era was not a ripe moment for new risk-taking initiatives like domestic reforms or mutual disarmament. A bipartisan majority of Congress was aggressive in supporting America's new fight in the Cold War. Domestically, while willing to continue such proven New Deal mainstay programs as Social Security and the minimum wage, the majority was not in favor of a program of extended reforms. Thus, although Democrat and former New Dealer Truman won an upset victory in 1948, Congress, which returned to Democrats after two reactionary years of the Republican-led 80th Congress, still had a crossover conservative majority that voted down Truman's Fair Deal of extended reforms but ardently supported the hard-line Cold War stances that Truman had initiated at home and abroad.

Congress approved new military contracts with industry, especially after 1949, when Mao took over China and Stalin announced the Soviet Union had the atomic bomb. Government spending expanded the postwar economy. The already broadened middle class—now beginning to move in droves to the suburbs with fathers supporting stay-at-home wives and children—simply wanted to play it safe, hold on to its new possessions, purchase more, gain status amidst neighbors, and not look back to the hardships of war or Depression.

The nation's chronically unaided poor, such as the millions of migrant workers, enfeebled elders, and rural poor were of no concern to the new comfortably prosperous middle class. They were virtually invisible to the nation because media rarely focused on those millions in the bottom underclass. The New Deal and the long 1940s economic boom had permanently left them outside. These poor were dread reminders to the new consumer class of Americans of the harshest times of the jobless Depression. In effect, these were the citizens of an America forgotten amid the new affluent, cautious conservative male-led late 1940s America.

FAMILY

The American family of the 1940s was the subject of a powerful myth of togetherness that overshadowed the wartime reality of broken up and scattered families. Closeness and mutual concern made up the ideal family that propaganda said America was fighting to defend. The military was fighting for family and country. Reality in wartime consisted of a total of 16 million, sons, brothers, fathers, husbands, and some daughters gone far away from the family to fight the war. Rooted at home, grandparents were once part of an extended family all living under one roof on a farm or in a small town, but during the war this tradition was shattered as married daughters with families tended to move away to wait on crowded bases or work in boomtowns until their husbands returned from the fighting. During the war, families faced separation and loneliness.

Myth of Family Life

President Roosevelt had declared the Four Freedoms as the goals that America was fighting for in the war, but it was Norman Rockwell who grounded these goals in the collective imagination by painting traditional family images for each of these abstract freedoms. His four illustrated freedoms, headed "OURS . . . to fight for," appeared everywhere as posters and on the cover of the popular *Saturday Evening Post*. For the poster "Freedom from Want," the image is an iconic Thanksgiving table with an extended family seated, each member warmly smiling, while at the head of the table, grandmother sets down the giant roasted turkey that grandfather is about to carve.

Mother carrying a child outside a wartime nursery. There were not nearly enough such centers to accommodate children once mothers were called upon to work on the home front. (Library of Congress)

Reality of Family Life

Actual conditions for the American family in wartime was often just the opposite of Rockwell's "Freedom from Want." The average Thanksgiving dinner was more likely served by a harried, tired mother with teens and small children around a kitchen table in a tiny apartment in a crowded multifamily dwelling in a strange, new location far from home. The dinner would more likely be meager, consisting of what the mother was able to obtain with ration stamps, given the frequent wartime food scarcities.

The father, in reality, is absent, overseas in the military, still safe—everyone hopes. The grandparents are at "home" having Thanksgiving, just the two of them. The separation in the wartime families brings recurring loneliness and worry to each one. Scarce infant day care, new crowded schools, a difficult work commute, a new job, no mate, no father in the home, no old friends, no familiar neighbors—any one of these concerns might be on the minds of one or more of the members of this new wartime American family.

War, Marriage, and the Family

The global fight involved a mobilization of all of American society in the fullest realization of modern total war, and the civilian and military contribution was of equal importance for victory. Given this total reorienting of civilian life toward the goal of military victory, the American family underwent profound changes. Some marriages came after brief, intense affairs, with a soldier home on short furlough, or with a high school sweetheart suddenly called to war. Pregnancies often followed in the wake, and the father would not see the new child for a long time. On the other hand, overseas in the military, married men often gave in to long-repressed sexual urges through affairs, usually with prostitutes (in one poll 25 percent of servicemen admitted to adultery).

On the home front, wives remained faithful for the most part, but war created its own pathology for the single wife. With the new stress, women drank more, either at home or in bars; their rate of alcoholism came closer to that of men. Married women or single women also had affairs in greater numbers. The famous Kinsey Report on American sexual mores, taken from a wartime sampling, had found that 26 percent of all wives younger than 40 had committed adultery at least once, and that two of three single women had had sex before marriage.

With the war's end, long-separated married couples came back together; some marriages survived in spite of the strains of separation but others, especially the hasty couplings, came apart. The 1946 divorce rate in the country was the highest in the world, but it then fell as men and women remarried. In the same year, the numbers of new marriages skyrocketed, as did new births. The American family was reborn, and most marriages were now set to last.

Nuclear Families Increase over Prior Decade

At the end of the 1940s, the American family, especially as shaped by suburbia, was a stripped-down version from earlier. It consisted, in general, of two parents and an average of two children. The extended family living together was still very common during the Depression. What comes to mind is the iconic Joad family migrating from their dusted out farm in a jalopy on rough roads to the promise of a new beginning in California. In John Steinbeck's *Grapes of Wrath,* published in 1939 and made into a popular movie in 1940, the family consists of Ma, Pa, son Tom, daughter Rose of Sharon who is pregnant, her husband, and a good friend, a laypastor. All of their possessions are together packed onto their one car. All members of the group cooperate and pool their resources for the endeavor to overcome the many struggles of the journey. In contrast, in the 1950s, when the fear of atomic war caused a fad for backyard A-bomb shelters, the family was expected to have packed provisions only for the family members —typically, the father, mother and two children—no more persons.

Marriage as a primary institution of the family underwent changes in the 1940s that contrasted with prior aspects of this institution. Quickly arranged marriages before a justice of the peace became more common in war, and this trend was steadily making marriage a more secular ceremony than the religious one of the 1930s. With war causing the wide movement and mixing of persons, marriages tended to involve two persons of more diverse backgrounds than those earlier when there was a stronger adherence to the ties of each person's group and religion. Religion in the family from the 1930s to the 1940s became less uniform among the family members; more frequently, family members, including children, chose their own beliefs. This long-term result certainly owed a debt to the more permissive child-raising methods advocated by the famous pediatrician Dr. Spock.

When prosperity returned in the 1940s, couples again tended to marry at a younger age and to enjoy more economic security. Yet the divorce rate rose slightly throughout the decade. In 1940, there were 16.5 divorces for every 100 marriages. By 1949, the number of divorces per 100 marriages had risen to 23.1. The rate had dropped during the Depression from 17.4 in 1930 to 16.5 in 1940s primarily because divorced persons had less overall security than those who remain married, even in bad marriages.

There was a steady, long-term decline in the number of persons in a family, from 4.76 members in 1900 to 3.6 in 1949. With the growth of cities, families adapted to apartment living with less space. Whereas farms required many children for labor, this was no longer true in cities, and children were more often seen as economic burdens to a low-income family.

Children in the 1940s engaged in fewer family-centered activities; other institutions like schools and public recreation programs replaced activities previously done in or near the home. Because teens in the 1940s had their own expendable income, they developed their own subculture, which was often at odds with that of adults; this planted the first seeds for teen rebellion and generational conflict. These were matters that the poverty-burdened family of the 1930s had not encountered, when teens were still working to earn meager sums for family survival.

Rather than a producing unit, in the 1940s, the city family became a consuming unit, vital in its spending to the state of the overall economy. By 1949, the American family was the key element to the greatest consuming market ever in

A Hollywood Sociodrama of Veteran and Family

In 1946, the movie *The Best Years of Our Lives* became popular because it dealt with the contemporary drama of families and returning veterans. In it, the same small town is home to three different veterans. One is a middle-aged army sergeant with a wife and older children, and the other two are younger; one is an Air Force captain and the other is a sailor who lost both of his hands in the war and now has prosthetic hooks. The lives of the younger veterans are the most disrupted because they believe they have lost "the best years of their lives." Not so the sergeant, who, while heavily dependent on alchohol, has the easiest adjustment, making his homecoming a ritual to be remembered by taking his wife and grown daughter for a night out on the town. He has a long and solid enduring marriage.

The captain will have a gripping struggle to reenter civilian life. First, he suffers a humiliating loss of self-esteem, going from being a bombardier to a soda jerk, the only job he can find in the immediate dislocations of reconversion. His wife appears to have been having a long affair with another man. He is left to struggle on his own, with continuing insecurities. He is finally helped in his plight when the sergeant's daughter falls in love with him.

When the sailor's family rushes outside to greet him upon his return, his mother sees his prosthetic hooks and breaks into uncontrollable sobs. Both are engulfed in mutual hurt and embarrassment. He feels awkward and self-conscious as he learns to use his new hands. Standing out in public makes him feel all the more lonely and isolated from his fellow humans. The war had stolen his right to a carefree youth and an unredeemable innocence. Yet life will go on, and so will the young man now grown old.

the history of humans. The family steadily gained in purchasing power, although evidence suggests the black family did not share equally in the new consumer cornucopia.

Family and the Returning Veterans

American families of the 1940s experienced their greatest transition with the return of the veterans. The veterans had changed, and they came back to changed circumstances. Husbands rejoined wives, fathers were there once more for children, and sons and brothers suddenly reappeared. Adjustments needed to be made on the part of everyone, and yet not all were capable of making the adjustment. Divorces occurred in a record number in 1946.

At the time of the family reuniting, various family members had different vantage points. Sons who remained boys below draft age lacked role models while their fathers and big brothers were away at war; often slightly older male peers acted as role models for younger boys. Daughters were more independent. Wives were expected to relinquish their hard-won wartime autonomy back to husbands. Fathers were to replace mothers as heads of family. It is no wonder the frequent result was broken families.

War widows with children had the greatest struggle. With their husband's war deaths, these women were the hardest hit in any circumstance. Worst hit were those women who were let go from high-paying factory jobs when the men returned. A great challenge also awaited the woman or mother who welcomed back a husband or son who had been physically maimed or had been shell-shocked or suffered mentally from combat. Nightmares, high anxiety, reenacting traumatic moments in an unpreventable ways became a constant struggle for some veterans. But neither they nor their families knew this was a common, almost predictable symptom for a combat survivor (later this became known as post-traumatic stress syndrome). With lack of understanding, the veteran suffered in silence and often acted in ways that alienated his family or caused divorce.

Family and Effects of the Postwar Suburbs

After 1946, the extended family became a thing of the past, and the smaller, more mobile nuclear family became the norm. Separation of grandparents and grandchildren became the norm, even if this simply meant the former remained in the city, and the latter moved to the new suburbs. The telephone call was the most common link, along with occasional visits. Young families moved frequently, especially those in which the fathers were corporate middle managers. Companies shifted them around to different regions or divisions, as needed by top management.

Large family gathers to watch television, 1949. (Time & Life Pictures/ Getty Images)

The suburbs also separated the wife and children at home from the father at work with colleagues. The wife in the suburbs, if she once had been a war worker, may have occasionally felt a nostalgic longing for those old times when she made all her own decisions and felt more self-fulfillment. No matter the stress and worry, the woman's life

Convenience Is the Hallmark of New 1940s Foods

1940	Arnold Bread, Red Cheek Apple Juice, Dairy Queen soft serve ice cream
1941	M&Ms, Cheerios
1942	Tootsie Rolls packed in U.S. ration kits, Post Raisin Bran, Kellogg's Raisin Bran, Dannon yogurt
1944	Chiquita brand bananas
1945	Kraft Grated Parmesan Cheese, Welch's Junior Mints, Constant Comment tea
1946	Pillsbury pie crust mix, frozen French fries, Ragu spaghetti sauce, French's Instant Potatoes, Tupperware
1947	Pillsbury hot roll mix, Reddi-Whip, cake mixes, Lady Borden ice cream, Almond Joy, frozen orange juice
1948	V-8 Cocktail Vegetable Juice, Nestlé Instant Tea, Minute Rice, Nestlé's Quik chocolate milk additive
1949	Kraft sliced American cheese, Fritos Corn Chips marketed nationally, Sara Lee cheesecake

in war had seemed an adventure. Any longings like these, however, the new suburban homemaker quickly dismissed as she thought with satisfaction of her new detached single-family ranch home with a lawn and flowers on a quiet street with trees. Every day, media ads proclaimed that she was now the most privileged American homemaker in history. Enjoying the never-before-imagined new labor-saving electric appliances such as washers, dryers, dishwashers, and vacuum cleaners, she should not complain, only stay happy.

In the late 1940s, television sets in homes grew at a steady rate until, by 1950, the total was 10 million and growing exponentially. This powerful new mass medium (especially in its ad commercials) conveyed novel values and mores appropriate to a new national, middle-class family ideal in this novel mass-consumer society. Countless viewing families in this increasingly conformist Cold War era changed their personal attitudes and behavior to fit the norm of the mass family ideal. The new serial dramas on the small screens portrayed this ideal in countless ways. In time, with children's programming, the television set also would become an ideal babysitter.

This brave new family increasingly behaved like their suburban peers (usually equal in income strata and broad religious and social attitudes). This newly emerging middle class took cues from television about family, marriage, and child-raising methods. When a family moved, it was usually to another similar suburb where the network television programs remained the same.

RELIGION

Given the mass anxieties of World War II, the dawn of the nuclear age, and the start of the Cold War, the 1940s decade witnessed a dramatic rise in the number of churchgoers in America. Class and religion were significant qualities for those who were part of the mass migrations during the war (with Southern poorer denominations, such as Baptists or Methodists, increasing the numbers of those believers in the North and West). While a solid core of fundamentalist Christians remained in the South, others went westward across the South, eventually to Southern California, giving a much broader base across the country for this group. The Cold War heightened religion and democracy as the American ideals to oppose the ideology of atheism and communism in Russia. Fundamentalists and conservatives in religion generally are the same in politics. In the 1948 presidential election, Strom Thurmond's breakaway Dixiecrats, who favored racial segregation, represented an early example of the power of the Religious Right.

Threats from Communism and Science

Conservatives, including Catholics, saw communism as a threat to religion. International news accounts of Eastern Europeans being forced to forsake religion after communist takeovers fueled their fears. Because the resistance to the Nazi occupation in countries like Italy and France had included many leftists, the communists became heroes to many in these countries upon liberation by the Allies. In Italy, the Communist Party numbered roughly one-third of the population and was feared to be in a position to outvote the Western-supported Catholic Christian Democrats. The 1947 Marshall Plan giving billions to rebuild the middle class did much to halt the postwar trend in Europe toward placing hopes in communism.

In the United States after 1945, American families seemed called to return to religion. Various reasons combine to explain this; perhaps the most important was a mass yearning for a source of meaning that transcended the seemingly endless cycles of major world military conflicts. Scientific discoveries like the Dead Sea scrolls in 1948, which implied the birth of Christianity had an explainable evolution from the almost identical prior beliefs of a sect of Jewish Essenes, had the effect of making Americans all the more eager to proclaim their religious beliefs.

Religion's Broad Civic Aspect in America

The American approach to religion is unique. Being a practical-minded people in general, America's faithful tend not to emphasize deep intellectual or theological reasons for their beliefs. Instead, they tend to hold strong beliefs and give mutual tolerance toward a broad, almost generic sense of religion. As long as someone claims to have strong personal faith and believes in some religion—regardless of which variety—that person is accepted as part of the religious experience valued by Americans. Within this general framework, Americans grant much individual latitude in choosing a denomination.

The American way of life gives primacy to individual choice, which is the underpinning not only for the country's great religious diversity but also for its individualistic democratic politics. Similarly, its economic system emphasizes individual competition within a free enterprise system as the best and most efficient way to wealth. Because the country was first colonized shortly after the Protestant Reformation, the national foundations tended to be individualistic, Protestant, and Bible-based. The constantly moving frontier created opportunities for a wide range of Protestant denominations.

Overview of Religion in the Postwar Era

In the post–World War II 1940s, a general religious consensus developed, with most of the population's denominations deriving from Judeo-Christian foundations. According to influential theologian Will Herberg, the country's three major religious communities, Catholic, Protestant, and Jewish, share the Americanism of a general belief in religion, faith, and individual choice. If only in a conceptual sense, all three together represent the American religion or way of life.

The decade's rise in church membership is telling. Considering all religious bodies, the rise goes from roughly 65 percent to 85 percent, with Protestants of all types gaining in churchgoers 38 percent to 51 percent. Catholics followed with a gain of 21 percent to 28 percent. Some of the reasons for this decade's rise in church members, especially after 1945, include the anxiety at being the first humans to enter the nuclear age and because of a distrust of science for having revealed a dark destructive side.

Some upwardly mobile postwar families sought to gain in social status by joining certain more affluent denominations. There was a strong competition for membership among many denominations. Also, many parents of the millions of children born during the 1940s baby boom set a priority on religious training for their children.

Consistent with a more conservative and conformist time, a church community also gave individuals a sense of belonging. In the postwar years, there was a continuation of the movement from small towns and rural areas to cities, and the loneliness of the urban newcomers was often eased by joining a church or synagogue. The religious community would serve as a social center for new suburbanites as well as new city dwellers.

Religion and African American Migration

In moving out of the South in large numbers during the war and immediate postwar, African Americans kept their traditional allegiances to the Baptist or Methodist churches. In northern and western cities, they founded new, mostly all-black congregations. Church membership among all African Americans in the nation was 70 percent. The wide dispersal of the African American population during the 1940s helped give the nascent civil rights movement a national scope, base, and organization. Ministers were a majority of the leadership of civil rights movement. The movement's Southern base gained great encouragement and support from churchgoers in such places as Harlem in New York and the south side of Chicago.

1940s Conservative Christianity: A Historical Context

The rise in church membership during the 1940s is part of a long-term national trend; from 1926 to 1960, those claiming church membership rose 100 percent (the overall population gain was only 45 percent). This period encompassed such collective traumas as the Great Crash of 1929, the Depression of the 1930s, World War II, the dawn of the nuclear age and the beginnings of the Cold War in the 1940s, and the resultant arms race, which continued to 1960 and beyond. Given the mass anxieties of this new modern era, many Americans sought comfort in religion, either in a new denomination or in the faith that was part of a family tradition.

The Fundamentalist Fight against Science

The clash between science and modernism versus the Bible and old-time religion dates back into the 19th century and continued during the 1940s. In the period before the Civil War, many Americans based their faith on the considered truths of the Bible. With the theories of evolution put forth by Charles Darwin verified by modern techniques of dating used in geology and archeology, science provided hard evidence to overturn various biblical passages. Darwin's theory of evolution stated that through the processes of mutation and natural selection, the human species had evolved from apes over the course of eons; this refuted the literal biblical statement that God had created human beings in his own image. Using the new methods of modern science, geologists found fossils and rock strata proving the earth to be millions of years old, and not created in the biblical seven days.

Religious conservatives and fundamentalists (whose greatest numbers were in the South) refused to be swayed by such new discoveries and held to their absolutes as stated in the Bible. The growth in fundamentalism in the 1940s had its roots in earlier decades, of course, most famously, in 1924, at the famous Scopes Trial in Dayton, Tennessee, a young biology teacher named John Scopes was put on trial for teaching the theory of evolution in his high school biology class, a practice that violated the law of the state. Making headlines day after day nationwide, Clarence Darrow, the brilliant, Chicago-based lawyer, defended Scopes against the Bible-defending prosecutors who put up an array of famous witnesses, including the former Democratic presidential candidate, William Jennings Bryan. Darrow proceeded to destroy the opposition and won the case while making a laughingstock of Bryan. To the Tennessee jury, however, the Bible had won. The teacher had to pay a fine.

Outside the Deep South, however, the trial dealt fundamentalism a great setback, if not outright defeat. In cosmopolitan cities especially, it came to be considered the peculiar religion of the poor and ill educated in the poorest region of the country, the South. But over the next 25 years, left alone, ignored by intruding outsiders, the fundamentalist faithful grew in numbers and in the strength of their beliefs. During the migrations of poor tenant farmers during the 1930s and the movement of Southerners to work in wartime factories in the North and West during the 1940s, fundamentalist Protestantism had outposts outside the South but still was concentrated there. In 1941, Dr. Carl McIntire founded The American Council of Fundamentalist Churches. Many of the member churches represented were solely local congregations that believed biblical truth is absolute and that their believers should ostracize all followers of liberal Christianity as well as all scientific modernists and secularists. These churches were nondenominational, separatist, and fundamentalist; their followers had, by comparison, the lowest levels of education among Protestants

Evangelical Christianity, Billy Graham, and Revivals
More moderate evangelical Christians viewed fundamentalism as being too uncompromising and separatist. While also conservative and biblical, evangelicals, by contrast, practiced a public form of faith, called witnessing, that involved telling others of their experience with a God who caused many of them to be" "born again" or to perform miracle cures for fellow believers. Their emphasis was on a personal relationship to God who intervenes in the world to give grace and love to help save the faithful. Evangelicalism cuts across denominations. In 1949, Billy Graham, a young Baptist Evangelical minister, preached at a massive revival meeting in Los Angeles that drew tens of thousands. Because many attendees became born-again converts, this revival caused widespread notice in the national press that thereafter brought Graham steady backing from the vast conservative Hearst newspaper chain. In 1950, Graham, then 32 years old, began his "The Hour of Decision" radio ministry and shortly afterward was the first famous televangelist.

Suddenly, the conservative fundamentalists and evangelicals, heretofore associated largely with the South, burst onto the national scene through radio and television broadcast, with the added historical timing and advantage of providing many citizens with a ready-made ideology to oppose communism during the

Evangelist Billy Graham holds a revival in Los Angeles, November 1949. (Time & Life Pictures/Getty Images)

Cold War. This came at one of the country's darkest hours, in 1949, when the Soviets exploded an atomic bomb and the communists took over China.

Liberal Christianity

Modernism did not present nearly as big a challenge to religious liberals as it did to conservatives. The liberal denominations of Protestantism—Presbyterians, Episcopalians, Congregationalists—had some of the best-educated followers. Over the decades, they had made judicious compromises between biblical writ and scientific discoveries.

For liberal denominations of Protestantism in the late 1940s, the historical dilemma was that, beginning during the war, political conservatism was growing—aided by religious conservatism—and during the Cold War and the House Un-American Activities Committee (HUAC) hearings, liberals of all sorts became the suspected targets of those advocating 100 percent Americanism. The relativism inherent in so many aspects of modernist living—seeded by the initial theories of relativism in Einstein's work in physics—became anathema to the absolutist truths of conservative Christians, some of whom charged liberal Christians with being linked to this relativism by tailoring and retailoring the Bible to conform to constantly changing scientific discoveries.

Postwar Society and Religion

In the postwar 1940s, there was an astonishing rise in national prosperity and individual incomes. America quickly became the richest country in the history of the world. This phenomenon provided the underpinning to further spur the mass religious revival of the same years. The turning point was economic uplift, and with the unleashing of the pent-up consumer demand of the war years (over $150 billion), the national prosperity soared to record levels. For 25 years after 1945, the economy continued growing, matched for much of the time with rising church membership. A religious revival and an increasingly prosperous way of life were America's great bulwark in its struggle against the Soviets during the Cold War. Godless and without heed for individual wealth or consumer goods, communism was made all the more unappealing to the West. Moreover, the West emphasized that in a victory of communism, the threat was a forced mass conversion to atheism and loss of all private property.

The booming national economy had other aspects that either directly or indirectly helped to boost church membership. Giant corporations like IBM spanned the nation with regional marketing areas. This meant that firms like this regularly transferred marketing and sales employees. Relocated by corporations, families often sought churches or synagogues to provide an instant sense of community in a new faraway city, and to locate them within the appropriate class and income level.

Postwar Americans of all classes continued to move on a regular basis, possibly growing accustomed to this from the wartime migrations. Twenty percent of the total population shifted locales at least once each year. In the original suburb, Levittown, New York, 3,000 families left and were replaced each year, usually for reasons of work relocations. In many such instances, social reasons dominated religious reasons for joining a church or synagogue.

Religion, Advertising, and the American Way of Life

Religious groups were also quick to adopt successful marketing techniques (pioneered by corporations) to sell religion. Government was also eager to bring religion to the center of American life because it was so essential an aspect of the ideology that America used to oppose that of the Soviets. Presidents Truman and Eisenhower and FBI director J. Edgar Hoover gave endorsements to the unique American way of encouraging all individuals to have religion (the type was irrelevant) and faith (again, details were not necessary). Ministers, priests, rabbis, and government officials emphasized the importance of providing religious instruction for the young, in part to ensure that future generations of Americans would be anticommunist.

Religion and economics intertwined in other ways. As part of the new consumer culture, Americans had a distinct preference for religious items or entertainment. Bible sales rose dramatically. Movie and books with religious themes were box office hits and best sellers. Highway billboards advertised a coming religious crusade by a powerful evangelical preacher like Graham—who was seen by many as performing a great patriotic duty. In gaining converts and building even more postwar revival of religion during the Cold War, Bishop John Fulton Sheen and, in New York, Cardinal Spellman, would eventually perform a Catholic Revival, attracting converts and those fallen away from Catholicism by wedding Catholic faith with anti-communist crusades.

In their own conferences and workshops, ministers and priests learned to craft in these prosperous times a frequent type of sermon, one that avoided the negative and emphasized one's personal comfort and well-being as the will of God. Negative matters were deemphasized because people—maybe understandably after 15 years of economic depression, war, and a nuclear threat—were at church for good news and hope for the future.

Materialism, Consumerism, and Religion

In 1945, American currency did not carry the slogan "IN GOD WE TRUST." It wasn't until 10 years later that all bills were printed with this slogan, signifying a link between the material and spiritual realms. In 1945, our national pledge of allegiance did not include the phrase "one nation under God." Nine years later, this phrase was added, signifying the link between religion and patriotic nationalism. Building on trends begun in the postwar 1940s, in both instances Congress authorized the changes and president gave his approval.

A booming economy with widespread prosperity needed to be sustained for the government to continue the boast that a free enterprise economy provided better for its citizens than a communist one. The question was how to perpetuate an expanding economy. Certain valuable lessons had been learned from the New Deal and wartime economic policies of large government spending for defense. Soon this policy was to continue in massive outlays for new weapons to match the Soviets in the arms race and for expenditures to support anticommunist allies in fighting communism worldwide.

Government spending alone, however, would not have been the answer. America in the postwar was to lay the foundations for the growth of consumer capitalism or free enterprise based on advertiser-induced purchases of ever newer, ever changing consumer goods. Advertising was the crux of this type of economy; its aims were to manufacture desire for nonessential goods. Mass consumption made for mass production. The goal was to constantly expand consumption. For example, encouraging families to have two cars instead of one made for added production, as did other duplication of purchases like two or more phones.

The consumer culture that emerged in the postwar 1940s was fed by other developments, including planned obsolescence, which meant that a light bulb would last only so long before going out and creating the need for a new one. (In fact, technology allowed for much longer-burning bulbs, but these were not introduced to the public because sales would suffer.) Clothing fashions for men and women followed trends. Advertisements warned of being out of style. The formula was to create dissatisfaction with what one has (even though still perfectly serviceable) and create a desire for the new, soon to get old, then the next newest, and on ad infinitum. Many still usable consumer goods were thrown away in the process.

Consumer credit was also a big part of this new culture: encourage the purchaser to buy now and pay later. An unspoken guideline of this new consumer economy was do not defer gratification. Even experts believed this approach to hold the secret to a never-ending prosperity. Between 1945 and 1955, the national consumer debt would rise by 700 percent. A fine credit rating became a moral good and assuming manageable debt a patriotic duty. Consumer debt buoyed up the economy. When the individual bought an item for personal use, this could be seen as an unselfish act, an effort to maintain the common good by maintaining the factory jobs of those who produced consumer goods.

Throughout their history, Americans have had a constant struggle to balance materialism with ideals. The postwar 1940s were a variation on this theme, with a rise in religion combining with a rise in prosperity—both being championed as singular American achievements in its Cold War struggle with Russia. Yet there were times when the frenzied materialism undercut the deeper aims of religion. Still religion served the need for community in a mass society where individuals felt adrift and alienated from their true selves. Even though most readily voiced the age-old belief in idealistic individualism, the postwar corporate and religious worlds offered a combined formula for conformity—feel-good religion and a boost-the-country business philosophy.

NORMAN ROCKWELL ILLUSTRATES DOMESTIC ASPECTS OF THE 1940s

Norman Rockwell was the country's best-loved illustrator and most well-known artist. His steady flow of paintings used on the covers of the widely circulated *Saturday Evening Post* made many of his images indelible in the minds of Americans on the home front in the 1940s. For this reason, a sampling of his images from the decade will illustrate topics in this chapter. His was a sentimental, idealistic portrait of a country of materially comfortable, church-going, family-oriented people who worked to support the war and longed for loved ones overseas risking their lives in combat. Absent from the artist's vision is any evidence of the poor or vastly wealthy or of the good life lived on the home front, where many used heightened profits or wages to go to the race track, night

Norman Rockwell, the artist renowned for painting "everyday" American life, normalizes nurse as working woman in this painting. (Bettmann/Corbis)

club, or to Miami, the hot spot for popular luxury and entertainment at that time. The following Rockwell images from throughout the war, 1942 to 1944, reveal the artist's impressions of aspects of life on the home front.

Man as Soldier

During the 1940s Rockwell frequently portrayed the role of men as soldiers— as recruits and as adult officers. In a 1942 *Saturday Evening Post* cover titled, "Willie Gillis in Church," Rockwell shows us Gillis, the typical teen soldier of the artist's imagination meant to stand for all those in service. He was no ideal physical specimen but somewhat skinny, gangly, and awkward with a wide smile, auburn hair, and a mischievous quality that seemed to need to be suppressed at times for military decorum. The theme of this cover could be that while we are all God's children, in the military, the young Gillis is the most lowly, humble, and respectful in his pew. He is flanked by high-ranking military men front and back, with an arm and a shoulder displaying their insignia and badges, at this place of common worship, possibly at a stateside military post. During the war years, Gillis appeared 11 times on the cover of *The Saturday Evening Post*. The last Gillis cover, in 1946, showed him as a mature man at college carrying an armload of books, thanks to the G.I. Bill.

Family as Depicted in the Artist's "Four Freedoms"

Families on the home front during the war are depicted in two of the four sections of Rockwell's famous painting and ubiquitous poster for FDR's Four Freedoms. In "Freedom from Fear," he shows the ideal, middle-class nuclear family of two parents and two children, a son and a daughter. An especially treasured, comforting image for the public, it shows two young children in bed sleeping while the mother leans over to make sure their blankets are in place and the white-collar father looks on lovingly. From his hand dangles a newspaper with headlines "Bombings Ki . . ." and "Horror Hit . . .". The message is of a father feeling especially blessed that his children, at least for the moment, are free from the fear of nighttime bombings and mass killing of civilians in war zones. The inspiration for the image was the 1940 Battle of Britain, fought before the United States entered the war.

   Family appears again in Rockwell's "Freedom from Want." This time an extended family is portrayed at Thanksgiving dinner, with the grandmother at the head of the table setting down a huge roast turkey, soon to be carved by the grandfather at her side. This image is of middle-class super abundance in a genteel setting, again with a host of blissful younger family members, including young males of draft age, perhaps all with deferments for defense work.

The artist himself came under fire for this image which was unpopular with Americans who thought it unseemly in the midst of the genuine want of various war-torn populations. Europeans of the time criticized it as a callous boast of a feast proving American superabundance.

The Iconic "Rosie the Riveter"

Women in wartime were the subject of numerous *Saturday Evening Post* covers. The most iconic was Rockwell's 1943 depiction of Rosie the Riveter. Unusual in comparison to the work of many other artists depicting her, Rockwell's Rosie is truly androgynous, powerful, and appealing in equal parts. Her phallic rivet gun rests nearby. This seemingly fair Irish lass is clearly poised, capable, and confident, with or without the company of male co-workers. Her work boot rests on the copy of Hitler's *Mein Kampf,* which relegates German women to the traditional role of home and family.

Youth on the Home Front

The artist depicts youth of the time in the 1944 "Willie Gillis New Year's Eve" in which he makes the soldier's young girlfriend the central focus. She has framed photos of Willie arrayed around the walls of her bed where she is lying under the covers—not out partying, but loyal to him and so retiring early. Many young women of the time found themselves absent their beloved overseas and in a situation like this. In reality, many soldiers had relationships with women at home and overseas, and even Gillis had numerous girlfriends he corresponded with at home in addition to the loyal one depicted here.

"A Little Girl Observing Lovers on a Train" (1944) portrays trends of the war era—teen mores had loosened so that necking in public, in this instance in a railroad passenger train, was more acceptable to all. A young couple could be about to be married before he left for war, so the public became more accepting of public displays of affections. Railroads were the most popular form of travel in those years, and thousands of service people were on the move; the car in this painting is packed. A little girl of age six or seven looks over the back of her seat at the two lovers seated behind her; the lovers' faces do not show, but their legs are entangled. Childhood innocence is here gazing upon faster maturing teens in a changed, war-altered courtship ritual of shorter, more urgent duration.

The Postwar 1940s in the Artist's Vision

After the end of the war, Rockwell continued painting his insights into American domestic life. In his 1947 "Tired Salesgirl on Christmas," he shows a completely exhausted salesclerk leaning against a department store backroom wall, shoes kicked off aching feet, arms limp at her sides. She is exhausted after waiting on hundreds of customers in the children's toy department. Arrayed around her are child-size dolls, a toy car large enough to be driven by a child—all clearly higher priced items. Her balance book for the shift is in her lap bound by a rubber band. Christmas as the ritual day of proof of abundance in the new consumption economy was a favorite Rockwell subject. The artist's salesgirl also serves as an example of the lowered earning capacity and lessened job market for women after 1945, when returning servicemen replaced them.

"The Bridge Game" (1948) has a view directly above a card table where two couples sit playing cards. The viewer sees what cards each player holds. The image illustrates the "togetherness" theme of socializing in the postwar era, something greatly sought in the new suburban era. Cards and parlor games were one of the few arenas left where women could compete with and best men. However, according to the gender stereotypes of the time, women were often depicted as being slightly foolish.

In "Santa's Surprise" (1949), Christmas is again the event being anticipated in this image of a little boy aghast, mouth open, as he spies his father in a Santa Claus costume, with pillow stuffed over his stomach. On the floor, his mother is making alterations to the costume, letting it out from the previous year, when the wearer was likely thinner. Wrapped presents are piled up nearby, signaling the growing secular importance of December 25. The day has become the merchants' most important for selling out inventories, with countdowns like "Only X Days Left Until Christmas." Easy credit buying is a new feature of the late 1940s.

In "Shuffleton's Barbershop" (1950), Rockwell depicts a nostalgic, small-town main street after dark. The shop is closed, but there is enough street light to see that the room in back of the barber chairs is filled with the town's amateur musicians (all male) having fun playing music, likely at their regular time, on the regular night. The social worlds of men and women were often strictly separate domains in this era. The sexes socialized at gatherings such as cocktail parties and card games.

BIOGRAPHIES

Jane Bolin, 1908–2007

First African American Judge

Bolin became the first African American judge in the country in 1939 when New York City mayor Fiorello H. La Guardia appointed her to Domestic Relations Court (later Family Court), after two years as the first African American woman to work in the city's office of legal counsel. The appointment made international news. Bolin was eminently qualified. In 1928 she was the first African American woman to be admitted to study law at Yale and the first to graduate, in 1931. Her first decade on the court extended to 1949, when Mayor William O'Dwyer reappointed her. Bolin went on to serve 40 years in her post. As family court judge, she made reforms that included ending the assignment of probation officers based on race. A lifelong advocate of social justice and women's rights, the "lady judge" ruled on cases involving juvenile crime, battered wives, child-support payments to divorced women, neglect, nonsupervision, paternity, and adoptions.

Jane Bolin, first African American judge, ca. 1942. (Library of Congress)

Mother Cabrini, 1850–1917

The First American Saint of the Catholic Church

On July 7, 1946, Pope Pius XII canonized St. Francis Xavier Cabrini. It was ringing news throughout the world as the United States had its first saint. Mother Cabrini had been beatified in 1938, the second-to-last step in the process. Born in Italy the youngest of 13 children, she founded an order of missionary sisters. In 1889, the Pope sent her to New York City where she established numerous homes for orphans (in other American cities as well) and aided new immigrants. In 1909, she became a naturalized American citizen. She died in Chicago eight years later and was buried in Manhattan's Washington Heights, where she is honored by a shrine and a street named Cabrini Boulevard. She is considered the patron saint of immigrants.

John H. Johnson, 1918–2005

Multimillionaire African American Publisher

John H. Johnson, the grandson of slaves, was born in Arkansas and later moved to Chicago with his mother, a cook, after his father died in an industrial accident. John fulfilled the American Dream, literally going from rags to riches, after borrowing $500 from his mother in 1942 and founding the Johnson Publishing Company, which published the magazines *Ebony* and *Jet* for African American readers. These pioneered an unbiased view of the African American world. Johnson's success came early on when he persuaded brand-name corporations to advertise in his pages using African American models. When he died in 2005, his publications had a vast national and international circulation, and he had built a business empire worth half a billion dollars.

Reinhold Niebuhr, 1892–1971

Theologian, Author, and Founder of Christian Realism

A lifelong social activist and political socialist, Niebuhr was one of the most influential thinkers of the 20th century. Both denying liberal idealism as perfectionism and conservative traditionalism as outmoded, Neibuhr advocated a pragmatic concept of social justice based on relative circumstance and compromise called Christian Realism. It was developed in his series *The Nature and Destiny of Man,* two volumes published in 1941 and 1943. As a teacher at Columbia's Union Seminary, from 1928 to 1960, he influenced generations of ministers.

William Shockley, 1910–1989

Inventor of a Vital Component to Smaller Computers

In the beginning, computers were giant machines run with hundreds of vacuum tubes and prone to overheating. One invention, the transistor, eliminated vacuum tubes and reduced the scale so significantly that smaller computers were built for use in business and government offices—and eventually the home. Shockley led a small team to one of this century's great discoveries while working at Bell Laboratories in 1944. In only a few years, the transistor revolutionized the electronic world. Eventually this wartime inventor would improve his discovery and start Shockley Semiconductor, a pioneering business in what would become Silicon Valley. Shockley won a Nobel Prize for his work in 1956.

James Thurber, 1894–1961

New Yorker Writer and Humorist

Reaching middle age in the 1940s, Thurber wrote humorously of this gender-stretching decade as intensifying a traditional war between the sexes. In his stories and illustrations, wives are stereotypical nagging, niggling partners (which was objectionable to modern feminists) who browbeat their husbands. Reactions to these depictions brought laughter, mostly from male readers. Underlying Thurber's humor was an ever-present American phenomenon, male fear of the real or imagined power of the female. In 1941, Thurber published his best-known short story, "The Secret Life of Walter Mitty," which was part of the 1942 collection *My World—And Welcome to It*. The story was made into a film starring

Danny Kaye in 1947. To escape the endless harangues of Mrs. Mitty, Walter escapes into wildly funny grandiose fantasies.

Betty Trezza, 1925–2007

Pioneer Player in the Women's Baseball League

A women's professional baseball league began in 1943, started by the chewing gum multimillionaire, Phillip R. Wrigley, who wanted to maintain interest in the sport while most of the male players had left the big leagues to fight in the war. The women's league lasted until 1954 and proved an interesting example of new gender roles in that time of tumultuous relations between the sexes. Women like Trezza enjoyed a sudden new opportunity to showcase their athletic skills. Yet male founders still believed commercial appeal remained in having females retain their customary sex appeal. Players were required to attend charm school, venture out with chaperones, and wear uniforms with short skirts. Brooklyn-bred Trezza joined the league in 1944. As a fleet, strong-armed average hitter, she won fame in 1946 when she singled in the 16th inning to bring in the winning run for her Racine (Wisconsin) Belles in the women's championship series. The 1992 movie, "A League of their Own," starring Madonna revived those times.

The 20th-century humorist James Thurber brought humane intelligence and biting wit to stories and sketches that describe human foibles. Thurber's hapless heroes, such as the protagonist of his best-known tale, "The Secret Life of Walter Mitty," go unredeemed except in the hilarity of the moment. (Library of Congress)

REFERENCES AND FURTHER READINGS

Abrams, Richard M. 2006. *American Transformed: Sixty Years of Revolutionary Change, 1941–2001.* Cambridge: Cambridge University Press.

Bednarowski, Mary Farrell. 1984. *American Religion: A Cultural Perspective.* New Jersey: Prentice Hall.

Bundy, Beverly. 2002. *The Century in Food; America's Fads and Favorites*. Portland, OR: Collectors Press.

Cooke, Alistair. 2006. *The American Home Front, 1941–1942*. New York: Atlantic Monthly Press.

Fessler, Ann. 2006. *The Girls Who Went Away*. New York: Penguin.

Gluck, Sherna Burger. 1987. *Rosie the Riveter Revisited: Women, the War and Social Change*. New York: New American Library.

Honey, Maureen. 1984. *Rosie the Riveter: Class, Gender and Propaganda during World War II*. Amherst: University of Massachusetts Press.

Jacoby, Sanford M. 1997. *Modern Manors: Welfare Capitalism since the New Deal*. Princeton: Princeton University Press.

Lincoln, C. Eric, and Lawrence H. Maniya. 1991. *The Black Church in the African-American Experience*. Durham, NC: Duke University Press.

Marling, Karal Ann. 1997. *Norman Rockwell*. New York: Abrams.

Marling, Karal Ann. 1991. *Engendering Culture: Manhood and Womanhood in New Deal Public Art and Theater*. Washington, DC: Smithsonian Institution Press.

Melosh, Barbara, ed. 1997. *Gender and American History since 1890*. London and New York: Routledge.

Mettler, Suzanne. *Soldiers to Citizens: The G.I. Bill and the Making of the Greatest Generation*. New York: Oxford University Press, 2005, b.

Meyerowitz, Joanne, ed. 1994. *Not June Cleaver: Women and Gender in Postwar America, 1945–1960*. Philadelphia: Temple University Press.

Parfray, Adam. 2003. *It's a Man's World*. Los Angeles: Feral House.

Rockwell, Norman. 1960. *My Adventures as an Illustrator*. New York: Doubleday.

Susman, Warren. 1984. *Culture as History: The Transformation of American Society in the Twentieth Century*. New York: Pantheon.

Trager, James. *The Century in Food*. http://www.foodtimeline.org/fooddecades .html#40hors. Accessed August 21, 2008.

Migrations

OVERVIEW

America in the 1940s was a country on the move; roughly 30 million citizens moved during war away from a traditional home locale to a new place. Two mass migrations took place, one involving roughly 16 million into the military and an equal number who filled war jobs on the home front. When the war ended, one out of every two who had moved chose to remain in their new locations, primarily cities. Migration from the inner city to the new suburbs took place in the postwar era.

Americans have historically been a mobile people, but in the 1940s this occurred in a dramatic mass form. World War II was the prime factor for the initial uprooting of huge numbers of people. Since the country's beginnings in colonial times, its pioneers had spread steadily westward until the new nation eventually extended its western border to the Pacific Ocean; the first western state, California, joined the union in 1850. Other West Coast states, Oregon and Washington, followed. In the 1940s, the four western states gained the most wartime migrants. War contracts flowed into cities there to build factories and service ships to fight in the Pacific theater. Migrants came primarily from the South and Midwest. They were a mostly conservative group; they helped make the future Southern California into one of the bastions of traditional Republicanism (in 1946, Richard Nixon was elected to Congress from Southern California).

The Deep South in particular lost population during the war to Northern cities such as Detroit where people hoped for industrial jobs in the conversion to peacetime production. Workers who moved included the poor of both white and black races. The push to leave the South was longtime poverty. (In the 1930s Roosevelt had termed the region the nation's foremost economic problem.) The South was mired in a backward economy of sharecropping and outmoded segregationist attitudes about race and caste. Long resisting attempts at modernization and the introduction of industry, the region had remained rural. The Roosevelt administration successfully began the process of bringing the region into the mainstream with war contracts with southern cities with factories or valuable ports. In Alabama, Mobile and Birmingham became wartime boomtowns, not sizable enough to offset migration but still significant.

Nationwide, the overall result was that the once-isolated regional culture of the South—stock car racing, country music, evangelical Protestant religion, and the black musical tradition of blues and rhythm and blues—began to develop a countrywide audience of ex-Southerners in the North and West. When the new mass media of television entered the mainstream in the late 1940s, these aspects of culture telecast around the country would result eventually in such phenomena as televangelism and rock 'n' roll music. Also, a politically conservative South began to desert the Democratic Party (the Strom Thurmond Dixiecrats bolted the party over race issues in 1948) to favor or join in what in the future would be termed The Sun Belt, which stretched from Florida through Texas to Southern California.

The country's agricultural sector produced more in the 1940s with larger farms and fewer workers because new technologies in farming techniques and equipment allowed the excess of workers to go to manufacturing jobs in cities. This had been a trend ever since the advent of industrialism in the country in the early 19th century. For instance, the new McCormick Reaper had freed up many men to fight for the Union Army in the Civil War, possibly being a little-known but important factor in the North's victory. In much the same way, from 1942 to 1945, technology allowed farmers to reduce their workforce, and there was an influx of labor into the country's cities and military.

Following much the same pattern, Mexican American and Native American minorities migrated from farm work or rural reservations to serve in the military or to work in newly opened factories in the cities. There they often encountered racial prejudice which resulted in violent episodes such as the Zoot Suit Riots in 1943, in which youths of Mexican ancestry were targeted. Riots also took place that year in many northern cities against African American newcomers from the South.

Immigration represented another aspect of the movement of peoples in the country in the 1940s. U.S. immigration officials adopted a temporary worker program with Mexico. With China, the U.S. Congress reacted favorably to an ally fighting the Japanese, doing away with a policy from 1882 that banned all Chinese, and making generous exceptions to the operative 1924 Quota laws to admit immigrant Chinese. The government was less welcoming to Jews. With the world's Jewish refugees and survivors from Hitler's concentration camps clamoring for entry into the United States, the country held to a 1924 law restricting Jewish immigrants. Eventually President Truman backed the longtime Zionist dream of a new state of Israel. The new country was created by the United Nations in 1948 within the largely Arab Palestine, a former mandate of the British.

TIMELINE

1940   The draft begins a peacetime buildup with the registration of all males aged 21 to 30.

U.S. Military is ranked 48th in size in the world.

The number of illegal Mexican immigrants crossing the border is at an all-time low due to the Depression.

1941   The draft calls up 1.5 million men.

1942   The wartime draft call-ups rise to peak volume, eventually reaching millions whose names are chosen by more than 8,000 local draft boards.

In all, 16 million will serve in the armed forces during the war; 75 percent of those will be deployed overseas. Frontline fighters were a tiny percentage; most were in backup support services to the fighting men.

The South loses 700,000 African Americans in a massive out-migration to the North.

1943   Twin migrations reach peaks—soldiers going overseas and war workers changing home locales.

Detroit faces race riots after a migration of 500,000 to the city, including 60,000 African Americans.

The United States begins a program to allow temporary migrant workers into the country from Mexico.

The Zoot Suit Riots target Mexican youth who migrated to wartime cities.

Mexican Medal of Honor winner S.Sgt. Marcario Garcia is denied service by a white Texas restraunteur.

1944   The G.I. Bill of Rights is passed; this bill allows returning servicemen to go to college and buy houses in record numbers.

Mobile, Alabama, a Deep South boomtown port, grows 61 percent from 1940 to the start of this year.

Mexican deportees reach 25,000 after an average of 19,000 each year before the war.

1945   Millions in the service undergo mass demobilization.

By this year, those who served constitute 10 million drafted, with 6 million enlisted. Women serving for the first time in wartime armed forces number 350,000.

Agriculture has lost 11 percent of its workers due to greater efficiencies and better equipment.

1946   Soldiers demand to be sent home in the "Bring the Boys Home" riots in Manila.

The CIO begins the effort to unionize the South (Operation Dixie) and keep high wartime wages, which stems migration from the region.

1947   With wartime influx, California, Washington, and Oregon each had one-third population growth. The West in general grows, but these states lead the gains.

The Mexican temporary worker program ends after enrolling 350,000 participants since 1943.

1948   Migration to the suburbs hits a high volume.

College towns overflow with newcomers due to an influx of enrollments by veterans who receive government-paid education through the G.I. Bill.

1949   One in every two wartime migrants stayed in a new place in the United States.

The National Farm Labor Union (AFL) calls a strike against giant California grower DiGiorgio, ending the use of illegal migrant replacements.

THE MILITARY MIGRATION

In World War II, the military compelled a vast migration of 16 million mostly provincial Americans to leave their home. They migrated first on trains to scattered, distant training camps located all over the country. Once trained and ready, these Americans were sent overseas to exotic places previously unknown to many of them. The mixing of different types of Americans—old stock and recent immigrant offspring—in this generational adventure was itself a novel experience for most. For example, for the first time, the son of a third-generation Midwestern farmer of Norwegian stock might meet the first-generation son of a Sicilian immigrant grocer who was raised in New York. Catholics, Protestants, and Jews all came together for a common cause, trained and fought together, risked their lives together, and, in essence, intensely lived out the melting pot experience in the war years.

The Curious Situation of the Italian Americans Early in the War

After Pearl Harbor on December 7, the Americans declared war on Japan, and then Germany and Italy declared war on the United States. On December 8, 1941, the president issued executive orders 2526 and 2527, which declared all aliens born in the Axis countries of Germany or Italy to be enemy aliens. An alien was an immigrant who remained a noncitizen because of not completing the naturalization process. At this time, the Italian American minority totaled about five million. Approximately 600,000 did not have naturalization papers. Many had been original immigrants who had harbored the dream of someday returning in their old age to live in their native villages. The order now suspended the naturalization process for all enemy aliens and limited their travel and employment opportunities.

At the time of Italy's declaration of war, all Italian nationals in this country were ordered held until the end of the war. This included the crew and passengers on ships then docked in this country's ports and any Italian tourists or business travelers then in the country. These Italian nationals, along with a select number of longtime Italian immigrants now considered enemy aliens, were sent to the interior of the country to live the remainder of the war in a guarded relocation camp. Hundreds were held for the war's duration at Fort Missoula in Missoula, Montana. The Italians were in general well behaved but, nonetheless, their detention was forced upon them. Many older detainees from the Little Italys of the United States were bewildered; they never afterward spoke about the experience.

Following the attack on Pearl Harbor, Italian American citizens united behind their country's cause. The young men volunteered by the thousands to serve their country. Maybe more than any other American ethnics at the time, the Italian American servicemen were the most provincial, having habitually kept to tightly knit city neighborhoods. Being swept up in the migrations overseas and back, some became the most worldly. Joining with Americans of all other backgrounds, they felt an acceptance and appreciation from their countrymen that was not always there in the years before the war.

In the years before the United States entered the war, Italian Americans were strongly isolationist, and many had been proud of the progress and military stature of Italy under the leadership of Benito Mussolini. In 1940, when Italy declared war on England, Italian newspapers in this country were mostly favorable. But in the spring of 1940, when Roosevelt called Mussolini's surprise attack on France "a stab in the back," many Americans grew suspicious of the ethnic Italians. In turn, the Italians in the United States became fearful of this mainstream reaction toward them. All Axis aliens had suddenly become suspect. Marginalized Americans at the time of Pearl Harbor, the Italian immigrants and their descendents seized the chance to express their true loyalty to America by joining the ranks of the American military.

The Draft

The years from 1940 to 1942 constituted the peacetime buildup to full military mobilization. In 1940, Roosevelt got Congress to pass the country's first peacetime draft, which required all males age 21 to 36 to register at their draft boards, staffed by locals (the country would eventually have a total of 8,000 draft boards that determined who was fit, nonfit, or deferred). With general compliance, millions were on the rolls available for call-up. When a draftee's number was called in a lottery, the next step was to pass a physical and mental examination before being inducted into the armed forces. Beginning in 1940, the country's military was less than 500,000. By 1941, the military had 1.5 million.

Massive mobilization began immediately after Pearl Harbor. By 1945, 10 million had been drafted, along with 6 million enlisted men and 350, 000 women who had volunteered for the WACs, WAVEs, and other newly established women's auxiliary units. From 1942 on, a massive military migration abroad began. This movement of peoples left a domestic vacuum to be filled by another domestic migration of millions of civilians. By war's end, on the home front, 15 million Americans had at least one major change in residency.

The overseas migration had triggered the domestic migration. Inductees moved by railroad to their new military training camps, many in the South. There northerners both white and black suddenly encountered southern legal segregation for the first time in most their lives. Liberal-minded northerners did not wish to take seats in the front of the bus from African Americans; African Americans born in the north found it humiliating to have to sit in the back of the bus in the colored section for the first time.

After six weeks of basic training, the military gave each inductee a service assignment. About 75 percent, or 12 million, were deployed overseas; by the end of the war, one in nine Americans had gone overseas. This generation thus became the most traveled one to date and constituted the greatest number of Americans at any one time who were world wise or cosmopolitan.

U.S. soldiers leaving Pullman cars, ca. 1942. (Library of Congress)

The end of the war brought a massive demobilization. After being overseas, some for the full three and half years, this huge military machine achieved victory in 1945. Servicemen returned home based on a point system, with the first to go home the ones with most service time and actual combat time. Victory in Europe, V-E Day, occurred in May and three months later, victory came in the Far East (V-J Day). Thereafter the American military brass drafted plans for the military in the vast Pacific region to be redeployed to fight with local troops in places like the Philippines and China, which continued to fight communist insurgencies. In response, in early January 1946, tens of thousands of servicemen rallied in Manila and demanded to be sent home. "Bring the Boys Home" became the movement's name at home; in the Far East, servicemen revolted after the example of their Manila comrades. With fierce pressure at home and abroad, the War Department gave in to the popular pressure and brought these troops home. The Truman administration and Congress then haphazardly let millions return to civilian life with little social planning and a sharp drop-off in the size of the military.

With victory in 1945, a massive demobilization occurred, with the same vast group returning to the United States. Often the GIs returned to big cities where the new jobs existed, not back to the farms, ranches, villages, and small towns where their journeys had begun. In the postwar years, the G.I. Bill was indispensable in training and educating veterans to broaden the future middle class of the country and ensure its growing prosperity.

In the postwar 1940s, the booming U.S. economy managed to absorb most all of the roughly 30 million Americans engaged in the two migrations: the one overseas and the domestical one. The G.I. Bill was a great aid in that it gave veterans educational opportunities to prepare them for new jobs or some cash as they looked for work. The bill allowed a veteran either to enroll in college or to wait to decide his future by getting a livable allotment of $20 per week for 52 weeks. If not enrolling in college, a veteran could also have the cost of an apprenticeship or vocational school paid for by the government. The bill gave veterans a chance to share in the new prosperity in the country and erase the bitter memories of the Depression era they had left behind.

Most importantly, in many ways, the young man who had left was not the young man who was returning. Combat veterans suffered psychological damage in higher numbers than was ever reported to the public. But their families knew. Others had been disabled, and lived with lowered self-esteem for the rest of their lives. All had memories of seeing or being part of the most brutal aspects of darkest side human behavior.

World War II veterans in considerable numbers suffered from severe stress—or Post Traumatic Stress Disorder (PTSD), as it was known after the 1960s Vietnam War. It was referred to as battle fatigue before and after the 1940s fighting. Those with the condition suffered depression, sleep disorders, and especially nightmare episodes in which they awoke believing themselves to be in the middle of a battle exactly as if it was occurring again all over. At the time, there existed a taboo against mentioning mental illness or anything like it, and veterans often had to suffer this in silence. The war's most decorated combat hero, Audie Murphy, suffered from this into the 1960s, when he became addicted to sleeping pills Overcoming this, he addressed the problem of the stresses of battle on the emotions of the individual and became a spokesperson for veterans at this later time.

War Breaks Down Barriers for Ethnic Americans

By the time of war, ethnic Americans—Italians and other Eastern and Southern European immigrants—were first- or second-generation American-born children or grandchildren of the immigrants born in the old country. Many were assimilated to a large degree, having attended schools in this country and, many spoke only English. These groups still often resided in ethnic enclaves, even though the 1924 Immigration Act had restricted new immigration from these groups to tight annual quotas.

With the draft in 1940 and then, in first year of full-scale war in 1942, the migration of millions of ethnic and older stock Americans into training camps and then into command units and small fighting groups melted remaining parochial barriers among ethnics themselves and mainstream culture. Young men from the most diverse family backgrounds became buddies and depended on one another for their survival. In basic training, many a WASP had made the acquaintance of his first Jew or Italian and vice versa, but by the time all were fighting together on the front lines, these distinctions had come to mean very little compared with aspects of individual character like courage, endurance, and camaraderie.

In the postwar era, millions of returning servicemen looked back and saw their common war experience as a rite of passage; this was a bond for the whole generation. As a result, the country experienced a general easing of the old-time hostilities between ethnic neighborhoods and between the ethnics and native born WASPS. After the war ended, the draft also ended in 1945, but it began again as a peacetime draft in 1947 due the country's far-flung military commitments in the Cold War. One result was the forging of an "American" military which decreased the role of ethnic identity. The G.I. Bill then also helped bring a broad mix of veterans together to go to college in pursuit of the American Dream. Class and racial barriers remained stronger than ethnic divisions among white Americans.

World War II proved a great contrast to the war 20 years earlier. In 1942, the entire population of the country was mobilized for war; in 1917, this did happen to the same degree. The social dislocations in the form of vast migrations of citizens during World War II were therefore of much greater magnitude, especially after 1942. Six times more Americans went overseas than the Foreign Expeditionary Force that Woodrow Wilson sent to Europe.

The Great War (as World War I was called at the time) was primarily fought on a single front in the European theater and was characterized by huge opposing armies stalled by trench warfare. Far greater in scope—in fact, truly global and fought on two widespread fronts—World War II brought airplanes and tanks into full use. The trench war that had characterized World War I was no longer possible. At sea, new aircraft carriers served as moving airstrips from which to launch fighter planes in surprise attacks at the enemy, as happened when the Japanese struck at Pearl Harbor, with the Americans caught unaware.

The high ideals that animated American intervention in both wars differed mostly in tone. Americans and the doughboys sent to fight in Europe in 1917 had high idealistic goals. President Wilson had said this was "a war to end all wars" and this was "a war to make the world safe for democracy." He had his Fourteen Points for the peacemaking. Grand disillusionment was the result as Americans witnessed the victorious Allied European nations undermine these hopes and lay the seeds for a future world war. Wilson's League of Nations met defeat in the U.S. Senate as postwar Americans turned increasingly to isolationism.

President Roosevelt deliberately avoided setting war aims too high and instead set out the rather vague Four Freedoms. The GIs, in contrast to the doughboys, were not idealistic but very gruff, down-to-earth, and pragmatic in wanting just to get the job done and get home. Few could recite all four freedoms (only 13 percent) and many had confusion, at times, over the more abstract national goals. These soldiers fought a much more personal war: for one's own survival and that of buddies—no more, no less. Grunts, they called themselves, often bedraggled, dirty with a scruffy beard, exhausted but pushing on. Only a few individuals truly captured this American fighting man: one was the cartoonist Bill Mauldin who depicted the struggle through his GIs Willie and Joe, much beloved by the troops themselves; the other was the war journalist Ernie Pyle who wrote dispatches from the viewpoint and perspective of those in battle, not as if above the battle analyzing it the day afterward.

Battle Front and the Home Front: Connected by a Fighting Journalist

With many millions of citizens caught in the twin migrations inside and outside the United States, this great mass of dislocated Americans needed to feel connected. The war reporter Ernie Pyle was one link between the front lines and home front; in the most vital of ways Pyle was beloved by GIs (he was often in combat with them and shared their living conditions) and he was beloved by the readers of his six-times-per-week column from the front. Syndicated to over 300 newspapers, it had some 13 million readers. Some readers and soldiers even called it "Ernie Pyle's War."

During a time when the individual was often lost within the giant bureaucracy necessary to conduct modern war, Pyle wrote from the point of view of the individual soldier's experience of four or five individuals who were his buddies, forming the team vital to survival. Cosmopolitan while at the same time a product of a small town midwestern upbringing, Pyle bridged the gap between home and combat not with abstract strategies or accounts of overall battles and fighting ideals but with a focus on the battling grunt whose life depended on a few other grunts. This was the very concept of small-town sports: the individual star needs the other players or he is nothing.

Weary, bedraggled, tired to the bones, Pyle told stories of the real frontline man, who fought to survive another day but was willing to sacrifice all for a real buddy who would do the same for him. Very few of these men could recite correctly the Four Freedoms, the nation's war aims. Like Hemingway, Pyle shunned concepts such as freedom and liberty as being too abstract to be constantly on the minds of a fighting man without a bath for weeks, wearing the same clothes, scratched, wounded, with jungle rot fungus between his toes, in a situation of kill or be killed by an unseen enemy hidden in the fiery, hot, humid jungle of an island strategic for some reason beyond understanding.

Pyle reported from both theaters of war—first in Europe, covering the invasion of North Africa and then the Italian campaign. In Sicily, he wrote probably his most famous piece about an Army captain who movingly gave his life not as a noble hero but as common infantryman battling in the immediate instant— who became an Everyman fighting in service to his country but especially family and intimate loved ones, whose photos were likely in his wallet. In 1943, Pyle won the Pulitzer Prize for his war column; he went on to cover D-Day and the liberation of Paris.

In 1945, he accepted an assignment to the Pacific Theater, and there, only a few days before the war ended in Europe and a few months before the Japanese surrender, Pyle was killed on a lonely island by an enemy bullet surrounded by his adopted buddies, the fighting GIs. Buried in a shallow dirt grave on the island by fellow grunts, he was widely mourned at home and everywhere by our servicemen and women. Likely to miss him most were those far behind the front lines, providing vital supply needs—the forgotten individuals he included in columns: cooks, laundrymen, mechanics, and the occasional woman who was in the first U.S. war to officially include her sex in all branches of the armed services.

Ground combat itself, especially in the Pacific, became brutal early on as Americans realized their foe, the Japanese, believed surrender was shameful; instead the Japanese soldier believed he had to fight to the death to honor his family and his country. He believed his foes should likewise fight to the death, and the result was the enemy execution of many captured Americans; as a result, there was retaliation in kind, rarely if ever reported because of military censorship of all war information let to the home front.

Wartime censorship was widespread and very effective in showing the home front only a certain acceptable view of the war to keep civilian morale high, even during the early months of 1942 when the United States. was staggering from defeat after defeat in ground and sea battles and coming perilously close to overall defeat. For the first 21 months of the war, no images of American war dead appeared to people at home; afterward, some select photos of corpses began to appear, largely to motivate defense workers to spur production and cut the growing absenteeism. A similarly thorough censorship had existed during World War I.

Military life itself made for the most crucial change of all in 16 million young men that the government had compelled to migrate from home and live a new, dutiful, hierarchical, regimented way of life for the duration of the war. It had major effects of their lives, especially as more of these veterans more easily adapted to the mid-management levels of the military-style management structure adopted by corporations in the postwar. The lesson was that individualism needed to be sacrificed for the good of the group. In domestic life, the prior military training also made social conformity more easily the norm in the late 1940s, and especially in the collectively more conservative political spectrum based on broad-based anticommunism.

During the six weeks of basic training, the military's goal was to break down the individual's sense of self (thus the buzz-cut hair changed personal appearance to a group standard) and then rebuild that individual to blend with his basic fighting unit. This way the individual was expected to learn that his own survival and the survival of his close comrades were one and the same. Forged in boot camp, the basic fighting unit of men remained intact through mutual danger and loss of members, which made the bonds between them even closer. The individual began to matter less and less as the survival of all was predominant.

Nonetheless, Army life itself was based on inherent inequalities of assignment and rank whether enlisted or career military. Because segregated African American soldiers were barred from combat, more educated whites tended to have behind-the-line desk positions, and college-educated whites were often officers, the front-line combat troops were disproportionately disadvantaged whites. Many of these had come from relatively marginal home and work backgrounds and naturally were less socialized and more antiauthoritarian. Grunts risking their lives were at times commanded by higher-ranking officers who had little of the savvy or knowledge of the fighting man experiencing the battle. Mistakes by commanders led to a raw hatred of them by the rank and file. But, as military success was based on the idea that the lower ranks needed to obey authority, the military proved a separate authoritarian society existing within a civilian democratic society.

Termed the "Greatest Generation" these individuals had endured a Depression-era upbringing and then went through two migrations in the 1940s—one overseas to a victorious war against dire threats to democracy and the other a return migration home to help sustain domestic prosperity with renewed will to win the new Cold War.

The Flag-Raising Photo at Iwo Jima: Facts and National Symbol

In all of World War II, the single most famous photo of the fighting was of five Marines and one Navy corpsman on the summit of Mount Suribachi raising the U.S. flag during the critical battle for Iwo Jima. The battle was strategic because the rocky island was near enough to the Japanese main islands to allow American bombers a much-needed place to land to refuel or get repairs. Associated Press photographer Joe Rosenthal took the photo on February 23, 1945, on only the fifth day of a roughly 35-day battle against 21,000 diehard Japanese who would fight to the death. More than 6,800 Americans were eventually killed at Iwo Jima.

In this award-winning photograph, which served as the model for the Marine Corps War Memorial, U.S. troops raise the American flag on Iwo Jima on February 23, 1945. Strategically, the capture of the small island almost a month later was crucial to the United States because it was an ideal site from which to bomb Japan. (National Archives)

The combat photographer had climbed the 546-foot mount to reach the peak at just the right moment to witness the second flag-raising, one with a bigger flag mounted on sturdier sections of heavy pipe so as to be seen all over the island where the fighting was raging. Swinging his Speed Graphic camera, set at 1/400, he just caught the shot of the spontaneous action (luckily he'd just appeared that second after first deciding not to make the steep climb to the top). He had no idea this would be an iconic photo. Three of the six flag raisers were to become casualties at Iwo Jima; the other three returned home as heroes.

Back on the home front, the photo alone became a national icon, symbolizing for all citizens the special, precious fighting spirit of a indomitable people. The image became a metonym for the Good War, remaining as such through the end of the war, into the start of the Cold War, and beyond into the rest of the century. Almost immediately after it reached the United States, the photo was reprinted in countless newspapers and magazines; it was produced on 3.5 million Treasury Department posters advertising one of the last great drives for the public to buy war bonds. Helping in this effort were the three surviving flag raisers who promoted the war bond drive at rallies where they reraised the flag time after time in a way that cheapened the original spontaneous act. No matter, in 1945, the image was placed on a three-cent postage stamp. Rosenthal won the Pulitzer Prize.

What was it that made the photo so singular in the American imagination? With the war and business becoming increasingly bureaucratic en masse, the photo showed a small team of six, each an individual but all representative of the enduring rural and small-town values of an America fast disappearing with the growth of huge cities. In 1945, especially for those at home and fighting on other fronts, the photo was an image of national unity, representive of how we are all in this fight together and unconquerable amid the immediate lived individual experiences of dislocation and disconnectedness associated with the mass migrations of so many millions of Americans. In a time of great upheaval at home with families separated from loved ones, the great effort required of the six to place the heavy pole and fluttering flag on the hill served as a visible symbol to viewers of the great burden borne by a free people to defend liberty.

In the ongoing Cold War, the image gained an even larger symbolic presence; in Arlington National Cemetery, it served as the image for a War Memorial to the Marine Corps. After the fall of communism in 1990 and the official end of the Cold War, the symbolic image went on inspiring a people. In 1995, the government issued a new 32-cent stamp with its image. (Alas, in the celebration of the image, some salient facts of the case were lost: the three originally involved in the act were taken stateside, portrayed as heroes for publicity purposes, discharged, and then largely forgotten, left to struggle with the problems of readjustment. One, a Native American named Ira Hayes, became an alcoholic and died prematurely in 1955; the others struggled with survivor guilt.)

"The Good War" became the term used for the generation's military victory; after future American wars with more ambiguous aims and results, World War II became known as "the Last Good War" because it began with defense against an aggressor's unprovoked attack. The government had called upon this generation to defend the country through massive overseas deployment; in the fighting the returning servicemen and women in this generation had lost "the best years of their lives"—the span between ages 18 and 21. But what they lost in innocence they gained in early knowledge of the tragic sense of life. This gave them far more maturity than those who would follow shortly after them.

While it went without question that the country would owe great gratitude to this generation for its fight, the generational myth has grown so powerful at times that it glosses over some compromised and less than glorious aspects— from the carpet bombing of a civilian site like Dresden to the incarceration of

Japanese American citizens without trials. The myth almost glorifies the war in general. The American military was not without its own questionable actions and strategies. More importantly, the American public in this conflict became accustomed to the visible, open, democratic government operating along with a parallel, invisible, closed, authoritarian government. People participated directly in the first but only indirectly in the second. The prime example of this is the secret Manhattan Project and the atomic bomb used by President Truman without public knowledge. The greatest decision of the 20th century by the world's greatest democracy was made without the knowledge of its people or by a majority of their vote.

Americans believed that the use of the bomb ended the war and made possible the return of many who undoubtedly would have lost their lives if the United States had invaded the Japanese home islands. Historians have questioned if the timing of the bombs sought to end the war before Russia entered the eastern front and shared the spoils of war. But it was also the case that the Americans were demanding unconditional surrender by the Japanese; without this, the Japanese would have continued to fight to the end. Indeed, the Allies strategically bombed civilian populations in German cities in retaliation for Germany's bombings of England and other European cities. Dresden was carpet bombed with an all-consuming fireball that killed tens of thousands of civilians and destroyed a world heritage city for little actual military gain. Tokyo was virtually helpless against American bombers that dropped countless powerful conventional bombs. One saturation bombing set fire to all of inner Tokyo, and its wooden dwellings fueled an inferno so vast that it killed more humans than either of the later two atomic bombs.

REGIONAL MIGRATIONS

During the early 1940s and the war, the country underwent huge population shifts, as large numbers of people left certain areas and went to regions where the most wartime jobs were being created. Out-migration was a phenomenon of both the South and the Midwest while in-migration was a constant in the North and the West.

Highway of Hope: Route 66 and the Road to Golden California

A certain highway became the fabled road that migrants traveled to go west to California, a legendary place that lured all with the promise of reaching the American Dream. Americans imagined it as a cross-country symbol of the way west—more than a mere two-lane highway that began in Illinois, traversed Missouri and

Kansas and moved across the barren, sparsely populated southwest of Oklahoma, Texas (the Panhandle), New Mexico, and Arizona to California. The highway covered 2,500 miles.

In the *Grapes of Wrath* (1939), author John Steinbeck tells the story of the Joad family who flee the Dust Bowl by traveling the better part of their migration west on Highway 66; a year later the movie, starring Henry Fonda, shows the family's old overloaded jalopy crossing the Colorado River over the highway's famed bridge into California. In 1946, Nate King Cole recorded his hit record, "(Get Your Kicks on) Route 66," and thereafter the "Highway" was known as the more memorable "Route." The song's writer, Bobby Troup, a recently discharged Marine veteran, had traveled U.S. 66 to Los Angeles, California, from St. Louis, Missouri, earlier in 1946. The song with its rhymes etched itself into the imagination of America. Fame then made it the way to get to California.

From its origins as a Native American trail to an auto road of paved sections, Highway 66 was connected in 1925 as one of the number-designated highways, U.S. 60, in the new federal system (transcontinental routes ended in zeros). A year later when a powerful Kentucky governor got the federal government to designate a different highway going through his state as U.S. 60, the first highway from Chicago to Los Angeles was given the off-beat number U.S. 66, destined to be the best-known way west for most of the 20th century.

Beginning in 1956, the Eisenhower administration would put into effect the Interstate Highway Program and began building a separate but parallel freeway system with limited access; by the 1980s, the new freeway system had been built over the top of large sections of the famed U.S. 66 and had overshadowed other stretches of the highway. Sixty years after becoming part of the federal transcontinental highway system, the famed route lost its designation but not its place in the American imagination.

Migrations and Resettlement

Fifteen million Americans had moved throughout the country during the war. After 1945, one of every two Americans stayed in their new place; California, Oregon, and Washington all had populations one-third greater following the war. In the postwar years, a new migration began, with millions of people emptying out of the inner cities and going to the suburbs. The earlier wartime migrations continued but with far fewer people as prosperity began growing more widespread and included the regions that had earlier emptied of so many residents.

Where out-migration occurs, there usually is a push or cluster of unfavorable aspects causing people to risk moving elsewhere for greater opportunities. The Midwest in 1940 was a rich agricultural region where farmers, due to new technologies and crop-raising methods, produced more efficiently and thus required fewer hired hands. The South in 1940 was overwhelmingly rural and poor due to a sharecropping tradition of farming, a lack of industries, and a rigid social hierarchy and a racist caste system of segregation between the black and white

Beginning in 1941, men and women from all corners of the United States flocked to war production centers for jobs to help make the country the arsenal of democracy. Huge airplane plants and shipyards on the West Coast drew hordes of willing workers. With the war over, cutbacks and mass layoffs started migration eastward, but not in the same proportion as the trek westward in pre-war days. Speeding past one of the Highway 66 markers, Edmond M. Snow and his family head back to Minnesota after four years of war work at the Consolidated Vultee Aircraft plant in San Diego, California, August 23, 1945. His plans: To buy a small farm with savings from his war jobs. (Bettmann/Corbis)

races. African Americans in the area from 1940 to 1945 had the opportunity to find wartime jobs elsewhere, so they left discrimination, poverty, lynching, and voter disenfranchisement in the South. Poor southern whites (at the time referred to as hillbillies by northerners) also fled in hopes of making better lives in the North and West.

The North and West experienced waves of in-migration due to the pull of better jobs and brighter futures. In the North, Michigan gained the most population of the northern states because the government gave an overwhelming number of war contracts to Detroit's former automakers, who had converted their assembly lines over to the production of tanks and bombers. The government subsidized the building of vast new factory complexes like Willow Run.

In the West, the Pacific coastal states all made great population gains, but California led. Government spending on increased war production in this region created new jobs attracting migrants. Closest to the Pacific theater of war, these states had geographic advantages in getting contracts. Airplane manufacturing for the war became a predominant industry in Los Angeles. Shipbuilding took hold in the San Francisco Bay area with the town of Richmond in the East Bay being the prime manufacturing facility for Edgar Kaiser, whose new assembly-line methods began making new merchant or Liberty Ships in record time. The West topped all regions in gaining record numbers of new migrants during war and the postwar.

By 1945, one in five Americans had migrated during the war and, in the postwar, eight million would choose to stay in the new place. Others returned to their place of origin but with greater expectations. In the largely nonunion South, for example, many postwar workers sought union protection and the higher wages and better working conditions that had become the standard in defense factories.

Operation Dixie

Operation Dixie was a CIO-led campaign to unionize the South to retain the region's economic gains in wartime. In its war industries, the region had undergone promising beginnings of a would-be modernization that, if fully successful at that time, would have stemmed out-migration from the South and, in the larger sense, changed the mass migration pattern throughout the country. Wartime government contracts let to southern industry had mandated standards of higher wages, better working conditions, and, most importantly, the unionization and integration of the workforces in these plants. Benchmarks had been reached; by 1945, the CIO had organized 800,000 workers including African Americans, and compared with all other regions, the South's wages had risen proportionally higher than the rest.

In 1946, the CIO organized Operation Dixie to both maintain these gains and further organize the South's industries: textiles, tobacco, and lumber. A huge union drive went into effect with hundreds of organizers fanning out through the 12 target states and establishing many local offices. Unfortunately, the union organizers only partially anticipated the depth of opposition from archconservative elites, politicians and businessmen who believed the war years were a necessary but temporary adjustment. This conservative coalition would insist labor return to prewar conditions of a low-wage and racially divided workforce. Company towns so common in the region became fortresses from which the elite archconservatives would fight with ferocity against the union organizers from outside the region. Their weapons would be traditional appeals to white racism and outright violent threats and actions against what they often branded "communist" unions wanting to take over the South and make an integrated workforce against tradition.

Operation Dixie foundered from the beginning because of local regional resistance; it ultimately failed because of a larger national anticommunist campaign against the more radical branches of the union movement, especially the CIO. In the rising tide of what would later be called McCarthyism, Union officials' were diverted from organizing the South to defend the CIO from charges of that unAmerican communists controlled the union. Intraunion factional disputes and national political fights over the issue also drew energy away from unionizing the South. But mostly, the die-hard antimodernism of southern conservatives and their political representatives in Congress proved too formidable a foe at the time.

Southern Out-migration

In the postwar era, wartime migrations would continue but with less urgency; young Americans especially continued to move from the South, off the farms and to the cities. A new migration began in the late 1940s, as people emptied out of the crowded apartments of the inner cities to move to spacious single-family homes of the new suburbs. Some saw this as a migration pattern come full circle, starting with an original migration from farm to city, then with a generation moving to the green suburbs almost in homage to farm origins but still with commuter access to the business-centered city.

The South, the area losing most migrants in the 1940s, had long been the country's most depressed region. In 1937, President Roosevelt had recognized the region's economic potential, but in much of the region, textile mills were its only real industry. Nearly 100 years after the Civil War, with the exception of the Virginia tidewater tobacco region, the South was agriculturally a one-crop economy based on the growing of cotton.

Land ownership was highly concentrated because one person owned a large acreage and rented parcels of it to be farmed by poor white and black share-croppers. The owner staked the cropper to a year's seed and provisions, and at harvest, the cropper gave half of the crops to repay his landlord. A bad harvest put a cropper in debt, unable to pay back that year's loan; with time, many croppers became indebted servants, bound to the land with an accumulated debt impossible to pay back.

The South held out little real hope to sharecroppers for upward social mobility. The cropper and his family were locked into a meager station of life. Poor whites held on to a thread of "superiority" by clinging to their racism against African Americans. But, in turn, racism and the sharecropping system provided major stimuli for the Great Migration of rural African Americans to the North in the early 1900s. The flow spiked in response to the new jobs of World War I and during the prosperous 1920s. Harlem, for instance, grew both in area and in numbers, and there was parallel growth in other Northern urban black communities. The Depression slowed this flow North, but a new factor pushed rural southern African Americans out in record numbers by the early 1940s—the mechanical cotton picker.

Westward Ho

The 1940s migration pattern of moving from the South and Midwest to the Far West had happened before in the 1930s during the Dust Bowl. Poor farmers from Arkansas and Oklahoma and the lower Midwest had lost their topsoil to the heat and winds, which forced them to head for the imagined golden land of California. *The Grapes of Wrath* by John Steinbeck, published in 1939 and produced as a movie in 1940, captured the Joads, one family in this massive exodus cross country. After overcoming challenges and loss, they reach California just as unwelcome then subject to exploitation as farm workers.

The 1940s saw a continuation of two deep historic trends in American migration: the movement westward and the movement from farms to the city. During World War II and the postwar, Americans moved westward in greater numbers than at any other time in their history, aside from the earlier movement of pioneers from the eastern seaboard over the Appalachian Mountains into rich farmlands stretching from there to the Mississippi River. Urban growth also continued in the war years with migrants from farms; this trend had begun with full-scale industrialization in the latter half of the 19th century. The 1920 census stated that for the first time more American lived in cities than in small towns or on farms.

Migration had been made easier by the 1940s. Trains provided low-cost passenger travel over a vast national railroad network. Auto ownership was widespread due to Henry Ford's introduction of the affordably priced, durable Model T Ford in the 1920s. In the years after, the country developed a better network of two-lane roads along with a network of gas and service stations. During the war, millions of migrants used autos to migrate to new opportunities, although gas rationing and the tire shortage created problems for all except commuting defense workers who got special rations.

New Migrant Culture

When the war ended and the soldiers came home, the question remained: would the domestic migrants move back to their places of origin? Fifty percent, or roughly 8 of the 15 million, chose to remain in their new destinations. The veterans in the postwar set new patterns of migration, to the suburbs often from their parental dwellings in the cities. Colleges and universities had a new migrant population of older students; the freshman class was a mix of those aged 22 or older along with customary 18-year-old students. Once veterans obtained their degrees, the careers they began would set them on a path moving about the country, away from and far different than the work patterns of their parents' generation, especially those long residing in ethnic neighborhoods.

The G.I. Bill benefits made possible both affordable loans for these first-time homeowners and the money for tuition and living expenses for these first-time college students. Millions benefited; they began the new patterns of social mobility that constituted new suburb-to-suburb immigration patterns.

Poor southern whites and African Americans migrating North and West to cities like Los Angeles, New York, Chicago, and Detroit created a new urban cultural form that drew on their rural past. These urban and regional areas inherited aspects of the migrants' rural cultural traditions: country music, the blues, and rhythm and blues. All of these music styles were slated to have deep influences on national popular culture. Black music provided the seeds for 1950s rock 'n' roll. Rather than simply being regional, each of these types of music gained a wider national urban audience as did such rural southern pastimes as stock car racing and African American–style dances and slang.

In religion, Southern Baptists gained a northern foothold from both the poor white and African American migrations, and southern evangelical and Pentecostal religions cropped up in Los Angeles where in 1949, the Reverend Billy Graham gave his first breakthrough gospel crusade. The new mass medium of television would greatly aid the national dissemination of these formerly isolated aspects of southern culture. Fundamentalist Christianity, many from all over the country found out for the first time, served as the perfect antidote to atheistic communism.

Thus, the 1940s migrations from the South and Midwest to the North and West brought about permanent changes in the ways Americans thought of themselves. In the boom cities and towns with defense jobs, a mix of migrant peoples had to learn to understand each other enough to cope with new dwellings and jobs. The West Coast went from having a scattered population in relatively sleepy cities, such as the 1930s Los Angeles of the Raymond Chandler detective novels, to being one of the country's greatest population areas. New houses were springing up like wild flowers in Los Angeles; housing developments grew to be "suburbs all in search of a city," as the writer Dorothy Parker satirized Los Angeles. By 1949, the state of California had grown by 72 percent over its population in 1940.

The new migrants also fueled the growth of suburbs in the east. In New York City, the population excess of wartime migrants and returning veterans began to spread eastward, with suburbs replacing farms on Long Island, and northward, with the new auto-based suburbs surrounding the stately old interurban trolley and train suburbs of Westchester County.

FARM TO URBAN MIGRATION

America from 1940 to 1945 witnessed the greatest short-term reshuffling of people in its history; by end of the war, one in every five citizens had moved. The greatest number of these migrants left farms or rural areas and went to cities.

The South and the Midwest were the places these farm persons left, and they went to the large cities of the North such as Detroit, Cleveland, and New York and large cities of the West such as San Diego, Los Angeles, Portland, and Seattle. Smaller towns in the South landed contracts for defense plants or shipyards and instantly exploded in population, often beyond the capacity of local schools and hospitals. These were the classic boomtowns of the war.

Boomtown Los Angeles in the 1940s

Los Angeles in the 1940s had its largest, most transforming period—in size and population, physical look, and widening of its economic base. Due to the huge financial input of government war contracts to the city, it drew migrants from elsewhere, especially farmers from the Midwest, and it developed an industrial sector to offset its traditional agriculture and petroleum sectors. In 1940, the city had a population of just under one and half million; 10 years later it was near the two million mark. The city, including its sprawling outlying unincorporated areas, was fast becoming the metropolis of the West Coast, the equivalent to New York City on the East Coast.

The migrants who came during wartime stayed after war's end. Few went back home. Thousands more came to Los Angeles to make it their new home in the postwar years. Jobs remained plentiful as California's economic base widened to make it first in the country not only in movie-making but also in such new areas as aircraft and sport clothing manufacture. The now industrial Los Angeles was nearly the largest center for making car tires and assembling cars.

Native-born Angelino Fletcher Bowron, Los Angeles mayor from 1938 to 1953, presided over the explosive growth of this boom metropolis. By 1948, the city was getting 10,000 newcomers each month, and most intended to stay. The challenge was to keep providing a steady supply of new homes in new neighborhoods with new schools and ever-extending electric, water, and sewage lines. Bowron's administration did a commendable job in building an infrastructure to keep pace with the incredible population growth. In 1948, the city laid 50 miles of new water main tunnels each month. Since first being elected in 1938, the mayor had built over 30 new schools. In the three years following the end of war in August 1945, the city had over 400,000 new phone users. In water, it consumed nearly 500 million gallons per day in an area that had been desert, seemingly only yesterday.

Rural agricultural distress helped push migrants to the city. Agriculture in general underwent changes during the war; there was an 11 percent decrease in the numbers of farm workers coupled with a 15 percent increase in production. Larger, less marginal farms used greater and more effective fertilizer and more and better machinery. The more viable farms absorbed smaller ones and, in growing larger, benefited from economies of scale. Crop prices doubled during the

Nine huge Liberty cargo ships at the outfitting docks of California Shipbuilding Corporation's Los Angeles yards, nearly ready to be delivered to the U.S. Maritime Commission, December 1943. (Library of Congress)

war. Of all groups, already secure farmers gained the most in prosperity during World War II. In the postwar, family farms gave way to corporate agricultural enterprises, known as agribusinesses. The first to become well known were in the rich Central Valley of California. Profits rose three times over, and greater crop worth increased land values against which farmers borrowed to make greater technological gains. Moreover during the war and after, farmers enjoyed government support in ensuring a set price for certain crops. Migrant labor, of course, did not get such help, and insufficient farm work drove many to seek opportunity in the nation's industrial cities.

Farm distress pushed migrants, but opportunities in the cities may have been as important in attracting them. Industrial cities become a magnet for those leaving the land. During the war, with many men were off fighting, the home war industries had a great demand for workers. Leaving the agricultural areas, workers came to take the new multitude of jobs in munitions factories, shipyards, plane factories, and army facilities. This influx transformed cities; for example, San Diego, a quiet prewar port town, experienced a boom with a new giant plane factory, an expanded shipyard and busier port, and the biggest of all naval bases and two large nearby army bases. No longer sleepy, the downtown was open 24 hours a day. Theaters never closed and one café had ten bars and a dance floor for thousands. Military paydays brought pandemonium.

Urban areas changed racially during the war as well as 700,000 African Americans left the farms of the South to get factory jobs. Detroit, for instance, had an overall in-migration of 500,000, of which 60,000 were African Americans. Tensions mounted over housing and jobs, and African Americans were forced to reside in a teeming, overcrowded area called Paradise Valley. Older ethnic workers fought for sole possession of their work rights, and in 1943, Detroit experienced the worst race riot of the war. Northerners also practiced racism, not in a legal fashion, but by informal custom—de facto segregation. Poor whites also did not fare well: locals termed rural white migrants from the South hillbillies or poor white trailer trash.

Southern Economic Development

Beginning in 1940, and especially with entry into the war, American farmers had a fear of repeating the earlier disaster of World War I, when their boom war production and profits had ended in a severe postwar depression due to over-production and a huge surplus with little or no market. During the prosperous 1920s, agriculture remained a sick part of the economy, but then help came in 1933 in the form of the government-supported Agricultural Adjustment Administration (AAA), which paid farmers subsidies to take land out of use to bring production in line with the market. The New Deal brought other benefits such as rural electrification (1935) and a strong effort to keep small farmers in business through loans for resettlement to better land or purchase of their own land.

New Deal programs only mitigated more basic problems with southern agriculture, however, and migrants began to exit the area in growing numbers. Ever since the advent of full industrialization after the Civil War, the long-term migration trend in the country was from the farms to the cities. In the 1930s, this migration was accelerated by natural disaster in the form of the recurrent dust storms that swept away the valuable topsoil of the lower Midwest and Arkansas and Oklahoma. The destination for these migrants even at this earlier time was also California, which ads portrayed as golden land of sun, fruit, and the glorious Hollywood of the Silver Screen.

During the war, the government encouraged the movement for bigger farms and the consolidation of cropland, conceding that the small farms did not have the efficient production capacity needed in the wartime emergency. Until 1943, farms enjoyed steadily rising profits though because of the lack of effective price controls on food products bought by the consumer. The cost of living rose alarmingly until, against farmers' protests, the government finally brought inflated food costs under effective price controls and rationing. Beginning in the postwar period, farmers, with the help of the powerful Farm Bloc of lobbyists, again secured government help in the form of price supports and the purchase of surplus farm produce for a postwar devastated, starving Europe.

A dramatic yet lesser-known development of the war years was government defense contracts given to places in the South in a deliberate effort to initiate industry and jobs in the poorest region of the country, still strongly rural. The plants soaked up local pools of the unemployed, including those leaving southern farms to obtain this new industrial work in the region. From southern farms to southern industries became a subtheme of migration contrary to the larger national migration of rural people out of the region.

Overall, this development would prove very significant for the future of the country. A region with a more balanced economy and a greater chance to develop and progress was the result of these first wartime government projects. The industrial base was more diversified for the first time and less dependent on the textile mills. Wage scales rose momentarily along with general prosperity, yet the southern oligarchy was still determined to keep the unions out and maintain relatively low wages after the war—something that attracted even more industry from other regions, especially the North.

Except for the Deep South, the states of the region all experienced growth during the war, and in some instances even significant in-migration from the North. For instance, Texas grew by 20.2 percent and the South Atlantic border states of Maryland and Virginia grew by an average of 25 percent, the latter benefiting greatly from Washington, D.C., which went from being a sleepy town to a booming government center in the war years, with tens of thousands of new civil servants and military and business people. Florida nearly doubled its population.

Mobile, Alabama, was a classic new southern boomtown. Benefiting from a fine port and new war industry, the city grew by 61 percent between 1940 and 1943. Outside the movie theaters and cafes were long lines, something never before experienced by longtime local residents. New migrants lived anywhere in any possible space: trailers, rented basements and garages, shacks, and packing crates.

Mississippi's experience was unusual; the state actually lost overall population during the war, but this was not true for the small town of Pascagoula with its fine shipyard. The town's population grew fourfold during the war. Longtime locals resented the new migrants, tried to reject them, and made them feel inferior, calling them "idiot hillbillies," and "low-life trailer trash." Schools were overwhelmed, as was the waste disposal system that was forced to dump raw sewage into the river, doing great damage to the ecology of the area. Yet, overwhelming as some as these developments were at the time for some of these places, the war provided the seeds for the bloom of the Modern South.

The Sun Belt Emerges

The Sun Belt of the future was taking embryonic form in these years as the South gained industry and attracted population even from the North. In general, in a belt across the South from California through Texas to Florida, there was enormous population gain. In political terms, the House of Representatives, in which representation is in proportion to population, the southern states stood to gain power.

The industrial northeast also gained population and representation in the House, but eventually, as these northern states lost their industrial base (with many firms going to the low-wage South), there was a concurrent out-migration to the Sun Belt. In a harbinger of the political cast of this region in the future, in 1946, the Sun Belt region of Southern California elected to the House of Representatives Richard Nixon, who deployed what would become his signature "dirty tricks" to defeat the well-regarded New Deal incumbent, Jerry Voorhis, with spurious allegations that he was a communist supporter. Nixon would become the winning vice president on the Eisenhower ticket in 1952 and, mobilizing a backlash of Middle American resentment against the reforms of the 1960s, would win election as president in 1968.

The first Sun Belt president, Lyndon Baines Johnson, a Texan, was vice president under John F. Kennedy. Johnson ascended into office following the assassination Kennedy in 1963. The next year, the country elected him president. The region was in turmoil as the white South finally gave way to integration of the races in public facilities due to the strong push in the 1950s and 1960s of the combined power of the civil rights movement, the federal courts, and the enforcement by the military of new laws. The New South of integration was a long time coming.

White Southern Diehard Support of Segregation in the Late 1940s

Sen. Strom Thurmond (D-S.C.) led a delegation out of the 1948 Democratic convention because President Truman backed an equal rights plank for African Americans. Calling for continued segregation under his new State's Rights Party called the Dixiecrats, Thurmond ran on its banner for president, lost the election, but split his old party by taking four states of the deep South. Segregation now and forever was the call of his supporters—something a wide majority of all white Southerners backed, although in a milder form not warranting a vote.

Segregation between the races by the late 1940s had been in effect for three generations, so grown children, parents, and grandparents had all lived with this separation of the races in the use of all public facilities. White southerners had come to see it as a natural way of life in the 11 former states of the old Confederacy.

With the integration of the South and the consequent full blooming of the Sun Belt, it is easy to forget the attitudes that supported die-hard segregation in this region in the late 1940s. White supremacy was so strong it defeated Oper-

*An African American man uses the "colored entrance" to a segregated cinema during
the 1940s. The doctrine of segregation established by the U.S. Supreme Court case*
Plessy v. Ferguson *(1896) determined the social landscape of separate facilities that
persisted even after the landmark desegregation case of* Brown v. Board of Education
(1954). (Library of Congress)

ation Dixie, the union movement targeting the region in 1946, and it caused the
Democratic Party to moderate its civil rights push in the 1950s. Whites had various attitudes or rationalizations supporting the white enactment of the battery
of laws separating African Americans into a subordinate status in their society.

The racism involved was so ingrained that it evoked an instant, unthinking
defense. "Both races wanted this" was one defense. The Bible supposedly had
irrefutable proof that God approved of segregation. Atheistic communists were
the ones behind the push for integration, along with the Northern radical unions
and liberals in the federal government, said white southerners. Integration would
cause a mixed race population in America, thus causing the eventual disap-
pearance of what they thought to be the superior race. Opinion polls from the
region at that time show a majority favored this stance strongly.

Fortunately, some liberal white southerner leaders—ministers, newspaper
editors, and educators—were scattered throughout the region, and as the civil
rights struggle grew in intensity, they followed their own consciences and not
the inherited belief system. Others born and raised to believe white racial dogma
without question listened to the new issues presented in the civil rights debates

and changed their minds. Such southerners played an important role in bringing integration to the South.

In the end, such liberal southerners became a minority in their region as the conservative Republican Party became dominant over the increasingly civil rights–oriented Democratic Party. Democrats had been the single party in the region since the end of Republican Reconstruction. No more. Thurmond and his breakaway Dixiecrats in 1948 foreshadowed a future seismic regional political change in the country.

Politically, another impact of the rural-to-urban population shift during the war was that African Americans became influential voting blocks in northern and western cities. Those with fresh memories of the injustices in the South backed civil rights actions in the North. They also rebelled against the hypocrisy of the subtler northern racism, police brutality, and unfair housing restrictions.

Agribusiness

In the postwar, farmers often became executives of huge agricultural corporations run on strict managerial business standards. The family farm still existed but generally only those run with up-to-date scientific methods of agriculture and modern business management techniques. Fewer persons producing greater amounts was the overall trend in agriculture, and this freed up workers to continue migrating to the cities and the suburbs. In 1900, one in three Americans still lived on farms; in 1990, only 2 percent were still on farms. The 1940s was a critical decade of transition in this process. With the aid of government subsidies and price supports, small farms were increasingly displaced by large agricultural businesses.

MINORITIES AND MIGRATION

Native Americans

Native Americans in the 1940s underwent a major migration. They left reservations in the largest numbers ever to go to distant training camps and then overseas to combat or to cities to work in war production plants. In these cases, Native Americans fought or worked closely alongside a majority from the dominant culture. Matching others in the jobs at hand, they proved their worth and gained pride in their accomplishments.

Extending into the early 1940s, Native Americans had enjoyed new policies favorable to their cause under President Roosevelt. The New Deal inaugurated a renaissance in Native American customs and mores, which were gravely endangered at the time. Allowing the Native Americans a strong bicultural tribal and national identity, the Roosevelt administration was willing to let them set a slower pace for assimilation.

When war came, Native Americans from all tribes volunteered in great numbers—approximately 25,000—and their journey of migration began from training camps to overseas combat in all theaters of the war. Unlike African Americans, Native Americans served in integrated units, and over half were in the Army. Their decorations for combat were numerous; two won the Congressional Medal of Honor for outstanding bravery, and conspicuously so, given the overall small indigenous population.

Native Americans became, like all other infantry soldiers, closely tied to their buddies for survival. White comrades could see for themselves that Native Americans were patriotic Americans and ordinary humans like themselves. Western novels and movies had portrayed Native Americans in narrow stereotypes of noble primitives or savage barbarians. The GI could see his Native American combat buddy was just another grunt like himself—no better, no worse, and in the same awful dilemma of war.

By 1940, Native Americans had lived for six years under the 1934 Indian Reorganization Act (IRA), which had inaugurated a new era after 47 years of government policy that had sought to force assimilation onto the tribes. Under the Dawes General Allotment act of 1887, all Native Americans were strongly urged to abandon their old tribal ways and become isolated family homesteaders (rather than families grouped togther by tribes), adopt farming (rather than continuing their nomadic ways), become strong individuals (rather than dependent on a tribe), and send their young off to boarding schools to learn Christianity (to replace the age-old tribal religion).

The IRA reversed this policy—after two generations had been indoctrinated in its deracination reform. President Roosevelt was hopeful about his new program, and he made particularly good appointments to carry out his goals. Most outstanding was the new Commissioner of Indian Affairs, John Collier, a lifelong scholar and advocate of Native American self-guidance and returning control to the tribes.

Into the 1940s, Collier urged Native Americans to revive their waning tribal languages, rituals, customs, beliefs, and the near-forgotten ways of making their crafts. Their cultures, in these years, were slowly being restored. At the time, the Commissioner's hope was for Native Americans to preserve their ways while also adapting their own ways to the mainstream culture. His policies slowed down the pace of their adapting to the country's mainstream culture. Yet, significantly, the federal government by way of the Interior Department overseeing the Bureau of Indian Affairs had the only say in the future paths of a minority of tribal people. Moreover, the government still retained the same goal as ever—integration—even if its method and pace had changed from 1934.

In the postwar more than ever before, Native American veterans and defense workers chose to reside and work in the broader world outside the reservations while retaining vital aspects of their own cultures. Other Native Americans returned to the reservations in 1945 but with some new attitudes that they would help their tribes take advantage of some of the modern ways of the white culture—higher living standards, better mainstream schooling, and more modern technology.

One of the myriad ways Native Americans had absorbed the uses of new technology was in the field of new communications like radios and walkie-talkies. They had especially distinguished themselves as combat communications teams because they used their native languages as code to confuse the enemy. The Navaho were of great importance in doing this in the Pacific, completely confounding any Japanese who intercepted the messages. "Windtalkers" was their special name for themselves. Skill in communications could help one get work in the broader world or could be taught to reservation peoples. Native Americans' modest adaptation to modern western culture through a war experience that tied Indian language to new technology supplemented Collier's program for a assimilation tempered by the preservation of Native culture.

Henry Bake and George Kirk, Navajo Code Talkers in a U.S. Marine artillery regiment, relay orders over a field radio in December 1943. A group numbering approximately 400, the Navajo Code Talkers developed and implemented a code based on their native language for use in military telephone and radio communications during World War II. The code was never broken. (National Archives)

However, for most of the postwar era, the white public engaged in an ardent public debate over the "Indian Question." The strong feeling was the sooner Native Americans would assimilate, the better. Patience was running short as to how much longer these indigenous peoples ought to be allowed to retain and nurture their own native tribal cultures while postponing assimilating into the mainstream culture. The white public was ignorant of the specifics of Native American culture and unresponsive to new thinking in cultural anthropology that valued and sought to maintain Native Americans' tribal ways, especially when this called for taxpayer money. Why weren't the Native Americans more like other ethnic immigrant groups that had come to America and adopted the ways of the new nation?

The Native Americans' experience in World War II had two results: first, Native Americans integrated in greater numbers, but, second, white culture thought this should be done faster and with the abolishment of reservations altogether. The growing mainstream conservative swing before and after the war distained New Deal programs as coddling people, as not helping them become independent. The result was an expedient postwar policy that moved 25,000 from reservation to war and then sent thousands of others to cities. There, they might earn the highest incomes of their lives, but at the price of losing much of their heritage.

The tragedy was that the general public was willing to destroy tribal culture once and for all, not because postwar America could not afford tolerance of diversity—it was, after all, the richest nation the earth had ever seen. Rather, it was because the tribes insisted on maintaining different ways in a time of conformity, a time when the average American wanted to use money for personal consumption and pay greater taxes only for defense, not for what seemed like a welfare program for Native Americans. Tribal governments with independence and growing cultural distinctions seemed like the federal government was building obstacles to assimilation. The white push was increasingly to terminate the reservations and compel assimilation.

The government's duty was to the future, Roosevelt said during war after he vetoed a crucial bill already passed by both houses of Congress to grant the California Native Americans their claim of $100 million for the lands that the United States took from them by conquest in 1850. The Native Americans, the president felt, were wrongly asking the government to honor commitments long past. To this same way of thinking, the future was quick assimilation, given a jump start in the recent war, and not a return to the tribal past. Assimilation had always been Roosevelt's hope for the Native Americans throughout his New Deal, and after what he imagined as their reward for wartime contributions. Unfortunately, this view did not take into account the majority democratic leanings of the Native Americans—indeed, they had remained wards of the state, a conquered people in the white government's view, regardless of NRA or Dawes Act.

Mexican Americans

Mexican Americans resided mostly in the Southwest and the West in 1940 and 1941. They included the following categories: citizens (Mexican Americans), legal aliens (Mexicans with official status and in process of becoming naturalized citizens), and illegal aliens (Mexican citizens not authorized to be in the country). In the popular mind, though, all were lumped together as "Mexicans," and this whole minority group suffered great discrimination by the Anglo majority, especially in Texas but also in other states like California. Most Mexican Americans were engaged in the lowest paying, seasonal jobs in agriculture. Children often attended separate schools and most were early dropouts. Little social opportunity beckoned to them. They lived in "barrios"—segregated housing communities enforced by whites in cities and small towns.

Nonetheless, when war came, this minority of Mexican Americans, like so many other minorities, disproportionately volunteered to serve in the military, in numbers well in excess of their percentage of the total population. The military gained some 250,000 to 300,000 Hispanics, many of whom were not yet citizens but legal aliens. They served in integrated units and found little discrimination in the military in comparison with their experience in civilian society. Many became noncommissioned officers and a few even commissioned officers— telling evidence that bias often took a backseat in wartime when it came to recognizing leadership qualities and courage in combat.

Mexican Americans counted an astounding 11 winners of the Medal of Honor. Mexican Americans tended to volunteer for the most hazardous missions, perhaps as a reflection of machismo, but also perhaps to challenge bias that belittled them. In any case, as combat fighters they more than proved themselves fighting alongside Anglos. A great number became paratroopers and displayed a willingness to risk jumping from planes to land and fight behind enemy lines.

The 36th Infantry Division from Texas was the fighting unit for many Mexican Americans; its casualty rate was the third highest of all combat units. The 88th Infantry Division—the notorious "Blue Devils"—was another fighting unit with many Mexican Americans and legal aliens (the latter were not free to choose an arm of the service so the Army claimed and placed many in this division).

On the wartime home front, many Mexican American citizens and legal aliens moved from the farms to the city to work in defense plants. It was the first time many of them had lived in the city. Their wartime earnings exceeded any in the past. In factories, they became accustomed to working alongside Anglos and were accepted more because of the need for work cooperation.

The lure of jobs with good earnings in the wartime economic boom that drew large numbers of additional illegal immigrants from Mexico into the country complicated the reception of those Mexican Americans and legal aliens already in the country. By 1940, the number of illegal crossings of the border by Mexican nationals had reached a low point as the Depression had left the United

States with few available jobs even for its own citizens. Deportations were particularly harsh and effective in the 1930s but the advent of America's boom wartime economy and the continued prosperity in peacetime quickened the pace of border crossings.

The Anglos felt great anger over this influx, especially because illegal immigrants' medical and education expenses came at taxpayer expense. Both the U.S. and the Mexican governments tried to stop these wartime illegals but to little avail; still, an average of 19,000 per year were deported through 1944 when the number spiked to 25,000.

Mexican Americans Settle In

In the postwar era, a significant number of Mexican Americans, having gained confidence from their combat duty or defense jobs, were spurred on to gain skills or training to carry them over into jobs in the mainstream culture. The wartime migration from fields and barrios to serve their country overseas or in new cities gave many a worldliness that lent a broadened perspective on possibilities for themselves and their families. Many furthered themselves by taking advantage of the G.I. Bill to get an education, while others, no longer willing to accept the confinement of the barrio, used money saved in wartime to purchase nicer homes outside.

Mexican American assimilation and resettlement was complicated by systemic patterns of discrimination. Spanish speakers had traditionally faced fierce discrimination in general and were denied equal opportunity in employment, jobs, education, and housing. Socially, they were stigmatized as being lazy and unwilling to learn proper English and content to remain to themselves living in harsh conditions. This was not true, yet this Anglo stereotype served as justification to some states in the West and Southwest to pass laws that placed Mexican students in separate schools because of the language barrier. Even so, the teaching was so ineffective the minority students who did master English were not integrated into the main public schools. In Texas and other states, discrimination toward Mexicans was an everyday occurrence, and some areas permitted businesses such as bars, cafes, hotels, and parks to ban Mexicans. Cemeteries and churches also were segregated spaces for Anglos and Mexicans in some places. Such discrimination continued in wartime affecting Mexican American servicemen home on furlough or in basic training.

At home during the war, the government began a new approach to the problem of excess immigration from south of the border. In July 1943, it initiated a new program that allowed large numbers of Mexican nationals to legally cross the border and do farmwork for a temporary period of 180 days, with potential rehire for the next 6 months before having to return to their own country (later, these temporary farmworkers would be known as braceros).

While the braceros program sought to stem the tide of illegal immigration, its primary goal was to create a critical pool of cheap agricultural labor. Workers

Mexican laborers register for temporary employment in the United States in Mexico City in 1943. (Howard R. Rosenberg, "Snapshots in a Farm Labor Tradition," Labor Management Decisions, *Winter–Spring, 1993)*

were in short supply in the war years and the large growers in California were calling for some relief. Through this program, the growers were responsible for paying a livable wage and ensuring that their temporary workers were shuttled back and forth to Mexico according to agreed upon work periods. Between 1943 and 1947, some 350,000 temporary workers participated in this program. In 1947, it was cancelled for lack of efficiency, then later reinstated.

The program did little to stop illegal immigration; great numbers continued arriving in these years. Overall, the population swell of Mexicans in the 1940s brought greater public awareness of them and actually intensified discrimination in California and other places where such discrimination was not as prominent before the war. In California, another factor contributed to the heightened discrimination against Mexican Americans—once the Japanese had been removed to concentration camps inland from the coast, the new major public scapegoat became the Mexicans. The Hearst newspaper chain and the Los Angeles police department within months of the departure of the Japanese had played up a new problem—a rise in the crime rate caused primarily by the influx of unwanted and often underemployed Mexicans, especially their young people.

Spanish-speaking and often newly urban, Mexican American youths faced great discrimination when the authorities blamed them for a notable rise in juvenile delinquency. The youths rebelled by becoming hepcats who wore baggy zoot suits with chains, defiant outsider duds that in 1943 in Los Angeles provoked a famous riot and beatings by servicemen while police looked the other way. The press reports had stirred the public into a frenzy until all the Mexican youths became pachucos, another word for thugs.

Prejudice against Spanish speakers had been traditional in Texas, but some deplorable wartime instances showed the hostility that persons reach to keep a minority in their place, especially after Mexican Americans had gained great distinction in frontline fighting. One instance took place in 1943 in a small south Texas town, where a waitress in a café refused S.Sgt. Marcario Garcia a cup of coffee. He became angry and a fight took place, Garcia was beaten and was the only one jailed after the fight. Garcia later won a Medal of Honor for his heroic actions in battle in Germany.

In another instance, a decorated Mexican American was refused entry to a Colorado nightclub; he argued, a crowd beat him, and he was killed. In this case, Mexicans boldly came to his defense with thousands signing a petition to arrest the club owner. He went free instead. The biased press accounts of the whole incident incited younger Mexicans to great antagonism. No longer would they stand passively by and submit to such treatment without at least demanding justice, even if justice was as unlikely as before.

In the postwar, Mexican Americans—unlike other groups of ethnic American immigrants—continued to confront problems unique to their group. Because Mexico was just across the border from the United States and not a sea away, Mexican Americans who were achieving some measure of success were regularly threatened by competition for jobs, housing, education, and other opportunities from new migrants. As important, they were constantly in danger of having their accomplishments undercut by public hostility toward large groups of new arrivals depicted in lurid press accounts as breaking the law. The image of Mexican Americans as lawbreakers, and of course, those who did break the law—worked to sterotype all deprived the hardworking loyal citizens of the status and respective that was their due.

When the temporary worker program was reinstated, it was operated with continued inefficiencies and proved an obstacle in another way. In 1946, the National Farm Labor Union received a charter from the AFL and in 1949, it called members out on strike against the giant grower de Giorgio. In need of strikebreakers, de Giorgio got these readily from illegal immigrants and braceros. The NLRB ruled against the company for doing this, but the strike was already lost.

On the positive side, postwar hope came to many who had mixed with Anglos in the frontlines and factories in war. For the first time in a significant way, Mexican Americans began to realize the power of their concentrated voting blocs, especially in the large cities. Like the African American urban minority, they would leverage their votes to get better treatment. Mexican Americans also for the first time began to be elected to city councils and local schoolboards.

Puerto Ricans: The Unusual Case of Near-citizen Immigrants

Puerto Rico and its island residents provide an unusual case involving people who had many of the advantages of American citizenship yet lived in a quasi-colony of the United States. Puerto Ricans were granted citizenship without voting rights in 1917. Especially prized, each adult had the freedom to leave and return without being considered a member of a foreign land. After the United States defeated Spain in 1898, Congress eventually allowed Puerto Rico to claim its own status as an island commonwealth, a political entity partway between statehood and full independence.

Migration to the mainland United States had been but a trickle in the years up to the late 1940s because the island was rural and most residents were small farmers. In the postwar 1940s, however, these small farmers began a vast exodus off the island as large farms absorbed smaller ones due to greater efficiency and mechanization. Cities suddenly mushroomed due to a United States policy of luring American industries into tax-free zones on the island. These new factories, which mostly served industry and manufacturing, did not provide enough new jobs to absorb nearly all the now unemployed from the farms.

Migration to the mainland United States, primarily New York City, began for the first time in large numbers immediately after the end of World War II. One primary reason for the growth in immigration was because the price of a flight to the States had fallen to within reach of even the poorest families. The result was an eventual total of 40 percent of all its residents would become part of the flow to America, and the barrio of East Harlem in New York grew larger than all of the island's cities except for the capital, San Juan.

IMMIGRATION

Chinese Americans

In 1942, in the first full year of all-out war in the Pacific, America found China to be a valuable ally in their mutual struggle against the fierce military machine of Japan. Due to these changed attitudes about the Chinese at home and abroad, Congress repealed the Chinese exclusion Act of 1882. The way was then opened to more liberal laws regarding Chinese immigration.

The Immigration Act of 1924 was based on a quota system with each country's immigration to the United States based on census data. Prior to that, 1890s to 1914 Great Immigration allowed millions of immigrants from Southern and Eastern Europe—Jews, Italians, Greeks who were of different religions and ethnicities than mainstream America. The 1924 quotas gave high preference to the pre-1890s immigrants from Northern Europe—Protestants largely from England, Germany, and the Scandinavian countries. The Chinese, of course, were totally excluded until 1944 when Congress passed a law allowing 105 persons per year of Chinese ancestry, with a 75 percent preference going to those born and residing in China. The law also granted the resident aliens of the country's Chinatowns the right to become naturalized citizens of the United States.

Chinese American immigration completely turned around during the 1940s; the number allowed into the country went from zero in 1940 to some tens of thousands per year by the end of the decade. The dominant American attitudes toward the Chinese underwent a transformation, changing from distrust to affirmation. The reasons were various, but most importantly, by 1940 the Chinese had valiantly fought an eight-year Japanese invasion and occupation of Manchuria. After Pearl Harbor, with U.S. entry into World War II, America was allied with China, which received military aid and lend-lease. Americans were appreciative and began to see their own Chinese American minority in new ways, eventually allowing this minority to benefit from immigration changes and economic opportunities. The real change in migration would follow the rise of Mao in China in 1949 and would conform to the emerging anticommunist policies of the era. Taiwanese would be welcome to America as refugees from communism.

While the Chinese mainland was embroiled in a vast civil war between Nationalists and Communists headed by Mao, the U.S. Congress in the postwar period, in the flush of a growing anticommunist mania, enhanced what was to be nationalist "Chinese" immigration, which was in reality from Taiwan. In 1946 and 1948, amendments to the immigration law specifically gave additional quota allowances to Chinese wives. Resident-alien husbands in this country had assurance that their alien wives and children were to have preference in yearly quotas. A couple, similarly, had entrance for their alien children. Eventually, the unmarried were admitted, initially under age 18, then age 21. The law's aim was to correct the prior imbalance between the sexes in this minority. Earlier Chinese immigration had been primarily of men, who lived in "batchelor societies." The new provisions, were justified as family unification, a policy that would become general only in the 1965 revision to the Immigration law. The War Brides Act of 1947 was especially important in this regard. Having married a Chinese woman, any American citizen could have his war bride gain permanent entry to America. These numbered approximately 6,000.

Chinese American Mobility

Chinese in America beginning the decade were a small minority, largely segregated into Chinatowns across the country. The Chinese Exclusion Act of 1882 had forbidden any Chinese immigration. Prior to the Act, Chinese immigrants to America had been primarily males recruited for gang labor needed to build the transcontinental railroads. West Coast laborers had perceived the Chinese immigration to be a wage-reducing threat of "coolie labor" and, along with other groups, had pressured Congress to bar the race.

Thus, in 1940, those in the Chinese ghettoes across America were descended from the population of Chinese existing here from 60 years earlier, and this 1940 population was overwhelming skewed with males outnumbering females by a 2.5 to 1 ratio. Resident aliens for the most part, the Chinese in America had largely been denied naturalization, the process by which a resident alien becomes U.S. citizen.

However, by mid-war, the country abolished exclusion and began to allow for some Chinese immigration. Economic advantages came to the Chinese Americans as the wartime demand for labor gave them entry to work that was closed to them previously. By the end of the decade, this thrifty minority built a middle class that started to move from their traditional Chinatowns to outlying mixed city neighborhoods. With a more pluralistic upbringing, attending mixed schools and often excelling, their children had greater aspirations than their parents; the children were often more Americanized and were at odds with their parents' traditional ways. Assimilation into the mainstream came easier to the children who, through education, often achieved the American Dream, due primarily to the mainstream's changed attitudes to this minority starting in the 1940s.

Dwelling in their exotic Chinatowns, this minority spoke their own language and adhered to their own customs; the mainstream American public had viewed them with avoidance and distrust. A stereotype prevailed of a sly, clannish, secretive group. But many mainstream Americans had begun to change these attitudes for the better beginning in the 1930s. In the years of the Great Depression, America became aware that its Chinese minority had one of the lowest rates of relief (compared to all other ethnic and racial groups) even though these people were among the poorest and most limited in their job opportunities. The reasons for this, the public was to learn, were rooted in antimaterialist Chinese cultural values: what was desired was limited and simple. Moreover, hard work resulted in even tiny amounts being saved on a regular basis. Chinese mutual aid societies provided a support network, whose self-help method preventing the need for relief from the general society, something many individuals—both among the Chinese and in the dominant society —thought of as shameful and to be avoided at all costs. Thus, in coping

Wong Ruth Mae Moy, a young Chinese girl who survived the Canton bombings, is working on an aircraft engine part, 1943. (Library of Congress)

with the hard times in general, the Chinese had won the admiration of their adopted country.

Jewish Americans

Anti-Semiticism has had a long, sad, and persistent place in America's history. It may never have been more vicious than in the decade before the war and that history shaped anti-Semitic government policy during the war as well. From the 1929 crash to Pearl Harbor, a considerable sector of the American public along with national leaders and elected officials engaged in more open anti-Semitism than had previously been the case. In a mind-boggling way, these bigoted individuals made Jews the scapegoats for both capitalism and its enemy, communism. In the Depression years, this minority seemed only too convenient to blame for whatever ills that plagued persons who were unable to understand the overall impersonal economic forces that had caused their fates.

Opponents of the Roosevelt administration were especially guilty of virulent prejudice, accusing the Roosevelt administration of openly favoring Jews. The isolationists of the America First Committee such as world-famous flight hero Charles Lindberg thought America's Jews were pushing the country into war against Germany with its openly anti-Jewish policies, ones that some isolationists like Lindberg favored.

Jewish Americans in 1940 and 1941 continued to be victims of 1930s anti-Semitism, the worst of any decade in the country's history. Throughout the decade, Congress made no exceptions to the tiny annual quota allotted to immigrant Jews under the operative 1924 Immigration Act. This stance shut the door on the large numbers of Jews seeking escape from Hitler's anti-Semitic policies before the war, and from the Holocaust (most Americans distrusted occasional reports as propaganda and could imagine such deaths, if true, being only near 100,000). In the postwar, the many Jewish displaced persons (some survivors of the Holocaust) remained barred from entry to the United States, although a partial or full exception to the quota could have been made by congressional law.

With the attack at Pearl Harbor, the country united for survival and victory, and all its ethnic and racial groups came together to fulfill the common goal. Anti-Semitism lessened. The small Jewish minority contributed a large percentage of their total numbers—some 12 percent or near a half million—to the military. Jews were in all branches of the military, but 25 percent were in the Air Force; of these, 20 percent were pilots and the other 5 percent in air support positions such as gunners or navigators. One in three Jewish dentists and doctors enlisted. Those who long had been members of the armed forces during war reached the highest ranks: 19 generals of all ranks, 1 admirals, and 2 rear admirals. Fighting with valor, over 30,000 Jews were given awards for bravery.

Military units constituted men from all classes, regions, and ethnic groups in the country, and for the first time in many instances, Jews, other ethnics and long-time natives were mixed together as buddies in fighting units. Prejudices of all kinds tended to ease in such circumstances. In war movies of the time, the typical platoon consisted in an almost formulaic way of an Italian, a Jew, an Irishman, and a WASP—a portrayal that was not far from the truth.

Many individual Jews made many outstanding contributions to eventual victory; those ranged from the physicists Albert Einstein and Robert J. Oppenheimer to a less-well known wartime admiral, Ben Morel. Admiral Morel made one of the chief combat contributions in U.S. Naval history when he created and commanded the Seabees, the unit that constructed runways, roads, and anything needed for the use of Navy ships and their land fighting force, the Marines. By war's end, the military had grown to 250,000 Seabees, and many of their feats had become legendary. *The Fighting Seabees* was a wartime movie starring John Wayne.

When the war ended, the country learned firsthand of the genocidal horrors against European Jews perpetrated by Hitler. Public expression of anti-Semitism became shameful. Yet a quieter prejudice continued to exist against Jews and other ethnics by exclusion from private country clubs, certain residential areas, elite colleges, and old tradition-bound professions.

World circumstances were dire for the many displaced Jews seeking a nation for refuge. The United States admitted only a few Jews, but in Europe it did help build large refugee centers for those who were without a country after the war, Jews and non-Jews alike. Britain had halted all Jewish immigration to Israel within their mandate of Palestine because of the strident protests of the region's Arabs and their respective nations.

Therefore, another postwar turning point for American Jews came with the question of whether this country should open its doors to large numbers of the world's Jews. American Jews were split with some saying yes but others against it. The latter group, which was more often made up of German Jews, reasoned that so many Jews (many who would be Eastern European) in the United States would cause a renewal of anti-Semitism here. Congress, at any rate, did not vote to make this a real possibility.

Another turning-point debate among American Jews was whether their displaced brethren constituted more than a dispersed religious race and whether they should be considered an independent nation of Jews from all the nations of the Diaspora. This was the renewed Zionist cause; roughly half of Jewish Americans supported it, especially after the Holocaust. Many Jews reasoned that if murderous anti-Semitism could arise in a nation like Germany where the Jewish population had been long assimilated, then Jews worldwide needed to build a refuge—a nation of their own. A near-majority in the United States opposed this solution. But, for the lack of any other alternative, almost all Jews were willing to extend money and support to the cause of a new nation, provided another solution did not become possible.

Because of the Paris peace conference that ended World War I in 1919, the British had a mandate over Palestine, a portion of which was once the land of the Biblical Israelites. In the 1920s, the British had granted the Zionist leaders the Balfour Decree, which offered the right of return to the world's Jews, but virtually from that time on, the British overseers had put more and more restrictions on the actual process of Jews returning to Palestine because of violent Arab protests and resistance. In 1939, the British, needing to secure oil for the war, conceded to the Arabs by halting all Jewish immigration. This policy continued after the end of World War II.

The new United Nations provided a forum in which the world heard the argument of Zionist spokesmen in the context of the wartime plight of the Jews after the recent Nazi war crimes trials at Nuremberg. With great leadership and skill operating on this new world platform, the dream of a new nation open to all of the world's Jewish people began to take shape. In 1948, with the support of the United States and the power of the United Nations, the State of Israel came into existence. Immediately after, it had to fight for its existence against an all-fronts invasion by surrounding Arab nations, who had never been asked to cede this land. Israel triumphed against heavy odds. Jewish Americans were the new country's distant supporters. Granting citizenship to all Jews in the world, the new state filled with newcomers from Europe and the Near East. Few Jewish Americans took up the offer to go live in Israel but instead reaffirmed their commitment to reside in this country. However, they did give strong support for the new state.

BIOGRAPHIES

Fletcher Bowron, 1887–1968

Mayor of Los Angeles from 1938 to 1953

Bowron was a throwback. Los Angeles in 1938 was a city rotten with corruption and mismanagement but that year the citizens voted in a neoprogressive, honest ex–Superior Court judge, Fletcher Bowran. He would serve his native city extremely well for the next nearly 15 years. With wise structural reforms, he relentlessly drove corruption out of city government but especially in those agencies that directly serviced the public, such as the police and utilities. The electorate rewarded his efforts by reelecting him four times. Skill and competence in managing the war's boom effects on his city won Bowron a national reputation, and in 1948, he appeared on the cover of *Time* magazine. In the postwar period, the slow-talking, near-Puritanical reformer pushed through huge projects in public housing and desegregation. In 1953, during the McCarthyite atmosphere, he lost the votes of moderates and, thus, his mandate in the office. Yet possibly no other mayor of this city is as responsible for the look and feel of the modern Los Angeles as Bowron.

Albert Kahn 1869–1942

Noted Jewish American Industrial Architect

Prior to the United States' entry into the war, Kahn had honed his specialized skills and training to become an expert at designing and constructing the much-needed new military factories for the Allies and the United States. Kahn's genius was meeting a tremendous demand to either convert or expand peacetime industries with factory buildings, layout, and equipment designed for consumer

Albert Kahn, Jewish American industrial architect (1869–1942). (Bettmann/Corbis)

goods, or to construct new ones designed for the altogether different manufacture of war materials. Credited with making possible the existence of so many of these factories in record time and thus increasing the flow of vital war materials to all Allies, Kahn did as much as some generals to win the war. The Ford bomber plant at Willow Run, Michigan, was his masterpiece. A huge single building 16 football fields long, it was then the largest industrial building in the world. Jobs within its interior alone created a strong single pull drawing migrant war workers.

Breckenridge Long, 1881–1958

State Department Head of Immigration during the War

A patrician typical of State Department officials at the time, Long served as assistant secretary of State in charge of all immigration or refugee matters during the war. Regarding letting in Jewish refugees, he held to the strict provisions under the Immigration Law of 1924 based on a unbalanced quota system favoring WASPs and allowing in few Jews or other ethnics who had come to the country in large numbers during the period of open immigration up to 1924.

By mid-war, with contradictory reports on Hitler's camps, Long made it policy to withhold more reliable reports about these matters for fear it would create a clamor for masses of Jews to be let into the country. Long often masked his will to do little by referring to Roosevelt's long-standing policy of letting nothing be a diversion from the aim of winning the war. Giving into Jewish pleas, Long contended, was going to needlessly antagonize Arabs, whose lands held great oil preserves crucial to the war effort. A report by Secretary of the Treasury Henry Morgenthau, Jr., and hearings by Congress uncovered Long's complicity, and in 1944 Edward Stetinius, Jr., took responsibility for immigration, quickly creating a War Refugee Board.

Breckenridge Long, State Department head of immigration in the war (1881–1958). (Library of Congress)

Joe Louis 1814–1981

African American Heavyweight Boxing Champ

African American migration to northern and western cities during the 1940s created a sense of dislocation and disorientation for many, but amid this diaspora, certain figures in the African American world stood as constant and unifying symbols of race pride, strength, and endurance. Joe Louis was one such figure—his reign as heavyweight champ of the world stretched from the hard luck 1930s (in 1934 he turned pro, and in 1937 first won the title) into the war and the postwar era. When Louis fought, America's African American ghettoes had their radios tuned in; with Louis's victory, tenements often emptied onto the streets in celebration. When Louis defeated the pride of Hitler's fighters, Max Schmelling, in the 1930s, this was especially true—Louis, the son of a sharecropper, had disproved any Nazi claim to be a "superior race." Victories continued for Louis; in 1946, he defended his crown for the 22nd time with his knockout of Billy Cohn. In 1948, he defended again with a knockout. On March 1, 1949, Louis announced his retirement after 11 years as champ.

Lucy Randolph Mason, 1882–1959

CIO's Representative in the South

Lucy Randolph, or "Miss Lucy" as she was called, was the CIO's leading roving representative in the South from 1937 to 1953; most importantly, she performed this often dangerous job with success throughout the war and the antiunion strife of the postwar period. Born to a distinguished southern lineage in Richmond, Virginia, she developed a social conscience early in life and joined with the YWCA in the fight for racial justice and with the unions for fair labor standards. CIO president John L. Lewis recognized her talents and appointed this gray-haired southern lady to be the CIO ambassador; Mason would roam the South and open the way for interracial unionization under wartime labor statutes of the federal government. In 1944, she did work in the region for the CIO Political Action Committee, seeing that union workers both black and white voted; in doing so, she helped Roosevelt win his fourth term. In the late 1940s, she organized interfaith, interracial groups that called for fair wages through unions. Her 1952 memoir, *To Win These Rights,* has an introduction by Eleanor Roosevelt.

Audie Leon Murphy, 1924–1971

U.S. Combat Hero of World War II

Murphy, a 2nd lieutenant, ended his three years of frontline service in the Army as a Medal of Honor winner with an additional 32 awards and medals for bravery, the most granted anyone in the military history of the country. A legend in his time and a unifying figure of national pride, Murphy fought in the European theater and single-handedly killed a recorded 240 enemies, with numerous others being wounded or taken prisoner. Born to into poor Texas sharecropper family, he went in as an Army private and rose to fame by means of his extraordinary bravery and leadership. In 1945, his photo appeared on a *Life* magazine cover and his good looks led the actor James Cagney to invite the veteran to make movies in Hollywood. Acting was a challenge for him to learn but in 1949's *Bad Boy,* he had his first starring role, and from there went on to make a total of 44 feature films, mostly westerns. In 1949, his autobiography, *To Hell and Back,* was a best seller (the 1955 movie became the biggest Hollywood blockbuster until *Jaws* in 1975). On May 28, 1971, he died in a small plane crash.

Joe Rosenthal, 1911–2006

Associated Press Combat Photographer in World War II

Rosenthal was a combat photographer in World War II who covered the Pacific Theater. Prior to his taking the iconic photo of the Iwo Jima flag raising, he had covered the American island-hopping campaign toward the main Japanese home islands including a string of often-dangerous invasions: New Guinea, Guam, Peleliu, and Anguar. Ironically, the military had rejected him for service because of poor eyesight. During the war, he was a photographer for the AP but quit in 1946 to join the *San Francisco Chronicle,* where he worked for 35 years before retiring. He died in 2006 at the age of 94. For the greatest photo of the war, he received a few thousand dollars, his employer gave him a bonus in war bonds, a prize from a photo magazine, and a few paid radio appearances.

REFERENCES AND FURTHER READINGS

Bailey, Beth, and David Farber. 1994. *First Strange Place: Race and Sex in World War II Hawaii*. Baltimore, MD: Johns Hopkins University Press.

Bernstein, Alison R. 1991. *American Indians and World War II*. Norman: University of Oklahoma Press.

Honey, Michael K. 1993. *Southern Labor and Black Civil Rights: Organizing Memphis Workers*. Urbana: University of Illinois Press.

Krim, Arthur. 2006. *Route 66: Iconography of the American Highway*. Chicago: University of Chicago Press.

Mason, Lucy Randolph. 1952. *To Win These Rights: A Personal History of the CIO in the South,* Foreword by Eleanor Roosevelt. New York: Harper and Brothers.

Murphy, Audie Leon. 1949. *To Hell and Back: The Epic Combat Journal of World War II's Most Decorated G.I.* New York: Henry Holt and Company. Reprint New York: Owl Books paperback, 2002.

Polenberg, Richard. 1980. *War and Society: The United States 1941–1945*. Westport, CT: Greenwood Press.

Sitton, Tom. 2006. *Los Angeles Transformed: Fletcher Bowron's Urban Reform Revival, 1938–1953*. Albequerque: University of New Mexico Press.

Terkel, Studs, ed. 1977. *"The Good War": An Oral History of World War II*. New York: Random House.

Popular Culture in the 1940s

OVERVIEW

During the 1940s, popular culture had two distinct phases. During the first half of the decade, Americans focused on the war and hope for victory. This focus provided overarching themes to the entertainment industry. Nationwide audiences desired both escape and hard news. The movies, with their preshow newsreels, and radio each fulfilled these needs and reached all-time peaks of popularity.

The postwar 1940s saw the rise of television, the newest, most powerful medium of mass entertainment. Television allowed advertisers to demonstrate their products. This new medium immediately drew corporate dollars away from the traditional print and radio broadcast media. Its rise also threatened the movie industry. Television was an ideal means to sell products to Americans. It was a primary catalyst to postwar mass prosperity and stimulus to the blossoming consumer society.

Radio was the first significant national mass media form and in the 1940s it continued to play a central role in the culture. It allowed an undifferentiated mass of listeners—from all levels of society, rural or urban, poor and wealthy, white and black, all religious and political hues, at home or in the car, to hear a broadcast of news in real time. Radio broadcasts of news on the war front gave audiences a national focus and common purpose. Live news broadcasts kept huge national audiences up to the minute on the war, both before and after the

United States was a participant. More importantly, radio formed public perceptions of the course of the war. Nearly all families had a radio set.

Radio was intimate. Speaking personally, it seemed, to every listener, President Roosevelt informally addressed the nation in his regular "fireside chats." He used this format to explain his recent decisions and policies in ways understandable to all. Each listener imagined Roosevelt in a fireside chair with his terrier, Fala, relaxing in the White House, and talking in a conversational voice so close that it seemed their leader was right beside them. Roosevelt was a genius in his ability to use the medium of radio to build support for his policies and to maintain his political majorities through four elections. When he died in April 1945 all Americans, supporters and opponents, grieved openly, believing they had lost a close friend as well as a great leader. To many youth, he was the only president they had known.

Radio's Golden Age began in the 1930s and continued through the war. Various weekly radio series such as *The Lone Ranger* and *The Jack Benny Show* were long running, with broad-based audiences prior to the war. When American society underwent new changes and stresses with the country's entrance into the war, radio offered the continuity and comfort of their favorite shows, both for Americans on the home front and those posted abroad who received broadcasts. *The Lone Ranger* and *The Jack Benny Show* ran for 22 and 26 years, respectively, which brought a sense of personal familiarity across varying social contexts—Depression, war, and postwar prosperity.

During the war, the movie industry also played a major role in building morale and providing an escape from the horrors of the war. Movies provided a release from society's concerns and the industry enjoyed peak profits. Many prospering war workers had the money to go into a dark theater and see the latest offering on the big screen. Viewers could lose themselves in the engrossing story on screen. One appeal was that the movies counterbalanced the immediacy of radio war news. Most films of the wartime 1940s offered escapism for those on the home front, many of whom were deeply lonely and missed faraway loved ones.

Musicals, with songs, dances, and gaiety, were especially popular (they had long served as a home-grown form of people's opera). War movies were usually uplifting with victorious, brave heroes and American soldiers presented as clean-cut fighting boys (combat buddies were a predictable array of ethnics). Enemy combatants were stereotypical barbarians—Germans, Japanese, and Italians—all without redeeming human traits. Actual war news often preceded the movie features, as brief, heavily censored newsreels.

Wartime moviegoers found a comforting continuity in following the reappearances of favorite stars. The studio system, then at its peak, signed stars for long contracts, and publicity departments spent millions to keep up the relationship between the fan base and the star. Fans followed the making of a star's next movie and read fan magazines that revealed the exciting, exotic personal lives of the stars. Gossip magazines shocked fans with stories telling of stars caught up in personal tragedy, ones who tumbled from the heights of success due to scandal, murder, or suicide. Certain sectors of society found wartime diversion in following these lurid, gossip-fueled tabloid stories of stars.

Mass media were important cultural forms, but they were also political instruments, most especially of the war effort and emerging Cold War to follow. Government and military censorship prevailed during the war. Official censors determined society's freedom of information regarding all images and words coming from foreign fighting fronts. They decreed that no media for the home front could show dead American soldiers, only masses of enemy dead. Society could not see any images of sexual carousing, drunkenness, or extreme battle fatigue of this country's fighting men. Broadcast radio news of war had to pass censors linked to the military or the government's official censorship office, the War Information Board (WIB).

During the postwar 1940s, both the movie and radio industries suffered decline or a leveling off of business. Radio had no war on which to focus and struggled to find a successful new format with the right balance of music, news, and shows. Moreover, the movie industry, and to a lesser extent radio, had to confront the head-on challenge of the powerful, new medium of television, which was gaining popularity by the month. Both older industries were slow to adapt to the quick changes in the trends of society, including its growing conservative mood in politics, family life, and work.

The movie and radio industries suffered as well from the anticommunist crusade. HUAC focused on the entertainment industry, alleging that many entertainers had once had associations with the Communist Party and were subversives. Some actors, writers, and producers had been involved with leftwing causes in the 1930s; others remained committed to social justice campaigns, which were now suddenly made suspect and illegal with the pointed suspension of constitutional rights to assembly and free speech. As a result, the entertainment industry as a whole was put on the defensive. Both movies and radio faltered and finally failed to implement radical experiments in content or technique as ways to become more competitive with their new challenge.

Meanwhile, in the late 1940s, television began to move to the center stage of mass entertainment. When not directly confronting the older industries, the new television networks co-opted their content. Movies over 10 years old were aired on television free. Television's new variety shows gave jobs and new careers to old vaudeville performers—those who had become radio stars and others who were otherwise forgotten.

By 1949, radio would find new purpose in music formats, featuring the Top 10 Hits. By slowly opening up to the power of African American song traditions to regenerate the nation's mainstream popular music, radio laid the foundations for rock 'n' roll. Similalry, the movie industry tried to capitialize on new technologies and had an upward business swing by introducing the novelty of drive-in theaters. These proved a good movie-going alternative for the growing audience of young married couples with new cars and a suburban home, who now had the option of the whole family going to the movies without having to get a babysitter.

TIMELINE

1940   *The Grapes of Wrath* starring Henry Fonda and adapted from John Steinbeck's 1939 novel is about the dust bowl migration of the landless, poor Joads west to California.

The Great Dictator, a Charlie Chaplin movie, satirizes Adolf Hitler.

Sergeant York, starring Gary Cooper, is a biography of the pacifist Appalachian farmer who becomes the greatest combat hero of World War I.

CBS Radio's Edward R. Murrow gives live news coverage of the London Blitz.

1941   Film noir begins; one of the earliest films is director John Huston's *The Maltese Falcon* with Humphrey Bogart, based on the novel by Dashiel Hammett.

The Pearl Harbor attack occurs on December 7.

1942   "Bluebirds over the White Cliffs of Dover" is a hit song.

Wake Island from director John Farrow, depicts a 1942 American defeat.

The Office of War Information becomes the official department of censorship.

"Any Bonds Today?" is a topical hit song written by Irving Berlin.

Life publishes photographer Dorothea Lange's photo essay depicting Japanese Americans removed from their homes and sent to internment camps.

1943   The year's hit tunes include "Swing the Quota" (for a new bond drive), "Ration Blues," "Rosie the Riveter," "I'll Stand Alone," and "Be Seeing You."

The war begins to favor the Allies.

Life publishes the first photo that censors allow of American war dead (none had appeared for the first 21 months of combat). The photo, by George Strock, depicts three anonymous Marine casualties on a beach in New Guinea.

1944   *Double Indemnity* is an early femme fatale version of film noir starring Barbara Stanwyck.

1945   "Till the End of Time" by crooner Perry Como is the year's best-selling hit; Irving Berlin's "Just a Blue Serge Suit" is also popular.

Joe Rosenthal takes the iconic photo of the war showing five U.S. Marines and a U.S. Navy corpsman raising the flag on Iwo Jima.

Life's Robert Capa, the most famous staff photographer, who covered the European Theater, publishes a photo essay of the Battle of Leipzig.

Victory in Europe, V-E Day, occurs on May 8.

Victory in Japan, V-J Day, occurs on August 14.

1946   *The Best Years of Our Lives,* a film about the problems of returning veterans, wins the Academy Award for Best Picture.

The Nuremberg war crimes trial and the atomic bomb test at Bikini Atoll are broadcast live on radio.

The radio and movie industries earn benchmark profits.

1947   The Truman Doctrine is inaugurated, which historians see as one marker of the beginning of the Cold War abroad; Taft-Hartley Act, which labor leaders called the "slave-labor" bill and would be deployed by business and the government to dismantle left-led CIO unions, helps inaugurate the Cold War at home.

The House Un-American Activities Committee (HUAC) begins hearings on Hollywood and other entertainment industries.

The World Series baseball finale is televised for the first time.

The Berlin Airlift brings entertainers, including Bob Hope, to perform during the holidays for the troops based in Germany.

1948   Radio is big business still, with 38 million listeners but few sales of new sets.

The radio show *Stop the Music* is tops for giving away merchandise.

Movie industry profits are down 45 percent from a peak in 1946.

Movie top box office hit is another of the silly "Road" musicals by Bob Hope and Bing Crosby.

As Democrats and Republicans both hold their conventions in Philadelphia, the up-and-coming television vies with radio and wins the mass coverage battle.

The U.S. Supreme Court rules that movie studios must divest of their chains of theaters.

Television surpasses radio and movies as the medium of future entertainment.

1949   President Harry S. Truman's inaugural address draws a television audience greater than all who saw all previous inaugurals in the country's history.

Drive-in theaters prove a new profit-making novelty for the movie industry.

African American music reinvigorates popular music through jazz (bebop), rhythm and blues, and the blues, especially the "jumpin' blues," a precursor to 1950s rock 'n' roll.

Popular culture has music revivals of folk and Dixieland; popular dances include comebacks like the 1920s Charleston and Swing, with bands like Benny Goodman's. The Stan Kenton Band introduces "hot jazz."

WAR AND POPULAR CULTURE

The world war in all its phases—first in Europe (1939–1941), then with the entry of the United States after Pearl Harbor on December 7, 1941, and extending to V-J Day on August 14, 1945—had a major influence on the content and business prospects of all forms of popular culture, including radio, movies, music, and advertising. More importantly, war work raised the income levels of many who during the Depression had little extra income to spend on entertainment. By late 1942, many Americans had the extra money to see a first-run movie. Entertainment's mass audience increased during the war to encompass more affluent youth, who, as first-time consumers, began the first teen culture in the country.

The national economic boom began slowly in the prewar years, 1940 and 1941, and rapidly expanded from 1942 onward, until the workers on the home front enjoyed full employment from the all-out production of war materiel for the soldiers abroad. Blue-collar employees at defense plants worked a six-day week and earned a great deal of additional pay from overtime; that worker's weekly paycheck was often greater than that of a white-collar worker of the time. A driller, for instance, earned $110 per week while the white-collar worker made $35. Defense contracts made for handsome profits and thus suitable high-level salaries. War work created a vast number of persons with fat savings and little to spend it on in the way of goods (because these were scarce and rationed). This opened the way for spending on entertainment of all kinds.

Government defense spending resulted in a great boom for legal and illegal forms of entertainment. Boomtowns often had bars and casinos with gambling going around the clock because the local defense plants were running three shifts for 24 hours non-stop, every day except Sunday. A day of rest became the big day in wartime to go out and have a good time. Liquor flowed. Bootleg operations came back at times when a shortage caused a temporary halt in the normal supply of booze. Illegal gambling often occurred in many places. Miami, the hot city in the war years, had big-time gambling in its swank casinos and nightclubs.

The movie industry had record attendance during the war. Of all the movies brought out between 1942 and 1945, two-thirds were escapist entertainment—musicals, comedy, standard drama—and only one in three were related to the war. After reading the day's grim headlines, Americans turned to movies to forget, at least for a short while, their fears and worries of the present.

Movies about the current fighting had distinct phases. In the first six months of 1942, with America losing the fight all across the Pacific, movies like *Wake Island* and *Guam* showed surprisingly realistic depictions of American defeats. But Hollywood and the government did have a positive objective for their negative depictions: they hoped to frighten Americans into realizing the country was at war with a fierce opponent, the Japanese, and that victory was not a sure matter.

Once the war began to turn in favor of the Allies in 1943, the war movies depicted American victories against bumbling, stereotypical enemies, and often neglected to include other Allied forces. Short newsreels before movies gave action images and information about recent battles. Unbeknownst to the public, these were cut and edited for positive effect to please military censors whose aim was to maintain high civilian morale.

Casablanca, the War's Finest Anti-Nazi and Pro-Allies Movie

Hollywood produced a propaganda war film, *Casablanca,* which had its premiere on November 26, 1942. *The New York Times* instantly dubbed it one of the top 10 movies of the year. In 1943, it won Academy Award for best picture, best director, and best screenplay. The movie became an instant classic. *Casablanca* had significant social impact. It boosted home-front morale and increased the common will to contribute to the war effort. The movie's message was that the Allied cause required deeply personal sacrifice—consequently, ordinary Americans needed to make similar sacrifices for victory. The movie wove its anti-Nazi message so skillfully into the overall compelling story that most moviegoers deeply felt it but were not aware of the propaganda. Subtlety of this sort was absent from later propaganda feature films that Hollywood made about the war.

Casablanca also gave many viewers a greater understanding of the complex sociopolitical concerns of the Axis enemies in North Africa (for instance, giving an understanding of the opportunistic Vichy French). Such knowledge proved immediately timely with the announcement that American troops would attack the Germans first in Morocco. At the time the movie opened, the Allied Expeditionary Force had landed in North Africa in the real port locale of Casablanca and within weeks had driven the Germans from this previously held territory. This helped the film; which was promoted on its posters to be "As Exciting as the Landing at Casablanca."

Not touching on the war directly, the movie takes place in the port city of Casablanca, which is controlled by the Vichy French. Its main setting is Rick's Café American, a nightclub owned by Rick Blaine (Humphrey Bogart), a veteran of the Spanish Civil War. The nightly gathering of drinkers at the cafe includes a host of unsavory characters—Nazi officers, French collaborators, and black marketers, as well as undercover resistance fighters. When Ilsa (Ingrid Bergman), a former lover of Rick's, walks in one night with her husband, a French resistance fighter on the run, the complications begins. She and Rick still love each other.

At this point, the movie initiates the underlying message that the individual's personal needs can run contrary to social necessity. The individual needs to be part of the huge collective effort to protect the many against the unprincipled enemies of free people everywhere. Sacrifices must be made. Rick is the individualistic American (the home viewer identifies with him) who faces the question: to sacrifice or not. Should he take Ilsa, fly away, and leave her freedom-fighting husband to his fate? Or should he give up his love of a lifetime for a greater cause?

In the end, to secure the freedom of the husband in the French Resistance, Rick sacrifices and gives the couple the two passports he'd been saving for his own use. Rick's cohort Sam, the black cafe pianist, provides the haunting background songs like "As Time Goes By" with its unforgettable first line, "You must remember this." At the movie's end, the message once again is the need for personal sacrifice to ensure the greater good, a future free of fascism.

Six weeks after the invasion, with Casablanca liberated by the Americans, the Allied leaders made it the site for an important conference. Roosevelt and Churchill met there and confirmed their resolve to free the world of tyranny. They decided on a single coordinated military strategy and adopted the position of unconditional surrender for each enemy, Germany, Italy, and Japan.

Radio as the Dominant National Medium of the Time

Radio was the prime form of mass media at the time. Americans recognized a host of long-familiar radio voices—ranging from FDR to the otherwise anonymous singers of advertising jingles. The nature of this sound medium for many of its listeners was that these beloved voices were disembodied from the speakers. The listeners only rarely had the chance to see photos of the real persons announcing the news, reciting a commercial, or acting in a radio drama. Radio was a paradox; it was both personal and impersonal.

Radio was also the prime source for breaking news. During the attack on Pearl Harbor and the following day's declaration of war, radio collected all levels of society into one immense, undifferentiated community of millions of listeners, all hearing at the same instant the exact same words being spoken by the same voice. Radio was the first electronic media with nationwide networks linking a

President Franklin D. Roosevelt delivers one of his popular fireside chats, a series of evening radio talks to the American public. Roosevelt used these chats to explain New Deal programs during the Great Depression and war policies during World War II. (Library of Congress)

vast series of relay points and radio stations. Radio could instantly gather millions to create an unseen, unknown, coast-to-coast mass audience eager to tune into breaking news. It was the sole source for war news as it was happening, and the networks developed the real-time broadcast early in the war.

The pioneering CBS team of war correspondents led by Edward R Murrow developed this live-broadcast format, most notably at the 1940 Battle of Britain. All summer, CBS supplied Americans with regular reports of besieged Londoners coping with the destruction and firestorms caused by Luftwaffe bombers and of the British fighter pilots daily defending their isle in costly air battles. As a result, some listeners on the home front more readily became interventionists.

Radio was also a powerful political medium. Extremely adept in the best use of this medium, President Roosevelt from 1940 until his death in April 1945 maintained a faithful national community of regular radio listeners. Throughout the war, he continued his "fireside chats" via radio with the American public, explaining the progress of the struggle in a warm, homey understandable way.

Radio was also a main source of entertainment that offered daily installments of soap operas, ongoing dramas, and comedy shows. Radio programming as entertainment was twice as common as news or programs related to war. Escapism was again a preferred mode for war-weary listeners. Sports contests also were engaging dramas that allowed hundreds of thousands of listening fans to forget for a while the worrisome ongoing drama of war.

The public heard music of all sorts on the radio; new and old songs played on recordings or played by orchestras in live broadcasts from faraway hotel ballrooms in big cities. Whether swing bands or individual crooners like Frank Sinatra or symphony orchestras, the radio was the source for music lovers, from bobby-soxer teens to oldsters. Every age group danced to music played on the radio.

Advertising, after Pearl Harbor, in deference to the war, de-emphasized the seeming ubiquitous selling of a product that had become traditional in peacetime. Wartime advertising was minimal because production had ceased for many well-known consumer items. Still, almost all large businesses continued advertising their product brand name by linking it in some manner, direct or indirect, to the ongoing war effort. In war contracts, the government had agreed to cover these phantom ad expenses. From an American business perspective, corporations needed to sustain consumer loyalty to their brand names if they were to quickly regain and build mass purchasing power at home and abroad in the postwar years.

Echoes of Earlier Social Trends, Views, and Values

Popular entertainment during World War II built on the legacy of World War I (1918–1919) and trends within the culture of the 1930s. One classic example is seen in the award-winning 1930 film *All Quiet on the Western Front,* a film which reflected powerful isolationist sentiment in the United States at the onset of the decade of the 1940s.

American isolationism developed in reaction to World War I, and the *All Quiet on the Western Front* gave popular expression to these sentiments. The movie was adapted from the antiwar novel by the German pacifist author Erich Maria Remarque. A powerful, realistic rendering, it tells of the horrors and futility of trench warfare and of the tens of thousands of lives lost in vain in single battles without military gains.

The movie follows a whole group of young, idealistic Germans through enlistment, training, and first assignment to the front lines. Then come the horrors of war—combat experiences, the casualties and death, the trench life of mud, squalor, rats and shelter, and sleep in the subhuman trench dugouts, like the caves of early man. Battle hardened, their lives forever altered by trauma and loss, the few survivors struggle to go on with their lives as the deprived and degraded losers of the war. On the other side, the victorious soldiers are, along with the losers, hard pressed to see glory in any of it.

The film reflects the sentiments of the powerful 1930s antiwar majority in the United States (before Pearl Harbor, polls consistently found more than 50 percent of Americans were against U.S. involvement in World War II, even though most did favor providing financial aid to the Allied side). The majority of Americans thought the United States should never have entered World War I. They rued the fact that the Europeans, fueled by long national hatreds, had begun another barbaric world war in 1939. It seemed they had learned nothing from World War I. A movie and novel like Remarque's served to strengthen the resolve of the country's isolationists. Before Japan's attack on U.S. troops at Pearl Harbor, only a quiet minority wished for a declaration of war against Hitler.

Other films, however, expressed alternative views which also had an audience. Thus, *The Great Dictator* (1940) starring Charlie Chaplin provides a cultural expression of interventionist sentiment. The film reflects pre–Pearl Harbor sentiments against Hitler and for American support of the Allied war effort against the dictator. Onscreen, the famous "little tramp" plays Hitler himself, and in doing so, ridicules and makes a buffoon of this very powerful, hateful, living dictator. Laughs from the viewers greeted such aspects as his uncanny miming of Der Fuhrer's histrionic gestures, facial grimaces, and ranting speeches. A little Jewish barber who resembles the dictator, Hinkel (Chaplin), suffers amnesia following the World War I and wanders back to a country already under heavy restrictions against Jews and where all little people suffer the brute oppression of their maniacal leader. Our hero flees to a neighboring country where citizens mistake him for the occupier's brutal dictator. Finally, Chaplin shows he is the opposite of Hitler when he mounts a platform and gives a speech full of human compassion, empathy, and brotherhood. The movie had pointed appeal for interventionists.

From 1940 to 1945, popular entertainment also continued various trends that had emerged in the Depression era. During the 1930s, people turned to entertainment to escape the dreariness of joblessness and lack of a future. The Hollywood studios offered escape in a variety of forms, from musicals to screwball comedies like those of the Marx Brothers. The public needed escape during the war years and found it in some of the same forms—in zany musicals, like the 1940s "Road" movies of Bing Crosby and Bob Hope.

Radio, too, provided threads of continuity from the 1930s into the 1940s. Many radio comedy shows that had won big audiences in the 1930s—Amos 'n' Andy and Jack Benny—continued. Their radio scripts added subtle and appealing bits of topical war-related material (the government in cooperation with the radio networks used this gentle propaganda only on alternate shows to avoid seeming heavy handed). The continuity of radio shows was comforting to many listeners and provided at least one unbroken thread in an otherwise scrambled new world of continuous war-induced changes on the home front. Another unbroken thread linking both decades was the president's familiar soothing voice in his continuing "chats" explaining the solutions to first, the Depression, and then the war.

Wartime Entertainment: The Case of Two Great Movies

The bombing of Pearl Harbor marked the transition from the popular culture of the 1930s to that of the 1940s. Some classic movies function as metaphors for society in such passing moments. Two movies in particular—*Gone with the Wind* (1939) and *Grapes of Wrath* (1940)—serve this function. Drawing each on the past of the Civil War and the social strife of the Depression, offers a strong domestic focus far removed from the present overseas outbreak of world war. These foci appealed of course to isolationist inclinations to concentrate on matters inside their own country.

These two movies also divide into two broad types, the romantic and the realistic. While each subtly augurs the transit to society's future concerns, *Gone with the Wind* is in the romantic mode of nostalgic escapism to another idealized past era of the nation's history. *Grapes of Wrath* realistically portrays the social class conflicts, rural poverty, and desperate western migrations of the poor at the end of the Depression.

Gone with the Wind
In the dull and still grim late 1930s, when Europe again clamored for war, the American public had a great craving for diversion and immersion in an expensive, glittering, spectacular public event. In 1939, the movie *Gone with the Wind*, adapted from Margaret Mitchell's recent all-time best-selling novel, was that event. The story led entranced readers out of the present back 100 years to the

life of Scarlett O'Hara, a beautiful, willful, and fiery heroine. The story opens on Scarlett's Georgia plantation, Tara, among the antebellum aristocracy, and follows her through the white South's tragedy—the shock and humiliation at losing all in the burning of Atlanta, the sadness of defeat in the Civil War, and the suffering and painful redemption under the peacetime Yankee occupation. Scarlet O'Hara was the strong woman rising up from the ashes, the love of her life was the handsome rogue, Rhett Butler, and the proper suitor was Ashley Wilkes. Her slave and domestic maid remained loyal, even after she was freed. Other of her plantation slaves thought of Tara as their dear home and were distressed at their liberation in the wake of the northern Army.

Millions had read the book, the country's all-time best-selling novel; so the movie had a huge, waiting, ready-made audience. A Gallup poll before the premier predicted 56 million Americans were eagerly waiting to buy tickets. Why did all strata of society find such appeal in this particular story? First, this story encapsulated the South's peculiar myth that, prior to 1861 and the Civil War, the region enjoyed a golden age, especially in race relations. This myth was still believed by many southerners in the 1940s, which provided the historic justification for continued white supremacy.

In the ideal antebellum society, Southern white supremacists contended, the two races had lived in harmony because each race knew and accepted their rightful order. In this narrative, African Americans as a whole embraced their inferiority and gave thanks to their white superiors for the paternal system of slavery and the gift of the Christian religion. This system was so because of the very nature of God's universe. The North's blundering victorious armies had upset this Eden-like time.

The second reason for the story's grip on the public was it came at a timely social moment. It had dual and conflicting messages about war as then debated by two segments of citizens. To isolationists, the film's depiction of war's aftermath brings a worse world; to interventionists, the story had an opposite message—it fulfills a noble aim such as maintaining one nation living thereafter in peace.

Third, the story featured a strong woman aristocrat who was brought to poverty and ruin but who struggled back; this theme had a hopeful appeal to those still struggling with the effects of the Depression. This hope was especially resonant with the "invisible" woman of the Depression, the wife who had become the sole support of her family, able to work as a domestic or office worker while the husband remained unemployed. A social stigma made the man ashamed to acknowledge his reliance on a woman.

Finally, the movie served as a type of compensatory myth for the nation as a whole. For older Americans in other regions, the movie provided nostalgia of another sort; their own lost golden age of the prosperous 1920s had been destroyed by the 1929 crash. Now they again faced the unwelcome prospect of war in Europe with the unsettling prospect their world was about to be transformed again. No wonder they, too, held to the nostalgia of a lost golden age. In sum, this story beckoned to all America like a national Rorschach test; this grand screen spectacular, *Gone with the Wind,* was true escape from the harrowing present of 1939.

The movie became an all-time blockbuster. Some wondered if it would earn back the staggering $4 million it had cost to make (which was an unbelievable sum at the time). In fact, it earned back its costs many times over and held the record for the biggest earning movie in Hollywood history for many years.

The Grapes of Wrath

In 1940, Hollywood made a movie of gripping social conflict: *The Grapes of Wrath,* adapted from John Steinbeck's Pulitzer Prize–winning 1939 novel. The story created much controversy with conservatives attacking the author as a leftist for siding with the downtrodden and for showing the more shameful underside of life for many rural poor in this country of plenty.

Defenders saw Steinbeck's story as a moving echo from the nation's history of the pioneer poor going west in search of better lives. Touchingly, it also showed the old-time extended family all unified in the face of adversity—three generations leaving home for an unknown future (ironically, real American families of this type were to be imperiled in a few short years by the wholesale dispersal to war and war industries of individual family members).

Upon reaching their golden land of California, these poor migrants learned that this land no longer had a frontier. They were nearly turned back by angry mobs and police. Ironically, migrants such as these who were forced to live as dirt poor temporary farm-workers, in a few years would find the best-paying jobs of their lives as war workers in the cities. The wealthy growers, meanwhile, were left desperately lacking enough fieldworkers to bring in their crops.

The novel and movie tell the story of the poor dispossesed Joad family, driven from their tenant farm in the South by dust storms and the human greed of others. In their ancient jalopy loaded with all their paltry belongings, they go on their harrowing journey westward into the setting sun, part of the larger migration of the time of so-called Arkies and Oakies. Along the way, many people despised the Joads as unwanted white trash. The migrant poor, however, formed a slowly moving road community (a modern version of the covered-wagon trains). Sharing the same hardships, they offered aid and showed kindness to each other.

When they arrived at the state border, the Joads met resistance from native Californians who did not want this penniless, pitiful lot allowed into their West. Once let in, the Joad family suffered exclusion, oppression, and even death because of their subjugation by the large growers who owned the land. The growers exploited the farmworkers by demanding long hours at miniscule wages while fighting any attempts by unions to organize these workers.

The controversy started by the novel created a ready-made silver screen audience. Book purchases had made it a best seller. The movie, starring Henry Fonda, was also a great success at the box office.

Sergeant York: Screen Symbol for a Peace-loving Society Ready to Answer the Call to Defend the Country in War

A year later, a popular film biography, *Sergeant York,* heralded a 1941 transition from (alleged) neutrality to all-out aid to the Allies short of the United States entering the war. Some, like FDR, worried that if there was to be a victory over Germany, entry into the war needed to be soon. Not all regions of the country equally took this position: the South was the region of the country by 1941 most solidly in favor of going to war against the Axis enemies. A October 1941 Gallup poll showed 88 percent of all southerners had this sentiment. Reasons for southern support for entry into the war were various. First, given the region's high percentage of Anglo-Saxon ancestry, its people naturally sided with Britain. Second, a poor exporting region, the South had counted on Britain as its best overseas customer. Third, the region was distinct in having a long martial tradition with pride and a readiness to fight for a worthy cause.

Advocates for intervention gave the highest urgency in 1941 to a declaration of war on Germany because of the ongoing devastation of the American merchant fleet by Nazi U-boats operating near our shores. The enemy submarines easily sunk these lightly armored ships, causing thousands of merchant seamen to drown and the loss of valued cargoes headed for the Allies. These merchant seamen were among the greatest unsung heroes of the war. The movie was based on the the life of the man who became the greatest American hero of World War I, Alvin C. York.

This story of the first world war promoted an active defense of the country, and resonated with Americans eager in 1941 to fight the Nazis. And Southerners took particular pride in this story. The region was the birthplace of the real hero, and it was there that he learned his remarkable skills as a rifleman. This living legend, Sergeant York himself, was in attendance at the premier in New York City. At the movie's end, he stood and gave a short speech imploring the nation to join the Allies and his countrymen to again unify and do the right thing, as he'd done in World War I. The audience loudly applauded.

A country boy and crack marksman from the hills of Tennessee, York, who was played by Gary Cooper, was a deeply religious pacifist who struggled with his conscience about going to war. In the end, he decided to enlist and fight for the greater good of his country. Joining with the tens of thousands of other doughboys, he went "over there" to Europe and entered into combat. While at the front driving back the Germans, he—nearly singlehandedly—captured 132 Germans. The movie featured accurate, realistic battle scenes.

Wartime Hollywood and the U.S. Government

On December 7, 1941, the country was instantly united in declaring war against the nation that had secretly attacked America and destroyed its fleet in the Pacific. For the first six months, rendered almost helpless in that Pacific Theater of war, the country suffered a series of devastating defeats to the Japanese. Hollywood's war films in 1942 and 1943, *Wake Island* and *Bataan,* replicated these shocking defeats. In the former, the movie follows a young group of trainees until all are killed as the Japanese overran Wake Island.

These 1942 movies made clear to the public that the nation had begun an uphill fight for survival. "Remember Pearl Harbor!" continued to be the rallying cry for all home front Americans. Yet, since war had begun so suddenly, the government mobilized to give people needed orientation and a morale boost through better "understanding" (from the U.S perspective, of course) of the war— of Allied war aims, of the moral and political faults of our enemies, and of the winning progress of the Allies. In 1942, the Office of War Information (OWI) began this effort and managed all sources of public information to these ends. Signaling a turning point in national culture, the entertainment industries cooperated in this effort and gave the public largely uplifting, but many times also informative, fare (for example in the censored, yet documentary, newsreels shown before feature films).

Mauldin Cartoons of Gritty Grunts: Wartime Realism Emerges

Where did the America public get its most realistic view of actual American fighting men? One source was the war cartoons drawn by Bill Mauldin, who traveled with the soldiers and shared their lives day to day. Never as glorious and patriotic as depicted at home in John Wayne's many triumphalist war movies, the Mauldin cartoons depicted war through his two cartoon soldiers, the grungy, unshaven GI buddies Willie and Joe. The two fought to protect their buddies (never mind to protect the whole abstract nation or to realize the Four Freedoms that most soldiers could not repeat). The real grunt's hopes were immediate and earthy: survive another day to have the privilege to sleep in mud, march in rain, see buddies die—luckily, rather than be maimed. Originally printed in the Army newspaper, *Yank,* to show the combat life and get a laugh from the living breathing fighting men, in time, newspapers at home picked up and printed the cartoons.

Bill Mauldin became well known as a cartoonist during World War II when his cartoon strip about two combat soldiers, Willie and Joe, was featured in the nationally syndicated Stars and Stripes *publication. Mauldin's successful career included two Pulitzer Prizes. He died on January 23, 2003. (Library of Congress)*

Unlike other soldiers in past American wars, these GIs dispensed with idealistic aims of victory and fought merely to get the job done and survive. Period. The Mauldin cartoons showed exactly this. In one, a weary grunt holds out a cigarette to the other. "I'm offering you this since you saved my life yesterday." In another, Mauldin deftly separates the actual wartime experience from the official home front report of it. Here amid rain, one of his weary grunts with rifle slung over shoulder escorts three even more bedraggled enemy prisoners through muck, all with heads down and morose as the caption reads: "Fresh, spirited American troops, flushed with victory, are bringing in thousands of hungry, ragged, battle-weary prisoners. (News item)" The troops loved these cartoons because they spoke to their actual experiences, whereas they often laughed derisively at the fake, superhero antics of actors like John Wayne in the combat movies from home shown on outdoor screens in the Pacific and Europe. Mauldin's images had deep social impact and made lasting impressions and memories for many of the front-line fighters who brought victory in the war.

Noir Film and Wartime Social Anxiety

World War II brought about vast changes in the dynamics of American society. The new crime film subgenre, film noir, just beginning in wartime, most closely reflected some of the changing gender roles for the sexes. In doing so, it encapsulated the wartime status anxieties, especially that of the lower-middle-class men at home, such as white-collar clerks, along with other men who did not go to war.

Conditions in wartime America challenged how many men saw themselves and forced many to ask hard questions about their manliness and status: How does society view me? How does the other sex view me? Do they view me as weaker, since I was ranked 4-F in the draft physical? Do they view me as past a man's prime, since I'm too old for the draft? Have I lost my social status, since women war workers can earn more than I can as an accountant? Besides, most male blue-collar war workers now make much more money than me and many other midlevel white-collar males. How much farther down will I fall? Wartime society's sudden status upheavals made certain males feel more insecure, and the new noir film genre's appeal came from its depictions of what were men's (and, as we shall see, women's) conscious and unconscious reactions to these changes.

A group of women newly empowered in the workplace created the other important part of the underlying sociopsychological appeal of the new film genre. In 1942, with America now a combatant, the role of women in relation to men changed drastically as well, as some females took over the jobs males left when going to war. That the majority of women continued their role of homemaking was easily lost on those who saw changes all around them. The new inclusion of women in the labor force created a new arena for male anxieties. A woman fully independent with enough money of her own does not need to depend on a man. This new female empowerment was a matter dealt with only indirectly in normal society but more directly in wartime film noir.

The crime film metamorphosis to wartime noir was evident in a variety of changes. First, in the new film genre, bold women became the seducers, performing a role reversal from earlier screen parts, and reflecting the stronger aspect of women in the real wartime society of Rosie the Riveter. Second, male leads turned indecisive, hesitant, and weak. Third, the man often was subjugated to the sexual powers and manipulations of an overpoweringly strong woman, in the new role of the notorious femme fatale. She sought monetary gain for her own selfish interests, usually by luring this confused, insecure male to perform the necessary crime.

Film noir movies began showing in 1941. The director Billy Wilder's *Double Indemnity* (1944) is an early example of the femme fatale version of noir crime. Set in Los Angeles, this movie has a sultry wife (Barbara Stanwyck) play to a timid insurance salesman (Fred Mac Murray) to help kill her allegedly abusive husband and collect the life insurance. With his common sense resisting her amateurish plan, the salesman, like many noir male leads, cannot seem to stop himself from going along, almost helpless against his lust for the sexy, scheming wife who claims to have never loved a soul (and likely never will). The insurance company investigator (Edward G. Robinson), a higher paid colleague and friend with an insidious sneering smile, becomes the salesman's hunter in the tense final scenes.

Noir films were often adaptations of prewar 1930s hard-boiled crime novels by noted tough-guy writers, for example, James C. Cain, whose novel, *Double Indemnity,* was the basis for the film. The noir movie would prove to be a lasting genre, continuing into the postwar and after. Many produced in the war years became classics; Hollywood often remade them later, using color film and contemporary actors. Being urban-based, dark in mood, showing an underside of American life where corruption lies both with the lawful and the lawless, these films captured the wartime feelings of many. Beneath the otherwise morally uplifting versions of entertainment, the noir film revealed the underlying paradoxes and perplexities of wartime society.

POPULAR CULTURE IN THE POSTWAR 1940S

With the war's end, increased public prosperity brought greater mass consumption, and popular culture grew in variety and vitality. Entertainment seekers in the period had more disposable income to spend on paid entertainment options. More of these existed than during the war. Advertisers had larger budgets to spend in a new variety of outlets. Thus, all varieties of entertainment became more competitive and each industry competed harder for the larger revenues available from advertisers or the paying consumer.

In 1946, the country converted back to a peacetime economy (for example, suddenly removing wartime price controls on most commodities). The tumultuous result was almost instant rising inflation and a higher cost of living for all. This caused drops in profits and audience size for most forms of entertainment. But by the end of 1947, the transition smoothed out, the wartime boom resumed, and certain parts of the show business industry recovered to register better profits than in the war's peak entertainment profit year, 1945. In fact, two traditionally strong popular culture media—radio and film—languished, each settling into overall flat or downward business trends in the postwar 1940s; it was the new medium of television that spurred the postwar entertainment growth.

Still a big business, radio had reached its peak in 1945. As the major medium in war, radio had built a strong audience. In 1948, it still counted 38 million listeners and $60 million in profits for the industry. Growth, on the other hand, was almost nonexistent. Sales of radio sets were static. Americans owned roughly the same number of sets as in 1936. The networks' offerings of stars, popular shows, and comedies were generally the same fare as they had been for years.

During these years, radio began a host of give-away shows like *Winner Take All* and *Stop the Music* as a way to compete with television. The latter show in 1948 had a peak giveaway with winners awarded commercial goods amounting to $165,000 per week. Thus, through its ads and the heralded gifts of the sponsors of these shows, radio became a prime promoter of the country's rapidly forming consumer culture.

After 1946, the movie business declined but still remained competitive. The movie industry also suffered from an attack by HUAC. With the solidification of the conservative majority in Congress, the support for HUAC became stronger. With the start of the Cold War, liberal Democrat Truman authorized government loyalty oaths and lists of proscribed organizations. The congressional conservatives' hunt for subversives only gained momentum. This meant it was only a matter of time before the long-suspect Hollywood stars would be called forth to answer to often unfounded allegations and emotional charged accusations. Newspaper headlines, shrill newsreels, and especially television created a mass audience for this congressional investigation. Public interest was high because so many called to testify were stars. By 1947 and the beginning of the Cold War, the HUAC search for communists within the movie industry and its hearings had stigmatized Hollywood and the film industry. The industry slumped because of these hearings and the direct threat from the other newest medium of home entertainment. By 1948, profits had slid 45 percent in three years. In 1949, the industry ordered layoffs and slashed budgets.

Road to Rio *movie poster. The film was the highest-grossing movie of 1948. (CinemaPhoto/Corbis)*

Movie fare in the postwar years covered a spectrum, beginning in 1946 with a series of critically acclaimed serious movies based on real social problems like those of the returning veterans. The Academy Award for best film that year was *The Best Years of Our Lives* on that very theme of the veterans. Other subjects covered included alcoholism and mental illness. No matter the worth of these films, the majority of the movie-going public still wanted pure escapist fare and proven patriotic stars. So, by 1948, the box-office leader would be another zany musical comedy in the "Road" series with Bob Hope and Bing Crosby. A year earlier during the Berlin Airlift and with the HUAC first targeting Hollywood, Hope had traveled to Berlin during the holidays to entertain American troops blockaded by the Soviet Army.

Commercial Television Starts a Revolution in Social Communications

In contrast to radio and film, television's growth was on an upward curve. Television was a novelty that drew Americans away from radio and films in droves. The new medium enthralled Americans and by 1949, the country had 10 million sets. Across the country, American homeowners had purchased television sets or planned to buy one soon. Screens in millions of living rooms showed seemingly wondrous new images. Home entertainment had a new appeal because of the magic of this new device.

The television industry followed a steady growth pattern. Its future was extremely promising, according to all the various indicators of the time. In October 1947, the first World Series was telecast, and bars and saloons with sets showed up to a 500 percent gain in customers. As to the overall media audience for baseball games, a growing number of fans preferred to watch on the screen, rather than to listen on the radio.

With a growing mass audience now able to see an image of the merchandise being advertised, Madison Avenue advertisers ventured to buy time on the new medium. The Walter J. Thompson Agency was the first to record $1 million in the sales of televised ads.

Politicians grew aware of this new advantage in campaigning—a far distant unknown voter could now see as well as hear the candidate, live or in an ad. They took notice of the emerging mass audience to be reached by television. In January 1949, President Harry Truman gave an Inaugural Address watched by more Americans than had watched all other combined inaugurals since the founding of the nation.

Postwar Sociopsychological Changes

The dark, pessimistic film noir genre, started in the war years, grew during the postwar period, expanding its select but sizable audience by creating on the big screen a metaphor for the compacted new anxieties of Cold War. Americans (especially certain veterans of the recent war) were drawn to film noir as the Red Scare in domestic life created a new appeal for the basic plot: A moviegoer could now ask, Is this beautiful women a paid Soviet agent? Is there never an end to armed struggle in the world? A combat-traumatized veteran might wonder if a future nuclear war would leave no survivors and no victors.

There was a "veteran factor" in the appeal of film noir. Veterans were prone to anxieties in part because of stress due to several life-altering changes. Most of them had abruptly left their familiar way of life in the military. Then they had come home to a country that had radically changed during the war and was still changing, from obsessions with nuclear disaster to strikes and job losses, changing expectations among blacks and women who had worked or fought in the war, and so forth. These changes could be dizzying and left many veterans disoriented. Many searched for their own identities anew, struggling to find a new role for themselves in this changed society.

Veterans who had left regular combat duty and quickly returned to civilian life often had special problems. From a world of kill or be killed, those in frontline combat soon found themselves in the world of peace-abiding, lawful civilians. War trauma afflicted many but they had little recourse for help.

Veterans in large numbers also experienced dislocation in their personal lives. Reliant on the military for housing, food, clothing, income, and purpose to daily life, veterans now thrust into civilian life were expected to be independent and self-supporting by finding a job in the competitive job market, where women and, sometimes, blacks appeared in greater numbers than before the war.

Women seemed more powerful in general as many a married veteran renewed a relationship with a wife who had also grown more capable and independent— self-supporting in his absence and without dependence on him for financial or emotional support. The wives of some had showed their independence by having an affair. Others' wives simply could not understand what traumatic incidents their husbands had experienced in war. Many of their husbands were incapable of expressing the emotions connected with their horrific experiences of combat.

Within the larger society and greater global world, veterans and other Americans experienced dizzying instabilities in their postwar world. Enemies such as the Japanese and the Germans that they had fought with so much loss of life became sudden friendly nations and soon even allies of America. Once the Cold War started in 1947, it seemed to some vets that their cause in World War II was being passed by without full acknowledgement of their contributions. Former allies like Russia and China were soon enemies.

If this was the case, many a veteran and citizen asked, who could one trust? Anxiety grew with the unveiling of native stock Americans as homegrown communist spies who had given away government secrets. The threat of war with a nuclear-armed Russia only increased a sense of betrayal. A great fear took hold of people. Victory was to have vanquished altogether a fear of another war. Giant impersonal forces beyond the control of anyone seemed to make all feel helpless. Experiencing this, many a male especially felt stripped of his clear prewar sense of traditional masculinity.

Viewpoints about the Role of Women in Film Noir

Lovers of noir film have long debated gender questions. Is film noir a genre that provides women with newly empowered roles? Or does it serve more traditional ends by putting women back into a traditional role?

The former argue the genre did make more room for roles involving a powerful woman. They hold that no matter the end, the femme fatale is not passive but acts with assertiveness and decisiveness. The man is newly passive and weak—his fate either to be saved or doomed by the graces of this alluring yet also newly empowered woman.

The latter contend that because the femme fatale is fated to die, this is not a new role but the old one. This is punishment for the nonconforming, nonpassive woman. The second woman who often appears in a secondary role in a noir film often is the more sympathetic female. In this role, she might portray the more traditional, conforming wife who rescues her husband from being set up for a crime by the femme fatale. Her deed comes, even though she lacks the magnetic allure and forcefulness of her rival.

Postwar Film Noir

Postwar noir films more that most others captured the feelings, both conscious and unconscious, of many experiencing this new culture of the country after the war's end. Émigré film directors from Europe had injected Freudianism into these films for the first time in a significant way. Postwar screen noir characters often possessed a doubleness or a shadowed side that controlled their conscious actions. Thus, a noir film viewer's underlying fear might be of a good citizen being unconsciously lured into working for a Soviet spy.

In almost all noir films of this period, there are traits reflective of aspects of the larger society. The war veteran returned to civilian society felt a certain alienation and lack of psychological stability. Given all the above, postwar society was filled with mass feelings of instability and hostility. Noir would mirror this on screen.

The 1946 film *Blue Dahlia* encapsulated many of the stresses and problems of the postwar readjustments in a changed society. Veteran Johnny Morrison (Alan Ladd) returns home to discover his wife Helen (Dorothy Dowling) has been having an affair while he was away at war. He confronts her. He defends the male role of protecting a dependant woman while she asserts for herself a new role as an independent woman. She now is free to do what she pleases, when and how, including making her own moral decisions. She feels free to abandon the traditional role of wife as defined in the past.

They fight, and she baits him into losing his temper and being violent to her. Confused, insecure, and threatened, Johnny thus unwittingly becomes a prime suspect in her later murder. In the interim, he finds consolation among his Navy buddies, the sole group he feels accepts and understands him. Women altered by home front years confuse him as he struggles to find a way to adapt to this radically changed world. The stability he finds still lies in the familiar war experience.

Helen is a version of the femmes fatale, the female in the noir movie who uses her sexuality to manipulate men into getting her the thing—money, the murder of someone—she craves. Dangerously powerful, she takes advantage of the customary insecure male character in all noir films because he invests her with sexuality and then is obsessed and overpowered by it until he will do anything at her bidding.

Film noir also often featured a lead woman character who was strong but good and was active (not passive as in the past) in doing right by the weak wronged man that was her husband or secret love. As a result, the "good woman" could redeem him from the lures of a femme fatale.

Postwar Radio and the Fading of the Golden Era

Radio eyewitness reporting of news continued after the war. The networks provided live coverage for such epic events as the Nuremberg trials, in which the Allies tried various German leaders for war crimes. Proof that this country was continuing its nuclear research came with live reporting of the A-bomb test at Bikini Island in 1946 (this island's name lent itself to a new women's bathing suit made shortly afterward by the French but with future appeal to daring sun bathers in the United States).

Radio was more established and traditional than other media; in this regard, its drama and comedy series and its topmost stars and shows continued to flourish into the postwar. Comedians Bob Hope, Jack Benny, and Red Skeleton, humorous shows like *Abbott and Costello, Amos 'n' Andy,* and *Fibber McGee and Molly,* among others, remained solidly popular with listeners who had been fans from before the war. Fans with more serious tastes found radio dramas more to their liking on the Lux

Bud Abbott (top) and Lou Costello, chattering comics of the airwaves, ca. 1940s. (Bettmann/Corbis)

Radio Theatre. While radio commanded a huge audience throughout the 1940s, that audience in the postwar would remain the same or would gradually decline in the nighttime hours when television began to steal radio's audience for dramas and comedies. Radio executives feared that this decline signaled their media would retain only the large audience of housewives for daytime soap operas (so-called because of their many ads for soaps and detergents).

Music was the one long-standing staple of radio that would prove to be its salvation for the future—hit tunes played in endless sequence, most especially in cars where there was no competition from other media. Both live and recorded music listened to in cars or homes would become the medium's specialty. New and changing hits would provide an exciting and dynamic format that could be combined with old classics. In this sense, as a format, radio before and after the war was marked by innovation as much as continuity.

Transforming the Business of Mass Media

By 1948, the show business industry knew that the entertainment of the future would be based on television. In that year, the sign that the new medium had turned the corner was the outright struggle—radio versus TV—to better satisfy the public in broadcasting the political conventions of both Republicans and Democrats (each held in Philadelphia). Once both were over, the indication was that the public strongly preferred the telecast coverage. While radio had previously provided real-time news, it now seemed slated for a secondary role in this regard.

CBS founder, owner, and board chairman William Paley also looked to television as the likely future for his network when he made a dramatic talent raid on a rival radio network, NBC. Paley put comedian Jack Benny and show *Amos 'n' Andy*—NBC's number one star and series—under contract with the distinct aim of turning these into televised shows in preparation for his network's future. Making a series for television was a difficult undertaking because the hour was filmed live; the actors had only one chance to give a mistake free, flawless performance. In 1951, the first prerecorded dramas began on television.

Radio raced to attract advertisers and sponsors away from television by holding various contests whereby the winners would take away every type of merchandise imaginable—vacations, autos, furniture, homes, and anything new and alluring that a postwar business wanted to publicize to the noncontestant viewers. Vicariously, the viewers felt similar desires as the contestants to buy their own versions of the contestant's free prizes. These contests signaled that because of an ongoing shift to TV viewers, the older medium of radio was getting desperate.

Movie studio executives also felt desperation then about how to deal with television. If a film was 10 years or older, it was available free to a TV network to be shown on screen. The turning point in 1948 was when TV showed itself unstoppable, and the traditional entertainment industries—radio and movies—had to adapt or continue to lose their hold on the future. With this being the case, some movie executives used spot advertisements on the new medium to build excitement for the premier of a new motion picture. If you can't fight them, why not join them—was the thinking on the part of some in Hollywood.

Other Hollywood moguls fought to preserve their market control. In-home entertainment of film on television was conceded while Hollywood focused on preserving its control of the out-of-home experience. In this regard, in 1948, the movie studios all suffered a resounding defeat at a decision by the U.S. Supreme Court that ruled the studios had to sell their chains of theaters. That same year, the industry's profits dropped from a peak of $90 million in 1946 to $55 million.

The New Media Impact on Traditional Social and Political Patterns

Postwar entertainment brought enormous societal changes. One of the most important was television's effect on national patterns of family life. Younger children became fixed viewers, and parents had to turn off sets to get them to do schoolwork. With sports events on, husbands often watched for long hours while wives felt left out, ignored, and isolated. Owners of the first sets often were deluged with neighbors curious for a look then continuing to stay on for long periods without invitation.

Television in the late 1940s, it was learned, was the medium that could get a more favorable public reaction to the image of a certain person than was possible for that person to gain in a real-life presentation. Sen. Robert Taft, for example, in the campaign buildup to the 1948 election, was widely disdained for his conservative views (he was author of the antiunion 1947 Taft-Hartley Act) and for his brittle political personality; yet TV coverage made him appear a much warmer candidate who had reasonable views. Thus, he overcame his distinct drawbacks and won reelection.

While struggling in the late 1940s, the movie industry developed one new profitable arm of business—the auto theater or drive-in theater. In this new venue, movies were shown outdoors on a big screen and the viewers watched in parked cars, each with a speaker mounted to the car window. Such an enterprise had little overhead and high profits, sometimes near 50 percent, most of which came from concessions such as popcorn and hot dogs obtained at intermission. Young married couples with boom babies particularly enjoyed this type of entertainment because no babysitter was needed; young children went along and slept in the car. These were termed "passion pits" because teen couples alone in a car often engaged in heavy petting.

THE NATIONAL PASTIME

Baseball continued as the top national sport, and during the 1940s, it had many benchmark developments. Baseball underwent a transformation of generations —an earlier era was ending with the retirement of great stars like Babe Ruth and a new era had begun with young and rising stars. The war interrupted the continuity of the sport, with nearly 350 major league players enlisted in the military. United in their own backing of the war, fans expected their stars to serve in the military. To replace them, teams gathered numbers of rag-tag players (often too old or unfit for the draft) so major league baseball could continue during the war (the president decreed this good for national morale). To make up for the lost manpower, a new national league of professional women players began in 1943. And the Negro League, with segregated players, continued its long tradition during the war. The Negro League also contributed many players to the Majors after Jackie Robinson broke the color barrier in 1947 by signing with the Brooklyn Dodgers.

Jackie Robinson is shown in his Kansas City Monarchs uniform. Before Robinson signed with the Brooklyn Dodgers and became the first African American to play major league baseball, he played in the Negro Leagues with the Monarchs. He then signed with the Dodgers and began his major league career in 1947, winning the first Rookie of the Year award that year. Robinson also won the Most Valuable Player award in 1949, and he was inducted into the Baseball Hall of Fame in 1962. (Library of Congress)

The New York Yankees continued as the dominant team in baseball in the decade. Great familiar rivalries continued, and the Boston Red Sox were usually in a pennant race with the Yankees in the American League. Sometimes the Cleveland Indians, with their fireballing pitcher Bob Feller, won the pennant over both Yankees and Red Sox. In the National League, the cross-town rivals, the Dodgers, won the pennant several times and met the Yankees in a classic "Subway World Series."

The Yankees and the Red Sox also had the Major Leagues' best two young rising stars in Joe DiMaggio and Ted Williams. Both achieved heights in the sport not matched by others for many decades after. Both were inducted into the Baseball Hall of Fame shortly after the end of their careers, each having set at least one individual record likely to stand for ages.

After Pearl Harbor, these two stars and many others from 1942 on went into the military. Williams with his keen vision (tested at better than 20/20) became a fighter pilot flying dangerous combat missions; DiMaggio elected the much safer course of playing exhibition games for the pleasure of the troops. Most would not return to the Majors until 1946; some not at all, having become casualties.

In the wartime Majors, fans witnessed some novel aspects. A disabled outfielder had only one arm yet managed to catch the ball, hold it under his chin, toss his mitt off, and throw from the outfield. One team hired a player of small stature to pinch hit—his strike zone being so small, a walk was almost a guarantee.

The legendary Negro League also helped sustain interest in the sport during the war, although its stars, too, enlisted in large numbers. Most importantly, the top African American star baseball players were often the equals or better than their matching stars in the white major leagues. Catcher Josh Gibson was called the African American Babe Ruth for his power hitting and homerun production. Pitcher Satchel Paige was easily the equal of any of the top white pitchers of his day. Yet many greats like these were either in their late careers, retired, or dead by the time the chance existed for their race to enter major league baseball.

In the postwar years, the big story was the integration of the Major Leagues starting in 1947 when the Dodgers signed second baseman Jackie Robinson. A year later, the opposing American League followed suit when the Cleveland Indians hired the second African American player, Larry Doby, whose power hitting lead them to win the 1948 pennant.

In 1946, the returning veterans who had been players and stars in the prewar era rejoined their old teams to the delight of fans. The restaffed teams again playing at full potential excited the fans who had patiently awaited their stars' safe returns. Stars like DiMaggio and Williams had their careers shortened by the war interval, missing the prime years of their careers. Their overall lifetime career records had suffered, but almost all felt the duty to their country came first.

Baseball in the 1940s continued to be part of the Golden Era of Radio (television was making inroads but could not match the number of radio sets or mass of listeners until the 1950s). Broadcasters linked to a team became voice-famous; Dizzy Dean, who had finished his own Hall of Fame career as a pitcher for the St. Louis Cardinals, found a new role as a national announcer for the radio networks. Another famous radio broadcaster was Red Barber, who throughout the 1940s, became the beloved voice of the Brooklyn Dodgers. Their radio careers continued through the postwar, and in the early 1950s, they also did the newer telecasts of games.

The stars of the Major Leagues were expected to join the military. Baseball fans of the war years were distinctive in this patriotic demand. With a relatively fair draft law conscripting millions of young men across the spectrum, rich, poor, WASP, ethnic, immigrant, black as well as white, professional athletes were no exception. Pearl Harbor had united a nation in support of the war and its unanimous aim of survival with victory on both fronts.

African Americans and Wartime Professional Baseball

African Americans continued playing in the professional baseball leagues that paralleled the white male Major Leagues throughout the 1940s. The Negro Leagues had been a well-organized, segregated aspect of professional baseball for a number of prior decades. Teams had nationwide fame—not only among blacks but also whites—and, for instance, the Kansas City Monarchs, the longest chartered (since 1920) and the most winning, were the African American version of the New York Yankees with matching stars.

The 1940s Negro League

African American teams drew mixed audiences consisting of blacks and whites of both sexes; the teams sometimes attracted many more fans than their white hometown counterparts. The Homestead Grays (formed in a town near Pittsburgh) in wartime had the distinct advantage of playing in the stadium of the Washington Nationals, in the nation's capital. The latter had a team with a notoriously poor record. The Grays consistently drew more fans than the Nationals, mainly for their better quality of play.

In African American professional baseball, the organizational structure was very similar to that in the white major leagues, with teams competing in an American and a National League and the pennant winners in each going on to play in the Negro World Series Championship, usually involving a best-of-seven series. In the World Series of 1942, Kansas City took the title in four straight games over Homestead, which was the traditional leader in the East, winning nine straight league championships up to 1945. The Birmingham (Alabama) Black Barons were the American League pennant winners in 1943, 1944, and 1948. The Newark Eagles won the 1946 Negro World Series.

Other teams playing in the 1940s Negro Leagues included the Indianapolis [Indiana] Clowns, the New York Black Yankees, the New York Cubans, and the Philadelphia Stars. Although many players of the 1940s on these teams missed their opportunity to play in the Major Leagues, nonetheless, many were subsequently voted into the Baseball Hall of Fame in Cooperstown, New York, for their stellar play in the prime of their careers in African American baseball. These included the Eagles' outstanding third baseman, Ray Dandridge, and the New

York Cubans' top player, Martin Dihigo, who could perform at a high level at every position on the team in addition to being a fine hitter. The Homestead Grays contributed a host of future Hall of Famers from their gloried team of the late 1930s and early 1940s. These included first baseman Buck Leonard, catcher Josh Gibson, battery mate pitcher "Smokey" Joe Williams, and the outfielder "Cool Papa" Bell, among others.

Players had ringing nicknames such as "Pepper," "Piper," "Cool Papa," "Woody," "Goose," and "Choo-Choo." Owners were at times from the worlds of African American entertainment or from the professions, for instance, the New York Black Yankees were co-owned by Bill "Bojangles" Robinson, the tap-dance star, and the entrepreneur Jim Semler.

Women's Professional Baseball League

The Women's Professional Baseball League began during wartime in 1943. It was a novel alternative to sustain interest in the sport while the men's big league teams struggled with the loss of so many name players to military duty.

On the home front in the war years, Africans American and women players often shared similar circumstances; foremost was that many of each for the first time began living in cities and earning the most income of their lives. The older African American and newer women's league helped build a larger and more pluralistic fan base for professional baseball. Wartime fans had more leisure time and disposable income than had been the case for years. On at least one occasion, both minorities' pursuits of better opportunities intertwined; the owner and chief executive of the black Newark (New Jersey) Eagles, Effa Manley, was the first woman to own a professional sports team.

Fast-pitch baseball identical to the men's sport became the norm in the women's league in 1944, a year after its founding. In the initial year, the women had been required to play in a version closer to softball. But the women were ready and very able to play the men's game of hardball. Their fans relished it.

The team owners, mainly males, insisted on a dress and conduct code. They selected the uniform less for sports purposes than for sexual allure and insisted that women players wear short skirts with knee-length socks. Lipstick had to be worn during the game as well as off the field. Short hair was not favored. Dresses were to be worn instead of slacks when traveling on the road.

The women's league lasted 11 years, ending in 1954, and in the 1940s included 11 teams. The decade's top team was the Rockford [Illinois] Peaches who won the title in 1945, 1948, and 1949. The Racine (Wisconsin) Belles won in 1943 and 1946, followed by the Milwaukee Chicks (later the Grand Rapids [Michigan] Chicks) in 1944 and 1947.

In 1992, 49 years after the league's founding, director Penny Marshall made a movie loosely based on the origin, teams, and games of the women's baseball

Sophie Kurys, star of the Racine Belles of the All-American Girl's Professional Baseball League, slides into the bag as a player from the South Bend Blue Sox looks on, June 27, 1947. (Bettmann/Corbis)

league. The impressive cast of *A League of Our Own* included Tom Hanks, Madonna, Geena Davis, and Rosie O'Donnell.

Rising New Stars

A generation of famous baseball teams and stars from the 1920s and 1930s existed in the collective memory of many Americans entering the decade of the 1940s. However, many teams and players had left their glory days in the past. By 1940, a new generation of future baseball greats had just begun their careers, a few in stunning fashion with storied rookie years. For example, the New York Yankees 1920s World Series championship team had former stars like Lou Gehrig and Babe Ruth who were ending their careers. After a record run of playing in 2,130 straight games, first baseman Lou Gehrig in May 1938 scratched his name from the day's starting roster. Doctors discovered Gehrig's tiredness came from a lethal nerve disease. On July 4, 1939, the Yankees had a Lou Gehrig Appreciation Day and a packed stadium cheered their dying hero. In 1948, retired slugger Babe Ruth had his last day in the stadium he "built" when, dying of cancer, he went for the final time to the batter's box before cheering fans.

Meanwhile, during the interval from 1938 to 1948, the national sport had a rejuvenation. The Yankees signed a star rookie Joe DiMaggio in 1938; Joe had held out for a time after being offered a first contract of $25,000, a very high price for the time. He knew his worth even then. He would go on to become an incomparable centerfielder and legendary hitter known as the "Yankee Clipper." The Boston Red Sox had their own formidable rookie sensation in Ted Williams, who in his first season hit .322 with the power to produce 145 RBIs and 31 home runs. Williams would emerge the best hitter in the modern baseball era, with a lifetime batting average of .344, the fifth best in the history of the sport. Williams' rival, DiMaggio, helped the Yankees become the nemesis of the Red Sox, beating them repeatedly in pennant races to go on to win the World Series.

In 1941, the last peacetime baseball season, the two young emerging heroes of the sport each set a record likely to be among the hardest ever to shatter. Williams batted .406, the first to hit over .400 in decades and the last to do so to the present. DiMaggio got at least one hit in 56 straight games in the same year, a record of the same magnitude as that of Williams.

In 1942, the first year of American entry into war, hundreds of professional baseball players enlisted or were drafted, including DiMaggio and Williams along with the Cleveland Indians' fast-ball throwing phenomenon, Bob Feller, likely the then–best pitcher in all of baseball. Legally deferred because of his need to care for a dying father, Feller nonetheless voluntarily signed up with the Navy (a rookie in 1939, Feller, in his war-abbreviated career, won 266 victories with an astounding 2,581 strikeouts). DiMaggio enlisted in the Army in 1943, serving easy duty playing exhibition games for the pleasure of troops. Williams, however, became a fighter pilot, risking his life in combat missions.

In 1946, these veterans returned to baseball and continued their winning ways. Williams was named the League's Most Valuable Player in 1946, a distinction he won again in 1949. In 1947, he won the Triple Crown (best batting average, most home runs, and most runs batted in). Yet the same year, the Yankees, led by DiMaggio, beat the Brooklyn Dodgers by four games to three in a close World Series. It was the first series to be televised. In 1949, DiMaggio signed a then-stunning $100,000 per year contract.

The Integration of Baseball

In 1947, major league owner Branch Rickey broke the color barrier when his National League Brooklyn Dodgers signed Jackie Robinson, formerly of the Negro League's Kansas City Monarchs. The Cleveland Indians of the American League the next year signed the second African American to play in the majors, the Eagles' Larry Doby, a consistent power hitter. Major league baseball thereafter was to become a leading arena for racial integration (along with the U.S. military after Truman's 1947 order to integrate the armed forces).

The Negro Leagues continued in existence as late as 1962 with the Monarchs becoming a main supplier of big league talent. The Birmingham team won its last championship in 1948, with a teenager named Willie Mays at centerfielder; Mays would go on to a Hall of Fame career in the majors. The Indianapolis Clowns won their league pennant in 1952 with a switch-hitting, homer-hammering lad named Hank Aaron, who would go on to break Babe Ruth's lifetime home-run record.

The Monarchs produced the most talent of all for the majors, starting with the pioneering Jackie Robinson. Satchel Paige, well past his prime, went on to pitch some memorable seasons in the majors. Others were perennial All-Stars in the majors, such as Elston Howard and Ernie Banks. Doby played with Newark before 1948 when he was the first African American in the American League. Eagles star pitcher Don Newcombe went on to win a hurler's top awards with the Dodgers: Rookie of the Year and Best Pitcher of the Year, the Cy Young award, and the MVP Award. The New York Cubans contributed future American League All-Star, Minnie Minosa, who had led his Negro league team to the 1947 World Series before getting his opportunity to go on to the big leagues.

Pop Music of the 1940s

In general and important ways, although music would come to constitute a larger share of postwar radio programming, the war and postwar periods are continuous in their appeal to a popular music audience; for example, music—always a staple of wartime radio—became even more so from 1946 to 1949. Also, the radio continued to play songs favored by many generations, binding the populace into communities of listeners throughout the decade. The two musical periods also showed marked contrasts, the most obvious being that few songs after 1946 had lyrics related to war.

During the wartime period, listeners could hear pop music on radio in their cars, homes, or public places and on phonographs or jukeboxes. Listeners could hear in real-time on the radio the live sounds of big bands, sweet or hot, or crooners singing at a concert.

New records heard on wartime radio usually were created in a quick, standardized manner. Songwriters in New York City most often wrote the lyrics. The Brill Building on Broadway just north of Times Square was famous for its offices of lyricists, accompanying musicians, and their agents. A record studio would buy the song and have it recorded by a selected musical group or singer. Studios publicized it, radio network chains played it, and record sales indicated if it was a hit.

Many songs, thus, had an emphasis on events of the present. They mirrored the events of war at home and abroad and the resultant changing moods of the public. Most of the time during the war, songs, like movies, provided escape by tapping into sentimental feelings or nostalgic longings. War songs constituted only about one-third of new recordings. The public as well as servicemen overseas preferred escape to message songs. Escapist songs sometimes had only a hint of war, such as the 1942 hit tune "Bluebirds over the White Cliffs of Dover." Most often, a song had no distinct tie to war, but it expressed a nostalgic longing easily associated with war as in "She'll Always Remember," another popular 1942 tune. In the same vein, crooner Perry Como had 1945's best-selling song, "Till the End of Time."

The war's iconic song, in fact, lacked any direct connection to war but was a rousing patriotic tune. "God Bless America" was made famous by Kate Smith, who sang it on hundreds of occasions. The lyrics had been written by the renowned song writer Irving Berlin late in World War I but had gone unrecorded for more than 20 years.

Benny Goodman, the "King of Swing," ushered in the big band era and delighted a generation of fans. Known for lilting tempos and high ensemble standards, he improvised seamlessly, constantly exploring harmonic and instrumental possibilities. (Library of Congress)

Songs related to the war effort on the home front were numerous and covered a variety of subjects. After the Japanese attack on Pearl Harbor, a morale-boosting song, "We Did It Before (And We Can Do It Again)" became popular with Americans who were urged to remember the earlier victory in 1919. The seven national bond drives provided many occasions for songs that urged listeners to buy—"Any Bonds Today?" (a 1942 hit by Irving Berlin); a year later came "Swing the Quota." The limitations and shortages of goods provided a theme for a song, "Ration Blues," in 1943. Female factory workers were the inspiration for "Rosie the Riveter."

As the war progressed, enduring love became the theme of many songs. One warned men, "Don't Steal the Sweetheart of a Soldier." Other songs reassured servicemen abroad of the faithfulness of the sweethearts or wives left at home—in 1943, two were, "I'll Stand Alone" and "Be Seeing You." By 1945, with the end in sight, the man in uniform yearned for his old civilian look, and high on the charts was another of Berlin's songs, "Just a Blue Serge Suit."

In the postwar period of the 1940s, popular music retained many of the same themes while seldom referring to topical issues. The wartime theme that the woman would be left waiting for her man continued. New recording artists included Rosemary Clooney (with her hit, "Come On A My House"), Frankie Laine, Patti Page, and the soft swooner Nat King Cole, a African American singer of sophisticated love songs.

Swing bands, which had faded during the war due to transportation problems and crowded hotels, came back. The Benny Goodman Band led the way. Swing was the music beloved by the departing servicemen but the young teen generation preferred the new crooners like Sinatra or the jazz of hot-paced bands with scat singers. Stan Kenton's Band was the ultimate. While the returned veterans spurred a revival of the big swing bands and the dances popular when they had been teens in the 1930s, the Jitterbug became the dance of the young.

Society's Pop Music Tastes

There was much similarity in music that was popular in World War I and II. During both wars, popular wartime music reflected the ongoing war and public reaction. On the home front, the two world wars also shared many common themes in pop music. Conserving of necessities, so more fuel and other goods were available for national defense, served as the subject matter of songs in both wars. Songs also prodded the public to raise money for Liberty Bonds or the later War Bonds. "We'll Do Our Share While You're Over There," was the common promise of the home-front workers in both conflicts. So was the song, "Don't Try to Steal the Sweetheart of a Soldier" that had an echoing later song. Single women of both wars might have sung of being left behind with many available men called away to war; "A Good Man Nowadays Is Hard to Find" was sung first in World War I.

Popular music in the two periods similarly reflected some of the debates over American entry into the wars. During the peacetime the buildup of 1914–1917, before American entry into War War I, public opinion was divided with the majority strongly for neutrality and a growing minority desiring entry on the side of the democracies and especially England. With Woodrow Wilson's reelection in 1916 on the slogan "He Kept Us Out Of War," the musical theme was a non-war preparedness song, "My Country, Are You Calling Me?" With 1917 and the draft, a hit focused on the humorous inductee in army training camp, singing "Oh, How I Hate to Get Up in the Morning," and then, "I'm in the Army Now," and "Over There."

With isolationist sentiment strong in the years leading up to the country entering World War II popular songs bore a resemblance to the more light-hearted

World War I songs. In 1914 with the start of the war in Europe, the English troops' favorite song was "It's a Long Way to Tipperary." In the years before America's entrance into World War II, the song became very popular among Americans concerned about the distant war. Similarly, songs such as "I Didn't Raise My Boy to Be a Soldier" strove to keep America neutral and took on strong antiwar tones.

Popular music in the two world wars also expressed the differences of the two eras, separated by two decades and unique circumstances. For instance, in the earlier world war, music stores sold sheet music so customers could play the music at home on pianos while others sang; 20 years later, the music was already recorded on records. The major difference could be seen in the lyrics, though. Song lyrics during the first war expressed idealism, naive hopes, and vengeful attitudes toward aliens and enemies. For example, hatred toward the enemy was the theme of the 1917 popular song "Hang the Kaiser under the Linden Tree," while in the year of victory, 1919, a popular song pronounced "America Made the World Safe for Democracy." In 1945, song lyrics eschewed both the directness of the former song and overt idealism of the latter.

Foreshadowing the Roaring Twenties, a large portion of the pop music of World War I (as in the later one) was pure escapism; for instance, the craze for Hawaiian lyrics, many of them of the nonsense type. Dance for the younger generation took freer forms (comparable to the Jitterbugging bobby-soxers) as young men and women danced the war away doing the Ballin' Jack or the various steps accompanying the still-popular ragtime bands. Orchestras had couples doing the lively Foxtrot.

In 1917 to 1919, with the Great Immigration of the 1890s and 1900s still under way, the native-born WASP majority grew wary of unassimilated enclaves of ethnic Americans continuing to side with their country of origin instead of the new country. A 1917 song thus urged "Let's All Be Americans Now." Nothing of this sort seemed necessary 20 years later. Second- and third-generation American-born ethnics (the children and grandchildren of those in World War I) were more deeply assimilated and eagerly served and were accepted by native stock Americans in all fighting units.

The two world wars also had iconic songs with different geographic focuses. World War I's iconic song, "Over There," was written by George M. Cohan. The words were known and sung repeatedly by Americans in all walks of life on many different occasions. Soldiers overseas were selective about their preferences for home-front hits, but "Over There" was a favorite of soldiers as well as civilians. The publisher's sheet music version bought from lyricist Cohan sold an astounding half million copies in less than a year. Twenty years later, the second global war reflected the heightened sense that the war was an attack on America, as indeed events at Pearl Harbor had brought painfully home to Americans. The second war's best-known song was reflected in its title, "God Bless America," a theme that brought the focus back to America.

World War I also differed from World War II in the government's attention to popular patriotic songs. In World War I the Committee on Public Information headed by George Creel printed songbooks for public distribution and sent singing service groups around the country to stimulate patriotism and support for the war effort. Creel's Committee had a World War II equivalent, the United States Office of War Information, that was equally if not more politically active, spawning, for instance in 1942, Voice of America, but its officials took no active interest in popular songs.

Postwar Changes in the Business of Making Pop Music

With the end of war in 1946, the music industry enjoyed a benchmark year for profits and thereafter struggled to regain its wartime level. Postwar audiences had new and additional leisure time possibilities that offered more visual stimuli or outdoor fun. Moreover, public tastes in songs were undergoing a transformation, and the industry was slow to change to satisfy its new audiences.

In the late 1940s, new technologies transformed the pop music industry. In line with the flood of new consumer goods, the new model record player could play three types of records. New pop songs played on 45 revolutions per minute (rpm) records. Traditional favorites were on 78 rpm records, and classical songs were on new, long-playing 33 rpm records. Technological obsolescence was fast eliminating the now old 78 rpm record player and with it, changing the patterns of recording, selling and buying music.

New music industry technology affected song writing and the making of hit records. By 1948, the time-honored source of new song lyrics, Tin Pan Alley songwriters, was being eclipsed by unheard of songwriters from the hinterlands all over America—dramatically by Southerners who wrote country or western tunes, long referred to as "hillbilly music" by New York City record producers. Formerly restricted to a regional audience, these songs were now becoming hits on national charts. Wartime migrations of white Southerners to northern cities had created a national fan base for the music, along with westerners who identified with the gritty lyrics of these songs and their mainly rural, small-town singers.

Hit records were making the charts by a new method that also bypassed the older ways of the industry. A local radio disk jockey, it was discovered, could take a catchy song (written by an unknown and made by a small, independent record company) and make it a hit by constantly playing it. Soon word of mouth would create requests for it causing other deejays to start playing it. Many were country songs written by newcomers—"Jealous Heart" and "You're Breaking My Heart." Many became hits and then classics, such as little-known songwriter Vince Smith's duo of "Chattanooga Shoeshine Boy" and "Tennessee Waltz."

Tin Pan Alley lyricists suddenly facing competition from songwriters all over the country changed their minds about southern and western music tastes, aimed in these new directions, and soon began giving this war-broadened national music audience what it wanted: country and western tunes. Sophisticated New Yorkers began writing hillbilly songs—some catchy enough to make the charts.

Social Continuity and Changes in Postwar Music

The American public thrust into the beginnings of a dangerous unknown postwar future embraced song lyrics that could tell tales in folksy ways of simple human emotions and experiences. Songs of lost love, gambling fate, and the common ups and downs of life, matters easily understood on the ordinary human scale, rose on the charts. Continuing the escapism of prior popular culture during the war and then in the postwar period, these songs avoided reminding listeners of current topical issues or events. Thus, popular music throughout the 1940s had as one of its constant themes a return to older simpler times, and this was to hold true for two decades (even in the tumultuous 1960s, where it simply took the form of a return to a lost golden age of loving community).

It would be another 20 years before topical lyrics would again become a focus of mainstream songs and music, but the origins of this shift lay in the 1940s, too—in the folk song revival of the late 1940s. One of the favorite groups was the Weavers. Favorite revival tunes made popular by the Weavers included "Good Night Irene." The folk cantata, "Ballad for Americans," a WPA New Deal product, made famous by the baritone Paul Robeson, was even sung at the Republican Convention in 1939, the Republicans apparently unaware that Robeson and the Ballad's authors were well-known leftists.

Jazz Goes International and the Domestic Rise of Rhythm and Blues

American music continued to have an international impact, especially the one original strain of music developed in the nation—African American jazz. Duke Ellington and Louie "Satchmo" Armstrong played their brand of jazz in war-torn Europe to tens of thousands of appreciative fans. African American jazz stars found France a favorite country because the color barrier was negligible compared with the postwar United States.

Music that had future import for teen popular culture was the late-1940s black-soundings of blues and rhythm and blues. African Americans created this music and wrote the songs. Independent, small, mostly African American studios recorded the music. Broadcast as race music on only a few radio stations, this music would be the future basis for the early rock 'n' roll of the 1950s. Big Arthur Crudup, an African American blues singer, had a initial record, "It's Alright," that later became a cover record by Elvis Presley. The manager of Presley had long been looking for a white who could sing black. African American musicians Fats Domino, Little Richard, and others sang race music in the late1940s but would become early crossover rock 'n' roll artists of the 1950s.

Louis Armstrong was one of the 20th century's most important jazz innovators and performers. (Library of Congress)

CENSORSHIP, IMAGES, AND PUBLIC OPINION IN THE 1940s

The War Information Board (WIB), under its formal censorship division, carefully manipulated American public opinion. During the war, the military had full discretion in censoring certain war images for publication and public consumption that they thought would give a negative impression of America while authorizing others that they thought would create a positive national image. Thus, the censors shaped the public's image of the war. A photo, in the view of the censors, was indeed worth a thousand words. Thus, the wrong one, they assumed, might be demoralizing to the American public.

Government and military censors wanted to avoid this, and for the first nearly two years of the war, no photos of any of the country's dead servicemen appeared in the press while enemy dead appeared in large numbers. This winning phantom body toll, it was believed would reassure Americans at home. even when the country was facing near defeat in the first six months of war in the Pacific.

When the WIB first allowed images of American dead to be published in late 1943, it was for a specific new purpose, to mold public opinion at home. With a growing number of civilians sensing the nearness of victory, the WIB did not want complacency to affect the production effort by causing absenteeism or union problems. By showing images of those who had made the ultimate sacrifice in war, it was hoped those at home would be motivated to recommit to their wartime factory work. A 1945 government poster put up in factories made the point emphatically by using an actual combat photo of a lone dead GI face down in mud. The photo's caption read: "This happens every 3 minutes" and below, "STAY ON THE JOB and GET IT OVER."

Life Magazine—War Reports and Timely Images

Life magazine was the great photojournalism magazine of the time and a critical source of information for many Americans who trusted its images to convey the truth. The *New Yorker* film critic Pauline Kael remembered, "During the war years, the whole spirit of the country seemed embodied in *LIFE* magazine" (Terkel 2004, 123). In September 1943, the magazine published George Strock's photo of three dead Marines face down on a beach in New Guinea—it was the first photo of an American casualty since Pearl Harbor. With a staff of famous photographers, the magazine followed with other photos, notably, a series in April 1945 by its best-known photographer, Robert Capa, that was part of photoessay of the battle for Leipzig.

Capa covered the European Theater and did famous photos of the London Blitz, D-Day, and the liberation of Paris. In the Asian Theater, *Life* had Eugene Smith, who covered the battles but, significantly, did an empathetic shot of a Japanese mother and her terrified infant, innocent civilians, caught in shelling. Censors systematically suppressed sympathetic images of enemy civilians, yet this image somehow got through. On the home front, the great Dorothea Lange had provided the series of photos for an essay of the removal of the West Coast Japanese families to internment camps. The government censored her photos for showing too much sympathy for the Japanese Americans.

World War II had a single great iconic photograph, the five Marines and one Navy corpsman raising the American flag on Mount Suribachi after conquering it in the early days of bloody battle on Iwo Jima. This was the second flag to be raised on top Mount Suribachi.. The first flag raising was photographed by Sgt. Louis Lowry, a photographer for *Leatherneck* magazine; the first flag was too small to be seen from the beaches so it was replaced with the larger flag. Largely volcanic and barren, the island was nonetheless strategic as the closest refueling base for planes bombing the enemy's main islands. Combat photographer Joe Rosenthal took the photo that was reprinted all over America as emblematic of the tough but winning war effort of Americans. Significantly, the battle for Iwo Jima was not over at the flag raising but raged for more than four weeks longer; nonetheless, the image stirred great patriotism in the public at home and was useful for that purpose alone.

Society, War, Gender, and Photojournalism

At the time of Pearl Harbor, *Life* magazine—a mere five years old—presented something new in the magazine world. Rather than use a photo or two to merely illustrate a news story this new publication intended to let a series of photos tell their own visual story. It would specialize in what its founder and publisher, Henry Luce, termed the photo essay.

During World War II, this new weekly covered the ongoing events in a more compelling way than any other publication. Its consistency gained the public's attention because of its unusual photo-essays. It shaped public and political discussion of the wartime generations of Americans. Its vaunted success was not surprising given that Luce had already succeeded with *Time* (1922) and *Fortune* (1930) and had an almost unerring sense of new and innovative ways to convey news and information to ordinary Americans. The camera had come into its own with light, easy, fast, and fine-focused models a journalist could use under almost any circumstance. With a complementary photo story, the written story had more credence.

Life welcomed women photographers. Margaret Bourke-White would be the most famous of the war years. It was her photo that appeared on the magazine's first cover—an image of her 1936 photo story of 10,000 New Deal relief workers constructing a huge hydroelectric dam in Montana. Specifically, the image showed one of the workers' wild Saturday nights in this almost all-male boomtown reminiscent of earlier western mining camps.

As war correspondent in 1941, Bourke-White found herself the only member of the foreign press in Moscow

Margaret Bourke-White was one of the 20th century's most prolific photojournalists. As a commercial and industrial photographer and staff photographer for New York-based magazines Fortune *and* Life, *she pioneered the photo-essay, documented wars and disasters, and became as famous for her fearless pursuit of images as for her photographic virtuosity. (Library of Congress)*

when the Nazis began their surprise attack on Russia, their erstwhile ally. Her photos of the approaching Germans from the roof of the American Embassy provided a fine and unforgettable photo-essay. After this, she became the first women ever to be given U.S. Army credentials as a combat photographer and later the first allowed to fly on combat missions. In 1945, she was with General Patton's army as it liberated the concentration camp at Buchenwald. Her shocking on-site photos of the Nazi atrocities in this death camp are visual proof even to this very day against the spurious deniers of the Holocaust.

Public Communication and Postwar Global Realities

With the end of war, the country went in an entirely new direction as friendly nations during war changed into enemies in the postwar, and former enemies became friends with dizzying speed. The changes could be difficult for many Americans to absorb all in such a short time. Moving and still images helped to reshape these views of other nationals just as had been the case during the fighting.

Germany and Japan Reimagined

War movies had portrayed the Japanese and Germans in one-dimensional stereotypes making these nationals especially odious to the American public. With victory and the defeat of their fascist governments, the former hated enemies became sudden allies spurred by Americans' need for allies against communism. Along with other postwar anxieties, not a small number of Americans were confused by these sudden crossovers. One was Dellie Hahne, a nurse's aide in the war who recalled: "The OWI . . . did a thorough job of convincing us our cause was right. We were stopping Hitler and you look back at it and you had to stop him. . . . A few years later, when we started to arm Germany, I was so shocked. I'd been sold a bill of goods—I couldn't believe it. . . . I picked up the paper, and read our sworn enemy was now our ally." She concludes by saying she was disillusioned" (Terkel 2004, 117–118).

Russia and China Reimagined

The story of wartime Russia, Hahne remembered in this way: "Russia was the enemy from the time I was born right up to '40. Then Russia became our ally. It was funny no one stopped to think that was a complete turnabout. As soon as the war was over, we dropped Russia. During the war, I never heard any anti-Russian talk (Terkel 2004, 118).

Public information and images repeatedly changed to shape and reshape public opinion toward the Soviet Union; from 1940 to 1947, the attitudes of Americans to the leading communist nation went from hatred, to affection for an important ally, to distrust bordering again on hatred. In midwar, a Monsanto

Chemical ad showed the face of a clean-cut, handsome "All-American type" Soviet soldier holding a cup of tea, with the copy beginning, "Ivan knows . . . Sweetness is a Materiel of War." The ad goes on to relate how the company had developed an artificial sweetener for Ivan to use in his tea break on the bitterly cold Eastern Front. The sweetener was needed because the invading Germans had taken over the sugar beet–growing areas of the Ukraine, depriving good Soviets like Ivan of their traditional source of natural sugar (Roeder 1993, 143).

The Rise of Domestic Conservatism

The postwar era with its wholesale switching of allegiances was aided by the underlying public fear that arose against the view of monolithic communist nations with nuclear weapons and a program of world expansion. Thus, the sweet Ivan, valiant fighter against the Nazis, became the common man, Ivan the Terrible, a cog of the state.

The Chinese were similarly reimaged as automatons. China, a wartime ally when fighting the Japanese, had a post-1945 civil war that Mao and the communists won in 1949. This drove the small, defeated fragment of pro-American Nationalist fighters off the mainland to Taiwan. By 1950, the vast majority of Chinese became enemies, as had Stalin's Soviet Union only a few years before. Americans believed both had one aim, to overthrow the West.

In Congress, Democratic and Republican conservatives who were becoming dominant over old-time liberals gave strong backing for the view of these countries as implacable enemies. Newspapers, *Life,* and other magazines helped shape public opinion in these new directions. Photographic images were as convincing as ever, whether a photo of a Hollywood star testifying before HUAC with the caption giving a select preferred way to read the image or a photo of a stereotypical stodgy, blocky Russian diplomat taking an opposition stance to his appealing American counterpart.

War and Society: Government Propaganda Shapes Social Perceptions

Although the government curtailed the WIB and ended strict government censorship at the end of the war, the amount of classified information kept from the public, nonetheless, steeply increased because of the advent of a largely "cold," covert war against what was portrayed as a worldwide communist conspiratorial menace. Many images were stamped "Top Secret" and not released to the public. The government, for instance, wanting to prevent enemies from using it for anti-American propaganda, suppressed from public view any photos of the horrifically maimed Japanese survivors of the atomic bombs. These images would not get a public viewing for 20 years.

With fervid anticommunists searching for a conspiracy of hidden communists in government, it was not uncommon for a "doctored" photo (one with the image of an alleged communist cut, pasted, and smoothed onto the image of a gathering of known communists) to provide "proof" of past associations. The Federal Bureau of Investigation (FBI), in domestic matters, and the new postwar Counter Intelligence Agency (CIA), in foreign affairs, took over the role of censorship in peacetime that the WIB had during war. One rule in the game of shaping public opinion held constant for all these agencies—never revealing information was a more effective propaganda method than using information for purposes of persuasion.

Government Censorship and Racial Attitudes

The African American experience in wartime is a good example of government censorship. In wartime, censors eliminated most and used only certain photos to shape the African American military experience for home consumption. The process created a false panorama of that experience. Although African Americans often performed unpleasant details like mass burials, no home photos depicted this, nor were African Americans shown at integrated social events or getting awards for noncombatant job excellence. Photos of wounded African American soldiers the censors rarely released because the Army felt the African American newspapers at home tended to overstate the heroic portrayal of these men. African Americans might well have been the invisible soldiers. Bowing to widespread racial prejudice, censors justified this policy as being in the interests of national unity.

In the postwar period, the domestic African American experience continued to remain unknown to most white Americans because big-city white newspapers rarely if ever showed photos depicting African Americans except in instances of violence or crime. Of course, these select depictions distorted or merely confirmed white racist views of African Americans. The *New York Daily News,* in these years the largest circulation newspaper in the city, actually had an editorial policy that forbade photos showing images of African Americans. Its rationale, in part, was that the city's African American press such as *The Amsterdam News* covered African American life, but whites did not buy African American newspapers so were ignorant of the life of African Americans even in the most cosmopolitan city in the country. The most prominent reason, however, was, de facto segregation in the news, as in housing, jobs, and public facilities. In short, censorship of information both reflected and created negative or positive public attitudes toward African Americans.

BIOGRAPHIES

Arthur Crudup, 1905–1974

Blues Musician

Arthur Crudup migrated to Chicago from Mississippi in 1940 as part of the decade's African American migration; he was an example of an African American artist bringing northward a unique blues sound that was destined to be one of the musical seeds in the evolving synthesis of black and white music that later became 1950s rock 'n' roll. Crudup originated a number of hit records on the African American song charts that were rerecorded by Elvis Presley. In fact, Presley claimed Crudup was his favorite blues singer. "That's All Right Mama," "My Baby Left Me," and "So Glad You're Mine" were three Crudup songs that became later Elvis hits.

In his own right, Crudup was an innovator in the long tradition of African American blues. With crude guitar licks and growling out his original songs, he was discovered singing on the Chicago streets and eventually signed by RCA Victor Records. In the mid-1940s, he recorded "Who's Been Foolin' You," and "So Glad You're Mine," and a few others that were hits in his evolving style, termed rockabilly.

In the 1950s onward, his career faded until, in the 1960s, bluesmen tracked down this now living legend and found him doing migrant labor. In the late 1960s, he had a successful comeback, and by the early 1970s, Crudup at last was making a decent living from his music. He died in 1974.

Louis Jordan, 1908–1975

African American Rhythm and Blues and Jazz Great of the 1940s

The 1940s were the prime decade for this African American singer and saxophonist, the one musician with the strongest claim to be the first rock 'n' roll singer, although Jordan felt that it was just a new name for the African American tradition of rhythm and blues, of which Jordan was the undisputed king in the 1940s. A jazz innovator as well, Jordan and his band, The Tympany Five, played hot jazz that evolved into the "jump blues" style with one-line humorous asides breaking forth from the fast jazz. Jordan was the dominant singer on the 1940s R&B Hit Chart or "the race music chart," the segregated listing.

Jordan recorded 18 No. 1 hits—a record at that time on that chart—in his peak decade. Many pop music scholars consider his 1949 "Saturday Night Fish Fry" the first rock 'n' roll record.

During wartime, in 1944, he recorded two of the most memorable hits of the time—"GI Jive" (a crossover No. 1 hit on national charts as well) and "Is You Is Or Is You Ain't My Baby," his first million-record seller. In the postwar 1940s,

Black rhythm and blues and jazz great Louis Jordan (1908-1975). (John Springer Collection/Corbis)

he continued a series of R&B favorites like "Caledonia," his all-time top hit, "Ain't Nobody Here But Us Chickens," and "Boogie Woogie Blue Plate."

Jordan's music influenced such later rock bands as Bill Haley and the Comets and the great rock singer and guitarist Chuck Berry who claimed Jordan was the greatest influence on his music. Jordan failed to see the distinction that new African American rockers such as Little Richard and Berry claimed for the new pop music. In the 1950s, Jordan's career slowed greatly. Twelve years after his death in 1987, Jordan was voted into the Rock 'n' Roll Hall of Fame in Cleveland, Ohio.

Bill Mauldin, 1921–2003

Cartoonist

Mauldin's name is most often linked to World War II and his cartoon GIs, Willie and Joe, the scruffy, down-and-dirty duo who endured the war with a realism experienced by most front-line soldiers. Mauldin himself was a solder, and in 1943, he was wounded and won a Purple Heart. The same year the military newspaper *Stars and Stripes* carried his cartoon creations. Soon these appeared in syndication in home front newspapers. In 1945, he won a Pulitzer Prize, the first of several for a man who went on to become one of the most famous in his field.

While most are familiar with his GI duo in war, Mauldin went on in 1945 and 1946 to portray the same two characters struggling to adjust to the new peacetime culture. Satirizing politicians the way he did military officers, one cartoon shows a jalopy loaded with a household's goods stopped while a man wearing a uniform sits writing. Beside him, his baby-laden wife says, "Don't bother Daddy. He's writing a sequel to *The Grapes of Wrath*."

Having his own difficulties readjusting to the home front, Mauldin used his edgy, opinionated cartoons to attack many targets that his editors were terrified to offend—the FBI, HUAC, the KKK—and the one they most feared, Sen. Joseph McCarthy. In 1948, his cartoon syndicate refused to renew his contract. In 1949, he was without an outlet for his work. Yet, Mauldin, talented and with the courage of his convictions, would not only endure but prevail the rest of the century.

Bert Parks, 1914–1992

Radio and Television Quiz Show Host

Radio quiz shows proliferated in the postwar 1940s, and *Stop the Music* with host Bert Parks was the biggest of all. The show, a unique combination of entertainment, quizzes, and stellar prizes, was introduced in 1948. It was an overnight sensation. Parks had a special magnetism. The show's format involved Parks or one of the vocalists singing part of a tune, backed by the house orchestra, until the music stopped. A person from the audience was asked to identify the song. If the first person failed, another was asked until the tune was discovered. The radio listening audience was vast. Listeners would vicariously participate to see if they knew the song before the contestant did.

Winners' prizes were the most generous of all of the give-away radio shows at that time; a winner could take away a cash prize of more than $20,000. Sponsors supplied brand-name products and travel for the prizes; these ranged from new cars to trips to Europe. A commodity give-away show like this stimulated and influenced the forming of a new, vast postwar consumer society.

The show came to television the next year, and ABC made it a hit with Parks, the same cast, and prizes. The network also kept it on radio, where it also remained a top show. The key element in the success of both shows was the deep audience affection for Parks; he continued with high ratings through the 1950s and 1960s and hosted other quiz give-away shows.

In 1955, Parks became the master of ceremonies for the annual Miss America Pageant; he is best known for this later role, one he held for 25 years, during and after his years on quiz shows.

Max Roach, 1924–2007

Bebop Innovator

Jazz innovator Max Roach revised the rulebook for drumming in the 1940s. He was a member of a group of pioneers that included Dizzie Gillespie, Thelonius Monk, and Charlie Parker who transformed jazz during the war years and immediate postwar period. Bebop had its roots in jazz, but its adventurous, unpredictable rhythms modernized the form. "You can't write the same book twice," Roach told the *New York Times*. "Though I've been in historic musical situations, I can't go back and do that again." Born in North Carolina and raised in Brooklyn, Roach studied piano as a boy and took up drums before reaching high school. After graduating from Boys High School in 1942, he worked briefly with Duke Ellington's band, and played with Charlie Parker in after-hours jam sessions in Harlem.

He went on to play with Parker, Gillespie, and other bebop innovators. By the end of the decade, he solidified his place in musical history when he recorded "Birth of the Cool" with Miles Davis. He went on to lead his own band, and he

American singer Kate Smith in 1936. In 1938 she introduced Irving Berlin's "God Bless America" to the country and it has been associated with her ever since. On September 21, 1943, Smith appeared on a CBS telecast that raised $39 million for the war effort. (Library of Congress)

continued his individualistic approach to composing, recording, teaching at the University of Massachusetts. He continued to perform and lead his own bands into the 21st century.

Kate Smith, 1907–1986

Top Pop Singer Who Made "God Bless America" an Anthem

Singer Kate Smith had the distinction of being the first to sing the now famous patriotic song "God Bless America," written by Irving Berlin 20 years earlier during World War I. Never sung or recorded, the song had been filed away by the famous Tin Pan alley songwriter and forgotten. In 1938, Smith wanted to commemorate the 20th anniversary of the armistice ending the earlier war and asked Berlin if he could provide her with a patriotic tune. He remembered the one filed away in a trunk. On November 10, 1938, on her top-rated weekly radio show, *The Kate Smith Hour,* she sang it to millions of listeners whose vast heartfelt response has made the song a patriotic favorite ever since. She recorded it and sang it on hundreds of occasions during the war; the song became indelibly linked to her (although others like Bing Crosby also sang and recorded it). Berlin considered it his most famous composition. Her version of the song took deep root early in the war decade. In 1940, at the national political conventions, President Roosevelt and his Democrats along with opposing Republicans fought to be the most closely linked to the song by Smith.

A 1943 musical had her recreate her earlier recording episode that made the song famous. The song's popularity also benefited from the singer's fame throughout this decade when her variety show had a top rating along with her daytime talk and news show, *Kate Smith Speaks*. At midcentury, she entered the television phase of her 50-year-long career; the song continued as a patriotic favorite, and in the 21st century, after the 9/11 disaster, it was frequently sung and invoked to rouse the people to national unity.

John Wayne, 1907–1979

Movie Actor Popular as a War Hero in Combat Films

During the war years, John Wayne was not eligible for the military because of a hearing defect, but in film he became the big screen's iconic fighting man and war hero. In acting the role, he was a natural with a strapping physique and a gruff, no-nonsense manner—tough but with heart. After playing the six-gun cowboy in 1930s mostly B westerns (with the exception being his lead in John Huston's 1939 classic *Stagecoach*), Wayne became the star during and after the war in a series of combat films fashioned loosely on real battles. His war films were generally box office successes. These included *Flying Tigers* (1942), *The Fighting Seabees* (1945), *Back to Bataan* (1945), and *They Were Expendable* (1945). Most were formulaic, with the good guys represented as complex and human Americans, the bad guys depicted as stereotypical enemies. Their aim was to boost home front morale. Wayne's breakthrough war movie, *Iwo Jima,* came in 1949. It was a huge hit. The cast included three of the iconic photo's six actual flag raisers, Ira Hayes, John Bradley, and Rene Gagnon. Onscreen, after being led up Mount Suribachi by Sergeant Striker (John Wayne), the trio of veterans mimed their originally spontaneous action of planting Old Glory. Republic Studios had a large budget for the film, but the Marine Corps helped by lending extras. A filmic reminder to the public of the World War II battle triumph was important in this peak Cold War–year when Russia became a nuclear power and mainland China a communist power. The film made a huge profit and was voted one of the 10 most popular of that year. A turning point in Wayne's career, the film won him an Academy Award nomination, and for the first time, he appeared on the list of the 10 Most Popular Stars. His fame continued, and in 1969, he won Best Actor Academy Award. As late as 1995, 16 years after his death, he was voted America's Favorite Movie Star.

REFERENCES AND FURTHER READINGS

Appy, Christian, ed. 2000. *Cold War Constructions: The Political Culture of United States Imperialism, 1945–1966*. Amherst: University of Massachusetts Press.

Basinger, Jeanine. 2006. *The World War II Combat Film: Anatomy of a Genre*. New York: Columbia University Press.

Crowther, Bruce. 1988. *Film Noir: Reflections in a Dark Mirror*. Hyperion Books.

Doherty, Thomas. 1993. *Projections of War: Hollywood, American Culture and World War II*. New York: Columbia University Press.

Erenberg, Lewis A., and Susan E. Hirsch 1996. *The War in American Culture: Society and Consciousness during World War II*. Chicago: University of Chicago Press.

Gaddis, John L. 1972. *The United States and the Origins of the Cold War, 1941–1947*. New York: Columbia University Press.

Hannesberry, Karen Burroughs. 1998. *Femme Noir: Bad Girls of Film*. Jefferson, NC: McFarland.

Hilmes, Michelle. 1997. *Radio Voices: American Broadcasting, 1922–1952*. Minneapolis: University of Minnesota

Hixson, Walter L. 1997. *Parting the Curtain: Propaganda, Culture and the Cold War, 1945–1961*. New York: St. Martin's Press.

Hopkins, Jerry. 1970. *The Rock Story*. New York: New American Library.

Jackson, Walter. 1990. *Gunnar Myrdal and America's Conscience: Social Engineering and Racial Liberalism, 1938–1987*. Chapel Hill: University of North Carolina Press.

Kammen, Michael. 1999. *American Culture, American Tastes: Social Change and the 20th Century*. New York: Basic Books.

Kaplan, E.A., ed. 1980. *Women in Film Noir*. London: British Film Institute.

Klein, Marcus. 1970. *The American Novel since World War II*. New York: Fawcett Premier.

MacDonald, Fred J. 1979. *Don't Touch That Dial: Radio Programming in American Life, 1920–1960*. Chicago: Nelson Hall.

Maltin, Leonard. 1997. *The Great American Broadcast: A Celebration of America's Golden Age*. New York: Dutton.

Roeder, George H., Jr. 1993. *The Censored War: American Visual Experience during World War II*. New Haven: Yale University Press.

Saunders, Frances Stonor. 1999. *The Cultural Cold War: The CIA and the World of Arts and Letters*. New York: New Press.

Terkel, Studs, 2004. *The Good War*. New York: Pantheon.

Tuska, Jon. 1984. *Dark Cinema: American Film Noir in Cultural Perspective*. Westport, CT: Greenwood Press.

Wagnleitner, Reinhold, and Elaine Tyler May, eds. 2000. *Here, There and Everywhere: The Foreign Politics of American Popular Culture*. Salzburg: Salzburg Seminar.

Winkler, Allen. 1978. *The Politics of Propaganda*, New Haven and London: Yale University Press.

Wood, Michael. 1975. *America in Movies*. New York: Dell.

People and Events in the 20th Century

THE 1900s

THE 1910s

THE 1920s

THE 1930s

THE 1940s

THE 1950s

THE 1960s

THE 1970S

THE 1980s

THE 1990s

1940s Index

About the Author

Mark Ciabattari is a cultural and social historian who teaches in the English department at the City University of New York, John Jay College of Criminal Justice. He is a widely published cultural critic and essayist and the author of three books of fiction, most recently *Clay Creatures,* presented by the Pirandello Society at the 2005 Modern Language Association conference. He has, for the past decade, presented a series of public lectures on "Literary New York," "The Literary History of the Hudson Valley," and the "Literary East End of Long Island."